Electronic Commerce in Small to Medium-Sized Enterprises: Frameworks, Issues and Implications

Nabeel A. Y. Al-Qirim
Auckland University of Technology, New Zealand and
Deakin University, Australia

IDEA GROUP PUBLISHING
Hershey • London • Melbourne • Singapore

Acquisitions Editor: Mehdi Khosrow-Pour
Senior Managing Editor: Jan Travers
Managing Editor: Amanda Appicello
Development Editor: Michele Rossi
Copy Editor: Maria Boyer
Typesetter: Jennifer Wetzel
Cover Design: Michelle Waters
Printed at: Integrated Book Technology

658.872
A45e

Published in the United States of America by
    Idea Group Publishing (an imprint of Idea Group Inc.)
    701 E. Chocolate Avenue, Suite 200
    Hershey PA 17033
    Tel: 717-533-8845
    Fax: 717-533-8661
    E-mail: cust@idea-group.com
    Web site: http://www.idea-group.com

and in the United Kingdom by
    Idea Group Publishing (an imprint of Idea Group Inc.)
    3 Henrietta Street
    Covent Garden
    London WC2E 8LU
    Tel: 44 20 7240 0856
    Fax: 44 20 7379 3313
    Web site: http://www.eurospan.co.uk

Library of Congress Cataloging-in-Publication Data

Electronic commerce in small to medium-sized enterprises : frameworks,
issues, and implications / Nabeel A.Y. Al-Qirim, editor.
       p. cm.
Includes bibliographical references and index.
   ISBN 1-59140-146-1 (h/c) -- ISBN 1-59140-263-8 (s/c) -- ISBN
1-59140-147-X (ebook)
   1. Electronic commerce. 2. Small business--Technological
innovations. I. Al-Qirim, Nabeel A. Y., 1966-   .
   HF5548.32.E364 2004
   658.8'72--dc22
                                                         2003017708

British Cataloguing in Publication Data
A Cataloguing in Publication record for this book is available from the British Library.

Electronic Commerce in Small to Medium-Sized Enterprises: Frameworks, Issues and Implications

Table of Contents

SECTION IX: E-COMMERCE OUTSOURCING AND THE IMPACT OF ASPS ON E-COMMERCE SUCCESS IN SMES

Foreword

This edited book represents a unique contribution to e-Commerce research in small business as it addresses the more recent significant issues affecting the small business sector. The research coverage is comprehensive and addresses the practicalities of ecommerce adoption by small and medium enterprises. The chapters together demonstrate clearly the contribution Information Systems researchers can make to systems adoption by business and the crucial nature of their research for the real world.

The book also points other researchers to main issues pertaining to e-Commerce, theory and methodology. This book's timing is significant as it addresses the next step in taking e-Commerce research in small business to a further level of sophistication.

Prof. Brian Corbitt
Deakin University, Australia

Preface

Small to medium-sized enterprise (SME) research can be traced as far back as the 1960s (Brigham & Smith, 1967). However, SMEs were largely ignored for a long time, until the emergence of several reports—including the Bolton Report (1971) in the UK and the Wiltshire Report (1971) in Australia—which focused on highlighting the significant contribution of SMEs in these countries. Since then, research in small business has grown steadily, examining different perspectives pertaining to SMEs and their environments. Over the past 24 years in particular, there has been a continual growth of different academic journals and conferences focusing on SMEs research (e.g., *Journal of Small Business Management, The International Small Business Journal*) (Hill & McGowan, 1999). However, information systems (IS) research in SMEs started to surface in the 1970s (Schollhammer & Kuriloff, 1979) and has since grown steadily.

A common theme in this research points to its fragmentation and its failure to provide conclusive evidence about IS penetration or success in SMEs. Another theme emerging from this research points to different deficiencies at the different contextual levels (technological, organizational including managerial, environmental, individual) and to the lateness of the SMEs in adopting IS. Electronic commerce (e-commerce) research did not differ a lot from the IS research, pointing to the laggardness of SMEs either in terms of adopting and utilizing e-commerce or to the same impeding contextual factors highlighted above. In addition, due to its novel nature (early 1990s), e-commerce introduces unique features of its own and affects organization in an unprecedented way. Thus, capturing its multifaceted perspectives has proven to be challenging. A common theme in the earlier e-commerce research in SMEs reports the scant adoption of e-commerce technology in general and of EDI technology specifically.

The next wave (in the late 1990s) of e-commerce research in SMEs benefited from this initial research and attempted to devise different measures and factors aiming at capturing e-commerce successes and failures in SMEs. What could be synthesized from this research is that e-commerce is characterized by multi-faceted perspectives and represents phenomena too large and complex to be encapsulated within one study, one discipline, or one methodology. Still, what makes SMEs decide to adopt e-commerce is not conclusive and remains the subject of considerable debate among researchers. However, in this era where the Internet and its underlying technological infrastructure is well established, economical, and reliable in most countries, there is a consensus among researchers about the large-scale adoption and usage of e-mail as an efficient communication tool, Internet browsing as an information retrieval tool, and simple Web pages as a pointer to the physical location of a given SME company and its products. How significant is the actual use of these technologies and tools in business in SMEs? This leads naturally to the question of what makes SMEs adopt or reject e-commerce? And, further, how deep is the actual penetration of e-commerce in business? How to devise measures, which could capture these perspectives, is the challenge facing researchers.

At this stage of e-commerce maturity where technology, telecommunications, and applications are in a much better status than they were in the early 1990s and e-commerce researchers are aware of the complexities of the e-commerce field, this book emerges to introduce different strategies and topics in order to benefit those interested in researching e-commerce in SMEs. This edited book calls not only for more cooperation between the different disciplines to assess the significance of the variety of theories and methodologies for e-commerce research in SMEs, but also for the use of mixed approaches to unveil e-commerce perspectives. Above all, researchers should be aware of the complexity of the e-commerce field and the fact that unlike any other technological innovation, e-commerce impacts organizations immensely and holistically. This initial call, supported by the contributing chapters, attempts to shed some light onto this challenging research area, and to help pave the way for other researchers, policymakers, and professionals to adopt, adapt, and extend the different concepts, tools, and models highlighted in this book, and to examine their effects in their own countries.

Organization of the Book

The book consists of 20 chapters organized into nine sections addressing different research areas surrounding e-commerce adoption and usage in SMEs. The contributing authors came from different countries in Europe, Asia, the U.S., Australia, and New Zealand. Different theories and frameworks are introduced. The proposed methodologies ranged from interpretive (action research) to positivist research, dominated mostly by surveys, to hybrid approaches. The details of each of the different sections are explained next.

Section I: E-Commerce Research in SMEs

The first section addresses e-commerce research in SMEs, highlighting research procedures, theoretical frameworks, implications, and challenges. Based on e-commerce research, Chapters 1 and 2 attempt to provide a reflection on how SMEs behave in the e-commerce arena. Both chapters provide insightful coverage and critiques of different e-commerce issues in SMEs and address theoretical, methodological, and professional issues and implications.

Section II: Social and Cultural Impacts on E-Commerce Adoption in SMEs

One chapter represents the second section of this edited book. The author of Chapter 3 argues that, unlike the earlier e-commerce adoption research in SMEs, which has taken place within a business discourse, considering the diverse rationalities on which many SMEs are based is extremely important. In comparison with large businesses, the author contends that SMEs' business rationalities are more complex and are intertwined with the non-economic rationalities of social, community, and family life. It is by addressing this social formation, embedded in a wider social and cultural context, that reasons accounting for some of the otherwise inexplicable problems in establishing e-commerce relationships can be explained, along with the (apparently) irrational resistance of many SMEs to well-meaning advice and direction. Evidence in support of the author's argument is drawn from five research studies in Australia.

Section III: Factors Impacting E-Commerce Adoption and Use in SMEs

The third section aims at addressing e-commerce adoption and use in SMEs. The emphasis in this section is to identify factors, drivers, impediments, and other issues affecting e-commerce success in SMEs. The investigative nature of the different chapters in this section attempts to unveil part of the complex reality that characterizes the e-commerce field in SMEs. Chapter 4 provides extensive background about the main issues pertaining to e-commerce adoption in SMEs and, accordingly, suggests four broad contexts against which e-commerce adoption can be measured. The chapter then investigates e-commerce adoption in SMEs in the UK and Denmark by undertaking large, random, multi-stage stratified survey research. The chapter reports interesting facts about factors and challenges affecting e-commerce strategy in SMEs. The authors provide some response to some of these challenges and suggest a future research agenda.

Chapter 5 examines the challenges and barriers that SMEs experienced in e-commerce adoption based on a nationwide survey conducted by KPMG–Norlan Norton Institute (NNI) in Australia and New Zealand. The chapter address important issues pertaining to the adoption behavior of SMEs, trust between organizations, and perceived impediments. The chapter then sums up the findings alongside four contexts: technological, organizational, environmental, and social issues.

Section IV: E-Commerce in Developing Countries

One chapter represents the fourth section in this edited book. Chapter 6 represents a unique contribution to the e-commerce research in SMEs, as it sheds some light into e-commerce adoption in the remote country of Samoa, a developing island country in the South Pacific with a poorly developed infrastructure. With the aim of increasing e-commerce adoption and diffusion in that country, the chapter addresses the issues faced by SMEs in Samoa, highlighting different accelerators and impediments.

Section V: Adoption and Diffusion Patterns of E-Commerce in SMEs

In a continuation of the investigative nature of the chapters in Sections 3 and 4, Section 5 aims at introducing new measures and concepts, which could further explain the adoption behavior and patterns of e-commerce in SMEs. Chapter 7 examines the impact of seven factors (organizational, technological, and environmental contexts) that influence the variations of e-commerce adoption decisions of SMEs. Based on the e-commerce adoption decision, this chapter classifies firms into three main groups, namely adopters, prospectors, and laggards. The significance of the developed adoption model is investigated using one large survey research in Thailand.

Chapter 8 views the Internet as a cluster of three elements: e-mail systems, Internet browsers, and other, more advanced technologies. The chapter attempts to examine the level and nature of Internet usage alongside these clusters by undertaking a survey research in SMEs in Ireland. These categories proved useful in identifying the extent of e-commerce usage among the SMEs. According to the preliminary analysis and due to the importance of website technology to SMEs, the chapter focuses on identifying and categorizing the diffusion pattern of website development using the theory of mimetic IT adoption patterns. The chapter identifies two potential hybrid diffusion patterns and discusses their implications for policymakers and professionals.

Driven by the importance of strategic websites, Chapter 9 focuses on website implementation practices in SMEs in the UK. The chapter provides a comparison between the adoption practices of two groups of SMEs: SMEs that identified a need to adopt a Web presence, "Need Pull SMEs"; and SMEs that are pushed into adoption mainly due to the change agents efforts, "Technology Push SMEs." Using an Internet-based survey and semi-structured interviews, the chapter reports interesting results about the effective adoption and implementation of websites by both groups.

Section VI: Successful SMEs in E-Commerce

The chapter in this section aims at targeting successful e-commerce stories in SMEs. By following such an approach, the chapter aspires to provide exemplar cases and frameworks to follow by low or non-adopters. Chapter 10 provides an empirical analysis of successful Irish SMEs engaging in e-commerce and draws out the most successful combinations of factors, which attribute to a successful SME e-commerce project. The chapter investigates the factors that influence the degree of success of such an SME e-commerce project, highlighting the implementation issues. The chapter surveys and interviews SMEs in Ireland that had been accredited for their business use of the Internet.

Section VII: E-Commerce in the Supply Chain in SMEs

Following the richness provided by the preceding sections about different issues surrounding the e-commerce adoption and usage criteria in SMEs, this section addresses e-commerce penetration in SMEs along the supply chain. Chapter 11 proposes an analytical framework that identifies the triggers for value chain transformation that could encourage SMEs to adopt e-commerce. The analytical framework is built on key concepts extended from the literature. The authors adopt the multiple case studies approach using semi-structured interviews with B2B SMEs from different countries in Europe. The chapter produces different insights into the objectives and practices of SMEs introducing e-commerce in different types of value chains.

One of the key success factors for mass customization is the adoption of an e-commerce strategy to create efficiency in the supply chain. However, the process is not straightforward, and Chapter 12 introduces the application of a product model and highlights how inter-organizational product models can be applied to support knowledge distribution within the supply chain, via very economical "configurator" software. The chapter depicts the procedure for building product models and the corresponding complete software development lifecycle of the product starting from the analysis phase and ending with the maintenance phase. The chapter shifts the focus from acquiring internal efficiency to efficiency of integration with suppliers in order to create competitive advantages.

Driven by the importance of helping SMEs to adopt and utilize e-commerce, Chapter 13 highlights the importance of establishing efficient links between industry and research institutions. It is by this tight coupling between researchers and SMEs that satisfactory results can be generated. The chapter investigates the dissimilarities that exist within the literature. The chapter's findings of SME e-commerce utilization focus on case studies drawn from the automotive industry in Austria. Accordingly, the chapter proposes a framework where these dissimilarities could be bridged by connecting university research and regional SME networks in Austria. The chapter uses a multi-method approach for data collection combining grounded action research, surveys, semi-structured interviews, and document analysis to introduce interesting insights about e-commerce use in the value chain of the automotive industry.

Chapter 14 introduces the industrial district concept, a structure that can be used to manage relationships between SMEs. The authors contend that the introduction of e-commerce to these industrial districts could improve the collaboration among the SMEs and hence creates value along the entire supply chain. The chapter describes six models and highlights their strategic importance for the successful implementation of a usable and effective electronic solution for procurement in different industrial districts.

The authors of Chapter 15 contend that re-engineering among small firms has not yet occurred, and points to the importance of re-engineering internal processes for firms to benefit from e-commerce. Examining firms in the context of their Web-based business strategies, this chapter enumerates not only the factors that have been critical for successful re-engineering of core business processes in three SMEs in the U.S., but also the extent to which re-engineering plays a part in their competitiveness.

Stemming from the phases of the lifecycle of a virtual enterprise, Chapter 16 introduces a methodology for developing a new e-commerce tool for collaborative supply chain and development (CSCDD). The chapter provides an interesting comparison between some of the existing tools for CSCDD such as ERP and supply chain planning (SCP), and accordingly, proposes a method to model supply chain activities. This could help SMEs to design the strategic model of supply chains in which they are collaboratively involved. The realization of this tool is of significant importance to the literature in general, and to SMEs specifically.

Section VIII: New E-Commerce Avenues for SMEs

This section proposes new directions, which could guide SMEs in exploring new avenues pertaining to their e-commerce initiatives. The chapters in this section highlight hidden areas in the e-commerce field and provide solutions where the SMEs could increase their adoption of e-commerce. Chapter 17 highlights the importance of the new information age (e-commerce) to SMEs and how, by focusing on knowledge-based products and services, SMEs could tap into unprecedented opportunities. To compete effectively in the market-place, the authors contend that SMEs must integrate and leverage their existing knowledge (intellectual capital) and create new knowledge. However, not all SMEs are equipped to benefit from these opportunities. Accordingly, the authors investigate factors affecting SMEs' participation and success in knowledge-based economies, and provide a set of guidelines for SMEs to exploit the opportunities provided by this knowledge-based economy. Chapter 18 introduces the concept of the use community and regional portals as an impor-tant part of the online strategy of SMEs. Portals generally represent an advanced stage of development of business websites. SMEs are more likely to use portals than develop them. A potential list of benefits that portals can provide to SMEs is provided, and two existing regional portals in Australia are contrasted against the generic e-mall to determine the benefits that portals are currently providing for SMEs.

Section IX: E-Commerce Outsourcing and the Impact of ASPs on E-Commerce Success in SMEs

Continuing the preceding section, and in accordance with the IS and e-commerce literature in SMEs, this section explores their e-commerce outsourcing patterns and points to the importance of the application service providers (ASP) model as one solution to acquire professional and economical e-commerce capabilities. Chapter 19 evaluates the ASP busi-ness model and identifies the potential risks that SMEs could face if they remotely outsource applications using the ASP model. The chapter reports the result of survey research and interviews with IT professionals in the UK. Fourteen key aspects of the ASP model are analyzed in the light of 11 potential risks of traditional IS/IT outsourcing research. Accord-ingly, the chapter shows many risks associated with the ASP model and portrays a future research path to further validate the research results. Chapter 20 highlights the impact of the ASP model on e-commerce success in SMEs and reports its advantages and the associ-ated risks. The chapter investigates the process by which SMEs can establish cooperation with ASPs using a five-stage model. New concepts and ASP models are introduced.

This book represents an initial step in this theoretical and professional direction by ad-dressing an important entity in the economies of featured countries. It is hoped that the contributions herein will assist in providing insights into some of the vagueness that surrounds e-commerce adoption and penetration in SMEs. It is left to other researchers and professionals to further investigate and/or extend the issues highlighted in this book.

References

Bolton, J. (1971). *Small Firm: Report of the Committee of Inquiry on Small Firms.* London: HMSO.

Brigham, F., & Smith, V. (1967). The cost of capital to the small firm. *The Engineering Economist, 13*(1), 1-26.

Hill, J., & McGowan, P. (1999). Small business and enterprise development: Questions about research methodology. *International Journal of Entrepreneurial Behaviour & Research, 5*(1), 5-18

Schollhammer, H., & Kuriloff, H. (1979). *Entrepreneurship and Small Business Management*. New York: John Wiley & Sons.

Wiltshire, F. (1971). *The Committee of Inquiry on Small Business*. Canberra: AGPs.

Acknowledgments

The editor would like to acknowledge the help of all involved in the collation and review process of the book, without whose support the project could not have been satisfactorily completed. A further special note of thanks goes to all the staff at Idea Group Inc., whose contributions throughout the whole process from inception of the initial idea to final publication have been invaluable.

Most of the authors of chapters included in this also served as referees for articles written by other authors. Thanks goes to all those who provided constructive and comprehensive reviews. Special thanks to the publishing team at Idea Group Inc. In particular to Jan Travers and Michele Rossi who continuously prodded via e-mail for keeping the project on schedule and to Mehdi Khosrow-Pour whose enthusiasm motivated me to initially accept his invitation for taking on this project. This book would not have been possible witout their ongoing professional support.

In closing, I wish to thank all of the authors for their insights and excellent contributions to this book. I also want to thank all of the people who assisted me in the reviewing process. Finally, I want to thank my wife and children for their love and support throughout this project.

Nabeel A. Y. Al-Qirim
Editor
Auckland University of Technology, New Zealand and Deakin University, Australia
June 2003

Section I

E-Commerce
Research in SMEs

Chapter I

A Framework for Electronic Commerce Research in Small to Medium-Sized Enterprises

Nabeel A. Y. Al-Qirim, Auckland University of Technology, New Zealand and Deakin University, Australia

Abstract

It is believed that the recent emergence of electronic commerce (e-commerce) in the early '90s could provide different opportunities to small to medium-sized enterprises (SMEs) in overcoming part of their technological, environmental, organizational, and managerial inadequacies. However, recent research portrays a gloomy picture about e-commerce uptake and use in SMEs. Therefore, the implication here is twofold. Initially, there is a need to generate more e-commerce research that could penetrate much deeper into main impending issues pertaining to the SMEs in their potential uptake and use of e-commerce. On the other hand, e-commerce is characterized of being embryonic but growing very fast and fragmented across the different disciplines, which makes the task of capturing its different perspectives a very complex one. The preceding two implications represent the greatest challenge for researchers and professionals interested in undertaking e-commerce research in SMEs. In line with the above implications, the first objective of this research aims at capturing the different e-commerce perspectives from the SMEs' point of view, and the second objective aims at capturing the e-commerce perspective from the theoretical and the methodological point of view. Addressing the preceding implications in this research could shed some light into some of the gray areas in the e-commerce research in SMEs.

Introduction

In recent years, small to medium-sized enterprises (SMEs) have been shown to contribute significantly to national economies. It was in the 1970s that researchers first began to highlight the critical role of SMEs, not only in maintaining healthy and dynamic economies within industrialized nations, but also in introducing inventions and innovations (Cameron & Massey, 1999; Iacovou, Benbasat, & Dexter, 1995). By utilizing their assets, such as being more flexible, innovative, and incurring lower overheads than larger enterprises, SMEs have proven their importance in the face of increased global competition (Blili & Raymond, 1993). Generally, SMEs constitute around 95% of enterprises, and account for 60% to 70% of employment within the countries of the Organization for Economic Cooperation and Development (OECD, 1997). New Zealand SMEs form a significant component of the national economic output (35%) in terms of their proportion (96%) and employees (41%) (MOED, 2000). SMEs in the United Kingdom (UK) represent more than 95% of all businesses, employ 65% of the workforce, and produce 25% of gross domestic product (GDP) (Ballantine, Levy, & Powell, 1998).

The recent emergence of the Internet in general, and the World Wide Web (WWW or Web) in particular has revolutionized business activities (Abell & Lim, 1996). Information technology is generating new products, and is the driving force behind new production processes, new forms of business organization, new scope for consumers, and new market opportunities (MOED, 2000).

The open standards of the Internet bring electronic commerce/business (e-commerce) within the reach of even the smallest firms and help to reduce the gap between large and small firms (Kalakota & Whinston, 1996; MOC, 1998). Businesses are embracing e-commerce in order to reduce costs, increase efficiency, and ensure better customer and supplier management (MOED, 2000). Small-business Internet commerce is defined as "the use of Internet technology and applications to support business activities of a small firm" (Poon, 1999). According to Poon's (1999) definition, a business activity can be internally or externally oriented, and of a transactional or strategic nature. E-commerce is becoming more and more essential as a business tool for organizations in general, and for SMEs in particular, to gain competitive advantage and to access global markets (Poon & Swatman, 1995). The online economy introduces unique opportunities to SMEs for open and free trade because it avoids tariffs and tax, while lessening the impact of geographical distances and time, which can serve to separate SMEs from potential opportunity (Abell & Lim, 1996; Cameron & Massey, 1999; MOC, 1998; Peters & Paynter, 1999). However, this perspective is a double-edged sword. Firms choosing to distance themselves from this new competitive tool risk falling victim to it and missing out on many of its promised benefits. Rather, it is the innovative firms that have been able to profit from this new technological development (Blili & Raymond, 1993). Electronic commerce shifts the power from the sellers to the buyers, suggesting that businesses in general, and SMEs specifically, are no longer in control of their traditional markets.

Implications in E-Commerce Research in SMEs

Opportunities provided to SMEs are only apparent, and not necessarily actual. The process is not straightforward, and highlighting what Internet commerce can offer and what others have experienced is a priority (Poon, 1999; Poon & Swatman, 1999a; Premkumar & Roberts, 1999). Despite the apparent media hype (Premkumar & Roberts, 1999), and the enthusiasm among academics (Adam& Deans, 2000; Abell & Lim, 1996; *Infotech Weekly,* 1997; Poon & Swatman, 1999a) and professionals (Deloitte, 2000; IDC, 1998; PWHC, 1999) about e-commerce, the available e-commerce research is fragmented and does not offer significant insights into true e-commerce success or failure and penetration in SMEs (Abell & Lim, 1996; Riggins & Rhee, 1998; Turban, Lee, King, & Chung, 2000). Existing empirical research focusing on the success factors of e-commerce (e.g., websites) is anecdotal and exploratory in nature, and therefore does not provide sufficient insights into the combinations of these factors (Liu & Arnett, 2000). Primarily, there is a lack of detailed knowledge about the owners of small businesses and the process of running small businesses (Blackburn & Stokes, 2000). There also remains a lack of knowledge about the nature and extent of SMEs' needs and the mechanism for delivering support effectively (Hoffman, Barejo, & Bessant, 1998).

The existing e-commerce studies were mostly surveys, exploratory in nature and focused mainly on the growth of the Internet in terms of usage, advantages, and impediments (Abell & Black, 1997; Abell & Lim, 1996; Adam & Deans, 2000; Deloitte, 2000; PWHC, 1999; Poon & Swatman, 1995, 1997, 1998, 1999a, 1999b). Similarly, issues concerning how and why businesses are using the Internet are also scarce (Adam & Deans, 2000; Abell & Black, 1997; Abell & Lim, 1996; Deloitte, 2000). In a recent study, it was found that 73% of surveyed small businesses were connected to the Internet. However, their potential use of the Internet in business was rarely explored (Waikato, 1999), which cast serious doubts about the effective utilization of the Internet and e-commerce by SMEs. Findings indicate a lack of knowledge among SMEs about e-commerce and its applications (Deloitte, 2000). Further, the strategic importance of e-commerce in SMEs was positively viewed, but emerged mostly within larger organizations (Deloitte, 2000). Despite the high adoption rates of e-mail, domain names, and websites, SMEs are lagging behind large businesses in terms of e-commerce adoption and its use in business (Deloitte, 2000). In spite of the perceived advantages, the Internet is used mainly as a communication tool; websites are used mainly for publishing organizational information only, and are rarely used in conducting commercial transactions. The SMEs' approach toward e-commerce adoption is usually more reactive than proactive, generally doing just enough to meet their buyers/suppliers' needs (Chen & Williams, 1998). This laggardness in e-commerce adoption applies equally to SMEs in countries as different as Ireland (Mcdonagh & Prothero, 2000) and the U.S. (Alexander, 1999; CB, 2000).

The shortage of detailed e-commerce research, however, is a result of the relatively recent emergence of e-commerce in the early '90s and the fact that it is still in the evolutionary phase, although it is progressing in a revolutionary manner in different directions. On the other hand, this could also be the result of the multi-perspectives that characterize e-commerce. Capturing these perspectives represents a significant challenge for researchers and professionals interested in examining SMEs and e-commerce. This can further fragment the e-commerce field across different disciplines. The recent calls from researchers in the IS field specifically—from groups such as the International Federation for Information Processing (IFIP)—for a wider interdisciplinary investigation of the multi-faceted perspective of the e-commerce field,[1] endorse the complexity of the field and the need for a larger collaboration among researchers from the different disciplines. Thus, this book's objectives are divided into two parts: firstly, there is a need to generate more e-commerce research tackling critical and contemporary issues in SMEs, and secondly, there is a need to establish a theoretical foundation for the e-commerce field, not the least from the IS disciplines. Thus, the first objective aims at capturing the e-commerce perspective from the business point of view, while the second objective aims at capturing the e-commerce perspective from the theoretical and the methodological point of view.

Theoretical Framework for E-Commerce Research in SMEs

The Impact of E-Commerce in SMEs

In addressing the first objective, one should note that e-commerce could profoundly impact organizations in different ways. Electronic commerce impacts organizations differently in the sense that it introduces a set of unique features. Past studies have found that facilitation factors vary according to the innovation type (Swanson, 1994). Issues such as security and legal concerns; the compatibility of the new medium with the organization and its employees, or in seeing customers through electronic interfaces rather than the traditional face-to-face interactions (social impact); and the complexity of the field and the lack of knowledge about the new field and its business models were only a few of the mentioned impediments. Further, e-commerce introduces unprecedented innovations and business models that were not possible before the emergence of the Internet. Riggins (1998) introduced a grid where various opportunities could be identified from the Web based on the strategic orientation of organizations. For example, the reverse auction model for airlines tickets (priceline.com), online auction, and watch ads and get paid model (cybergold.com) are but some of the relevant examples.

Much of the IS research examines the automation of internal systems and processes within organizations, e.g., transaction processing and back-office automation, and the emergence of inter-organizational systems and EDI. Earlier literature tackling the strategic impact of IT on organizational performance was confined to a supporting role. This perspective grew to encompass the strategic behavior and the essence of the corporate strategies of firms seeking greater dominance in the marketplace (Blili & Raymond, 1993).

This is mostly attributed to the emergence of the Internet. It is, therefore, important to emphasize integration and to explore the holistic impact that e-commerce has on organizations.

Innovations can be either radical or incremental (Afuah, 1998; Thong, 1999). An innovation is said to be radical if the technological knowledge required to exploit it differs significantly from existing knowledge. Incremental innovations, on the other hand, extend or modify existing knowledge bases, e.g., enhancements/upgrades. The introduction of technological innovations such as the Internet and its constituents (WWW, HTML, XML) and new business models support the view that e-commerce represents a radical innovation. It is therefore not surprising that Kalakota and Robinson (2001) defined electronic business as "the complex fusion of business processes, enterprise applications, and organizational structure necessary to create a high-performance business model." This definition implies that realizing such business models is challenging and hence requires advanced e-commerce capabilities, in addition to making fundamental changes to the organization itself (e.g., new communication/selling medium) with respect to external stakeholders, including customers, suppliers, and partners. Realizing this will govern the success or failure of a given organization's e-commerce initiatives. Electronic commerce has the potential to streamline internal (e.g., intranet) and external (e.g., buyers and suppliers, EDI, XML, extranet/VPN, websites, etc.) processes and to thereby enable organizations to transform their physical operations (e.g., bricks and mortar) to become virtual (e.g., dot com, clicks) (see Figure 1).

Figure 1: The Impact of Electronic Commerce on Organizations: A Transformation Path

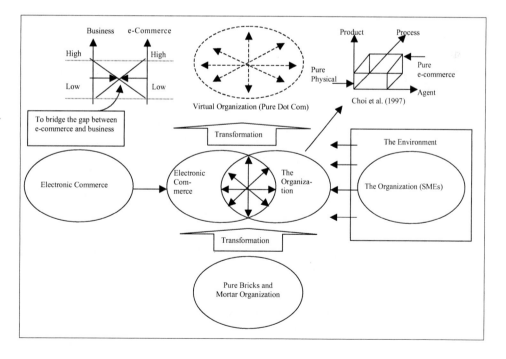

At the heart of the transformation process is the level of e-commerce integration between internal and external processes and systems (e.g., strategic e-commerce, outsourcing, change management, ERP, procurement, BPR, CRM, SCM, etc.) developing to enable organizations to develop successful and sustainable digital business models. Such organizations would be in a better position to digitize their processes, products, and delivery agents (Choi, Stahl, & Whinston, 1997). However, the preceding process depends in large part on issues pertaining to the product characteristics of these organizations, which in turn points to industry specifics (Al-Qirim & Corbitt, 2002b). Thus, addressing these perspectives could yield further insights pertaining to the e-commerce adoption and diffusion criteria in SMEs.

In addition to the product or industry perspective, the depth of the e-commerce impact (or transformation) depends on other internal organizational factors (e.g., product, management, structure, employees) and on the external environment (political, economical, social, technological (PEST) and micro forces such as competition, suppliers and buyers, partners, technology vendors) (Al-Qirim & Corbitt, 2002a, 2002b; Teo, Tan, & Buk, 1997; Vadapalli & Ramamurthy, 1997). SMEs are highly susceptible to environmental forces (Blili & Raymond, 1993). As a consequence, identifying the significant contexts and factors of e-commerce success in SMEs and explaining their impact is important to researchers and professionals. However, the depiction of the two extremes in Figure 1 (pure brick and mortar *vs.* pure clicks) does not imply that SMEs should elevate to the virtual marketplace eventually. On the contrary, depending on certain contextual impacts (highlighted above), organizations could be represented alongside the continuum separating the two extremes. For example, Adam and Deans (2000) suggested an inclination among organizations to migrate from both extremes towards a blend of bricks and clicks (Gulati & Garino, 2000). On the other hand, some organizations existed initially in the electronic marketplace and had never existed in the physical marketplace, e.g., online stock trading companies, auctions, virtual hospitals, virtual libraries, etc., while other companies may choose to have a physical presence.

In conclusion, the introduction of issues, concepts, implications, contexts, techniques, and tools to assist in unveiling the myriad facets that characterize e-commerce could contribute significantly to our understanding about the fast-growing and dynamic field that encompasses the Internet age. Accordingly, the editor posits the following broad questions, which are intended to be guidelines for researchers:

1. How can e-commerce impact SMEs (socially, politically, economically, technologically)?

2. How can SMEs respond to e-commerce impacts (organizational, culture, success and failure stories, BPR, SCM, change management, CRM, virtual organization, and new opportunities such as mobile commerce and ERP)?

3. How can SMEs develop successful e-commerce business models (clicks/bricks)?

4. How can SMEs measure e-commerce success in the adoption and/or diffusion stages (benchmarks, models, factors, predictive techniques using multivariate analysis and models, case studies)?

5. How can involved stakeholders influence e-commerce success or failure in SMEs (government, unions, interest groups, global trade and regulations, technology vendors, suppliers, and buyers)?

6. How can results be extended (or compared) from one country that defines SMEs as having 19 employees or fewer (MOED, 2000) to countries that define SMEs as having fewer than 500 employees (such as the U.S.)?

Theoretical Foundation

"The characteristics of electronic business are in direct conflict with the implicit assumptions underlying most academic research. Information systems research is challenging enough. The nature of the e-business domain presents even greater difficulties." (Clarke, 2001, p. 1)

In addressing the second objective, researchers are confronted by different hurdles. Researchers have suggested that the interdisciplinary nature of IS overlaps with the computer science and the business disciplines (Clarke, 1999; Mumford, 1991). This could extend to viewing e-commerce research as being part of the IS field. However, as IS is an applied discipline and lacks the presence of solid theoretical foundations, it is possible to utilize theories from other referenced disciplines (Clarke, 1999; Garcia & Quek, 1997) such as management, marketing, economics, etc. The risk, however, in adopting and/or adapting models from other disciplines is that the borrowed theoretical or methodological models might become stereotypical or distorted (Garcia & Quek, 1997).

In relying on the IS literature in small business as a reference theory, few insights into IS uptake and use by small business can be observed. In addition, often such research depicts mixed messages (Levy, Powell, & Yetton, 1998). In their review of the IS literature in small businesses, Harrison, Mykytyn, and Reimenschneider (1997) found that much of the earlier IS research in SMEs is exploratory or descriptive in nature, and concluded that the existing research focuses on selected business sectors and is fragmented in terms of the findings and the conceptual approaches used. Reimenschneider and Mykytyn (2000) found that early IS research on small businesses was dated, did not provide significant information about IS use, and was too industry specific. However, most of this research points to the devolvement of the small-business sector at the different organizational, technological, environmental, and managerial levels (Blili & Raymond, 1993; Cragg & King, 1992, 1993; Zinatelli, Cragg, & Cavaye, 1996; Levy et al., 1998). Thus, addressing such contextual impacts from within the different disciplines on e-commerce success in SMEs could contribute immensely to the e-commerce research in SMEs specifically.

The difference between large and small businesses is fundamental to their operations (Bilili & Raymond, 1993; Cragg & King, 1993; Harrison et al., 1997; Levy et al., 1998; Thong, 1999). Even among the SMEs themselves, larger SMEs are more likely to adopt e-commerce than smaller SMEs (Al-Qirim & Corbitt, 2002b). Enjoying significant resources and capabilities, large organizations were the frontrunners in reaping benefits from the Internet (Poon, 1999). Smaller businesses have much simpler structures, resources, and capabilities, and are more susceptible to environmental and internal constraints. Therefore their mortality rate is much higher than larger firms. Poon (1999), Thong (1999), and Jansen (1998) point to the following features, which characterize SMEs: simple, centralized organizational structure and decision-making (represented by the personality of the owner/CEO), a lack of financial resources and specialized skills (experts/expertise), short-term planning (reactive), target niche markets, vulnerable to start-up failures (especially in the first two years), hecticity and uncertainty. Blili and Raymond (1993) and Soh, Yap, and Raman (1992) confirmed these same features and pointed to others: less use of information and formal managerial techniques, a favorable attitude towards information systems but with fewer expectations, very simple IS in place (mainly accounting or administrative packages), and usually under-utilized, troubled, and risky. Understanding these specific characteristics is fundamental to e-commerce research into SMEs.

Thus, applying and/or adapting (Greenwood & Grimshaw, 1999) results from IS research from large businesses to smaller businesses is dubious at best (Jansen, 1998; Reimenschneider & Mykytyn, 2000; Thong, 1999; Thong, Yap, & Raman, 1996), and more accurate models targeting SMEs are required. Thus, researchers extending e-commerce models from large organizations and attempting to apply them to smaller businesses would risk bypassing two main perspectives highlighted above, namely, IS and e-commerce studies in small businesses. This could result in misdirecting the whole research endeavor and in having divergent or fruitless results. Harrison et al. (1997) pointed to the importance of this perspective (lack of frameworks and models in past IS studies in small businesses) and the need for suitable frameworks that would guide the research procedure. Therefore, researchers attempting to borrow reference theories or models either from IS or any other discipline, and trying to adopt/adapt them to their e-commerce research in SMEs, should take care to adhere to the most relevant issues pertaining to SMEs with respect to the different contexts and factors highlighted earlier (Al-Qirim & Corbitt, 2002a). A review of the technological innovation adoption literature on SMEs provides useful insights into factors influencing innovation adoption, but points to the need to introduce additional determinants of innovation adoption (Fichman, 1992) to SMEs research (Thong, 1999).

Driven by the importance of introducing more potential determinants to e-commerce adoption research in SMEs, Al-Qirim (2003) attempted to extend the technological innovation theories to e-commerce adoption research in SMEs. He identified potential constructs and factors from these theories and then checked their appropriateness to e-commerce adoption research using three case studies in New Zealand. The researcher endeavored to pinpoint and examine the most important determinants of e-commerce adoption in SMEs and to eliminate the least relevant ones. It is important to acknowledge that e-commerce introduces features that are unique and different from other innovations. For example, the proposed technological innovations determinants in SMEs (Al-Qirim, 2002) were revisited from within the e-commerce literature in order to justify the use of such innovation factors as potential determinants of e-commerce in SMEs (Al-Qirim & Corbitt, 2002a).

Research Methods

Electronic commerce research represents a new phenomenon and therefore imposes unprecedented challenges on existing research methods in capturing its multi-faceted perspectives. The related technology is changing so fast that people and organizations employing it are in a far from stable position. Most researchers do either quantitative (positivist) or qualitative (interpretive) studies. However, some researchers in the IS (Gallivan, 1997; Nissen, Klein, & Herschheim, 1991) and the e-commerce (Poon & Swatman, 1999) field have called for combining at least one method from each paradigm (positivist vs. Interpretive) within a given study. Poon and Swatman (1998) have indicated that "the survey provides the broad and unbiased overview and generic understanding of key issues related to small-business Internet use in a non-anecdotal manner. The multiple case-study research then served as a flexible and adaptive means to pursue the investigation of these issues in an in-depth manner." Others have suggested using multiple methods (or methodological pluralism) within the same paradigm (e.g., qualitative paradigm) (Galliers, 1991; Mingers, 1996; Myers, 1997) to achieve more rigor and validity (Garcia & Quek, 1997). Gallivan (1997) indicated that in studying the impact of new technologies on organizations such as e-commerce, the use of mixed-method studies provides opportunities to gather mixed-level data, which can be useful in linking the individual to the organizational level of analysis. Further, the use of a mixed-method approach could tie together positivist and interpretive researchers.

Gallivan (1997) asserted that in encouraging mixed-method studies, the "garbage can model" should be followed. In adopting this model, the researcher's preference for a certain methodology will shape the selected topic, not the research questions. On the other hand, combining methods is not a straightforward process and does pose serious implications (Mingers, 1996). In undertaking multiple research methods (e.g., surveys, focus groups, case studies), researchers can become confused by the issue of triangulation, e.g., contrasting the findings of one method by findings produced by another method, indicating that those findings are unlikely to be the result of measurement biases. However, this positivist view of triangulation is misleading, and direct comparison between methods is not always possible. Neither is validation by triangulation (Bloor, Frankland, & Thomas, 2001). Therefore, using different methods in the same research to generate different insights pertaining to the investigated issues is highly encouraged and a much more productive practice than engaging in attacking other methodologies.

Measuring E-Commerce Success (Benchmarking)

Some researchers measure e-commerce capability in small businesses by adopting measures such as the ability to sell/buy products and collect payments online, and even by the ability to deliver products entirely over the Internet (e.g., music downloads) (Adam & Deans, 2000; PWC, 1999). However (and as highlighted earlier), recent studies emphasizing the status of the e-commerce field in SMEs pointed to the laggardness of the sector in terms of adopting and using e-commerce. Therefore, studying advanced e-commerce issues such as selling and buying goods and collecting payments directly over the Internet is unlikely to yield useful results, and even if they exist, these results will be limited. Other e-commerce capability measures such as a change in the financial turnover since adopting e-commerce, increase in market share, number of customers, business activities, and sales enquiries are appropriate but not feasible, because the SMEs may not hold such figures in the first place, and even if they have retained such figures, it is highly unlikely that they would be inclined to provide such privileged information (Poon, 2000). Devising robust techniques and tools to detect true e-commerce use and success is essential to the e-commerce area in SMEs. Teo et al. (1998) and Thong (1999) have suggested that the use of continuous scales and measures could yield more accurate results, and that using multiple measures and scales within the same variable could yield more useful results. For example, Al-Qirim and Corbitt (2002b) introduced three measures to measure and to trace e-commerce adoption in SMEs where one of these measures was a continuous scale.

Defining SMEs

There is no agreement upon what constitutes a good definition for SMEs (Burgess, 1998; MOED, 2000; Zinatelli et al., 1996) except that they are managed directly by their owner(s), e.g., they own most of the shares, provide most of the finance, and make the majority of the principal decisions (Cameron & Massey, 1999). Cameron and Massey (1999) found that countries and agencies employ different qualitative and quantitative limits (Hailey, 1987) in defining SMEs. The criterion most commonly used is the number of employees, as it is a more reliable measure of firm size between different sectors of the economy. However, they highlighted other characteristics of these businesses: (1) personally owned, (2) managed and (3) not being part of a larger business enterprise. Premkumar and Roberts (1999) found that most SMEs tend not to divulge their sales revenue for confidentiality reasons and therefore utilized the number of employees as a measure in their study.

Another implication is in providing criteria where results from countries that define SMEs' size as being up to 500 employees (OECD, 1997) could be extended to other countries that define SMEs' size as being much smaller and vice versa. For example, the Ministry of Economic Development defines New Zealand SMEs as employing 19 or fewer full-time equivalent employees (FTEs) (MOED, 2000). However, for comparison purposes, MOED (2000) extended their definition of SMEs to include businesses employing up to 100 FTEs. Based on the type of industry, Burgess (1998) divided the SMEs into businesses belonging to the non-manufacturing (employing less than 20 people) or to the manufacturing (employing less than 100 people) sectors. Concentrating on New Zealand, Bollard (1988) limited the size of small manufacturing firms to less than 50 employees and very small firms to less than 20 employees. The preceding measures could facilitate the exchange of results across the different countries.

In accordance with the second objective, the editor posits the following broad questions, which are intended here as guiding criteria to researchers interested in e-commerce and SMEs:

1. What are the most probable guiding theoretical frameworks for e-commerce in SMEs (strategic alliances, strategic planning, corporate governance and decision making, marketing, consumer behavior, CRM, economy, finance (e.g., micro structure))?

2. What are the strengths and the weaknesses of the guiding theoretical frameworks?

3. How can researchers link the borrowed reference theory to e-commerce?

4. What are the best research approaches and methodologies for studying the impact of e-commerce in SMEs (case studies, surveys, action research, ethnography)?

5. How can combined research methods yield more significant results?

6. How can researchers triangulate their findings and increase their insight into the e-commerce reality?

Conclusion

This chapter addressed issues that are of importance to researchers, research students, policymakers, and professionals interested in the e-commerce field in general and in the context of SMEs specifically. The chapter addressed professional as well as theoretical issues relating to e-commerce, SMEs, theory, and methodology. It is by following such an approach that e-commerce research in SMEs could take on a shape of its own, and results could be shared transparently across different countries and institutions. As the e-commerce field is relatively new and fragmented across different disciplines, addressing issues pertaining to its novel perspectives and linking those with a reference theory is a priority and essential before undertaking a research endeavor.

This chapter introduced some of the implications that surrounded e-commerce research in SMEs and provided a framework where the different implications are progressed and are able to be addressed. This chapter points to other important issues that could contribute significantly to the progress of e-commerce research in SMEs. It is left to other researchers in the same field to expand on those issues from their perspectives and from the perspective of their countries.

Endnotes

[1] http://www.salzburgresearch.at/suntrec/IFIPTC8Conference/.

References

Abell, W., & Black, S. (1997). *Business use of the Internet in New Zealand: A follow-up study*. Retrieved August 8, 2000 from the Web: http://www.scu.edu.au/ausweb96/business/abell/paper.htm.

Abell, W., & Lim, L. (1996). *Business use of the Internet in New Zealand: An exploratory study*. Retrieved August 8, 2000 from the Web: http://www.scu.edu.au/ausweb96/business/abell/paper.htm.

Adam, S., & Deans, K. (2000). Online business in Australia and New Zealand: Crossing a chasm. *Proceedings of AusWeb2k—The Sixth Australian World Wide Web Conference*, Rihga Colonial Club Resort, Cairns (June 12-17).

Afuah, A. (1998). *Innovation Management: Strategies, Implementation, and Profits.* New York: Oxford University Press.

Alexander, A. (1999). Tuning small business for electronic commerce: Consultants say business consulting is essential, even in e-commerce. *Accounting Technology, 15*(11), 48-53.

Al-Qirim, N. (2002). A meta model of innovation adoption in small business: An electronic commerce perspective. *Proceedings of the 2002 Information Resources Management Association (IRMA) International Conference*, Seattle, Washington (pp. 1177-1181).

Al-Qirim, N. (2003). The innovation theories in retrospect: The case of electronic commerce adoption in small business in New Zealand. Forthcoming in *Proceedings of the IFIP Joint WG 8.2+9.4 Conference*, Athens (June 15-17). Published as a book chapter in *Information Systems Perspectives and Challenges in the Context of Globalisation*. Kluwar Academia Publishers.

Al-Qirim, N., & Corbitt, B. (2002a). Critical factors for electronic commerce success in small business: A meta study. *Proceedings of the 2002 Information Resources Management Association (IRMA) International Conference*, Seattle, Washington (pp. 798-802).

Al-Qirim, N., & Corbitt, B. (2002b). An empirical investigation of an e-commerce adoption model in small to medium-sized enterprises in New Zealand. *Proceedings of the 6th Pacific Asia Conference on Information Systems (PACIS 2002): The Next e-What? For Business and Communities.* Tokyo, Japan (September 2-4, pp. 343-362).

Ballentine, J., Levy, M., & Powell, P. (1998). Evaluating information systems in small and medium-sized enterprises: Issues and evidence. *European Journal of Information Systems, 7*, 241-251.

Blackburn, R., & Stokes, D. (2000). Breaking down the barriers: Using focus groups to research small and medium-sized enterprises. *International Small Business Journal, 19*(1), 44-67.

Blili, S., & Raymond, L. (1993). Information technology: Threats and opportunities for small and medium-sized enterprises. *International Journal of Information Management, 13*, 439-448.

Bloor, M., Frankland, J., Thomas, M., & Robson, K. (2001). *Focus Groups in Social Research.* London: Sage Publications.

Bollard, A. (1988). *Small Business in New Zealand.* Wellington: Allen & Anwin/Port Nicholson Press.

Burgess, S. (1998). *Information technology in small businesses in Australia: A summary of recent studies.* Retrieved June 27, 2000 from the Web: http://www.sbaer.uca.edu/websonar/WebSonar.acgi$SearchCommand.

Cameron, A., & Massey, C. (1999). *Small and Medium-Sized Enterprises: A New Zealand Perspective.* Auckland, New Zealand: Addison Wesley Longman New Zealand Ltd.

CB. (2000). Small businesses are using the Web, but are skeptical. *Community Banker, 9*(8), 44-45.

Chen, J., & Williams, B. (1998). The impact of EDI on SMEs: Summary of eight British case studies. *Journal of Small Business Management, 36*(4), 68-72.

Choi, S., Stahl, D., & Whinston, A. (1997). *The Economic of Electronic Commerce.* Indiana: Macmillan Technical Publishing.

Clarke, R. (1999). *Appropriate research methods for electronic commerce.* Retrieved March 16, 2000 from the Web: http://www.anu.edu.au/people/Roger.Clarke/ResMeth.html.

Clarke, R. (2001). *If eBusiness is different, then research in eBusiness is two.* Retrieved July 25, 2002 from the Web: http://www.anu.edu.au/people/Roger.Clarke/EC/EBR0106.html.

Cragg, P., & King, M. (1992). Information systems sophistication and financial performance of small engineering firms. *European Journal of Information Systems, 1*(6), 417-426.

Cragg, P., & King, M. (1993). Small firm computing. Motivators and inhibitors. *MIS Quarterly,* (March).

Deloitte. (2000). *Deloitte e-Business survey: Insights and issues facing New Zealand business.* Retrieved August 8, 2000 from the Web: http://www.deloitte.co.nz/images/acrobat/survey.pdf.

Fichman, R.G. (1992). Information technology diffusion: A review of empirical research. *Proceedings of the 13th International Conference on Information Systems,* Dallas, Texas, USA (pp. 195-206).

Galliers, R. (1991). Choosing appropriate information systems research approaches: A revised taxonomy. In H.-E. Nissen, H. Klein, & R. Herschheim (Eds.), *Information System Research: Contemporary Approaches & Emergent Traditions* (pp. 327-345). Amsterdam: North-Holland.

Gallivan, M. (1997). Value in triangulation: A comparison of two approaches for combining qualitative and quantitative methods. In A. Lee, J. Liebenau, & J. DeGross (Eds.), *Information Systems and Qualitative Research* (pp. 417-443). London: Chapman & Hall.

Garcia, L., & Quek, F. (1997). Qualitative research in information systems: Time to be subjective? In A. Lee, J. Liebenau, & J. DeGross (Eds.), *Information Systems and Qualitative Research* (pp. 444-465). London: Chapman & Hall.

Greenwood, D., & Grimshaw, D. (1999). Driving IS strategy at an SME. In D. Targett, D. Grimshaw, & P. Powell (Eds.), *IT in Business: A Manager's Casebook* (pp. 143-155). Oxford: Butterworth Heinemann.

Gulati, R., & Garino, J. (2000). Get the right mix of bricks & clicks. *Harvard Business Review,* (May/June), 107-114.

Hailey, J. (1987). *Entrepreneurship and indigenous business in the pacific.* East-West Center Research Report Series No. 9. Honolulu, HI: Pacific Island Development Programs (The Pacific Entrepreneur).

Harrison, D., Mykytyn, P., & Reimenschneider, C. (1997). Executive decisions about IT adoption in small business: Theory and empirical tests. *Information Systems Research, 8*(2), 171-195.

Hoffman, K., Parejo, M., & Bessant, J. (1998). Small firm, R&D, technology and innovation in the UK: A literature review. *Technovation, 18*(1), 39-55.

Iacovou, C., Benbasat, I., & Dexter, A. (1995). Electronic data interchange and small organizations: Adoption and impact of Technology. *MIS Quarterly,* (December).

Infotech Weekly. (1997, April 1). *New Zealand Internet use.* Retrieved May 15, 2000 from the Web: http://www.nua.net/surveys/index.cgi?f=VS&art_id=863080905 &rel=true.

International Data Corporation (IDC). (1998). *E-commerce booming in New Zealand.* Nua Internet Services. Retrieved April 30, 1998 from the Web: http://www.nua.ie/ surveys/index.cgi?f=VS&art_id=905354498&rel=true, and retrieved May 15, 2000 from the Web: http://www.nua.ie/surveys/index.cgi?f=VS&art_id=905354498& rel=true.

Jansen, A. (1998). Technology diffusion and adoption in small, rural firms. In T. Larsen & E. McGuire (Eds.), *Information Systems Innovation and Diffusion: Issues and Directions* (pp. 345-372). Hershey, PA: Idea Group Publishing.

Kalakota, R., & Robinson, M. (1999). *E-Business: Roadmap for Success.* Reading, MA: Addison-Wesley Longman.

Kalakota, R., & Whinston, A. (1996). *Frontiers of Electronic Commerce.* Reading, MA: Addison-Wesley Longman.

Levy, M., Powell, P., & Yetton, P. (1998). SMEs and the gains from IS: From cost reduction to value added. *Proceedings of IFIP WG8.2 & WG8.6 Joint Working Conference on Information Systems: Current Issues and Future Changes.* Helsinki, Finland (December 10-13). Retrieved June 5, 2000 from the Web: http://www.bi.no/dep2/ infomgt/wg82-86/proceedings/table-of-contents.htm.

Liu, C., & Arnett, P (2000). Exploring the factors associated with website success in the context of electronic commerce. *Information and Management, 38,* 23-33.

Mcdonagh, P., & Prothero, A. (2000). Euroclicking and the Irish SME: Prepared for e-commerce and the single currency. *Irish Marketing Review, 13*(1), 21-33.

Mingers, J. (1996). Combining research methods in information systems: Multi-paradigm methodology. *Warwick Business School Research Bureau, 239*(September).

Ministry of Commerce (MOC) (1998, November). *Electronic commerce: The 'freezer ship' of the 21st century.* New Zealand.

Ministry of Economic Development (MOED). (2000, January). *SMEs in New Zealand: Structure and dynamics, firm capability team, update report.* Retrieved May 5, 2000 from the Web: http://www.MOED.govt.nz/gbl/bus_dev/smes2/ index.html#TopOfPage.

Mumford, E. (1991). Opening address: Information systems research—leaking craft or visionary vehicle? In H.-E. Nissen, H. Klein, & R. Herschheim (Eds.), *Information System Research: Contemporary Approaches & Emergent Traditions* (pp. 21-26). Amsterdam: North-Holland.

Myers, M. (1997). Living scholarship. *MIS Discovery.* Retrieved January 2001 from the Web: http://www.auckland.ac.nz/msis/isworld/.

Nissen, H.-E., Klein, H., & Herschheim, R. (1991). A pluralistic perspective of the information systems research arena. In H.-E. Nissen, H. Klein, & R. Herschheim (Eds.) *Information System Research: Contemporary Approaches & Emergent Traditions* (pp. 1-20). Amsterdam: North-Holland.

OECD. (1997). *Small business, job creation and growth: Facts, obstacles and best practices.* Paris.

Peters, D., & Paynter, J. (1999). Application of electronic commerce in New Zealand. In F. Tan, P. Corbett, & Y. Wong (Eds.), *Information Technology Diffusion in the Asia Pacific: Perspective on Policy, Electronic Commerce and Education* (pp. 148-162). Hershey, PA: Idea Group Publishing.

Poon, S. (1999). Small business and Internet commerce: What are the lessons learned? In F. Sudweeks & C. Romm (Eds.), *Doing Business on the Internet: Opportunities and Pitfalls* (pp. 113-124). London: Springer-Verlag London Ltd.

Poon, S. (2000). Business environment and Internet commerce benefits—a small business perspective. *European Journal of Information Systems, 9,* 72-81.

Poon, S., & Swatman, P. (1995). *The Internet for small businesses: An enabling infrastructure for competitiveness.* Retrieved June 27, 2000 from the Web: http://inet.nttam.com.

Poon, S., & Swatman, P. (1997) Internet-based small business communication. *International Journal of Electronic Commerce, 7*(2), 5-21.

Poon, S., & Swatman, P. (1998) A combined-method study of small business Internet commerce. *International Journal of Electronic Commerce, 2*(3), 31-46.

Poon, S., & Swatman, P. (1999a). An exploratory study of small business Internet commerce issues. *Information & Management, 35,* 9-18.

Poon, S., & Swatman, P. (1999b). A longitudinal study of expectations in small business Internet commerce. *International Journal of Electronic Commerce, 3*(3), 21-33.

Premkumar, G., & Roberts, M. (1999). Adoption of new information technologies in rural small businesses. *The International Journal of Management Science (OMEGA), 27,* 467-484.

PWC. (1999). *SME Electronic Commerce Study* (TEL05/97T). Pricewaterhousecoopers, September 24. Retrieved April 10, 2000 from the Web: http://apec.pwcglobal.com/sme.html.

Reimenschneider, C., & Mykytyn, P. (2000). What small business executives learned about managing information technology. *Information & Management, 37,* 257-269.

Riggins, F. (1998). A framework for identifying Web-based electronic commerce opportunities. *Journal of Organisational Computing and Electronic Commerce.* Retrieved April 15, 1999 from the Web: http://www.cec.gatech.edu/papers/ecvalue.html.

Riggins, F., & Rhee, H. (1998). Toward a unified view of electronic commerce. *Communications of the ACM.* Retrieved April 15, 1999 from the Web: http://www.cec.gatech.edu/papers/unified.html.

Soh, P., Yap, S., & Raman, S. (1992). Impact of consultants on computerisation success in small business. *Information & Management, 22*, 309-313.

Swanson, E.B. (1994). Information systems innovation among organisations. *Management Science, 40*(9), 1069-1092.

Teo, T., Tan, M., & Buk, W. (1997). A contingency model of Internet adoption in Singapore. *International Journal of Electronic Commerce, 2*(2), 95.

Thong, J. (1999). An integrated model of information systems adoption in small business. *Journal of Management Information Systems, 15*(4), 187-214.

Thong, J., Yap, C., & Raman, K. (1996). Top management support, external expertise and information systems implementation in small business. *Information Systems Research, 7*(2), 248-267.

Turban, E., Lee, J., King, D., & Chung, H. (2000). *Electronic Commerce: A Managerial Perspective.* Englewood Cliffs, NJ: Prentice-Hall.

Vadapalli, A., & Ramamurthy, K. (1997). Business use of the Internet: An analytical framework and exploratory case study. *International Journal of Electronic Commerce, 2*(2), 71.

Waikato. (1999). *SME benchmarking survey*, 3rd Quarter, September. University of Waikato Management School Management Research Centre.

Zinatelli, N., Cragg, P., & Cavaye A. (1996). End user computing sophistication and success in small firms. *European Journal of Information Systems, 2,* 172-181.

Chapter II

E-Commerce and SMEs: A Reflection and the Way Ahead

Simpson Poon, Charles Sturt University, Australia

Xueli (Charlie) Huang, Edith Cowan University, Australia

Abstract

Since the middle of the 1990s when e-commerce[1] promised to transform the way business is done, curiosity about what impact it has on small to medium-sized enterprises (SMEs) was raised. Throughout the 1990s till this chapter was written, academia, industry, and governments around the world have carried out much research in this area. The efforts range from studying adoption of e-commerce to understanding what contributed to the success of e-commerce. Some focused on the technical issues while other looked at organizational and management concerns. Despite this wealth of added knowledge, there is only a fragmented understanding of how SMEs have benefited from e-commerce. In this chapter, we attempt to provide a reflection, based on the research published, on how SMEs have fared in the era of e-commerce. We conclude that further consolidation of the understanding will be developed by systematically refining research so far carried out.

Introduction

When the Internet was first opened up to carry commercial traffic, and a new class of domain names ended with .*com* was created, many predicted it would transform the business sector. Some compared it to Gutenburg's experiment in printing in the 15th Century. Others thought this was the dawn of the 'new economy'. It has almost been a decade since the first .*com* domain name was registered, and the world had embraced the era of 'dotcom' and disowned it as the era of 'dot-gones'. It is time to reflect on what impact e-commerce has had on SMEs and what future might be lying ahead for SMEs in the context of e-commerce.

In this chapter, we first provide an overview of key studies on SMEs and e-commerce. We then discuss the common issues addressed in the area and those which are still outstanding. We provide a number of future research trends, together with theories and models to be adopted, which may help to enrich and consolidate the domain of knowledge. Finally, we conclude that despite the fact that we have gained much understanding on how SMEs are using e-commerce for various purposes, there is still a need for further understanding, and such can only be obtained using an integrated approach and an examination of theories relevant to the field.

Overview of SME E-Commerce Research

The earliest e-commerce studies can be traced back to those published in 1994 (Barker, 1994; Cronin et al., 1994). Barker (1994) provided one of the first surveys on how small businesses used the Internet for business purposes. Cronin et al. (1994) discussed how e-commerce might change how competitive intelligence was being gathered. They also discussed briefly how small businesses could benefit from such a tool. In the next year or so, more research was published focusing on SMEs and e-commerce (e.g., Cockburn & Wilson, 1995; Dou, 1996; Fuller & Jenkins, 1995; Poon & Swatman, 1995). Since then, much has been published from the perspective of information systems, marketing, and management.

Research on the impact of e-business on SMEs so far is spread along the spectrum from technology adoption to management application (e.g., marketing and advertising). In this section, we briefly describe the research findings and issues adhered.

Technology Adoption of E-Commerce

Given the nature of youth in this field and its evolution, it is not surprising that earlier research in this field has focused on the adoption of e-business in SMEs. These early studies of SMEs' adoption of the Internet and e-commerce predicted how SMEs would benefit from this new technology. Although not always exact, some (e.g., Fuller & Jenkins, 1995; Poon & Swatman, 1995) of the predictions are true even to-date. For example, the key usages of the Internet as a communication medium and for information gathering are two such examples. In addition, these studies have identified a variety of the factors that motivate or inhibit the adoption processes among SMEs (e.g., Mehrtens, Cragg, & Mills, 2001; Mirchandani & Motwani, 2001; Poon & Swatman, 1997; Riemenschneider & McKinney, 2001-2002; Sathye & Beal, 2001; Van Beveren & Thomson, 2002). These factors include: (1) organizational variables, such as Internet to internal system integration, IT knowledge within a firm, and product characteristics; (2) managerial variables such as management enthusiasm, entrepreneurship, and management commitment; (3) e-commerce application variables, such as perceived benefits, ease of use, and costs; and (4) environmental and industry factors, such as industry characteristics and competition. Most of these studies are exploratory and empirically based.

Several researchers have drawn on theories from both the area of innovation diffusion and technology adoptions. For example, Riemenschneider and McKinney (2001-2002) borrowed the Theory of Planned Behavior (TPB), developed by Ajzen (1991), in their study of SMEs' adoption of e-commerce. The TPB proposes that the individual's adoption of technology is determined by his/her intention, which is dependent on three factors: attitude toward the behavior (the perceived association between carrying out the behavior and its benefits or consequences), subjective norm or normative beliefs (the expected approval from referent groups or individuals in the social or business context), and perceived behavioral control (the perceived facilitators or inhibitors in adopting the technology).

Such a deductive approach to studying the adoption of SMEs reflects a step forward towards utilizing concepts and theories in this field, potentially increasing the comparability between different studies and the generalizability of findings. However, one major concern in applying existing innovation diffusion and/or technology adoption theories to studying the adoption of e-commerce in SMEs is the level of analysis, and consequently the measurements of the concepts in the theories. The Innovation Diffusion Theory (Rogers, 1983), TBP, and Technology Adoption Model (TAM) (Davis, Bagozzi, & Warshaw, 1989) have all been originally developed from an individual's perspective. In other words, their level of analysis is individual. How valid these theories are still remains a question when they are applied to SMEs.

Indeed, the level of analysis greatly influences the validity of a study on the adoption of e-commerce among SMEs. By its definition, which is often based on the number of employees, SMEs comprises a wide spectrum of businesses, ranging from a single part-time owner business to those professionally managed organizations employing up to 199 people (Australian Bureau of Statistics, 2002). Such characteristics of SMEs inherently raise an issue of the level of analysis: individual or organizational level. Plus the role of the owner/manager has a strong influence on the direction of the company, far more than their large corporate counterparts. It is well accepted that issues at both levels in SMEs can affect the adoption processes. The question is which level of analysis is more appropriate, or if issues at both levels need to be considered in the research context.

Admittedly, how SMEs use the Internet and adopt e-commerce evolves as the technology and the infrastructure mature. The once-humble text-based Web browser has evolved into a Swiss army knife equivalent of an e-commerce suite—becoming the front-end of most e-commerce set-ups. Given the nature of the e-commerce definition, which is generally broad and thus includes many applications, a number of development approaches have been suggested. For example, in their study of best practice in the

Figure 1: Competitive Advantage vs. Investment in E-Commerce (Adopted from Poon, 2002a)

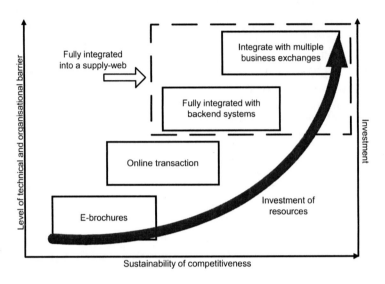

Europe, Jeffcoate, Chappell, and Feindt (2002) have identified three phrases—start-up phrase, growth phrase, and high volume business/maturity—in the development of an e-commerce business. They also clustered SMEs into three groups: gazelles, baby gazelles, and mice. However, it is not clear what e-commerce businesses they have studied. Poon (2002a, 2002b) also pointed out, as shown in Figure 1, that as SMEs try to get more ambitious about their e-commerce solutions, they are faced with both resource constraints and complexity. Although a more integrated and widespread e-commerce solution may bring more sustainable competitive advantage, something to be verified over time, many SMEs would find it too involved given their limited resources.

From a perspective of multiple applications of e-commerce, the Department of Trade and Industry (DTI), UK, has proposed an e-commerce adoption ladder (DTI, 2000, cited in Martin & Matlay, 2001), which consists of five stages, as briefly depicted in Table 1.

The DTI adoption ladder depicts the development of e-commerce in SMEs as a linear, staged, and well-planned process. It has been used by the UK government for benchmarking for the progress of SMEs in adopting e-commerce. However, this adoption ladder has received criticism because it does not reflect the inherent diversity and complexity of SMEs, and thus applies indiscriminately to target all existing SMEs (Martin & Matlay, 2001).

Management Applications of E-Commerce

Another stream of research focused on management applications of e-commerce. Given its broad definition, e-commerce has been hailed as having an umbrella of applications, including information searching, communication, marketing, customer relationship man-

Table 1: DTI Adoption Ladder of E-Commerce by SMEs Based on the Extent of Organizational Change and Sophistication

Stage	Brief Description
E-mail	Efficient internal and external communications
Website	Place in worldwide market; Window on worldwide suppliers
E-commerce	Order and pay online, reducing costs Maximize accessibility and speed
E-business	Integrate supply chain so manufacture and supply become seamless Minimise waste at every stage of the supply chain
Transformed organizations	Open systems information for customers, suppliers and partners New business models based on interworking between organizations and individuals

Source: Martin & Matlay (2001)

agement (CRM), e-tailing, e-procurement, and e-supply chain management (Kalakota & Robinson, 1999; Turban, Lee, King, & Chung, 2000). Even so, research published so far still confirms communication (often using e-mail) and information searching are the two key uses of the Internet (Huang, Soutar, & Brown, 2000; Telstra Corporation Limited, 2002).

The early studies of this research stream concentrated on small e-tailers, as they have been regarded as trailblazing small businesses in exploring the benefits and opportunities offered by e-commerce (e.g., Bhise, Farrell, Miller, Vanier, & Zainulbhai, 2000; Chen & Leteney, 2000; Phillips, 1998; Rosen & Howard, 2000). A variety of issues in implementing e-tailing have been described and investigated. For example, Rosen and Howard (2000) discussed several broad issues, including environmental factors (market size, growth trends, and physical environment), catalysts and deterrents, product characteristics, and type of property (e.g., malls, discount store, and power center). At an organizational level, Chen and Leteney (2000) have identified five key issues facing e-tailers: information, communication, transaction, supply, and distribution. More specifically, Bhise et al. (2000) focused on the delivery issues facing e-tailing. They described the challenges facing e-tailers and discussed three delivery approaches: outsource, selective builder, and integrators.

Using the Internet and Web for marketing has also received much research effort in studying SME e-commerce (Hamill, 1997). For example, Huang and Leong (2003) investigated the website objectives of SMEs. They found that SMEs' owners/managers set up their websites for a number of objectives, particularly for promoting company images, improving customer services, and enhancing products/services awareness. Leong, Huang, and Stanners (1998) also studied how SMEs' managers/owners perceived the marketing role of a website in relation to traditional media. They found that SMEs' managers/owners regard the website as being unique compared with traditional media because of its ability to provide detailed information and its low costs of marketing.

Despite that much research effort has been devoted to the issue of using the Internet and website for marketing and communication in SMEs, how e-marketing has impacted on the marketing outcome among SMEs is still not clear. Several crucial questions in studying SMEs and e-marketing still remain: What is the role of the Internet and website in the marketing mix of an SME? How does e-marketing impact on the bottom line of an SME?

Research also started to explore whether SMEs are better off becoming part of an industry-wide e-commerce infrastructure instead of owning an in-house e-commerce solution. Brown and Lockett (2001) explored the possible configurations of e-clusters and how SMEs might fit into such infrastructure to tap potential leverage. In its extreme, an SME does not need any investment into e-commerce except a PC and a browser suite. All the backend integration and information management will be centralized as part of the e-cluster management process.

Some recent studies have started examining the impact of e-commerce on SMEs and how to strategically manage e-commerce in SMEs (Shah & Dawson, 2002; Tetteh & Burn, 2001). Most early studies of e-commerce in SMEs only explored the *perceived* benefits and costs of implementing e-commerce in SMEs. How SMEs have *actually* benefited from implementing e-commence is a fundamental issue. To answer this question requires the development of a measurement matrix of e-commerce success. Unfortunately, little effort has been devoted to addressing this issue.

From a strategic management perspective, e-business can be regarded as being complementary to a firm's business strategy. Thus, many believe that conventional techniques for strategic analyses, such as external environmental analysis, Five Forces Model, and value chain analysis, are still valid (Dess & Lumpkin, 2003; Porter, 2001).

From a management perspective, how to successfully *implement* an e-commerce application has been an issue facing management researchers and e-commerce practitioners (Waddell, 2002). Implementing e-commerce requires organizational changes to a large or small extent. Thus, it falls into the discipline of change management, such as organizational development (OD) and/or organization transformation (OT). Despite the well-developed theories and concepts in the field of change management, such as contingency theory (for more details, see Stacy, 1996), researchers of SMEs and e-commerce have made inadequate use of the theories and concepts developed in the field of change management.

Challenges Facing SME E-Commerce Research

Despite the efforts to understand SME e-commerce adoption and management, the overall picture of how much SMEs have benefited from e-commerce is still a matter of opinion. There are a number of challenges facing researchers in this area.

Timing of Studies

SMEs' adoption and use of e-commerce is an evolving theme. It is very different from the adoption of other IT, such as PCs, which has reached a mature stage. Technology and services on the Internet are evolving as well as the knowledge and understanding of e-commerce among SMEs. Studies conducted in early 2000s would have different findings from studies in the mid-1990s. For example media streaming was at best scratchy in the mid-1990s, but is of quite good quality now. Also, many e-commerce platforms, be it B2B or B2C, were less well-developed but now are adopted by many small businesses. This leads to a chain of evolving results when referring to studies over the years. It is important not to just look at these results on their own, but to make sense of the evolutionary process of technology adoption.

What Constitutes an SME?

Studies on e-commerce use and adoption among SMEs often started with different assumptions of what SMEs are. On one hand there are definitions by governments (e.g., Holmes & Gibson, 2001) which define SMEs based on the number of persons employed, turnover, and/or ownership structure of a business, followed by further sub-classifications such as industry sector (e.g., manufacturing vs. non-manufacturing, agricultural vs. non-agricultural). By assuming SMEs within these categories are largely similar in their business processes, market orientation, management structure, and having a similar supply chain often led to variation in results. In fact, SMEs make up a very heterogeneous group where the owner's management style and orientation influence the firm greatly. The e-commerce orientation, experience, and perception of e-commerce success are different. For example, one SME may think it has achieved much by being able to use e-mail for marketing, but another may think its fully integrated supply chain management still needs improvement.

To ensure comparable results, it is important to have samples of SMEs not just classified by number of employees, but also other factors such as characteristics of goods, management philosophy, roles played on and the characteristics of the supply chain, among others. Without these added dimensions of sampling, results from e-commerce studies will be difficult to rationalize for extension of theories or generalization.

Cultural Context

One of the thrusts of studying SMEs' e-commerce experience is the belief that SMEs in different countries have different experiences. While it is likely that government policy, level of telecommunication infrastructure, and even the cultural orientation (Hornby, Goulding, & Poon, 2002) of the SME might have an impact on the benefit gained from e-commerce, increasingly the pattern of benefit based on e-commerce itself is getting similar. For example, e-mail is often cited as the most used application, and the Web is most often used to find information instead of other more advanced and sophisticated uses such as supply chain management. Indeed, using e-mail for communication purposes is often cited as the most valuable means of the e-commerce spectrum. Maybe the 80/20 rule applies to e-commerce too—with 20% of the tools and applications, 80% of the e-commerce needs are satisfied from an SME's perspective. If cultural context is to be investigated further, it is important to be more specific about what aspects of culture are to be investigated and what existing theories about cultural impact one is adopting.

Toward the Next Phase of SME E-Commerce Research

There are many challenging issues yet to be resolved in SME e-commerce research. The literature in the domain so far covers issues related to different aspects of how SMEs have been adopting and managing their e-commerce applications (Poon, 2002a). However, more solid studies on SME e-commerce, both qualitative and quantitative, are needed to enhance our understanding of SME e-commerce. Such studies should address a number of important issues regarding the research approaches adopted, concept and theory development, e-commerce developmental stage and applications, and research methodology used. We now discuss each of these issues in turn.

Toward an Integrated Framework

So far research into SMEs and e-commerce has not been much of a coordinated effort. Essentially, most of the studies published are focusing on SMEs' e-commerce activities such as adoption, usage, and issues related to specific topical factors such as management, supply-chain coordination, among others. While results from these studies have provided good insights into the early SME e-commerce situations, increasingly the domain is filled with more fragments of knowledge rather than bodies of integrated understanding. While this is typical in the formative years of the e-commerce domain, time has come for integrating existing 'fragments'. The results from different studies should be integrated into a more comprehensive picture about the e-commerce adoption and management in SMEs.

Multi-Faceted Approach to Studies

Often many SME e-commerce studies use a single approach to study a given problem and make conclusions based on the outcomes (e.g., a survey of a number of SMEs followed by statistical analysis). While this is a good approach, a multi-facet approach can generate reliable and valid insights into the research phenomena. The importance of triangulation, either in method, theory, measures, or observers, has long been emphasized by researchers in social sciences (Neuman, 2003). In addition, SME e-commerce researchers may consider longitudinal studies for investigating how SMEs implement their e-commerce and how e-commerce impacts on their performance. Poon (2002a) has proposed a research approach framework for studying SME e-commerce, as depicted in Figure 2.

Developing Theories in Future Studies

Lack of theory development is a common concern in studying SME e-commerce. Several factors can be attributed to such a shortage of theories and concepts in studying SMEs and e-commerce. First, it is well acknowledged that the SME sector is diverse and complex, which often makes generalization difficult. Second, e-commerce is a young, dynamic, and multi-disciplinary field. As a new field of inquiry, it usually starts with exploratory studies. However, as the inquiry evolves, more emphasis needs to be placed on theory development and enhancing our explanatory power. Such a theorizing process may start from ad-hoc classification systems, taxonomies, conceptual frameworks, and theoretical systems (Parsons & Shils, 1962). It may also originate from some "informal theoretical messages" (Weick, 1995) such as stories, a list of variables, then evolve into diagrams, concepts, hypotheses, and theory.

E-commerce inquiry involves multi-disciplines. Established theories including those on innovation diffusion, organizational science, and strategic management could be used. For example, neo-institutional theory (DiMaggio & Powell, 1983) could be useful in explaining the adoption process of e-commerce by SMEs. From this perspective,

Figure 2: A Suggested Approach to SME E-Commerce Studies (Adopted from Poon, 2002a)

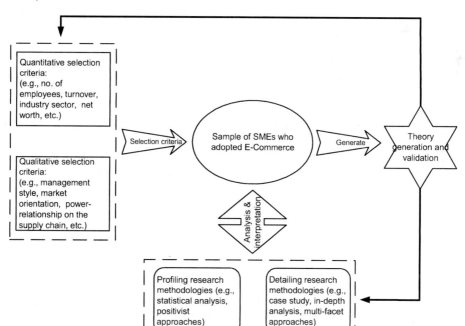

adoption of organizational practices, such as e-commerce in this case, can be attributed to three broad motives or processes: *coercive processes,* where organizations are forced to adopt some application; *mimetic processes,* where organizations copy their peers; and *normative processes,* where organizations make a decision on adopting a new practice because of internalization of norms or pressures by members of other organizations. So far most of the existing research on the adoption of e-commerce by SMEs has been largely described as normative processes, and the other two processes have not been adequately explored. These two processes can be equally important in explaining the e-commerce adopting process in SMEs. Anecdotal evidence from popular media has frequently reported that the coercive processes exist in some industries, particularly where large businesses dominate an industry network, such as vehicle manufacturing and oil exploration industries.

The three processes of adopting new organizational practice, as suggested by DiMaggio and Powell (1983), also raise an important research question whether early adopters differ from late adopters in their motives or pressures of using e-commerce. We may expect the early adopters could be more likely due to the normative pressures, while the later adopters are more likely due to mimetic or coercive pressures. Empirical research is needed to explore this issue.

Specifying the E-Commerce Application Under Study

Given the broad nature of e-commerce applications, future research into SME e-commerce needs to specify the type of e-commerce application under study for several reasons. First, the type of application can affect the adoption process because the investment and risks can differ widely from one application to another. For example, the amount of investment and risks in adopting a customer relationship management (CRM) package can be much higher than those for connecting to the Internet for market research and communication. Second, the antecedents of adopting a particular e-commerce application can be different, because of the level of technical and organizational barrier involved (see Figure 1). Therefore, a set of factors identified for a particular e-commerce application may not be readily generalized to another application.

Third, the nature of an e-commerce application determines the scale of change required by a firm implementing it. Consequently, the approaches used to manage such an implementation can be very different, ranging from organizational development to organization transformation (Waddell, 2002). Finally, the strategic analysis and performance measurement matrix for e-commerce application can be different too.

Conclusion

Although there were some encouraging results in the area of SME e-commerce research, the area is still in its infancy. It is important for the next wave of efforts to be focused on two aspects: an integrated approach to research and the application of well-established theoretical frameworks, particularly those that have been tested in a relevant discipline.

The area needs to go through a period of consolidation rather than generating more fragments of empirical puzzles. While empirical work will still be essential to further the understanding in this area, such can only be obtained by adopting a more systematic and coordinated approach. Like how small businesses collaborate to generate momentum and leverage, as researchers, there might be a lesson for us as well. By synthesizing results from the existing research and strategically developing future understanding, it will be possible to have a more consolidated body of knowledge of SME e-commerce in the near future.

Endnotes

[1]   The authors do not want to engage in defining what is e-commerce, e-business, and the many variants of definition, but use e-commerce as an umbrella term to cover them all.

References

Ajzen, I. (1991). The theory of planned behavior. *Organisational Behaviour and Human Decision Process, 50*, 179-211.

Australian Bureau of Statistics. (2002). *Small business in Australia* (1321.0). Canberra.

Barker, N. (1994). *The Internet as a reach generator for small business.* Unpublished master's thesis, University of Durham.

Bhise, H., Farrell, D., Miller, H., Vanier, A., & Zainulbhai, A. (2000). The duel for the doorstep. *McKinsey Quarterly,* 33-41.

Brown, D.H., & Lockett, N. (2001). Engaging SMEs in e-commerce: The role of intermediaries within e-clusters. *Electronic Markets, 11*(1), 52-58.

Chen, S., & Leteney, F. (2000). Get real! Managing the next stage of Internet retail. *European Management Journal, 18*(5), 519-528.

Cockburn, C., & Wilson, T.D. (1995). *Business use of the World-Wide Web.* Retrieved September 29, 2002 from Web: http://informationr.net/ir/1-2/vaperó.html.

Cronin, B., Overfelt, K., Fouchereaux, K., Manzvanzvike, T., Cha, M., & Sona, E. (1994). The Internet and competitive intelligence: A survey of current practice. *International Journal of Information Management, 14*, 204-222.

Davis, F.D., Bagozzi, R.P., & Warshaw, P.R. (1989). User acceptance of computer technology: A comparison of two theoretical models. *Management Science, 35*(8), 982-1003.

Dess, G.G., & Lumpkin, G.T. (2003). *Strategic Management: Creating Competitive Advantages.* Sydney, Australia: McGraw-Hill.

DiMaggio, P.J., & Powell, W.W. (1983). The iron cage revisited: Institutional isomorphism and collective rationality in organizational fields. *American Sociological Review, 48*, 147-161.

Dou, J.-M. (1996). French small business information through the Internet: A comparison with U.S. organizations. *International Journal of Information Management, 16*(4), 289-298.

Fuller, I., & Jenkins, A. (1995). *Public intervention in entrepreneurial innovation and opportunism: Short cuts or detours to the information superhighway?* Paper presented at the Babson Entrepreneurship Conference.

Hamill, J. (1997). The Internet and international marketing. *International Marketing Review, 14*(5), 300-323.

Holmes, S., & Gibson, B. (2001). *The definition of small business.* Retrieved September 3, 2002 from the Web: http://www.setel.com.au/smeforum2002/tp/BP01a.pdf.

Hornby, G., Goulding, P., & Poon, S. (2002). Perceptions of export barriers and cultural issues: The SMEs e-commerce experience. *Journal of Electronic Commerce Research, 3*(4), 213-226.

Huang, X., & Leong, E. (2003). Electronic commerce in SMEs: Objectives and initiation of websites. *Journal of Small Business and Enterprise Development,* (forthcoming).

Huang, X., Soutar, G.N., & Brown, A. (2000). *Product development in the net era: An exploratory study.* Paper presented at the 2000 International Council for Small Business Conference (June 6-8). Brisbane, Australia.

Jeffcoate, J., Chappell, C., & Feindt, S. (2002). Best practice in SME adoption of e-commerce. *Benchmarking: An Integrated Journal, 9*(2), 122-132.

Kalakota, R., & Robinson, M. (1999). *E-Business: Roadmap for Success.* Sydney, Australia: Addison Wesley Longman.

Leong, E., Huang, X., & Stanners, P.-J. (1998). Comparing the effectiveness of website with traditional media. *Journal of Advertising Research, 38*(5), 44-50.

Martin, L.M., & Matlay, H. (2001). "Blanket" approaches to promoting ICT in small firms: Some lessons from the DTI ladder adoption model in the UK. *Internet Research: Electronic Networking Applications and Policy, 11*(5), 399-410.

Mehrtens, J., Cragg, P.B., & Mills, A.M. (2001). A model of Internet adoption by SMEs. *Information & Management, 39,* 165-175.

Mirchandani, D.A., & Motwani, J. (2001). Understanding small business electronic commerce adoption: An empirical analysis. *Journal of Computer Information Systems,* (Spring), 70-73.

Neuman, W.L. (2003). *Social Research Methods: Qualitative and Quantitative Approaches* (5th ed.). Sydney, Australia: Allyn and Bacon.

Parsons, T., & Shils, E.A. (1962). *Toward a General Theory of Action.* New York: Harper & Row.

Phillips, M. (1998). *Success E-Commerce: 10 Case Studies to Show Small Business How to Profit from Online Commerce.* Melbourne, Australia: Bookman.

Poon, S. (2002a). Have SMEs benefited from e-commerce? *Australian Journal of Information Systems, 10*(1), 66-72.

Poon, S. (2002b). Management's contribution to Internet commerce benefit—Experiences of online small businesses. In S. Burgess (Ed.), *Managing IT in Small Businesses—Challenges and Solutions* (pp. 279-298). Hershey, PA: Idea Group Publishing.

Poon, S., & Swatman, P.M.C. (1995). *The Internet for small businesses: An enabling infrastructure for competitiveness.* Paper presented at the Fifth Internet Society Conference, Hawaii, USA.

Poon, S., & Swatman, P.M.C. (1997). Small business use of the Internet: Findings from Australian case studies. *International Marketing Review, 14*(5), 385-402.

Porter, M. (2001). Strategy and the Internet. *Harvard Business Review,* (March), 63-78.

Riemenschneider, C.K., & McKinney, V.R. (2001-2002). Assessing belief differences in small business adopters and non-adopters of Web-based e-commerce. *Journal of Computer Information Systems,* (Winter), 101-107.

Rogers, E.M. (1983). *Diffusion of Innovations* (3rd ed.). New York: The Free Press.

Rosen, K.T., & Howard, A.L. (2000). E-retail: Gold rush or fool's gold. *California Management Review, 42*(3), 72-100.

Sathye, M., & Beal, D. (2001). Adoption of electronic commerce by SMEs: Australian evidence. *Journal of E-Business, 1*(1), 1-11.

Shah, N., & Dawson, R. (2002). How to be an e-survivor in the current economic climate: E-commerce strategies and tactics to adopt for success. *Journal of E-Business, 1*(2), 1-13.

Stacy, D.A. (1996). Dominant ideologies, strategic change, and sustained performance. *Human Relations, 49*(5), 553-570.

Telstra Corporation Limited. (2002). *2002 Yellow Pages e-business report: The online experience of small and medium enterprises.* Retrieved September 15, 2002 from the Web: http://www.sensis.com.au/Internet/small_business/ypbi/sbpypbi_specialrpts.jhtml.

Tetteh, E., & Burn, J. (2001). Global strategies for SMe-business: Apply the SMALL framework. *Logistics Information Management, 14*(1/2), 171-180.

Turban, E., Lee, J., King, D., & Chung, H.M. (2000). *Electronic Commerce: A Managerial Perspective.* Prentice-Hall International.

Van Beveren, J., & Thomson, H. (2002). The use of electronic commerce by SMEs in Victoria, Australia. *Journal of Small Business Management, 40*(3), 250-253.

Waddell, D. (2002). *E-Business in Australia: Concepts and Cases.* Sydney, Australia: Pearson Education Australia.

Weick, K.E. (1995). What theory is not, theorizing is. *Administrative Science Quarterly, 40*, 385-390.

Section II

Social and Cultural Impacts on E-Commerce Adoption in SMEs

Chapter III

Small Businesses as Social Formations: Diverse Rationalities in the Context of e-Business Adoption

Tanya Castleman, Deakin University, Australia

Abstract

Small-business adoption of electronic business has been analyzed largely in conventional business terms such as benefits and costs, returns on investment, and competitive advantage. While these factors are important, small businesses are also embedded in social contexts which shape the rationalities with which they approach e-business. These rationalities are different from those that characterize larger businesses. They involve personal relationships, social esteem, lifestyle issues, and family considerations. Drawing on the theoretical work of Granovetter and Weber, this chapter examines interview data from a number of Australian studies of e-commerce by small businesses. These interviews illustrate the influence of the social context on the adoption (or deferral) of e-commerce. By recognizing that small businesses are social as well as economic formations, governments can tailor their programs to assist this important group of businesses in their approach to e-business.

Introduction

Large organizations have been active in implementing e-commerce techniques and have pioneered both the adoption of such techniques (e.g., EDI) and the transformation of the organization around them (e.g., BPR). The e-business issues that these organizations face can be understood in conventional business and organizational terms such as return on investment, implementation procedures, and change management challenges. In contrast, SMEs have been generally less active in e-business adoption and are often said to lag behind larger organizations. The smallest businesses are particularly late adopters. The problem of slow adoption by small to medium-sized enterprises is a recurring theme in the literature on e-business. This issue has been discussed in many countries and trading contexts. While much of this phenomenon can be explained as a rational response to business, the realities SMEs face (lack of resources, lack of skills, lack of trading power) do not fully explain what sometimes appears as irrationality in small businesses' reluctance to gain competitive advantage from e-business.

This chapter addresses the issue by considering the diverse rationalities on which many small businesses are based. It argues that these rationalities are often significantly different from the instrumental business rationality which motivates decision-making in large businesses. The argument is not that small-business people are irrational, but that their business rationalities are more complex and are often closely intertwined with non-economic rationalities of social, community, and family life, and this has consequences for the way they approach e-business.

The Sluggish E-Commerce Performance of Small Business

While we lack precise and widely agreed definitions of 'e-business' or 'e-commerce' (Wilkins, Swatman, & Castleman, 1999), the range of practices is easy enough to identify.[1] Shifting business activities from paper-based, local, face-to-face, and manual processes to electronic, dispersed, mediated, and automatic processes is the essence of e-business, whether in dealing with customers or suppliers. We are interested in the adoption of IT-enabled changes in business practice, especially related to the Internet, either in B2B or B2C applications. In this chapter, the terms 'e-commerce', 'e-business', or 'doing business online' are used interchangeably because they are all conceptualizations that relate to changes in business practices.

Although the indicators of growth show continued increases in business IT and Internet use (e.g., Telstra, 2002), the adoption trendlines have been disappointingly less steep than governments have hoped or practitioners have advocated. This has led many to wonder why small businesses are very often reluctant to recognize that e-business is advantageous and to embrace this change. The rationality of technological expansion is self-evident to many commentators and SME slowness is seen as a failing to be overcome through 'awareness raising' and support programs.

Recently, with greater sophistication and more sober views of the dot.com frenzy, the discourse has mellowed. There is clear acknowledgment that SMEs face both economic and organizational constraints. Lack of access to capital, cash-flow difficulties, limited IT skills, and heavy workloads are common problems of these companies, especially the smaller ones (DFAT, 1999, p. 35; SETEL, 2002, p. 4). But along with the new patience, governments and e-commerce experts are still committed to getting SMEs to move their business online with little questioning of its relevance or impact on the enterprise itself or its owners and operators.

Ultimately, most businesses will have little choice but to accommodate the spread of e-commerce. As electronic and Internet-based transactions become the dominant way of doing business, our concerns about SME adoption will abate. Until that time, there are issues of policy and practice to be addressed, considering at what cost this transformation will be made. We need to find ways of encouraging and supporting SMEs to move to greater and more effective online business, and to develop programs to prevent business failure of smaller companies that are excluded from opportunity by their lack of e-business knowledge and capability. But in order to do that, we need to understand the small-business context more broadly than we do at present and to theorize this context appropriately.

To develop a more sophisticated understanding, we should widen our theoretical framework and empirical lens to include social and cultural aspects as well as factors that relate directly to business operations. While small businesses are clearly economic entities, they are also social formations. In many cases we could argue that small businesses are *primarily* social formations and their economic roles are secondary. However, almost all discussion of SME e-commerce adoption has taken place entirely within a business discourse (see APEC, 1999; DFAT, 1999; NOIE, 2001; Poon & Swatman, 1999; Poon & Joseph, 2000) even when cultural factors have been acknowledged (Markus & Soh, 2002; de Berranger, Tucker, & Jones, 2001).

This chapter is particularly concerned with small and micro businesses, although they share many of the characteristics with businesses employing enough people to qualify as medium-sized. The context I discuss is principally Australian, but these are not especially Australian phenomena. Other countries have experienced the same difficulties in getting small business to move online (see, for example, Corbitt & Kong, 2000; Levy & Powell, 2002; Deschoolmeester & Van Hee, 2000; Golden & Griffin, 2000; Oliver & Damaskopoulos, 2002). My approach is to consider the small business as a social formation embedded in a wider social and cultural context. I consider the variety of rationalities that shape small businesses' decision-making and set them apart from larger companies (and certainly from very large ones). I argue that it is these complex and divergent rationalities that differentiate small companies from large ones, and that help account for some of the apparently irrational resistance of many small companies to well-meaning advice and direction to move with the e-business trend.

There is, of course, great diversity among the SMEs. Many small companies will think and act very like their larger counterparts, making business decisions including decisions about e-commerce that are immediately understandable in standard business terms. Many of the observations made here will not apply to them to any significant degree. But many small businesses inhabit a distinctive social context that shapes their approach to e-commerce. By understanding this context better, we will know what they may value in what e-commerce offers—that understanding can inform the way that awareness-raising, engagement, and other promotion activities are undertaken. It may also inform the way that electronic business processes are designed and implemented.

My analysis here is based primarily on a post-hoc examination of several qualitative studies of SME e-commerce experience that I have contributed to in recent years. None of the studies addressed the issue of social context directly, but in the course of interviews and focus groups, much about the participants' reasoning emerged. In those studies the social dimensions of the SME were largely 'noise', but a second look gives an insight into small-business life and its relevance to e-business use.

Economic Behavior and Diverse Rationalities

One of the ways of understanding business behavior is to focus on the rationality that underpins it. Most analyses assume that organizations and their members behave rationally to maximize business outcomes in terms of profit, growth, competitive advantage, sustainability, and so on. While business strategies may be culturally varied (Clegg, 1990) and some turn out to be unsuccessful, we take more or less for granted that the motivation behind these strategies is business oriented. That is, whatever the result, business decision-makers are oriented to achieving recognized business goals. Decisions to downsize, outsource, diversify, or consolidate are justified in terms of shareholder value. We recognize that these enterprises operate within a social values context that informs and constrains their options; there are social and ethical limits to economic choices. Activities which cause harm to people or the environment are frequently (but not always) rejected (see Tomasic, 2002; Rix, 2002). But the domination of the business case as the basis for organizational decision-making (in fact or in rhetoric) means that the economic behavior of large enterprises is, in the final instance, primarily oriented to business performance.

The promotion of e-commerce adoption is firmly grounded in this logic. Adoption of e-commerce has been advocated as a way of reducing transaction costs, gaining market share, streamlining business processes, achieving competitive advantage, and improving relationships with business partners for improved business performance (APEC, 1999, p. 12; Porter, 2001). When a large enough share of individual businesses use e-commerce to improve their competitiveness, then nations as a whole will become more competitive and prosperous (Porter, 1998, 2001; DFAT, 1999; NOIE, 2001). These are seemingly self-evident reasons, but it is worth noting that this advocacy does not promote e-commerce for non-business reasons (for example, because it is an interesting personal challenge, gives peace of mind, improves relationships with one's family or one's personal standing among one's friends). Why should it? Would it make any difference?

Kumar (1998) challenged the assumption that technology use is best seen in terms of 'technical-economic rationality'. Identifying a 'third rationality' (neither technical-economic nor socio-political) based on trust and collaborative relationships, he presented this as the most suitable explanation for the failure of an IOS in the Prato region of Italy. That case study well demonstrates the cultural and situational shaping of the family companies involved in that setting. Kumar portrays the centuries of social history in the Prato region as contributing to business practices at variance with the dominant, modern technical-economic rationality. In other contexts, multiple and counter-rationalities are also likely to be common. Even without the centuries-long established cultural patterns Kumar analyzed, third (and higher order) rationalities will shape business decisions.

There are sound theoretical resources to guide explorations such as these. In his influential work in economic sociology, Granovetter (1985, p. 483) drew attention to the fact that even in modern societies, economic entities are 'embedded' in the social context, much more than has been generally acknowledged. Networks of interpersonal relations are a key to understanding economic behavior, not an extraneous factor. Narrow rational choice models of economic behavior prevent recognition of embeddedness as a key explanatory element. Granovetter (1992, p. 5) showed that the narrow 'undersocialized' view of business rationalism shares a deficiency with the 'oversocialized' view of behaviorist social science: that the economic/social actor is someone who is not influenced by *current* social relationships and has no choice but economic and social conformity. Either of these views leads to unwarranted conclusions and fails to take into account the ways that real actors make decisions linked to their social and business lives. Instead, he argues:

> *"...the fundamental issue is not to get the right model of individual action, but rather to understand properly how variations in social structure create behavior that appears to follow one model or the other. The locus of explanation moves away from the isolated individual to a larger and more social frame of reference."* (Granovetter, 1992, p. 7)

Embeddedness is both structural and relational; it involves trust (Gulati, 1995; Gulati & Garguilo, 1999, p. 1446). It is a characteristic of large as well as small organizations, but for small enterprises, the embeddedness is strongly social and interpersonal. This is part of the reason that SMEs often do not show the same strategic rationalities as larger corporations and are uncomfortable with the efforts of governments and business groups to encourage formal structures and ways of doing things (Gibb, 2000).

The classic economic and social theories of Weber (1977) provide a useful concept for identifying and understanding how economic behaviors at the individual level articulate to the institutional or societal level. Weber's account avoided the pitfalls of both the under- and over-socialized views, and presented an alternative to the narrow economism of many of his contemporaries (see Zeitlin, 1997). Weber argued that the economic sphere is not made up simply of rational business calculations. He distinguished two main types of individual action, both of which were rational (i.e., made a choice of means to achieve goals), but which differed in the kinds of goals they sought. The primary economic activity was *instrumental rationality*, a form of action to achieve directly calculable business goals (such as profit and growth). This is the activity of the recognizable *homo economicus*, enshrined in classical and neo-classical economics (Granovetter, 1985, p. 481). But Weber argued that this was not the only basis for economic behavior. People could also act in terms of *value rationality*. This type of action was clearly rational in that it was oriented to achieve goals, but the goals were of a different type. They were not subject to calculation and not reducible to business outcomes. They included religious and ethical goals, well beyond economic calculation. Weber's classic and often-misunderstood study of the impact of religious ideas on economic behavior (Weber, 1985) demonstrated the independent operation of value rationality on business behavior and its wider implications.

SMEs are not strangers to instrumental rationality, but for these companies, value rationality is likely to be significant and in some cases may dominate business decision-making including decisions about e-commerce. This does not mean that small businesses are necessarily more ethical or have a greater interest in values *per se*, but that they are more likely to weigh personal, domestic, community, and lifestyle factors in business decisions than their counterparts in larger organizations have the choice of doing, especially at organizational level.[2]

There are several reasons that this is likely to be the case.

- Businesses and especially small businesses are commonly family based (Gilding, 2000), and the locus of work is often closely aligned with the family. In these cases, family goals are justifiably central to business decision-making (see Gersick, Lansberg, Desjardins, & Dunn, 1999; Riordan & Riordan, 1993).

- Small businesses may be traditional enterprises that follow long-established practices and principles (see Pahl, 1984). The modernization that has transformed larger, especially Western, enterprises into instrumentally rational formations has not yet transformed many small local auto workshops or retail outlets. Small-business networks are often local and face-to-face with traditional patterns of association and interaction.

- Some small businesses have been established by individuals who have consciously rejected employment in larger companies because this kind of livelihood gives them independence, flexibility, or freedom from supervision (even if the financial rewards are lower). Business owners may mistrust large organizations and government.

- Being a small-business owner may confer status and identity, and the satisfaction from this may even outweigh the economic benefits in some cases.

- Lifecycle issues are more likely to impinge on small-business decisions. The fate of a small business when the owner retires may be disappearance if it cannot be sold or passed on to a younger family member. Anticipation of the end of the company may precede the owner's retirement by a decade or more.

- The larger the enterprise, the more specialization it can afford and the less likely it is to rely on direct control. Smaller businesses are more likely to evince a jack-of-all-trades approach and the owner's fear of loss of control over livelihood and reputation.

- Some small businesses (especially if they are solely owner operated) are best seen as leisure activities that pay for themselves. The main goal has never been to achieve competitive advantage, growth, or significant profit.

To the extent that a small business shows these characteristics, its activities and decisions will be shaped by value goals and characterized by value rationality. These characteristics will profoundly affect how these businesses see e-commerce development and will shape their adoption (or non-adoption) decisions as well as their use if they do adopt.

Small-Business Life in Australia

Before exploring the evidence about Australian small-business rationalities and their e-commerce activities, let's examine their profile in the economy. A number of large-scale surveys provide a picture of this sector of the Australian economy.

The Australian Bureau of Statistics defines small business quantitatively as having fewer than 20 full-time (equivalent) employees, with medium businesses having between 20 and 199 full-time employees (ABS, 2002, p. 1). Small businesses are independently owned and operated, and closely controlled by their owners/managers who contribute all or most of the operating capital. It has been estimated that about 70% of businesses are family owned (Gilding, 2000). Micro-businesses with fewer than five employees are an identified sub-set of the small-business category. Small businesses comprise a key sector of the Australian economy, in 2000-2001 accounting for 96% of all private sector non-agricultural businesses and providing 47% of all private sector non-agricultural employment (ABS, 2002, p. 7). Clearly this sector cannot be dismissed as irrelevant and it is growing (ABS, 2002, p. 13).

Computer use is directly correlated with the size of the business, but the gap is narrowing and a majority of businesses are computer enabled. Internet usage follows the same pattern, but the gulf between small and large business is much wider, with 25% of micro-businesses connected in 1998 compared with 86% of large businesses (ABS, 2000, p. 93). The lowest rates of computer use among small businesses in 1998 were found in the hospitality, personal services, and transport and storage industries. Internet use was also low in these industries. Most small businesses' use of the Internet was for e-mail and information gathering (ABS, 2000, p. 95).

Annual surveys show the Australian SME sector to be steadily increasing its use of computers, which has almost reached saturation level, and of the Internet. Various other e-commerce indicators have also shown an upward trend. The general picture, documented in the *Small Business Survey* (Telstra, 2002), does not illuminate the complexity of the processes that underlie these well-documented trends. But understanding this complexity will prevent nasty surprises as we move away from models that assume a unitary diffusion/adoption path shaped by easily identified 'drivers' and 'barriers'.

Small Businesses Context and E-Commerce

My purpose here is to draw out some of the underpinning small-business rationalities and to link these issues to their approaches to e-commerce. This material is drawn from five research studies conducted in Australia in the period from 1998-2001. Each study included in-depth interviews with people in key positions (typically owner-managers) of small businesses, and explicitly explored their thinking about and experiences of e-commerce. Although these were all self-contained studies, there was enough similarity in the line of questioning that it is reasonable to consider the results as a body.

Most of the information referred to here was not gathered through explicitly framed questions in these studies that were all primarily concerned with drivers, barriers, and resources. This is an inductive reading of insights which arose (or were offered to us) in the course of other discussions with small businesses about e-commerce. Sometimes these comments were made as interviewees explained why they are not interested in pursuing e-commerce or their disappointing experiences with it. In other cases, they arose as interviewees outlined their success with e-commerce and how they came to incorporate it in their businesses. Sometimes these were expressed strongly, sometimes more subtly, but even though the themes reported here were to some extent inadvertently discovered, this makes them no less real or important. Our participants were telling us something valuable about their orientations to e-commerce, whether or not we were knowledgeable enough to ask them about it.

Themes in E-Commerce Adoption by SMEs

I have characterized the material into five interlocking themes, which in practice appear as a seamless reality both to the participants and to the interviewer. These themes highlight the embeddedness of small-business life—in the family and community—which is different from the formally structured relationships in large organizations with their explicit separation of organizational and private lives. Some of the social character-istics of these small businesses were motivators for e-commerce adoption, but more usually they had mixed effects or inhibited its uptake. These themes helped us concep-tualize the small-business milieu and understand the divergent rationalities that guide the decisions of the owners. Their thinking is, in fact, largely rational, although not in exactly the same terms that apply in larger enterprises.

Business, Identity, and Control

For many of the people we interviewed, their business is a core aspect of their personal and social identity. To some extent, they *are* their businesses. This is commonly demonstrated in the ways they talk with pride (and sometimes with apprehension) about the future, competitiveness, and collaborative arrangements. In micro-businesses with few employees or none at all, this identification is very strong. The owners exercise direct

Table 1: Research Studies Dealing with E-Commerce Issues in SMEs

Date Published	Study	Nature of Study	Number of Cases (number of small businesses)
1999	Australian Companies [a]	Case studies of Australian companies successfully using e-commerce	**44** (22)
1999	Australian Exporters [b]	Case studies of Australian SMEs successfully using e-commerce in their export activities	**19** (11)
2000	Regional SMEs [c]	Action research study working with regional SMEs to determine e-commerce strategy	**30** (16)
2001	Small Restaurants [d]	Survey of small restaurant owner-operators on attitudes to e-commerce	**22** (22)
2001	Victorian SMEs [e]	Survey of SMEs exporting and using e-commerce or considering doing so	**25** (25)

[a] DFAT (Department of Foreign Affairs and Trade) (1999)

[b] Castleman & Cavill (2001)

[c] Castleman, Coulthard, & Hewett (2000)

[d] Chin & Castleman (2001)

[e] Castleman, Cavill, & Terrill (2002)

control over their business, not only because there is little scope for any other arrangement, but because they are personally committed and involved. An illustration of this attitude was the vehement response of one small-business owner, discussing website development and e-commerce.

> *"So that's when I realized again...what I know from building this business for twenty years...no-one's going to do it for you. If you want to do it, you have to do it yourself. If you don't know how to do it, you have to learn...We're only a small company and we haven't got money to throw away. As in building the business, you employ an accountant and he'll do the books, employ a solicitor and he'll do the legal aspect, but they aren't going to run your business. They couldn't care less whether you go broke or not. If you are running a business, you have to do it yourself or know how to do it yourself; if there are staff doing it, then you have to know what is being done."*

The challenges of understanding and then being able to use IT for business discourage many small-business people from investigating e-commerce, much less adopting it. It may threaten a loss of the direct control and intimate knowledge of the business of the owners, and as direct managers they are likely to fear loss of control. Not surprisingly, many small-business owners who have been early e-commerce adopters were already skilled at IT and comfortable about experimenting with it. The venture into e-commerce did not, for them, reduce their control and knowledge. The following extract represents a common fortuitous pathway of experimentation rather than conscious strategizing.

> *"My background is IT, so I was fairly aware of it as an everyday issue, and I think it was a case that everyone was starting to do it. If you are aware that your competition is doing something, then you try to do the same thing...It was really seat of the pants. If I take everything into consideration, it went reasonably well. Because we were sort of in new territory, without knowledge I don't know how we could have done it better. There was a fair bit of luck in it."*

The pride in the business can sometimes contain a hint of bravado. The business as an extension of the owner, is illustrated in the following extract.

> *"We are the experts! Our major source is the Internet, everything is on the Net. There are e-commerce websites, electronic marketing, it is all basically on the Net. Legislation of other countries [is] available on the Net. Australian Government Departments are also generally very good, almost better than anybody else in the provision of information on the Web."*

Independence, skill, and pioneering spirit are glimpsed through the stories of the successful, as the quote below highlights.

> *"We set up gradually over time; we had a lot of the skills to start with, but we have really developed our technical skills over time through thinking about the outcomes we wanted to achieve and then working out how to do it. The company basically figured the problems out...When the company started there were very few people doing e-commerce and nobody else seemed to know how to do it. We have developed a culture of looking for new information all the time Now we do training for other people, which is basically one on one and information sharing."*

For those who do not have such skills and confidence, however, the Internet and e-commerce may be forbidding technologies, threatening the loss of this control and mastery, undermining the owner's grip on the direction of the business.

Business Life/Daily Life/Social Life/Lifecycle

The small-business person is, in a real sense, always at work. The distinction between being at work and being at home is blurred, a traditional work pattern (see Pahl, 1984). This is particularly so for those who work from home and in family businesses. The social embeddedness of the small firm creates distinct rationalities in relation to e-commerce and business technology. Investment of either time or money are problematic in cash- and time-strapped small businesses, but this is not typically calculated with much precision (see also Tatnall & Burgess, 2002). To a significant extent, time (especially that of the owner) is valued in terms of its opportunity cost both for business and other activities, separately from calculations about other business expenses. This orientation may hinder investment in the intellectual capital a small business needs to acquire to move into e-commerce.

> "We're interested in] information that doesn't require time and resources to attain (such as lengthy workshops or exhibitions), and even more so, the resources themselves."

Another person, declining to be interviewed, provided a searing insight into the stresses many small-business owners face:

> "I work from 9 a.m. to 1 a.m., six days a week; I don't have time for my wife, I don't have time for my children, and I don't have time to worry about technology or spare half an hour for an interview!"

These comments suggest that when small-business owners say they don't adopt e-commerce because there is no real application for it in their business, they are using personal rather than strict business reasoning.

Getting members of such groups to e-commerce roadshows and other public events is difficult unless there are recognized advantages in either business or social terms. Cost, timing, profile, and ambience all become important in attracting a receptive audience.

Tasks and functions are less strictly divided in smaller firms, with initiatives (such as technical innovations) absorbed within the mainstream of business activities. The accounts below from two small companies illustrate this.

> "The firm acquired the skills necessary for e-commerce...by hiring people who offered those skills and perspectives, even if this was not their core role. Ability to contribute to the e-commerce activities of the firm was defined as one of the general selection criteria. The firm also rewarded people already on staff for developing their expertise in this area. They were encouraged to go to training courses and a large library of materials is held in the firm which also helped people develop this knowledge."

> "Our first sources of information about e-commerce and export were clients and partners who were interested in these developments. The company identified a small number of people who were known to be highly motivated to achieve this. Then these people were encouraged to approach the task in the way they saw fit and supported [doing] this. We ensured that they gained whatever skills were then needed to achieve their particular goals. At the beginning there were no kits or guidebooks explaining how to implement e-commerce—they just had to do it."

Business and Family Dynamics

Families are important to small business, from the family owned business with formalization of family relationships, to the informal web of association and assistance that is an integral part of family life. The following quotation illustrates these relationships and their relevance to e-commerce adoption.

> *"...talking to other people and hearing about it was probably the biggest [impetus for adopting e-commerce]. My son was actively involved in that situation. He certainly was the driving force behind it all. Me being a person not of the electronic age as such, I always said, 'Well, why the hell do you want to be involved with all this? It takes too much time.' It came from other people basically."*

In another case, a small-restaurant owner said:

> *"The reason why I decided to adopt e-commerce into my restaurant was because of my brother who is in the IT field. My brother has been very helpful in terms of setting up the e-commerce technology for my restaurant and teaching me how to use each form of e-commerce according to my business needs."*

For many small-business operators, family and domestic issues are paramount. The work-family balance agenda that struggles for acknowledgment in larger organizations is at the forefront of their concerns. They make decisions about business (and e-business) with their other roles in mind. This may result in 'failure' to adopt e-business techniques that would confer competitive or market advantages. This is well illustrated by the issues raised by one participant in an e-commerce workshop we ran in 2000 (Castleman et al., 2000; Castleman & Coulthard, 2001).

> *The workshop members discussed ways that Mary [the sole proprietor of a small but thriving gardening business] might use business-to-business e-commerce to manage a branch business in another town, reducing the need for her to drive there frequently. She might publicize her business on the Internet, but at this stage she doesn't need more business, just a more profitable business. Ideally, she would like to get a bit more time for her family. At this point Mary faces a dilemma. If she expands and organizes a branch business or a franchise, she will need to step her business up to a higher level. E-commerce may well help her achieve this. But that move will also involve new demands, perhaps a significant investment outlay of family funds and more work stress. On the other hand, unless she makes a move, she may well find that a competitor (or several) could move into the area, perhaps one which uses e-commerce effectively.*

Larger businesses may, of course, also be family enterprises, and many of the considerations about succession, power, and incorporation of family members are similar (see

Gilding, 2000). But for small businesses, family issues impinge more directly on resources and operations involved in e-commerce implementation.

Relationships: Loyalty, Suspicion, and Competition

Relationships are the foundation of small business. These are relationships with business partners, employees, customers, and advisors. They are built on trust and familiarity (even though at times these relationships may be somewhat edgy) and are a major source of information, favors, problem-solving assistance, and personal interaction. Many of the smaller enterprises rely on word-of-mouth, referrals, and personal recommendations for new customers rather than systematic marketing.

Relationships are maintained through telephone and face-to-face encounters. Some e-commerce applications replace business relationships with automatic data exchanges. The logic appeals to managers in large enterprises concerned with streamlining, automating, and minimizing unnecessary personal interaction in the service of reduced transaction costs. Small-business owners, however, depend on these relationships for repeat customers, business intelligence, and advice. Business methods that undermine these relationships not only disrupt the traditional routines of small-business operators, but threaten a valuable, though hidden, resource.

In many interviews, small-business people complained to us about the difficulties of finding IT providers they could trust to help them put their businesses online. They relied on their trusted contacts to make these decisions. A successful innovator with a well-worked out e-commerce strategy for his business, nonetheless based his development on strong relationships.

> *What were the* **most** *useful sources of information for e-commerce development?*

> *"Personal relationships. A programmer I worked with in designing my online system. Never did a formal course on e-commerce. Currently I have a close relationship with [a] small IT company. I don't want a $25,000 website with whistles and bells. It provides more than I need and I couldn't see the value for the money I would have to spend."*

Another small business owner with a successful online development articulated the importance of his network of relationships in the e-commerce venture:

> *"Certainly you must get an organization involved that is capable of setting up a Web page and doing it well. I have heard of people being burnt in that area. So a recognized company that is a specialist in that field is the crucial part. But how you access those providers in the first place is a bit of a hit-and-miss business anyway unless you have some recommendation from someone who has had a successful entry into that area who can say, 'Okay, use these people, they're very good.' That's about the only way of handling that aspect."*

Relationships with customers are also vital and the small-business use of e-commerce to maintain these relationships is not well addressed by focus on market expansion or eCRM (electronic customer relationship management). The following extract describes how a family pottery business uses the Web for maintaining this relationship.

> *The important thing with their business is to get the contact. They started off from being the village potter—that is where potters have come from. The big change is they now tend to be the village potter for people who live in Sydney, Melbourne, and some overseas. Even though they don't produce large volumes, their village has gotten very big. Customers still want to talk to them because of the personal aspect of pottery. The Web lets them to do that— they couldn't do that before...They deliberately have photos of themselves all over the website because they want to say it is about people making stuff. It is like the wine growers, the same sort of thing, it is about that village...*
>
> *That relationship just continues on in the Web. They chat to them online. It is a really easy way to communicate.*

A number of people feared loss of control if they shifted their business to e-commerce, even though they recognized the potential benefits. The passage below describes Peter, who owned and operated a small bakery and catering company, is a case in point.

> *Peter was deeply ambivalent about e-commerce. He strongly believed that e-commerce would increase the threat of competition in bakery goods through electronic tendering and ordering processes. E-commerce was also increasingly likely for the efficient supply of raw materials for his bakery.*
>
> *On the other hand, Peter was very clear that he preferred 'the face to face' and dealing directly with customers and suppliers. He was aware that he did not have the technical skills and feared he did not have the ability to develop an effective e-commerce strategy. Peter was resigned to the fact that e-commerce was very likely to become a businesses necessity for him to continue his wholesale trade. To compound the problem he could not identify a ready and trusted source of advice to consult for the development of a detailed e-commerce business strategy. There were too many unknowns.*

Governments and Gorillas

Influence from large trading partners and governments is a powerful influence on small businesses to adopt e-commerce, especially if they must do so to retain those customers. Not all government or large business e-commerce initiatives are so muscular, with many attempts to engage with and encourage small businesses to move to e-commerce methods. Many of the people who participated in the studies on which this analysis is based had ambivalent views towards government initiatives. On the one hand there was a strong articulation of independence:

> *"There are certain grants available for certain areas to help small business that we have utilized where possible and that has been quite successful for*

us. You get to a situation where you think you may require something and you go down the track of finding out whether there is any assistance available to help you do that. If there is, you accept it, and if there isn't, then you look for another avenue to solve your problem, but I don't really think it should come back in every situation to relying on the government to get you out of a problem."

We also heard more truculent expressions of the resistance to government intervention, as for example:

"The Government can help [Internet business] by keeping clear, no stupid legislation about censorship. Prohibition never worked."

But many also saw the government as the only effective agency to offer protection from the unscrupulous or incompetent practices of some IT vendors, a widely identified problem (DFAT, 1999).

Some respondents listed ways in which government leadership, program initiatives, and substantial investment in e-commerce support activities should be undertaken (sometimes the person was unaware that the government had already innovated in exactly the area they mentioned). The two views (for and against government intervention) could be held simultaneously. Fewer government interventions were suggested in the e-commerce area than in areas where governments provided other business support (Castleman et al., 2002), possibly because the people we spoke with were unfamiliar with government initiatives and contributions in e-commerce. Research in the UK, however, identified a tendency of SMEs to prefer existing sources of advice rather than government-sponsored advisors (Mole, 2002), suggesting that even considerable e-commerce support efforts will not necessarily gain great adherence from time-strapped SMEs, somewhat mistrustful of government.

Less antagonism was voiced towards the large corporate and customer organizations ('gorillas') which wielded substantial power over trading terms and not uncommonly insisted on particular trading platforms that were not particularly beneficial to their suppliers. These requirements (regardless of the benefits that accrued to the small supplier company) were accepted with resignation. A small manufacturer's description illustrates this orientation well.

"I'll move into e-commerce if it's not going to take too much of my time to administer it. I'm currently doing some e-commerce with [another organization] and I have to go into their website to do the credit card transaction. For me that's too hard. It needs to be easy and not cumbersome in processes.

I have an e-commerce mailbox with [a large retail outlet]—to deal with them you have to communicate with them this way. I have a third-party service provider for that because I didn't have the software or the know-how to do the scan packing of all the barcodes. So I was forced into doing it to supply them. I do get paid electronically by most of the businesses I deal with now, which is easier than receiving chouse. With the [retailer's] deal I had to use

a third party, so control went out of my hands and that is a concern. In [the]
future I would like to acquire that type of system myself."

Stepping back for a minute to interpret what these apparently contradictory attitudes mean, a common thread is caution about losing control of business through greater government regulation and a generalized small-business mistrust of government, co-existing with a view of governments being above the untrustworthy practices of many commercial operators. If powerful trading partners seem to be accepted as e-commerce leaders more readily, it may be because small businesses have grown accustomed to their requirements on many other trading issues. There are clearly tensions in these attitudes, and getting the e-commerce support 'product' and the 'pitch' for small business right requires understanding the fierce independence (along with the need for support) that small businesses have.

E-Commerce for Small Business Rationalities

How can we summarize the distinctive business milieu and rationality that shape many small businesses, and what are the implications for understanding their responses to e-commerce? Adopting Weber's distinction between instrumental (economic) rationality and value rationality, we have seen how small businesses make e-business decisions, taking into account family and personal factors. Providing for children's livelihoods, preserving family lifestyles, maintaining parental authority, cementing kinship links may all weigh in the balance, and may be more important than the bottom-line results. For many small businesses, growth and transformation through e-commerce will not be a selling point if it means that one's son or daughter will no longer take over the running of the business. What may be more attractive to such business owners is the potential of these technologies to reduce the stress of running the business by, for example, improving the cash flow and reducing excessive transaction costs by using electronic ordering and payment systems.

It is important that this orientation should not be understood as irrational, but as a distinctive type of rationality, one in which personal goals and relationships weigh heavily. Advocacy of e-business and e-commerce exclusively in terms of standard business benefits will fall on deaf ears in many cases, not because they don't understand the logic, but because they don't see that it applies to them. E-business with a more human face may well appeal to more small-business operators, but for that to be successful, the advocates (governments, associations, and providers) need to re-examine their approach. Understanding e-commerce in more contextual terms is a start. Helping small businesses see how it might contribute to their non-business goals would also improve its attractiveness and utility. If we are to forge suitable programs, it is essential to recognize that overcoming fears (of technology, competition, loss of personal control of the business, relationship change) is an unavoidable part of transforming business practices and that these fears are not unreasonable.

What elements should be part of a more effective campaign? The following points could guide efforts to engage SMEs in e-commerce:

- The technologies and applications must be easy and relatively cheap. Unless IT is a hobby or special interest of the business owner, he or she is more likely to be put off by enthusiastic description of the technology's capability than inspired by it. While some IT learning is necessary and beneficial for small businesses, a significant investment of time is not attractive. Jargonistic, technical discourse may sound impressive, but is clearly counterproductive with those whose understanding of the technology is rudimentary. A focus on the technology should be avoided in favor of a concentration on business and lifestyle benefits (ease of use, solution to business problems, time saving, stress reduction).

  The technically capable early adopters of e-commerce in small business were important pioneers, but they were atypical. The bulk of small businesses need assistance in learning to drive, not a course in motor mechanics. They also need to see how the vehicle will make their lives easier in particular ways.

- Arguments for e-business should understand that typically small-business owners' repute and identity are inextricably linked with their businesses. Fear of failure is more than just business logic. E-business solutions that have a small risk of failure (either symbolically or financially) and highlight achievable personal and business advantages will be more attractive.

- In presenting the benefits of e-commerce, too little attention has been given to lifestyle benefits. These are not relevant in large organizations working to conventional business case logic, but for small businesses this becomes very important. The business case that offers more leisure and family time and greater peace of mind as the result of fewer cash-flow problems may be far more compelling than a case with a higher dollar return on investment or a larger customer base.

- Promotion of e-commerce needs to show how it supports existing face-to-face business relationships rather than replacing them. The latter logic appeals to large enterprises concerned with streamlining, automating, and minimizing unnecessary personal interaction to reduce transaction costs. Applications which recognize that small businesses rely on personal contacts and allow them to cement relationships of trust, information exchange, and personal contact will be more likely to be used by this sector. Reinforcing this capability through product design, marketing, and support would work off these patterns of business alignment rather than chafing against them.

Conclusion

Small businesses are not just scaled down versions of their larger counterparts. Many or most have distinctive social characteristics, which means that their owners design and operate them to achieve a variety of goals, many of them family, interpersonal, and community oriented. Their *value-oriented* rationality has implications for the way owners approach decisions about e-commerce. It is not reducible to economic costs and benefits, but includes concerns about life matters that are more off-stage in large organizations. There are good reasons for accepting that the embeddedness of economic activity (Granovetter, 1985) is especially important for theorizing the small business with its higher incidence of direct owner control, family ownership, diffuse social relationships intertwined with business relationships, and community associations. There is great variation in the way SMEs approach e-commerce and business itself, and the aim of this account is not to overstate differences in business behavior. However, complex value rationalities shape the activity of small businesses much more profoundly than value rationalities in business decision-making affect large enterprises.

What is sometimes described as the 'e-commerce journey' is varied. The socially grounded value rationalities of small-business operators and their employees can affect the way they see the benefits and negatives of e-commerce. These value rationalities need to be recognized and incorporated into analysis, practice, and policy. The strategies that result will enable the operators of small businesses to see the value in e-commerce for them and their businesses, and make it easier for them to participate in the digital economy.

Endnotes

[1]   I have used the term 'e-commerce' here to refer to the range of specific electronic transactions and 'e-business' as a more inclusive descriptor of electronic or online business activities not confined to transactions.

[2]   One counter to this trend is the growing interest in 'ethical investment', an orientation of investors to value as well as instrumental rationality.

References

Asia Pacific Economic Cooperation (APEC). (1999). *SME Electronic Commerce Study (TEL 05/97T), Final Report.* Telecommunications Working Group. Business Facilitation Steering Group.

Australian Bureau of Statistics (ABS). (2000). *Small business in Australia 1999.* Cat. No. 3121.0.

Australian Bureau of Statistics (ABS). (2002). *Small business in Australia 2001.* Cat. No. 3121.0.

Castleman, T., & Cavill, M. (2001). Voices of experience: Developing export capability through e-commerce in Australian SMEs. *Proceedings of the 14th International Bled Electronic Commerce Conference,* Bled, Slovenia (June 25-26).

Castleman, T., & Coulthard, D. (2001) On the fringe: Barriers to participation in the new economy in regional areas. *People and Place, 9*(2), 29-39.

Castleman, T., Cavill, M., & Terrill, L (2002). An integrated information strategy for e-commerce for export: Enhancing networking in an international business context. *Proceedings of the 15th Bled Electronic Commerce Conference—E-Reality: Constructing the E-Economy,* Bled, Slovenia (pp. 522-536).

Castleman, T., Coulthard, D., & Hewett, B. (2000). Riding on the Internet's back: Can rural communities use information technologies for economic development? *Proceedings of ACIS 2000,* Australasian Conference on Information Systems, Brisbane (December).

Chin, C., & Castleman, T. (2001). E-commerce for owner-operated restaurants: An exploratory study. *Proceedings of the 6th CollECTeR Conference on Electronic Commerce,* Coffs Harbour, NSW (December 3-4).

Clegg, S. (1990). *Modern Organizations.* London: Sage Publications.

Corbitt, B., & Kong, W. (2000). Issues affecting the implementation of electronic commerce in SMEs in Singapore. *Proceedings of the 13th Bled Electronic Commerce Conference,* Bled, Slovenia (pp. 474-494).

DeBerranger, P., Tucker, D., & Jones, L. (2001). Internet diffusion in creative micro-businesses: Identifying change agent characteristics as critical success factors. *Journal of Organizational Computing and Electronic Commerce, 11*(3), 197-214.

Department of Foreign Affairs and Trade (DFAT). (1999). *Driving forces on the new silk road.* Canberra.

Deschoolmeester, D., & Van Hee, J (2000). SMEs and the Internet: On the strategic drivers influencing the use of the Internet in SMEs. *Proceedings of the 13th Bled Electronic Commerce Conference,* Bled, Slovenia (pp. 754-769).

Gersick, K., Lansberg, I., Desjardins, M., & Dunn, B. (1999) Stages and transitions: Managing change in family business. *Family Business Review, XII*(4), 287-297.

Gibb, A. (2000). SME policy, academic research and growth of ignorance, mythical concepts, myths, assumptions, rituals and confusions. *International Small Business Journal, 18*(3), 13-35

Gilding, M. (2000). Family business and family change: Individual autonomy, democratization, and the new family business institutions. *Family Business Review, 13*(3), 239.

Golden, W., & Griffin, M. (2000). The World Wide Web: Saviour of small firms. *Proceedings of the 13th Bled Electronic Commerce Conference,* Bled, Slovenia (pp. 495-509).

Granovetter, M. (1985). Economic action and social structure: The problem of embeddedness. *American Journal of Sociology, 91*(3), 481-510.

Granovetter, M. (1992). Economic institutions as social constructions: A framework for analysis. *Acta Sociologica, 35,* 3-11.

Gulati, R. (1995). Does familiarity breed trust? The implications of repeated ties for contractual choice in alliances. *Academy of Management Journal, 38*(1), 85-112.

Gulati, R., & Garguilo, M. (1999). Where do interorganizational networks come from? *American Journal of Sociology, 104*(5), 1439-93.

Kumar, K (1998). The merchant of Prato-revisited: Toward a third rationality of information systems. *MIS Quarterly,* (June), 199-226.

Lawrence, J., & Hughes, J. (2000). Internet usage by SMEs: A UK perspective. *Proceedings of the 13th Bled Electronic Commerce Conference,* Bled, Slovenia (pp. 738-753).

Levy, M., & Powell, P. (2002). SME Internet adoption: Towards a transporter model. *Proceedings of the 15th Bled Electronic Commerce Conference—E-Reality: Constructing the E-Economy,* Bled, Slovenia (pp. 507-521).

Markus, L., & Soh, C. (2002). Structural influences on global e-commerce activity. *Journal of Global Information Management, 10*(1), 5-13.

Mole, K. (2002). Business advisers' impact on SMEs: An agency theory approach. *International Small Business Journal, 20*(2), 139-162.

National Office for the Information Economy (NOIE) (2001). *Taking the plunge: Sink or swim.* Department of Communication, Information Technology and the Arts, Commonwealth of Australia.

Oliver, J., & Damaskopoulos, P. (2002). SME e-business readiness in five eastern European countries: Results of a survey. *Proceedings of the 15th Bled Electronic Commerce Conference—E-Reality: Constructing the E-Economy,* Bled, Slovenia (pp. 584-599).

Pahl, R.E. (1984). *Divisions of Labour.* Oxford: Basil Blackwell.

Poon, S., & Joseph, M. (2000). Product characteristics and Internet commerce benefit among small businesses. *Journal of Product and Brand Management, 9*(1), 21-34.

Poon, S., & Swatman, P. (1999). An exploratory study of small-business Internet commerce issues. *Information & Management, 35,* 9-18.

Porter, M. (1998). *The Competitive Advantage of Nations.* New York: The Free Press.

Porter, M. (2001). Strategy and the Internet. *Harvard Business Review, 79*(3), 62-79.

Riordan, D., & Riordan, M. (1993). Field theory: An alternative to systems theories in understanding the small family business. *Journal of Small Business Management, 31*(2), 66-79.

Rix, S. (2002). Globalization and corporate responsibility. *Alternative Law Journal, 27*(1), 16-22.

Small Enterprise Telecommunications Centre (SETEL). (2002). *Accelerating the uptake of e-commerce by small & medium enterprises: A report and action plan by the SME E-Commerce Forum Taskforce, July 2002.* Also available on the Web: http://www.setel.com.au/smeforum2002.

Tatnall, A., & Burgess, S. (2002). Using Actor-Network Theory to research the implementation of a B2B portal for regional SMEs in Melbourne, Australia. *Proceedings of the 15th Bled Electronic Commerce Conference—E-Reality: Constructing the E-Economy,* Bled, Slovenia (pp. 179-191).

Telstra. (2002). *2002 Yellow Pages® business index: E-business report, the online experience of small and medium enterprises.* Australia: Telstra Corporation.

Available on the Web: http://www.sensis.com.au/Internet/small_business/ypbi/ sbpypbi_specialrpts.jhtml.

Tomasic, R. (2002). Corporate collapse, crime and governance—Enron, Andersen and beyond. *Australian Journal of Corporate Law, 14,* 183-201.

Weber, M. (1977). *From Max Weber: Essays in Sociology.* Translated, edited by H.H. Gerth & C.W. Mills. London: Routledge & Kegan Paul.

Weber, M. (1985). *The Protestant Ethic and the Spirit of Capitalism.* London: Unwin Paperbacks.

Wilkins, L., Swatman, P.M.C., & Castleman, T. (1999). What's in a name? Conceptual issues in defining electronic commerce. *Proceedings of the European Conference on Information Systems,* Vienna.

Zeitlin, I. (1997). *Ideology and the Development of Sociological Theory* (6th ed.). Upper Saddle River, NJ: Prentice-Hall.

Section III

Factors Impacting E-Commerce Adoption and Use in SMEs

Chapter IV

Business Issues in the 21st Century: An Empirical Study of E-Commerce Adoption in UK and Denmark SMEs

Michael Quayle, University of Glamorgan, UK

John K. Christiansen, Copenhagen Business School, Denmark

Abstract

This chapter explores the business issues affecting the level of implementation of e-commerce adoption in small to medium-sized enterprises (SMEs). Results of a survey of 256 UK and 140 Danish small firms suggests those SMEs in both countries that have developed e-commerce capability have not done so strategically and have yet to enjoy significant cost and time savings. The survey also identifies the challenges faced by SMEs. Finally, the authors suggest paths that might be followed in seeking to achieve effective performance and wider adoption of commerce.

Context

Business issues can be categorized into the drive for competitiveness, critical factors that emerge from that drive, and power relationships. Arguably all those issues affect one of the biggest strategic opportunities in business history, namely, e-commerce. The drive for competitiveness is influenced for example by instability of the U.S. economy, perpetual local wars in Eastern Europe and the Middle East, the pace of technological change, fluctuating oil and fuel prices, and globalization per se. Allied to this instability is the desire for product/service improvements, cost reduction, and the efforts by major purchasers to push risk as far down the supply chain as they can. Critical factors emerge from the drive for competitiveness. These include the need for a strategic approach to business, utilizing new technologies, meeting the logistics demands of the 21st Century, and ensuring the workforce updates its skills in a timely manner. Anecdotal evidence suggests that partnerships and trust now take a backseat to the old-style adversarial relationships. All this occurs as organizations (often encouraged by national government) implement or consider implementing e-commerce, which potentially provides opportunities for coherent procurement, improving buyer-supplier relationships, and eliminating time zone obstacles. It is in this context that research in the UK and Denmark has been carried out.

Literature Overview

There are government strategies for e-commerce. Generally the strategy has six strands. These are to establish a brand in e-commerce both domestically and internationally, transform existing business, foster e-commerce creation and growth, expand the e-commerce talent pool, provide leadership in international e-commerce policy development, and government online should be a priority. There is evidence of government online e-commerce (see Fee, Erridge, & Hennigan, 2001). Generally, however, there is a great deal of "hype" about e-commerce and SME survivability (Seppanen & Suomala, 2002). Indeed, there is evidence that those SMEs that have tried to implement e-commerce solutions (perhaps using the gut-feel approach) are dissatisfied with both the concept and service providers (O'Brien, 2000). Some are predicting a collapse of e-commerce! (Wallace, 2000). The world, however, appears to have made progress in implementing e-commerce. Anecdotally, the U.S., Canada, and Australia are the leaders. In Western Europe, Scandinavia leads the UK, Germany, Austria, Italy, Spain, and France; in Eastern Europe, Poland, the Czech Republic, and Hungary are progressing, but Internet access remains expensive. The Japanese perhaps surprisingly see the Internet as unreliable, preferring mobile phone commerce (m-commerce) where credit cards are not used and transactions are simply added to the monthly bill [see for example, Kotzab and Madlberger (2001) and Szwejczewski et al. (2001)]. Local economies contain a significant percentage of small to medium-sized enterprises (SMEs)—in many cases as much as 80% or 90% throughout Europe. While these SMEs are viewed with interest as suppliers, by customers who have coherent supplier development programs, e-commerce within the smaller firms receives little attention (Attaran, 2001). There is a limited amount of analysis of e-commerce in SMEs, although there is broad anecdotal agreement on a number of points. In particular there appears to be a scope for improving e-commerce, and a need to improve and develop credible methodologies for e-commerce implementation as SMEs strive to achieve competitive advantage (Benjamin, 2000; Albores, Ball, & MacBryde, 2002).

E-commerce can take a variety of forms, including electronic data interchange (EDI), mobile telephone, direct link-ups with suppliers, Internet, intranet, extranet, electronic catalog ordering, and e-mail. Its alleged popularity is due to a multitude of perceived operational benefits it can bring to purchasing practices (Soliman & Youssef, 2001). Examples of these benefits are cost savings resulting from reduced paper transactions; shorter order cycle time and the subsequent inventory reduction, resulting from speedy transmission of purchase order-related information; and enhanced opportunities for the supplier/buyer partnership through establishment of a web of business-to-business communication networks (Gulledge & Sommer, 1998; Dell, 1999). E-commerce can enhance supply chain efficiency by providing real-time information regarding product availability, inventory level, shipment status, and production requirements (Radstaak & Ketelaar, 1998). It has vast potential to facilitate collaborative planning among supply chain partners by sharing information on demand forecasts and production schedules that dictate supply chain activities (Karoway, 1997). It can also effectively link customer demand information to upstream supply chain functions (e.g., manufacturing, distribution, and sourcing) and subsequently facilitate "pull" (demand-driven) supply chain operations (Kalakota & Whinston, 1997). Despite such potential benefits, not every firm is ready to embrace e-commerce as a purchasing tool (Pawar & Driva, 2000). Some serious hurdles to the successful implementation of e-commerce include a host of security, legal, and financial problems, not the least of which are unquantified business cases for its introduction (Taylor, 1999; Min & Galle, 1999; Ramaseshan, 1997). In particular, the incoherence of the Web and concerns about security and flexibility limit the confidence of business in Internet-based trading systems (Prasad & Tata, 2000). Current e-commerce systems do not yet fully address these concerns, and most concentrate on bilateral relationships between sellers and buyers (van Hoek, 2001). The business processes supported can be quite simple (Quayle, 2001). In most instances, it is the buyers who dictate terms, yet many systems are very supplier-centric. Similarly, the issues that SMEs faces are not simply scaled-down replicas of large organization experiences and business processes (Sparrow, 2001; Ussman, Almeida, Ferreira, Mendes, & Franco, 2001; Wagner, Fillis, & Johannsson, 2002).

The perceived benefits of e-commerce can thus be encapsulated in Figure 1.

While one in 20 (5%) new e-business entities funded by venture capitalists succeed, the corporate world is going to have its fair share of failures (Carpenter, 2001). It is clear that while the corporate sector, publicly at least, would declare withdrawals from e-business being based on a poor return on investment, there may be other reasons centered around employees, suppliers, and organizations themselves. Feinstein (2001) suggests resistance from employees can take the forms of inertia, fear of previous failures, a general lack of faith in e-business, and future shock (the pace of change). Feinstein also argues suppliers are unwilling to dump their proprietary systems, and organizations generally lack equipment, time, and an unwillingness to use dot.com companies to develop e-

Figure 1: Perceived Business Advantages (Adapted from Hoek & Chong, 2001; Marrakech, 2000)

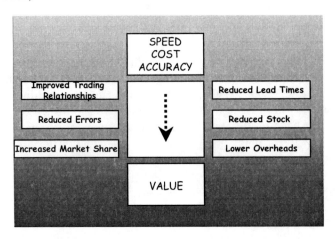

business capability. Gabbard (2001) suggests successful e-business has more to do with good procurement than electronics. In the last few years, a great number of large, established companies are developing e-business solutions; up until then, these companies were seen to only adopt the possibilities very reluctantly (*The Economist,* 2001). Studies have revealed that many companies fail since they do not recognize the special requirements that setting up a new type of business produces, and they do not recognize the need for organizational changes and project management of e-commerce projects (Kanter, 2001). Among the reported problems are: too little focus and too many small initiatives in the companies, problematic staffing and poor internal communication and coordination of e-commerce project, too few and too small ambitions (risk adverse), problematic selection and use of outside vendors for developing the solutions, too much copying of the "traditional" business processes, no real desire and resources to develop the e-business as a completely new business area, no focus on company-wide cooperation in cyberspace, not enough focus on online competitors, lack of training and focus on organizational implementation, and finally, there is often too little focus on learning from customers.

Most published case studies reveal that organizations that adopt e-commerce solutions are already involved in customer relationships at a distance (e.g., mail order or telephone-based sales and services). These organizations also tend to have a good understanding of computer-based systems before they embark on e-commerce solutions, and they usually do not opt for radical changes to their purchasing and customer supply systems—indeed paper-based systems are often maintained in parallel (Sriram & Bannerjee, 1994). Usually they modify and extend existing computer-based systems such as EDI, or they extend e-commerce options but retain older non-computing systems (St. Pierre, Parks, & Waxman, 1999). Nevertheless, the pace of business change, once the process of adopting e-commerce solutions has begun, can be very fast [see, for example, Fraser, Fraser, and McDonald (1999), Winser and Tan (2000), Croom (2001), and Murphy

(1996)]. None of these authors focus on either the business case for e-commerce introduction nor its introduction in SMEs. The implications are that the cost of change is undertaken without the benefits being clear (Wilcox, 1999; Ritchie, Brindley, & Peet, 1999; Croom, 2000; Wrennall, 2000).

Thinking strategically about e-commerce, its success is based on reach, affiliation, and richness (Evans & Wurster, 2000). Fundamentally, therefore, e-commerce systems need to be effective. Porter (2001) suggests the Internet merely provides a technological platform to aide gaining competitive advantage by building on effective strategy. The holistic and integrated approach is necessary to planning and implementing e-business internally and externally (McIvor & McHugh, 2000; Dekker & Meijboom, 2002). Suppliers, however, play a critical role in e-business by offering encouragement, training, incentives, and stressing the convenience of use (Deeter-Schmeiz, Bizzari, Graham, & Howdyshell, 2001). Smaller firms are also being squeezed by customers' desires for supply chain cost reductions, as well as being confused by which technical systems to use (Gulledge, 2001; Delfmann, Albers, & Gehring, 2002).

We need to remember also that the business world may be perceived as a slightly different place. The impact of September 11, 2001, has been (and is) wide ranging. We are, too, in a post-dot.com collapse period where uncertainty and changes in strategic direction have occurred. For example in Australia many IT functions have been eliminated and during 2001, 60% of IT managers left their jobs or were terminated (Orr, 2002). There is evidence from an eight-European-country study that e-business strategies have yet to mature (Cagliano, Canianto, & Spina, 2002). Indeed despite the proliferation of e-marketplaces, some organizations do not know such marketplaces exist (Carvalto, 2002).

Overall the literature and reality suggest four broad areas against which e-commerce adoption may be measured:

1. Customer relationships in terms of markets opened up; changes in relationships, pricing practices, customer expectations, product portfolio and face-to-face contact.

2. Supplier relationships in terms of changes to contractual practices, the supplier base, legal issues arising, and changes to face-to-face contact.

3. People management in terms of changes to working levels, working locations, business processes, skills needs, and organizational structure changes.

4. General information, for example, use of external support, procedures, increased sales, and reduced costs.

These four areas would appear to represent the difficulties associated with e-commerce adoption.

Despite these difficulties, SMEs remain interested in e-commerce. The research reported below provides an economic overview of the UK and Denmark, evidence of the adoption of e-commerce in SMEs, and the subsequent challenges that must be faced in achieving the required competences. Finally, some responses to these challenges are proposed for e-commerce in small firms, and a future research agenda is suggested.

Economic Overview

Denmark

This thoroughly modern market economy features high-tech agriculture, up-to-date small-scale and corporate industry, extensive government welfare measures, comfortable living standards, and high dependence on foreign trade. Foreign trade accounts for approximately two-thirds of GDP. While agricultural products used to dominate, industrial products now account for 75% of the export. Machines and instruments for industry are the principal export goods, followed by chemical products and industrially processed agricultural products. The former center-left coalition government has reduced the formerly high unemployment rate and attained a budget surplus, as well as followed the previous government's policies of maintaining low inflation and a stable currency, by tying the Danish Krone to the Euro. Since late 2001, a right-wing coalition is installed, focusing strongly on trying to reduce the tax burden in the longer run and supporting other liberal values. Problems of bottlenecks, and longer-term demographic changes reducing the labor force, are being addressed through labor market reforms. The unemployment rate is presently around 5.4%. The government has been successful in meeting, and even exceeding, the economic convergence criteria for participating in the Euro currency, but Denmark, in a September 2000 referendum, reconfirmed its decision not to join the other EU members in the Euro. Even so, the Danish currency remains pegged to the Euro.

The public sector plays an important role in the Danish economy, having around 33% of the workforce employed in this sector. With a total labor force of 2.8 million, the main industries are: food processing, machinery and equipment, textiles and clothing, chemical products, electronics, construction, furniture and other wood products, shipbuilding, and windmills. Denmark's main export markets are Germany (21%), Sweden (12%), the UK (8%), and the U.S. (5%).

UK

The UK, a leading trading power and financial center, deploys an essentially capitalistic economy, one of the quartet of trillion-dollar economies of Western Europe. Over the past two decades, the government has greatly reduced public ownership and contained the growth of social welfare programs. Agriculture is intensive, highly mechanized, and efficient by European standards, producing about 60% of food needs with only 1% of the labor force. The UK has large coal, natural gas, and oil reserves; primary energy production accounts for 10% of GDP, one of the highest shares of any industrial nation. Services, particularly banking, insurance, and business services, account by far for the largest proportion of GDP, while industry continues to decline in importance. The economy has grown steadily, at just above or below 3% for the last several years. The government has put off the question of participation in the Euro system until after the next election, circa June of 2006.

With a labor force of 29.2 million, the UK's main industries are: machine tools, electric power equipment, automation equipment, railroad equipment, shipbuilding, aircraft, motor vehicles and parts, electronics and communications equipment, metals, chemicals, coal, petroleum, paper and paper products, food processing, textiles, clothing, and other consumer goods. Its main export markets are Germany (12%), France (10%), The Netherlands (8%), and the U.S. (16%).

Research Aim

The purpose of this research, therefore, is to:

- Explore the degree to which SMEs have adopted e-commerce in the UK and Denmark;
- Understand the priority currently accorded e-commerce within SMEs in the UK and Denmark;
- Identify potential paths for UK and Danish SMEs to improve their e-commerce activity.

The Study

Deploying random multi-stage stratified sampling, questionnaires were mailed to the chief executives of 450 UK and 500 Danish organizations with a turnover of less than £20m, trading for at least seven years, employing fewer than 200 people, ensuring a wide geographical and industrial spread. With a 57% UK and 28% Danish response rate, the findings may be considered a substantive indication of the current trends.

Breakdown of the Survey by Industry

Table 1 gives the percentage breakdown of those companies that responded by sector.

Results and Analysis

The replies to the questionnaire were analyzed and the results are presented in the following sections. Two kinds of response were required from the questions. Some statements simply required an indication of agreement. In these cases the percentage of organizations indicating agreement is shown. The second type of question asked for a score (from 1-5) to indicate the importance given to an area. In this case the average scores of those answering the question are presented. The analysis gives the overall picture regarding priorities and adoption of e-commerce.

Table 1: Survey Sectors Responding

Sector	Percentage UK	Percentage Denmark
Manufacturing	35	33
High Tech	30	4
Electrical & Engineering	17	2
Packaging & Distribution	7	7
Finance Associated	4	37
Service/Utility	3	12
Construction	2	5
Agriculture	1	0

Business Issues

The research initially sought to establish the business issues of highest importance to the SMEs. The top 10 issues are given in Table 2.

The top three issues in the UK (leadership, strategy, marketing) are only concerned with a relatively narrow vision of what is required for the business to survive. In contrast, issues such as e-commerce, purchasing, R&D, and benchmarking do not appear to have great importance. The irony perhaps is that such issues are normally associated with innovation.

Table 2: Business Issues

Issue	Ranking UK	Ranking Denmark
Leadership	1	1
Strategy	2	2
Marketing	3	3
Supply Chain Management	4	6
Financial Management	5	5
Customer Management	6	4
E-commerce	7	
Purchasing	8	7
R&D	9	8
Benchmarking	10	
Change Management		9
Human Resources Mgt.		10

Table 3: E-Commerce Status

POSITION	UK %	Denmark %
In process of implementing	30	0
Implemented	59	22
Plan to implement	4	10
Considering	5	23
No plans	1	45
Tried and abandoned!!	1	0

The Danish survey produced somewhat similar results concerning the first eight issues, although ranking Supply Chain Management lower and Customer Management higher than in the UK survey. Noticeable in the Danish survey is that e-commerce did not make the top 10 issues at all, but that concerns about Purchasing, R&D, and Change Management and Human Resources Management are given higher attention by management. Not listed in the table, issues concerning Process Improvement, Legal Issues, Business Processes, Benchmarking, and Alliances & Partnerships are given a higher score than e-commerce in the Danish context. Actually e-commerce comes in as the lowest ranking of the issues mentioned by Danish managers. Noteworthy is also that if asking about R&D *and* Product Development, and not only about R&D, the question about R&D comes in as a number six on the list (instead of number eight).

Adoption of E-Commerce

Table 3 provides an overview of e-commerce implementation.

From Table 2 it would appear the UK is substantially ahead of Denmark in terms of implementation. On average, 10% of all purchasing activities are carried out electronically in the UK and Denmark. This is an encouraging overview and leads to establishing why companies had decided to implement e-commerce. The reasons given are in Table 4.

Surprisingly, it is the UK companies' own strategy to implement e-commerce rather than being customer driven as it is in Denmark. Perhaps Danish purchasers have grasped the e-opportunity. The top four reasons given for no e-commerce activity in both countries

Table 4: Reasons for Implementation

DRIVER	UK %	Denmark %
Supplier driven	3	17
Customer driven	8	74
Own strategy	89	9

Table 5: Customer Relationships

STATUS	UK %	Denmark %
Improved a lot	17	35
Improved a little	62	34
Not improved	22	31

are a lack of understanding of the business opportunity (38%), lack of technical know-how (32%), lack of workforce skills (26%), and the price of technology (4%). Other findings of interest in relation to customers are that those who have adopted e-commerce see it as primarily to communicate with existing customers and added value advertising. The results of improvements in customer relationships are given in Table 5.

Clearly, some improvement in relationships had occurred, but by no means could they be described as overwhelmingly positive. This is perhaps reflected in that business had increased in both countries on average by 10% as a result of being able to trade electronically. Only 10% in both the UK and Denmark experienced less face-to-face contact with customers.

In Denmark 35% report improved relationships with customers after implementation, e.g., due to closer relationships and by tying the customer closer to the company, while only 19% report changed behavior in customer relationships, and the same number reports that e-commerce had changed the attitude by customers—by modifications of expectations that they have towards the market. One third-report changes in trading arrangements after e-commerce implementation, and 19% of Denmark companies subsequently report changes in services and/or product portfolio of e-commerce implementation. In comparison, there appears to have been little improvement (17%) in UK customer relationships, a 10% change in product portfolio, and no significant change in face-to-face contact. Interestingly, very little changes in supplier relationships were observed; see, for example, Table 6.

There were no changes in local suppliers, but 2% in the UK and 1% in Denmark of new suppliers, respectively. The "new" suppliers were located in other areas of Europe. Similarly 95% of companies had not experienced any legal or IPR problems as a result of e-commerce activity. The most significant impact in terms of suppliers is that companies claim cost savings averaging 7%. In terms of general changes (in both countries) to trading, pricing, etc., 90% claim no change in their pricing policy, 90% claim no change

Table 6: Impact on Suppliers

CHANGE	UK %	Denmark %
Relationships	80% no change	81% no change
Face to face contact	92% no change	90% no change
More or fewer (suppliers)	87% no change	90% no change

Table 7: Barriers to Implementation

BARRIER	UK %	Denmark %
Time	24	30
People	27	30
Cost	20	30
Fear	7	5
Risk averse key people	7	5

in their product portfolio, and 90% claim there are no changes in employee working hours or locations. Some 62% of companies stated that skills updating had not been necessary, and 52% had not changed either their business processes or organizational structures. Barriers to implementation of e-commerce are given in Table 7.

Time was identified in terms of to gain the necessary knowledge, to develop websites, to update websites. The people constraints were finding someone to develop e-commerce; finding someone to drive it forward; and a lack of internal expertise in terms of knowledge, computer skills, and design capacity. Problem people were seen as finance and IT managers, with most staff seen as generally skeptical about e-commerce. In terms of fear, misuse of e-commerce, data corruption, and computer virus were the main elements identified. Costs were identified as prohibitive for wiring renewal, building facilities, and new computers. Allied to these costs, companies felt financing implementation (finding the financing), difficulties in quantifying benefits, and a reluctance of their customers to utilize e-commerce were all significant barriers.

Organizational Learning

Forty-eight percent of the UK and 50% of Danish who have implemented e-commerce have changed their business processes, suggesting that organizational changes and e-commerce are closely related; 25% of the Danish companies are disappointed with e-commerce implementation compared to 65% in UK. The typical UK and Denmark increase in business of 10% is minimal. The cost savings average of 7%, primarily due to reductions in supplier prices, is not dramatic.

Conclusion

Overall, the research does indicate some progressive approaches and awareness of e-commerce. Moreover, any organization, SME or larger, must manage itself; it may be that the SMEs' customers may be trying to manage suppliers rather than managing the interface. There is some case research (referred to elsewhere in this chapter) to show that good e-commerce can impact significantly on the profitability of the organization—in both public and private sectors. It appears that SMEs do not recognize this in the UK and Denmark, and see no real disadvantage in their own lack of e-commerce capability. Given their contribution to the UK and Denmark GDPs and employment, and the opportunities for economic development both locally and nationally, it would appear that developing e-commerce expertise in SMEs might be considered a key factor in industrial policy making in both the UK and particularly Denmark, where e-commerce adoption appears low. A subjective view of e-commerce is that it is mostly hype, and consequently companies have yet to fully utilize the concept. Similarly, companies may simply be risk averse with a greater understanding of costs than benefits. It could of course be simply a matter of timing—the general economic situation and the impact of September 11, 2001.

It is more likely, based on this research, that if organizations wish to maximize e-commerce, they need to revisit their business processes and overall business strategy. They need to decide perhaps if e-commerce is merely a tool to improve operational efficiency or e-commerce is a method of developing competitive advantage. For those who decide competitive advantage is their preferred role, there is a need to revisit their business processes. They need a generic e-strategy underpinned by clear objectives and a set of relevant critical success factors. We have to be realistic here, too. The development of e-commerce strategies is not easy. As well as the difficulties given in the literature overview of this chapter, this research suggests there are a number of contingent variables, a need for scenario planning, and a need for supply chain integration mechanisms. This is illustrated in Figure 2.

Clearly, in the trade and business "equation," strategy makers need to move away from a preoccupation with simply export promotion and market access. They need to realize that business and economic development depends on export delivery performance, fulfillment, and supply chain capabilities. The issue perhaps is convincing strategy makers (both in the public and private sectors) to pay equal attention to border in and border out supply chain support utilizing e-commerce.

Figure 2: Factors Affecting E-Commerce Strategy

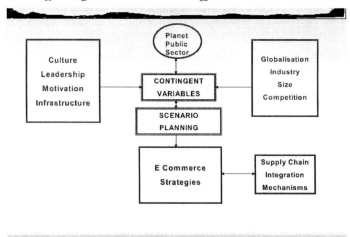

E-commerce represents a significant challenge. Food for thought here is that as the concept expands and more sources of supply become available, the desire to reduce the supplier base as part of strategic supply chain management may not be as important as it is currently perceived to be; what this does not recognize, however, is the partnership/ long-term business relationship, e.g., single sourcing and trust, that may have significantly more benefits to all concerned than maintaining a huge supplier base (Van Hooft & Stegwee, 2001). Given that 75% to 80% of all organizations' purchases have a transaction value of 500 Euros or less, there is a great deal to be said for e-commerce and the probability that transaction costs would be reduced (Aycliffe, 1999). There are, however, very few real studies on the business case for e-commerce introduction in SMEs.

SMEs could benefit by using e-commerce, both as a strategic business tool and to facilitate purchasing consortia. This needs recognition that effective e-commerce impacts on the all-important bottom line—both in the public and private sectors (Emiliani, 2000). SMEs do not appear to recognize this and hence do not see a problem with their own e-commerce capability. They perhaps feel low cost plus high quality equals winning criteria. In the 21ˢᵗ Century, delivery dependability, flexibility, innovation, plus low cost and high quality is the winning criteria. The way to achieve this is through grasping the e-commerce opportunity.

SMEs provide clear opportunities for economic development both locally and nationally. Developing SME e-commerce expertise is essential to sustaining (and in some cases, achieving) competitive advantage. SMEs appear to be aware of (if not embrace) the basic elements of e-commerce. The challenge perhaps is getting them to realize the same elements are also prerequisites for developing an organization's competitive advantage.

The future belongs to those who can use new technology to make themselves more efficient and develop better products and services (Weber, 1999). The results may not be instant; nevertheless, SMEs ignore e-commerce at their peril. The reality, however, is that businesses that really want to work with partners on the Internet ought to be prepared to do whatever it takes to get them there, including developing suppliers' purchasing expertise.

Future Research

The performance of SMEs is shaped by the commercial market, through expansion plans of purchasers and their ability to meet requirements. In order to meet these requirements, both workforce organization and process issues need to be addressed. Increasingly, as purchasers reduce their supply base, SME suppliers will be expected to meet international standards of performance, and this process may expose fundamental structural and potentially terminal deficiencies at all points in the supply chain. Research is necessary to establish key elements and disciplines of continuous improvement, with a particular focus on the purchasing functions and in particular e-commerce adoption both in public and private sectors. Are there sectoral models of e-commerce adoption that could be used by SMEs? Perhaps also beneficial would be some research into the leadership competencies needed to take forward e-commerce. Lastly, we'd like to see some research on the impact of September 11, 2001, (and subsequent events) on business issues and priorities.

References

Albores, P., Ball. P., & MacBryde, J. (2002). Assessing the impact of electronic commerce in business processes: A simulation approach. *Proceedings of the 9ᵗʰ EUROMA Annual Conference on Operations Management,* Copenhagen (June, pp. 15-26).

Alderman, N., & Thomson, A. (1998). *Supply chain management in capital goods manufacturing industries: Summary of the key issues* (pp. 2-7). BPRC University of Newcastle.

Attaran , M. (2001). The coming of age of on-line procurement. *Industrial Management & Data Systems,* 101(4), 177-180.

Aycliffe, R. (1999). Editorial comment. *Supply Management,* (March).

Benjamin, K. (2000). Spin to Win2. *E-Business,* (September), 32-36.

Cagliano, R., Canianto, F., & Spina, G. (2002). E-business strategy: How companies are shaping their manufacturing and supply chain through the Internet. *Proceedings of the 9ᵗʰ EUROMA Conference of Operations Management,* Copenhagen (June, pp. 201-213).

Carpenter, R. (2001). Faith no more. *E-Business,* (May), 34-40.

Carvalho, J. (2002). E-marketplaces criticality in Portugal. *Proceedings of the 9th EUROMA Conference on Operations Management,* Copenhagen (June, pp. 337-341).

CBI. (2000, July). *SME trends report* (pp. 10-12). London: CBI.

Croom, S. (2000). Impact of Web-based procurement in the management of operating resources. *Journal of Supply Chain Management, 36*(1) 4-13.

Deeter-Schmeiz, D., Bizzari, A., Graham, R., & Howdyshell, C. (2001). Business to business online purchasing: Suppliers' impact on buyers' adoption and usage intent. *Journal of Supply Chain Management, 37*(1), 4-10.

Dekker, K., & Meijboom, B. (2002), Adapting supply chain organisations to B2C e-commerce. *Proceedings of the 9ᵗʰ EUROMA Annual Conference on Operations Management, Copenhagen (June, pp. 391-400).*

Delfmann, W., Albers, S., & Gehring, M. (2002). The impact of e-commerce on logistics service providers. *International Journal of Physical Distribution & Logistics Management, 32*(3), 203-222.

Dell Company. (1999). *How stuff works.* Available on the Web: www.howstuffworks.com.

The Economist. (2001). E-strategy: While Welch waited. (May 19).

Emiliani, M. (2000). Business to business online auctions: Key issues for purchasing process improvement. *Supply Chain Management, 5*(4), 176-186.

Evans, P., & Wurster, T. (2000). Talking strategically about e-commerce. *Perspectives.* Available on the Web: www.bcg.com.

Fee, R., Erridge, A., & Hennigan, S. (2001). SMEs and government purchasing in Northern Ireland. *Proceedings of 10th International IPSERA Conference,* Sweden (pp. 377-387).

Feinstein, A.H. (2001). Hospitality industry services to embrace B2B. *Purchasing Today, 12*(5), 24-28.

Fraser, J., Fraser, N., & McDonald, F. (1999). Welcome to 'E' world. *Logistics Solutions, 1*(2), 18-21.

Gabbard, E.G. (2001). Establishing successful e-procurement. *Purchasing Today, 12*(8), 10-11.

Gulledge, T. (2001). B2B e-marketplaces and SMEs. *Proceedings of the 4th SME International Conference,* Denmark.

Gulledge, T., & Sommer, R. (1998). *Electronic commerce resource: An industry-university partnership.* ECRC Research Paper, Fairfax, USA.

Kotzab, H., & Madlberger, M. (2001). European retailing in e-transition. *International Journal of Physical Distribution & Logistics, 30*(6), 440-462.

Marrakech. (2000). *B2B E-Commerce White Paper.* Dublin: Marrakech.

McIvor, R., & McHugh, M. (2000). Collaborative buyer-supplier relations: Implications for organisation change management. *Strategic Change, 9*(4), 221-236.

Min, H., & Galle, W. (1999). Electronic commerce usage in business to business purchasing. *International Journal of Operation and Production Management, 19*(9), 909-921.

Murphy, E. (1996). Electronic systems alter the buying process. *Purchasing,* (February 15), 29-30.

O'Brien, L. (2000). SMEs blame suppliers for solutions failures. *Supply Management,* (March 9).

Orr, S. (2002). Post new economy strategic planning: Did we learn anything? *Proceedings of the 9th EUROMA Annual Conference on Operations Management,* Copenhagen (June).

Porter, M. (2001). Strategy and the Internet. *Harvard Business Review, 79*(3), 62-78.

Powell, P. (2000). *From SMEs to SMEEs.* CRISPS Seminar. University of Bath, UK (November 22).

Quayle, M. (2001). E-commerce usage in UK SMEs operating in the aerospace/defence sectors. *International Journal of Aerospace Management, 1*(3), 227-236.

Ritchie, B., Brindley, C., & Peet, S. (1999). E-commerce, IS development and risk management for SMEs operating in a global market. *Cyprus International Journal of Management, 4*(1), 4-18.

Seppanen, M., & Suomala, P. (2002). E-business in B2B wholesaler's supply chain. *Proceedings of the 9th EUROMA Conference on Operations Management,* Copenhagen (June, pp. 1315-1324).

Soliman, F., & Yousself, M. (2001). The impact of some recent developments in e-business on the management of next generation manufacturing. *International Journal of Operations & Production Management, 21*(5/6), 538-564.

Sparrow, J. (2001). Knowledge management in small firms. *Knowledge and Process Management, 8*(1), 3-16.

Sriram, V., & Bannerjee, S. (1994). EDI does its Adoption Change Purchasing Policies and Procedures. *International Journal of Purchasing and Materials Management, 30*(1), 31-40.

St. Pierre, J., Parks, C., & Waxman, R. (1999). Electronic commerce of component information workshop. *Journal of Research of the National Institute of Standards and Technology, 104*(3), 291-297.

Taylor, I. (1999). The debatable dozen. *Supply Management,* (December 2), 40-41.

Tikkanen, H. (1998). The network approach in analysing international marketing and purchasing operations: A case study of European SMEs' focal net 1992-95. *Journal of Business and Industrial Marketing, 13*(2), 1-19.

Ussman, A., Almeida, A., Ferreira, J., Mendes, L., & Franco, M. (2001). SMEs and innovation. *International Journal of Entrepreneurship & Innovation, 2*(2), 111-118.

Van Hoek, R. (2001). E-supply chains virtually non-existing. *Supply Chain Management, 6*(1), 21-28.

Van Hoek, R., & Chong, I. (2001). Epilogue: UPS logistics and practical approaches to the e-supply chain. *International Journal of Physical Distribution & Logistics, 31*(6), 463-468.

Van Hooft, F., & Stegwee, R. (2001). E-business strategy: How to benefit from a hype. *Logistics Information Management, 14*(1/2), 44-54.

Wagner, B., Fillis, I., & Johannsson, U. (2002). E-commerce adoption and e-supply strategy in the Scottish smaller firm. *Proceedings of the 11ᵗʰ IPSERA Conference,* Enschede, The Netherlands (pp. 721-733).

Wallace, P. (2000). Just wait for the gold rush to end. *New Statesman,* (February 21), 8-9.

Weber, T.E. (1999). How a purple box helps one company entice its customers online. *Wall Street Journal,* 81(September 20).

Wilcox, T. (1999). Net not seen as critical. *Supply Management, 4*(24), 13.

Winser, J., & Tan, K.C. (2000). Supply chain management and its impact on purchasing. *Journal of Supply Chain Management, 36*(4), 33-42.

Wrennall, W. (2000). Demystifying the supplier-customer interface. *Work Study, 49*(1), 18-23.

Chapter V

Perceived Barriers and Risks of E-Commerce Supply Chain Management Network Among SMEs in Australia and New Zealand

Pauline Ratnasingam, Central Missouri State University, USA

Abstract

Small to medium-sized enterprises (SMEs) have limited power in the Supply Chain Management Network (SCMN), as they come with limited resources to invest in advanced planning systems. This makes it difficult for them to cope with the latest challenges such as mass customization, which places higher demands on the company's ability to attune its production planning to customers' wishes and their suppliers in supply chain management. This chapter discusses the challenges (barriers and risks) that SMEs face today based on the findings of a survey that examined the extent of e-commerce adoption in Australia and New Zealand. The findings revealed how technical issues impact two groups of adopters, namely leaders and followers. Leaders refer to businesses that are willing to take risks and invest in IT, whereas followers refer to businesses that were more conscious of their IT investments. We conclude the chapter with key findings and implications to practice.

Introduction

E-commerce is impacting the way SMEs conduct business. Supply chains in practically every industry are at the beginning of a startling reinvention triggered by the rise of the Internet. Since the 1980s and with the emergence of logistics management, Just in Time (JIT) manufacturing and distribution, quick response (QR), efficient consumer response (ECR), vendor-managed inventory (VMI), materials resource planning (MRP), and others form the basis of a comprehensive "Supply Chain Management Network" (SCMN). Moreover, the increasing global competition, changing government regulations, technology innovation, new ways of retailing, and changing consumer needs represent issues that impact supply chain activities. The information, decisions, and processes in the SCMN are moving towards the Internet, and are breaking old paradigms of inter-organizational boundaries. Yip (2000) suggests that the impact of the Internet is more multiplicative than additive. For example, the automotive industry is rapidly embracing the supply chain management activities. Ford and General Motors have partnered with Commerce One to develop the American Automotive Network Exchange (AANX), an online marketplace that allows smaller suppliers to use custom-designed, Web-enabled applications to conduct real-time transactions with multiple Ford and General Motors organizations including: purchasing, financing, engineering, production control, and logistics. Another example, Sun Microsystems developed Web-based collaborative planning tools as a way to strengthen strategic relationships with key customers. These tools allowed Sun to exchange forecast and product status information with customers on orders, shipments, and promotions, and helped Sun to manage their products through the entire lifecycle. This capability has resulted in substantial reductions in lead times and forecast availability, improved inventory turns, increased customer satisfaction, and more efficient supply chain operations. As the supply chain evolves, using the Internet to support tighter coordination between business partners means that all information transactions and decisions that are the essence of synchronized supply chains will flow through the Web. Today customers place increasing demand for customized products, reduced delivery time, and reduced price. They are demanding innovation and personalization of not only the products, but also the associated service and delivery. Together with the general development towards globalization, and shorter product lifecycles, SMEs are forced to take action within several areas to compete on price and flexibility. This calls for new investment in flexible production systems, increased use of outsourcing, and optimized supply chain (supply network) activities to improve external coordination, and to achieve fast flows of high-quality products to customers.

One important pre-condition for effective SCMN is the sharing of information among partners in the supply chain. However, there exist various obstacles for the smooth exchange of information among partners in the supply chain. For example, a source of conflict arises when partners need to share information, and they do not want to release commercially sensitive data (Webster, 1995). Lummus and Vokurka (1999) suggest the following factors that may inhibit supply chain performance. They include:

- the absence of frameworks that can help establish alliances among supply chain partners,

- the lack of integrated information systems and e-commerce firms,

- the lack of trust inside and outside the company, and

- the lack of tools to measure the effectiveness of a supply chain alliance.

Moreover, it is becoming commonly accepted that by reaching customers through the Internet, SMEs can implement more effective target marketing and relationship building strategies with lower overheads (Nath, Akmanligil, Hjelm, Sakaguch, & Schultz, 1998). For many Internet-based EDI software, products and services are now being marketed, often targeted to SMEs without the computer expertise or budgets to implement VAN-based EDI (Mak & Johnston, 1997). GE TradeWeb, Premenos Templar EDI software, Sterling software, and AT&T have made it possible for Internet-based EDI. Premenos Templar claims that it provides Internet-based EDI with a secure transaction server that encrypts and authenticates orders, transactions, and messages sent over the Internet. Indeed, e-commerce can create economic value for buyers, sellers, market-intermediaries, and for the society at large (Bakos, 1998). However, this is not the whole story, as without proper integration of technology and people, much time and capital can be wasted. Thus, the hype and growth of Internet in B2B e-commerce has left SMEs with the pressure to remain competitive. In today's technology-driven and relationship-oriented arena of e-business, organizations are searching for many new ways to promote value and create competitive advantage into their inter-organizational relationships. With the failure of numerous well-funded dot.coms, the pressures remain for SMEs to stay competitive, and the focus has moved from how to *"get in the game"* to *"how to play the game."* In addition, the recent corporate scandals (e.g., Enron, Xerox, and Worldcom cases) derived from unethical business malpractices in the accounting and audit systems have under-mined the confidence of business partners. Furthermore, the spatial and temporal separation between business partners generates an implicit uncertainty around online transactions (Brynjolfsson & Smith, 2000). Therefore, the aim of this chapter is to examine the challenges, barriers, and risks that SMEs experience in e-commerce adoption based on a nationwide survey conducted by KPMG Norlan and Norlan Institute (NNI) in 1999. The research question designed for this study is: What are the barriers and risks that SMEs face in e-commerce adoption? The survey, titled "Electronic Commerce—The Future Is Here!," was conducted in Australia and New Zealand with the aim of determin-ing views of senior businesses and IT executives about e-commerce usage, benefits, barriers, and risks relating to e-commerce adoption. This chapter focuses on the barriers that SMEs experienced and the lessons learned in e-commerce adoption leading to two groups of e-commerce adopters, namely leaders and followers. The next section de-scribes the research method, followed by the background information and findings of this study.

Research Method

Previous research pertaining to e-commerce adoption mostly was conducted using surveys, but focused on business-to-consumer e-commerce, applying students as subjects. This study not only examines business-to-business e-commerce, but also business-to-consumer e-commerce and business-to-government e-commerce organizations.

The survey questionnaire was mailed to 1,000 companies in Australia and New Zealand; 289 completed questionnaires were received, contributing to an initial response rate of 28.9%. However, through e-mail, a number of organizations requested an extension of the survey return deadline. Consequently, a second round of the survey was carried out through a secure website. The extension contributed another 20 responses. Of the 309 responses, 146 were from Australia and 163 from New Zealand. The author was actively involved in the design and analysis of the survey. The project team, including the author, met and analyzed the findings using both quantitative and qualitative approaches. A quantitative data set was used for statistical analysis, and comments from the respondents led to pattern matching and explanation building. While all of us had access to the survey questionnaires received from the respondents, only two KPMG consultants were put in charge of data analysis. The rest of the team participated in the analysis of the findings that included interpreting respondents' comments and investigating possible reasons for the findings. This led to the design of a draft report that was later refined during a one-and-a-half-hour teleconference interview with team members from Melbourne, Adelaide, Sydney, Wellington, and Auckland.

Respondents' Profile

The survey sample consisted of more than 1,000 Australian and New Zealand organizations. In terms of the geographical reach, 35% of the responding organizations indicated they had a global reach, while 31% reported a national reach, 21% a regional reach, and 13% a local reach. Further, the nature of industry is likely to affect its propensity for adopting new ways of doing business. The two largest specific industry categories that participated in this survey were the manufacturing/distribution (28%) and the government services (13%). Figure 1 (pie chart) presents the respondents by industry types.

The size of an organization may be an indicator of the resources the organization can afford in e-commerce adoption. The majority of the organizations surveyed (75%) were SMEs. The remaining 19% had less than 100 employees, 14% had between 500 and 1,000 full-time employees, 11% had between 1,000 and 2,000, 9% between 2,000 and 5,000 employees, and 6% had more than 5,000 full-time employees.

Figure 1: Respondents by Industry Demographics

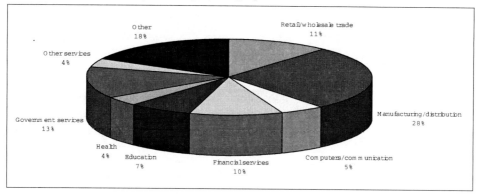

Key Findings

The findings indicated that 4% of the respondents have implemented smart cards, 6% kiosks, 9% automated teller machine technology, and 16% Interactive Voice Response (IVR). Similarly, only 17% of the respondents implemented certification authority technology. Furthermore, the volume of transactions came from the largest proportion of respondents (33%), who had between 1,000 and 10,000 electronic transactions per annum. Thirty percent had up to 1,000 transactions per annum, 20% had between 10,000 and 100,000 transactions, 10% had between 100,000 and 500,000 transactions, and 7% had more than 500,000 transactions per annum. More than half of the respondents indicated that their transaction value was over one million dollars per annum. The findings emphasized that despite an overall advance, much of the activity relating to e-commerce implementation remained in the *'talking stage.'* Most of the SMEs have also realized the importance of implementing e-commerce as a *'must do,'* due to competitive pressure from the larger firms. In the next section, we discuss the two types of e-commerce adopters identified in this study.

Types of E-Commerce Adopters

The findings revealed two groups of e-commerce adopters, namely leaders and followers, who displayed distinct sets of characteristics in terms of e-commerce adoption, implementation, and integration. Leaders referred to organizations that have achieved profit or productivity gains from e-commerce implementation, and followers referred to those that did not. With regard to e-commerce leaders are those for whom 'very good' or 'excellent' achievement of profitability and improvement benefits has occurred through e-commerce (or, in the case of non-profit organizations, 'excellent' achievement of productivity and improvement benefits).

We argue that leaders' characteristics may help to describe actions that followers might want to take (as lessons learned) in order to catch up and compete effectively with e-commerce. Characteristics of the leaders include:

- are smaller and more focused on business benefits in e-commerce,
- are more likely to be in the financial services and computer technology industries,
- have an aggressive cost focus,
- give e-commerce higher importance in their business strategies,
- have higher and more specific expectations from technology,
- are less likely to see barriers and better able to minimize those that may exist,
- demonstrate higher levels of integration of e-commerce across the board,
- are more likely to have implemented EFT, EDI, intranets, and extranets already, and
- are far more likely to be conducting marketing, public relations, and advertising via the Internet.

The findings revealed that followers lacked these characteristics. Further, in order to achieve potential benefits, organizations should follow characteristics of leaders that include being smaller and more focused on business benefits in e-commerce. Furthermore, organizations should give e-commerce higher importance in their business strategies, by having an aggressive cost focus, and higher and more specific expectations from technology.

Potential Barriers and Risks in E-Commerce Adoption

Respondents reported the perceived lack of security as one of the main barriers to the adoption of e-commerce technologies. The questionnaire pertaining to barriers and risks is in the appendix. The findings indicated that Australian VAN-based EDI implementation is just under the belt, and that most of the SMEs—in particular the followers—were resistant to change because of emotional insecurity for the fear of the reliability in the new system. They lacked the technical knowledge, skills, and expertise, and exhibited organizational inertia towards e-commerce adoption, whereas the leaders were aware of the control mechanisms in order to ensure security of their e-commerce transactions and systems. Based on the findings, this perception was even more remarkable as solutions for managing security had to be implemented in order to increase e-commerce adoption. The findings were consistent with the research outcomes of Chau and Turner (2002), who suggested that until a critical mass of e-commerce customers and suppliers are evident, the nature of the supply chain will remain a major hurdle to SMEs' utilization of e-commerce.

The findings also indicated that Internet-based EDI adoption in America took place two to three years ago. In the case of New Zealand, it was perceived to be more advanced than Australia, as VAN-based EDI was never implemented there in the first place. This paved the way for New Zealand businesses to implement Internet-based EDI, which aimed at achieving greater cost savings and increase in efficiency. Further, the growth in Australia was slow due to the lack of standard formatted document transfer (which implied that every trading partner will do it the same way). The current methods of standardization of the structure of data that is being interchanged across machines-to-machines interface totally ignored the way in which applications and programs are designed and operated.

Moreover, government policies, laws and practices, technical impediments, local and cultural factors add up to the obstacle. The manager of Edification stated that Australian adoption of the Internet is similar to the analogy of the *'herd mentality'*—it is like a waiting game to see if a group of trading partners already have experienced success, then the rest will follow suit.

Similarly, the research conducted by the Small Business Development Corporation of Western Australia indicated that SMEs were still not convinced by the merits of e-commerce or its relevance. Some of the reasons for the discomfort around security may be explained by ways in which most organizations have developed their key trading partner relationships over time. The highest ranked element for establishing trust between organizations, their customers, and suppliers is the existence of a long history of trading partner trust. This, coupled with a relatively low importance ranking for formal agreements between trading partners as a mechanism for establishing trust, means that organizations have not adjusted to the mindset required to effectively establish trust in electronic trading. It seems that while early adoption of these new business tools in Australia and New Zealand lags behind the United States and possibly Europe, the actual barriers to their widespread acceptance and use are more perceived than real.

The next section discusses barriers and risks SMEs experienced in e-commerce adoption in four categories: technological, organizational, environmental, and social issues.

Technological Issues

Security. Security was one barrier derived both internally (within an organization's e-commerce system and business practices) and externally (from the trading partner the organization is trading with and government policies, taxes, and audit procedures). Leaders were organizations that have gained from e-commerce adoption and had the technical knowledge and expertise on how to enforce security mechanisms and manage security issues, whereas followers lacked the technical knowledge and were reluctant to go online. Most SMEs fear that with the rise of Internet use, their ability to meet the needs and expectations of all businesses will be a concern. Despite the opportunities of Internet commerce, many businesses were reluctant to go online because they perceived the Internet as an intrinsically insecure environment (Bhimani, 1996; Cavalli, 1995; CommerceNet, 1997; Jamieson, 1996; Marcella, Stone, & Sampias, 1998; Storrosten, 1998).

Initial Implementation Costs. Startup costs for implementing e-commerce applications can be high. They include connection costs, hardware, software, set up, and maintenance costs (Iacovou, Benbasat, & Dexter, 1995; Nath et al., 1998, Saunders & Clark, 1992; Senn, 1998). Implementation costs included conducting an initial search costs, costs of writing contracts, and paying staff to update and maintain electronic databases (Senn, 1998). Other costs incurred were contractual, transmission, and coordination costs (Nath et al., 1998; Saunders & Clark, 1992). Further, technology and infrastructure costs increased, as organizations were required to implement compatible systems to receive messages from other trading partners.

Organizations need to first develop the necessary IT infrastructure applications, acquire the technical implementation expertise, and invest in training. They must also acquire e-commerce translation and mapping software, and contract with a communication medium or company (Riggins & Mukhopadhyay, 1999). Thus, high costs may create initial barriers to e-commerce participation, particularly among adopters who lacked the financial resources and top management commitment. Alternatively, leaders were committed, aggressive, and had the financial resources to implement e-commerce systems. Furthermore, the findings revealed that leaders were mostly from the data, communications, financial, and IT industries. Hence, they had the first-hand opportunity to experiment and learn about e-commerce applications and systems.

Lack of IT Infrastructure. IT infrastructure refers to IT connectivity, which is the extent SMEs are IT connected. IT connectivity in turn refers to IT compatibility, IS telecommunication infrastructure, and the extent of internal integration. The findings indicated that Internet-based e-commerce was in its formative stages in Australia and New Zealand, while the U.S. and Europe were two to three years ahead. Many trading partners lacked the skills, resources, and technical know-how for secure e-commerce, thus creating operational and technical risks. Saxena and Wagenaar (1997) conducted a study of EDI adoption at an organizational, industry, and country level. They found that one of the major barriers to successful EDI adoption was limited awareness of promotional activities in EDI use. This line of reasoning was consistent with previous empirical research, which also suggested that the lack of technical knowledge, expertise, and resources hindered IT use and e-commerce participation (Heck & Ribbers, 1998; Iacovou et al., 1995; Reekers & Smithson, 1996; Saunders & Clark, 1992).

Organizational Issues

Uncertainties. The most recent reverses in the dot.com have posed inherent problems for trading partners undertaking transaction exchanges on the Internet. Further, the proliferation of e-commerce applications have left most trading partners uncertain of e-commerce operations and unaware of the full potential of e-commerce technology (Ghosh, 1998). Uncertainties may arise when SMEs encounter barriers in communication (such as incompatible e-commerce systems or lack of uniform standards) that may lead to conflicts. Bensaou and Venkatraman (1996) classified three types of vulnerabilities: task, environment, and partnership uncertainties. Similarly, such matters inside an organization were seen as a roadblock even when EDI was first adopted (Emmelhainz, 1990; Nath et al., 1998; Premkumar et al., 1994).

Lack of Top Management Commitment. With poor internal management and a lack of top-level management commitment, implementing e-commerce even with the most advanced products becomes challenging. If management is unwilling to provide adequate financial resources, poor business practices might follow. For example, without full support an organization might neglect the need for a paper audit trail that would ensure the reliability of electronic certification and business continuity. Successful e-commerce adoption requires full top-level commitment, as many potential adopters are ignorant about the potential use of e-commerce technologies (Jamieson, 1996; Marcella et al., 1998). The findings revealed that leaders were committed and aggressive toward e-commerce adoption, whereas the followers had a laid-back attitude towards e-commerce adoption.

Environmental Issues

Competitive Pressure from other Trading Partners and the E-Commerce Environment. Electronic partnerships between buyers and suppliers or manufacturers and distributors have become increasingly inconsistent due to competitive pressures in the global environment that demanded quality (Premkumar & Ramamurthy, 1995). Iacovou et al. (1995) suggest that external pressures and organizational readiness may affect e-commerce adoption. For most organizations the biggest challenge is not if or when to consider an Internet commerce solution, but rather how to select the best Internet commerce strategies to develop and sustain competitive advantage (Raman, 1995). In today's hyper-competitive global marketplace, shareholders and customers are increasingly pressured by businesses to provide easy-to-use, online applications as a better way to conduct business (Premkumar, Ramamurthy, & Crum, 1997; Keen, 2000).

Pre-Adoption Negotiation—Startup and Restructuring Challenges. E-commerce adoption, unlike traditional information systems adoption, demands high levels of negotiation, cooperation, and commitment from participating organizations. Selecting transaction sets, negotiating legal matters, and defining performance expectations can burn up hours of staff time and also demand financial and technological resources (Senn, 1998). Furthermore, a survey conducted by Storresten (1998) revealed that 51% of the respondents cited an internal fear of opening their organization's systems to suppliers, as implementing e-commerce could affect critical business processes such as procurement, inventory management, manufacturing, order fulfillment, shipping, invoicing, payments, and accounting (Nath et al., 1998; Senn, 1998; Storresten, 1998).

Social Issues

Coercive Power. Coercive power is often exercised when trading partners lack cooperation. For example, trading partner A is likely to use coercive power when trading partner B does not cooperate. Previous research in EDI in the automotive industry has provided evidence of coercive power (Ratnasingam, 2000; Webster, 1995). Ford applied power when the EDI network was introduced. Ford made it clear to its established suppliers that they should use EDI. Ford did provide suppliers with initial training and its software to run on IBM machines. Suppliers with incompatible systems or with no systems at all were requested to find appropriate solutions as quickly as possible. Clearly, this was a situation where coercive power exercised by Ford was seen in establishing connections that involved the expense of the suppliers in buying new equipment. Dependence can arise due to limited supply alternatives or from an imbalance of power between suppliers and car manufacturers. Furthermore, the inconvenience of having to use Ford's system in addition to other systems for trading with other customers was another issue, especially at a time when the smaller suppliers were unaware of EDI's potential. Hart and Saunders (1997) suggest that organizations with greater power can influence their trading partners to adopt EDI. Their findings indicated that use of power was negatively related to the volume of EDI transactions. While electronic networks may facilitate easier exchanges, they may not necessarily lead to increases in the frequency of business-to-business transactions. Thus, power exists on two levels: (1) as a motive, and (2) as a behavior.

Figure 2 presents the potential barriers to e-commerce adoption.

Comparisons Between Europe and Australia/ New Zealand (ANZ)

On the security front, the findings claimed that while nearly half (43%) of Australia and New Zealand respondents indicated that security is one of the factors that had a high degree of influence on whether they moved into e-commerce, only 25% of the European respondents in a similar survey indicated that this was a high influence issue (Puchihar, Gricar, & Jesenko, 1999). Locally, those still wary about security cited identification and authentication high on the agenda, along with the need to implement firewalls.

Customer readiness falls behind security by one percentage point, and is comparable between Europe and Australia/New Zealand. In comparison with European results, Australia/New Zealand still appears to be running security-scared, despite technology solutions being made available and legislation pending.

Of equal concern are the uncertainties and lack of motivation to implement e-commerce activities. Survey results indicate that organizational inertia is 5% higher in Australia/ New Zealand than in Europe, with more than one in five (21%) of the Trans Tasman companies interviewed indicating they felt that they lacked the know-how to implement e-commerce into their businesses. Figure 3 presents a comparison of perceived barriers experienced by SMEs between Europe and Australia/New Zealand.

Figure 2: Potential Barriers to Adoption of E-Commerce

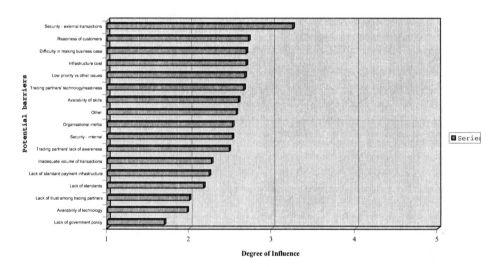

Figure 3: Perceived Barriers Between Europe and ANZ

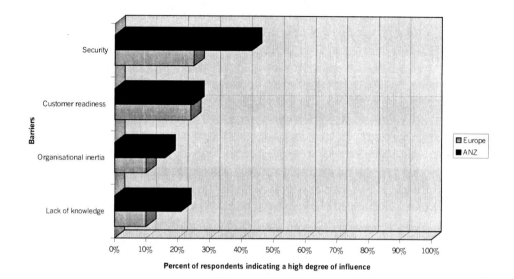

Future of E-Commerce in Australia and New Zealand

The future of e-commerce in Australia and New Zealand looks optimistic, although the survey was conducted in 1999, which was an exciting time for e-commerce development in the U.S. Most dot.com companies in America were implementing business plans in order to sustain their SCMN activities. In Australia and New Zealand, there were significant plans being made for increased activity and implementation. The Australian government has acknowledged the opportunities of e-commerce and is working with all Australian states and territories to coordinate efforts to reduce barriers to its adoption. The findings suggest that e-commerce is now reaching a critical mass and, while a number of elements continue to restrict its development, many of these, including the old security scare, are now being overcome.

Of all the industries surveyed, computers and communication showed the most aggressive stance and are reaping the greatest gains from e-commerce. This is not surprising, given the internal knowledge base, existing technology infrastructure, vested interest in promoting the channel, and predisposition of existing clients to employ technology in business transactions. The education and financial services sectors also displayed significant early adoption of e-commerce technologies.

Significant plans are afoot for implementation of e-commerce technologies, and we can expect significant growth in communication technologies, including company WWW sites, with 22% of respondents indicating they intend to implement websites. In the same timeframe, 25% intend to implement intranet, 27% extranet, 20% firewalls, 19% Electronic Data Interchange (EDI), and 15% certification/digital signatures.

Most of the businesses surveyed have been engaged in some form of e-commerce for some years now. Even though the greatest hype over the latest technology—that the

Internet will bring e-commerce to the fore—centers around its potential as a means of buying and selling, these functions have been done electronically for years. For example, order taking via EDI, call centers, and even fax was quite prominent. Even more common was the transmission and receipt of payment via Electronic-Funds-Transfer (EFT).

In order to overcome these barriers, SMEs should choose their trading partners and skills carefully, and start with a needs-based strategy, rather than a technology-based solution, as not all solutions meet their requirements. Furthermore, organizations should aim to develop an e-commerce strategy that complements the corporate strategy. The critical success factors required for implementing e-commerce in organizations can thus be summarized as follows:

- Start with a needs-based strategy rather than a technology-based solution, as not all solutions meet requirements and business processes of a trading partner, as some segments will not use the Web.

- Develop an e-commerce strategy which complements the corporate strategy.

- Aggregate the disparate investments in e-commerce that are likely to be found in any organization.

- Avoid layering costs onto the current distribution network and look for substitution between channels.

- Choose your trading partners and their skills carefully.

- Integrate across the entire organization in order to achieve large efficiency gains.

- Recognize that the transparent implementation and changing process is important both in terms of acceptance of the change and achieving expected efficiency gains.

- Distinguish between striving to win new markets or customers and gaining cost savings from process improvements.

- Develop a benefits register and measure your achievements against it.

E-commerce adoption among SMEs also suggests the importance of *'electronic partnerships.'* In fact, e-commerce, unlike other types of IT innovations, cannot be adopted and used unilaterally. Firms that are motivated to use e-commerce must either find similarly motivated trading partners, or persuade and/or coerce their existing trading partners to adopt e-commerce. This leads to interdependencies between organizations that arise from sharing e-commerce technologies in the supply chain management network and focuses on the importance of technical solutions, which create initial trust among the trading partners (Ratnasingam, 2001; Ratnasingam & Pavlou, 2003). Similarly, much of the failure to 'live up to expectations' is due to the perception that gains from e-commerce will be easy to achieve. It is assumed that benefits will be achievable within an overly optimistic timeframe that may also be due to inappropriate metrics being applied to measure the success of a venture.

Acknowledgments

The author who actively participated in this project would like to acknowledge KPMG-Norlan and Norlan Institute (NNI) for funding, cooperation, and administration of this survey.

References

Bakos, Y. (1998). The emerging role of electronic marketplaces on the Internet. *Communications of the ACM, 41*(8), 35-48.

Bensaou, M., & Venkatraman, N. (1996). Inter-organizational relationships and information technology: A conceptual synthesis and a research framework. *European Journal of Information Systems,* (5), 84-91

Bhimani, A. (1996). Securing the commercial Internet. *Communications of the ACM, 39*(6), 29-35.

Brynjolfsson, E., & Smith, M. (2000). Frictionless commerce? A comparison of Internet and conventional retailers. *Management Science, 46*(4), 563-585.

Cavalli, A. (1995). Electronic commerce over the Internet and the increasing need for security. *TradeWave,* (December 8).

Chau, S., & Turner, P. (2002). Four phases of e-commerce: An analysis of factors impacting on SMEs' potential to drive benefits from Web-based e-commerce: 34 Australian case studies. *Proceedings of the Information Resources Management Conference.*

CommerceNet. (1997). Barriers & inhibitors to the widespread adoption of Internet commerce. *CommerceNet Research Report #97-05,* April.

Emmelhainz, M.A. (1990). *A Total Management Guide.* NCC Blackwell.

Ghosh, S. (1998). Making business sense of the Internet. *Harvard Business Review,* (March-April), 126-135.

Hart, P., & Saunders, C. (1997). Power and trust: Critical factors in the adoption and use of Electronic Data Interchange. *Organization Science, 8*(1), 23-42.

Heck & Ribbers (1999). The adoption and impact of EDI in Dutch SMEs. *Proceedings of the Hawaii International Conference in Information Systems.*

Iacovou, C.L., Benbasat, I., & Dexter, A.S. (1995). Electronic data interchange and small organizations: Adoption and impact of technology. *MIS Quarterly, 19*(4), 465-485.

Jamieson, R. (1996). Auditing and electronic commerce. *Proceedings of the EDI Forum,* Perth, Western Australia.

Keen, P.G.W. (1999). *Electronic commerce: How fast, how soon?* Available on the Web: http://strategis.ic.gc.ca/SSG/mi06348e.html.

KPMG Norlan and Norton Institute (1999). *Electronic Commerce — The Future is Here.*

Mak, H.C., & Johnston, R.B. (1997). A survey of Internet strategies for EDI. *Proceedings of the CoLLECTer Conference,* Adelaide (pp. 126-141).

Marcella, A.J., Stone, L., & Sampias, W.J. (1998). *Electronic Commerce: Control Issues for Securing Virtual Enterprises.* The Institute of Internal Auditors.

Nath, R., Akmanligil, M., Hjelm, K., Sakaguch, T., & Schultz, M. (1998). Electronic commerce and the Internet: Issues, problems and perspectives. *International Journal of Information Management, 18*(2), 91-101.

Premkumar, G., Ramamurthy, K., & Crum, M. (1997). Determinants of EDI adoption in the transportation industry. *European Journal of Information Systems,* (6), 107-121.

Puchihar, A., Gricar, J., & Jesenko, J. (1999). Opportunities and threats of electronic commerce over the Internet in Slovenia's organizations. *Proceedings of the Global Networked Organizations' 12th International Bled Electronic Commerce Conference,* Bled, Slovenia (June 7-9, pp. 317-330).

Raman, D. (1996). *Cyber Assisted Business—EDI as the Backbone of Electronic Commerce.* EDI-TIE.

Ratnasingam, P. (2000). The influence of power among trading partners in business to business electronic commerce. *Internet Research,* (1), 56-62.

Ratnasingam, P. (2001). *Inter-organizational trust in business to business electronic commerce.* Doctoral dissertation, Erasmus University, The Netherlands.

Ratnasingam, P. (2001). The need for inter-organizational-trust in Web-enabled supply chain management. *Journal of VISION: Special Issue on E-Commerce: Systems and Management, 5*(1), 55-65.

Ratnasingam, P., & Pavlou, P.A. (2003). Technology trust in Internet-based interorganizational electronic commerce. *Journal of Electronic Commerce in Organizations, 1*(1), 17-41.

Reekers, N., & Smithson, S. (1996). The role of EDI in inter-organizational coordination in the European automotive industry. *European Journal of Information Systems,* (5), 120-130.

Riggins, F. J. & Mukhopadhyay, T. (1999). Overcoming EDI adoption and implementation risks. *International Journal of Electronic Commerce, 3*(4), 103-123.

Saunders, C., & Clark, S. (1992). EDI adoption and implementation: A focus on inter-organizational linkages. *Information Resources Management Journal, 5*(1), 9-19.

Senn, J.A. (1998). Expanding the reach of electronic commerce—The Internet EDI alternative. *Information Systems Management,* (Summer), 7-15.

Storrosten, M. (1998). Barriers to electronic commerce. *Proceedings of the European Multimedia, Microprocessor Systems and Electronic Commerce Conference and Exhibition,* Bordeaux, France.

Webster, J. (1995). Networks of collaboration or conflict? Electronic Data Interchange and power in the supply chain. *Journal of Strategic Information Systems, 4*(1), 31-42.

Yip, G.S. (2000). Global strategy in the Internet era. *Business Strategy Review, 11*(4), 1-14.

Appendix

Instrumentation of Perceived Barriers and Risks

The section below provides the questions used to examine barriers and risks in e-commerce. Please indicate the extent to which you agree or disagree with the following statements about your organization's risks and circle the most appropriate response (number). If you have no opinion on a question or a question that is not applicable, please check 0.

Perceived Risks of E-Commerce

Not Applicable	**Strongly Disagree**	**Neither Agree Nor Disagree**	**Strongly Agree**

1. *Our organization experiences compatibility problems with hardware and software*

    0   1   2   3   4   5

2. *Our organization experiences additional infrastructure and initial implementation costs*

    0   1   2   3   4   5

3. *Our organization experiences confidentiality concerns due to viruses*

    0   1   2   3   4   5

4. *Our organization experiences lack of adequate accounting controls*

    0   1   2   3   4   5

5. *Our organization experiences internal security errors that led to lack of integrity (i.e., delayed and inaccurate messages)*

    0   1   2   3   4   5

6. *Our organization experiences complexity in operating business transactions*

    0   1   2   3   4   5

7. *Our organization experiences task and environment uncertainties*

    0   1   2   3   4   5

8. *Our organization experiences trading partner reluctance to change*

    0   1   2   3   4   5

9. *Our organization experiences a shortage of training, knowledge, and awareness*

    0   1   2   3   4   5

10. *Our organization experiences poor reputation of trading partner*

    0   1   2   3   4   5

11. *Our organization experiences conflicting attitudes from our trading partners*

    0   1   2   3   4   5

12. *Our organization experiences lack of trust from our trading partners*

    0   1   2   3   4   5

13. *Our organization experiences opportunistic behaviors from our trading partners*
    0   1   2   3   4   5

14. *Our organization experiences partnership uncertainties from our trading partners*

    0   1   2   3   4   5

15. *Our organization experiences lack of security from our trading partners' system*
    0   1   2   3   4   5

16. *Our organization experiences a difficulty in identifying or quantifying costs and benefits*

    0   1   2   3   4   5

17. *Our organization experiences repudiation problems from our trading partners*
    0   1   2   3   4   5

18. *Our organization experiences authentication difficulties from our trading partners*

    0   1   2   3   4   5

19. *Our organization experiences availability of technology concerns from our trading partners*

    0   1   2   3   4   5

20. *Our organization experiences lack the standard infrastructure (e.g., data and payments concerns) for our payments*

    0   1   2   3   4   5

21. *Our organization experiences lack of government policies*

    0   1   2   3   4   5

22. *Our organization experiences poor business practices from our trading partners*
    0   1   2   3   4   5

Section IV

E-Commerce in Developing Countries

Chapter VI

The Potential of E-Commerce for Remotely Located SMEs: Case Studies from Samoa

Fuatai Purcell, Victoria University of Wellington, New Zealand

Janet Toland, Victoria University of Wellington, New Zealand

Sid L. Huff, Victoria University of Wellington, New Zealand

Abstract

This is a report on research carried out to identify the barriers to adoption, and opportunities that e-commerce offers for SMEs in the small island country of Samoa. The issues faced by SMEs in Samoa are relevant for all remotely located SMEs in both the developing and the developed world. The chapter will improve knowledge of the issues faced by SMEs wanting to adopt e-commerce, the driving forces that impact on the adoption of e-commerce, and the factors that are currently inhibiting the adoption of e-commerce. Diffusion of Innovation theory was used to understand the behavior of SMEs that led to their decision to adopt e-commerce.

Introduction

Rapid advances in information and communication technologies, especially the Internet, have created the "new economy" and brought about new ways of conducting business (Swatman, 1998), collectively referred to as e-commerce. E-commerce involves searching for information concerning products, services, advertising, and the buying, selling, and paying for products and/or services through the medium of communication networks, principally the Internet. E-commerce can benefit organizations of all sizes, and is particularly important for the small-business sector (Bright, 1997; Rommel, 1997; Huff & Yoong, 2000).

A number of studies have been conducted in recent years concerning the adoption and use of the Internet and e-commerce in small to medium-sized enterprises (SMEs) (O'Keefe, O'Connor, & Kung, 1998; Klein, 1998; Poon & Swatman, 1999; Huff & Yoong, 2000; Mehrtens, Cragg, & Mills, 2001). However, most of these studies focused on SMEs in *developed* countries. For *developing* countries, the situation is quite different.

There is still a big gap in Internet and e-commerce adoption between the developed and developing countries (Johnston & Acquaah-Gaisie, 2001; Licker & Motts, 2000) thus creating a "digital divide." A recent study conducted in India revealed that only 4% of the population have access to the Internet (Kiggen, 2001). Other recent studies also found that developing countries lag behind developed countries in the adoption of e-commerce, due to poor telecommunication infrastructure and the high costs of hardware (Tassabehji, 2000; Kiggen, 2001; OECD, 1998).

The few studies of Internet/e-commerce uptake that have been done in developing countries have focused on highly populated regions, including developing countries in South East Asia, Eastern Europe, South America, India, and Africa (OECD, 1998; Kong, 1999; Corbitt & Thanasankit, 2000). There is a dearth of research examining Internet and e-commerce adoption issues faced by SMEs in developing countries with smaller populations—such as Samoa.

Samoa is an independent island nation in the South Pacific, with a long history of political and economic stability. The country has a land area of approximately 2,934 square kilometers, and a population of approximately 169,195. The Samoan economy is made up of agriculture, fishing, handicraft production, small manufacturing goods, and one automobile-wiring manufacturing firm. More recently, tourism has become a valuable contributor to the Samoan economy. SMEs are central to Samoa's economic well-being, comprising 98% of the Samoan economy.

Relatively few SMEs in Samoa have attempted to adopt the Internet or e-commerce to date. The purpose of our research is to better understand the key factors that encourage or impede the adoption of the Internet, and e-commerce, by Samoan SMEs.

The key question being investigated was:

> *"What are the opportunities provided by e-commerce adoption for SMEs in Samoa, and what are the threats, and the barriers, to e-commerce adoption there?"*

Figure 1: Geographical Position of Samoa in the South Pacific

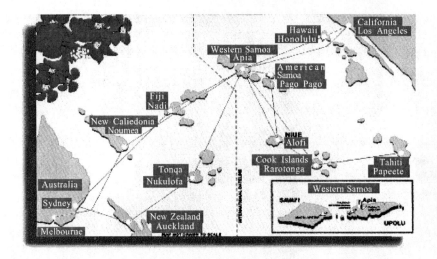

More specific sub-questions being investigated include:

- What is the level of understanding of e-commerce by SMEs in Samoa?
- What is the status of the telecommunication infrastructure?
- What are the financial implications of Internet access and website development compared to developed countries?
- What factors facilitate Internet adoption in Samoan SMEs?
- What are the benefits of e-commerce as experienced by the SMEs who currently have Internet access?
- What role is the government playing in e-commerce adoption by Samoan SMEs?

This study adopted the widely used Diffusion of Innovation theory (Rogers, 1983) to provide a theoretical lens for examining the Internet/e-commerce adoption phenomenon in the Samoan context.

Background

Internet in Samoa: Current Status

The Internet is growing at a steady pace in Samoa. The researchers interviewed the assistant manager and the senior technician of Computer Services Ltd (CSL), Samoa's largest Internet Service Provider (ISP), to obtain statistics on Internet connections. According to the assistant manager of CSL, they took over from an overseas ISP after

Table 1: Estimated Number of Internet Connections in Samoa (Source: SCL, 2002)

Name of ISP	Estimate Total Connections	Internet Access Cost
Computer Services Ltd (CSL)	2,150	NZ$ 9.00
LeSamoa	750	NZ$ 15.00
I Pasifika	570	NZ$ 10.00
Total Internet Connections	3,470 (2.04% of population)	Average NZ$ 11.33

it collapsed in 1998 with 268 Internet customers. As of September 2001, CSL has just over 2,000 Internet users. According to the Samoa Communications Limited (SCL), there are currently more than 3,000 Internet connections in Samoa, many of which connect government departments in the urban areas. Table 1 illustrates the approximate number of connections per ISP as of June 2002.

Internet adoption has been growing at approximately a thousand new connections per year in the last three years. While this is a rapid growth rate year-upon-year, the overall percentage of Internet connections in the country is still quite small, given an approximate population of 177,000. Most Internet users in Samoa reside in the central town and represent approximately 2.04% of the population. The Internet has failed to reach the more remote areas of the two largest islands of Upolu and Savaii. For example, the village "fale" (Samoan traditional thatched house) operators outside of Apia in Upolu and places like Falealupo in Savaii do not currently have access to telephones. This shows that, in common with other countries in the South Pacific, there is a rural urban divide in Samoa. Research has confirmed that a strong urban bias exists for Internet use in developing countries worldwide (UNDP, 2001). A similar divide exists between the high- and low-income earners, and between Samoans who have always lived in Samoa and those that have returned from other countries

SME Development in Samoa

SMEs in Samoa are generally smaller than in developed countries. According to the department of Trade and Commerce Industry, an SME is defined as a *"company providing goods and services employing five and less employees, and a manufacturing company employing 40 and less employees."* SMEs in Samoa can be divided into two categories: traditional SMEs and private sector SMEs. Traditional SMEs refer to family businesses, such as village grocery stores or those that sell their products at the local markets. With traditional SMEs, families use their own capital together with the assistance of relatives living overseas to start up the business. These SMEs are often a basis for prestige and raising the standing of the family in the village. Making a profit is not a primary aim of these businesses as long as they provide enough income to meet their day-to-day commitments to the family, church, and village (not necessarily in that order). Private sector SMEs are those that operate solely to make a profit and expand. This chapter focuses on private sector SMEs.

Table 2: New Small Businesses Registered 1994-2001 (Source: Samoan IRD, 2002)

Year	New Sole Traders Registered
1994	283
1995	345
1996	387
1997	402
1998	465
1999	575
2000	590
2001	630

According to data collected from the Samoan Inland Revenue Department (IRD), the number of SMEs has consistently increased since 1994 (see Table 2). This increase in new small businesses is due largely to the establishment of the Small Business and Enterprise Centre (SBEC), which provides business management training to those who want to start a business for the first time. The SBEC was established under a New Zealand Overseas Development Agency (NZODA) program in 1994, to provide advisory services to the small-business sector, modeled on similar centers overseas. NZODA has nurtured the development of SBEC, through funding its operational and development expenses, and through financing the capital fund securing the loan guarantee program.

SBEC has proven to be extremely successful, and following localization of its staff and translating its training materials to the Samoan language, it has extended its outreach to rural areas, developing a unique mix of services. The success of SBEC stems from the fact that it blends good business management practices with the Samoan culture and village way of life. In the last three years, about 83% of the SBEC's customers are "grass-root level" clients. Most of these people have never had an income before and have relied heavily on cash remittances from family members living and working overseas. The wide variety of SMEs in Samoa created through the services of SBEC includes small grocery stores in the village, tourism resorts, motels, fishing ventures, small food manufacturers using local products, small consulting firms, rental car operators, handicrafts, Internet service providers, and computer hardware shops.

Research Methodology

The methodology adopted for this study was a qualitative approach using "Case Study" research (Yin, 1994). The underlying principle used to select participants was to choose SMEs that used either the Internet only or those that used the Internet and had developed a website. A semi-structured interview guide was used to frame each interview (see

Appendix A for this guide). The specific criteria used for selecting the participants were:
- Small company providing goods or services employing five or less employees
- Medium manufacturing company employing 40 or less employees
- Must have access to a computer and the Internet
- Must represent one of four industry sectors selected for this study

E-mail and telephone were used to seek participants to take part in the study. Apart from the chosen participants, other subjects were also interviewed to gain further understanding of the issues expressed by the participants and to satisfy internal validity. Additional interviews were conducted with the following people:
- The Prime Minister of Samoa—about the role of government in terms of IT diffusion
- The Minister of the Department of Trade and Commerce Industry—to learn more about Samoan SMEs
- The CEO of Samoa Communications Limited (SCL)—to learn more about the status of the telecommunication infrastructure and find out first hand what is being done to improve the infrastructure
- The Assistant Manager of Computer Services Limited (CSL)—about the level of Internet adoption in Samoa
- The Assistant Manager of Small Business Enterprise Committee (SBEC)—to investigate the role of government in assisting SMEs

The additional interviews were also useful in validating the barriers of Internet and e-commerce adoption as elicited from the participants.

Interviews were conducted with 12 SMEs chosen from those that met the selection criteria in the manufacturing, tourism, retail, and consultancy sectors. The participants were owners and managers of SMEs. Due to the small size of Samoan SMEs, the owner is usually the manager who makes all the decisions. The interviews were conducted face to face in the workplace. They were conducted in English, or if a manager requested it, Samoan. Some of the interviews were conducted in a mixture of English and Samoan. For example, the greetings were always in Samoan, as it is a cultural practice to address the matai title a manager holds in the proper cultural manner. The interviews were tape recorded and transcribed. The transcriptions were sent back to the participants for checking. To further confirm the findings, the initial analysis of the interviews was discussed with the participants in a follow-up focus group setting.

Research Findings

The case study data were analyzed so as to discover and categorize the perceived opportunities presented by e-commerce and the Internet, and also the perceived threats and the perceived barriers to adoption. Table 3 summarizes the findings. The following discussion elaborates upon those findings.

Threats Associated with the Internet/E-Commerce

The main threats posed by adoption of the Internet and e-commerce by Samoan SMEs were:

1. Cultural threats
2. Decline in productivity
3. Exposure to undesirable information

Hofstede (1980) defines culture as "the collective programming of the mind which distinguishes the members of one human group from another." He emphasizes that culture is not the property of individuals but of groups. It has to do with what is considered proper, civilized behavior in that country. It includes, for instance, how to act toward strangers, colleagues, and family; how to address somebody; whether to look them in the face; and when to invite them home. Hofstede's model has been criticized for failing to take into account the emergent and dynamic nature of culture (Myers & Tan, 2002), however the model is a useful starting point for beginning to analyze the relationship between culture and e-commerce.

According to Hofstede's (1980) classifications, Samoa represents a high power distance culture. Power distance is defined as the degree of inequality among people that is accepted as normal by the population of that country. A high power distance culture expects different behavioral responses to be accorded to persons with different ranks within the societal hierarchy.

The Samoan high power distance culture is reflected in businesses there. An example of this is the failure of the first overseas Internet service provider (ISP) in Samoa. A private sector official explained that the first ISP in Samoa was an overseas company that failed because it did not understand the Samoan culture. They were doing business the way they did in their home country, which was totally different from the way business is carried out in Samoa. As one of the participants pointed out in reference to the first ISP in Samoa:

> "The reason why the first ISP failed was because they did not understand the business culture of Samoa. For example, they failed to understand that when a company does not pay the Internet access fee, you send the letter to the manager, not the clerk. Everything has to go to the manager."

Another aspect of the Samoan culture reflected in organizational culture is that the manager of an organization is seen as a father figure. Employees respect the manager and would not do or say anything that embarrasses the manager. A study of requirements elicitation in Thailand also found that the Thai culture has a similar impact on the organizational culture (Corbitt & Thansankit, 2000).

Participants fear that overseas investors attracted to Samoa through the Internet may fail to observe the respect Samoan organizations have for its culture. Participants also fear that more and more young people are surfing the Internet in digital cafes until closing

Table 3: Summary of the Issues that Impact E-Commerce Adoption by SMEs in Samoa

Summary of Interviews: Threats of the Internet	Summary of Interviews: Barriers of Internet Adoption	Summary of Interviews: Opportunities for E-Commerce in SMEs	Summary of Interviews: Factors of Internet Adoption
◆ Pornography ◆ Paedophile and child exploitation ◆ Culture ◆ Decrease in productivity of employees ◆ Quality of product may decline	◆ Cost to buy software and hardware ◆ Lack of skills ◆ Instability of the power supply ◆ Basic infrastructure not available ◆ Lack of awareness of e-commerce ◆ Older generation unwilling to change ◆ Lack of generic standard ◆ Huge resources needed to set up a unique supply chain for B2B transactions ◆ Lack of understanding on how e-commerce works ◆ Security of e-commerce ◆ Laws applicable to local e-commerce and other countries	◆ Cheaper advertising ◆ Increase market share ◆ Lower transaction processing costs ◆ Ability to transact business faster ◆ Country boundaries non-existent in doing B2B transactions ◆ Easy access to information ◆ Savings on manpower ◆ Improving employees knowledge ◆ Marketing local products to the world market ◆ Increase in tourism ◆ Increase in production of local products ◆ Available 24 hours, seven days/week	◆ Better and more efficient than phone fax and postal services ◆ Cheaper than phone fax and postal services ◆ Very useful for the business ◆ Faster medium to communicate with overseas customers and families ◆ Easy access to information ◆ Brings Samoa closer to the rest of the world ◆ Awareness ◆ Ease of use
Ranking of Threats	**Ranking of Barriers**	**Ranking of Opportunities**	**Ranking of Factors of Adoptions**
◆ Paedophile ◆ Pornography ◆ Culture ◆ Decrease in productivity	◆ Telecommunication Infrastructure is poor ◆ Instability of the power supply ◆ Cost of hardware and Internet access ◆ Lack of skills and knowledge ◆ No credit card facility ◆ Lack of understanding of e-commerce	◆ Cheaper and faster communication ◆ Marketing local products and services to the world market ◆ Availability of the Internet 24 hours, seven days/week ◆ Easy access to information ◆ Increase standard of living	◆ Awareness ◆ Better tool than what is currently available ◆ Useful for the business ◆ Ease of use

time, in which case they are likely to miss out in the traditional evening prayers and family meetings. As the manager of the Small Business and Enterprise Centre said:

> *"We do not want what happens in other countries, where employees take a company to court. In Samoa, the manager is always the owner of a small business and any issues are often settled outside of court using our cultural protocols."*

All the participants agreed that the Internet could reduce the productivity of staff because it is new and people are curious as to what this technology can do. Moreover, participants felt that their employees may spent a lot of time typing e-mails to their families and friends overseas because most of them do not have PCs at home. On the other hand, frequently using the Internet can lead to increasing experience. The issue here is that managers lack the knowledge of how to appropriately monitor employees who use the Internet as part of their jobs. One participant said:

> *"The other issue we found once the website was developed was low productivity because of the Internet's 'newness'. How do I know the employee is not surfing the Net or writing e-mails to families and friends? What do I do there?"*

Another participant pointed out that:

> *"Training staff was OK, but then I heard rumors that my staff were printing some obscene pictures from the Internet and distributing them. That means not only will productivity be reduced, but expenses will also be increased because my color cartridge and paper were used. It means that the Internet is a threat in itself."*

The Internet also provides easy access to pornography, pedophilia, and scams. It is already an established fact that pornography has been distributed through the e-mail. Yet, we found that none of the participants had an e-mail and Internet use policy in place. The participants explained that Samoan people would easily fall for such scams, as they have a limited knowledge of these cyber crimes and are gullible, particularly when there is a promise of quick cash. When the issue of Internet and e-mail policies was discussed with the Prime Minister, he pointed out that sometimes all the issues associated with a new phenomenon couldn't be resolved at once. He said:

> *"Well, that is something that we will gradually develop. It's a kind of chicken and egg exercise of deciding, you know. My own thinking is that we take what comes, and we must never be bogged down by the chicken-egg question of which must come first. We should move on in the interest of development; there will always be problems that we face across the way. And as we cross each bridge, we solve the problems one by one. But it is not a good strategy to determine first the evils before we proceed. We will never proceed. So I prefer that we learn by experience as we go along."*

Barriers to Adoption

This research found that the main barriers to adoption included:

1.   Poor telecommunication infrastructure
2.   Cost
3.   Instability of the electrical power supply

4. Lack of e-commerce skills, knowledge, and support
5. Credit cards are not easily available in Samoa

The state of the telecommunication infrastructure in Samoa is very poor. The CEO of the Samoa Communications Limited (SCL) explained that the Samoan telecommunications system has not been upgraded for at least five years. The cables have a relatively short life because there are no casings to cover the cables. They are laid directly into the ground, and the cables deteriorate quickly. Most of the cables and other telecommunication assets have passed their "use by" date, and it too expensive to replace them. However, the government has stepped in to drive Internet adoption in Samoa by adopting a range of measures including: deregulating the Post Office; approving the first privately owned Samoan bank to focus on lending to SMEs; putting time, effort, and money in improving its telecommunication infrastructure; and establishing an agency to provide assistance to SMEs. Work on laying fiber optic cables in the main town of Apia had already commenced during the data-gathering phase of this study.

The cost of hardware and Internet access is another barrier to the adoption of Internet and e-commerce by SMEs in Samoa. Internet access is much more expensive in Samoa than in New Zealand. For instance, in New Zealand, a typical flat rate for unlimited Internet access is NZ$24.95 a month (http://www.telecom.co.nz), whereas in Samoa, as confirmed by Computer Services Limited (CSL), the rate for unlimited Internet access is WS$330 per month, which is equivalent to about NZ$204 per month (CSL, 2001). The cost of a PC in Samoa ranges between NZ$2,000 and NZ$3,000 for the PC only, where as in New Zealand, one can buy a package of a PC, scanner, and printer for under NZ$2,000.

One participant, the owner of a computer retail business, explained that the high cost of computers is due to three main factors:

- Samoa's remote geographic position resulting in high delivery costs.
- High handling and processing fees for imports, such as duty, tax, etc.
- Poor power supply results in additional cost of uninterrupted power supply units.

"The other thing we learned was that we have opened ourselves to a much bigger market on the Internet, especially the business-to-consumer's section. We found that transportation was too costly to supply the products to a consumer rather than to a distributor, in the sense that we are paying to deliver the product to one person, which costs more than delivering a lot of products to a distributor. This issue is due to the remoteness of Samoa from the rest of the world. Most of the SMEs in Samoa experienced the same thing."

Power supply is one of the main barriers of Internet adoption in Samoa. The SMEs explained that often they are without electricity for periods of up to two hours twice a week. There is also never any warning of when to expect a power outage. Customers spent additional money to buy devices to protect their PCs from damage due to power surges.

There are only three sources of electricity in Samoa: hydro, solar, and diesel. Since it has been unusually dry in Samoa in recent years, there has been insufficient water storage for hydropower generation. The solar power system, though available, is limited in capacity, and the diesel is too expensive.

Lack of skills and knowledge is another barrier to Internet and e-commerce adoption among the SMEs in Samoa. To address this, Communications Samoa Ltd. and the National University of Samoa have formed a partnership to provide training to the local businesses as well as individuals. Most of the computer technicians and computer lecturers are from other countries. This is costing a lot of money not only for the SMEs, but for the government of Samoa as well. This study found that the lack of knowledge is due to the fact that the skills such as searching the Internet effectively, using search engines, and managing websites were not required before. Now that the Internet is becoming more important to SMEs, this lack of skills is the first barrier noticed. As the participant from the manufacturing industry sector explained:

> *"The main issue is not knowing what you are getting in to. I tried to do it myself, as it seemed easy to buy a disk then do it yourself, but it took me two years to try and do, to avoid costs. So in the end, I got people from Computer Services Limited to develop the website for me. The other issue is once the website was developed, I realized that I needed the resources to management it. However, there is a lack of skills, which means I have to spend money to get training for staff. We also found out from trying to develop the website ourselves that there are a lot of other things that we needed to understand, things that we did not know before, such as search engines, etc. We also found out that there is a need for the resources to manage electronic trading and to look for ways of sustaining doing business over the Internet."*

While the Internet is becoming more widely adopted by SMEs, Internet shopping is not common, as most SMEs do not have credit cards, because the banks in Samoa do not have credit card facilities in place. This is because Samoa has no central credit risk management system as exists in developed countries. For example, as explained by the CEO of Samoa Communications Limited:

> *"If a customer applies for a telephone line, SCL does not know if this customer owes money to the bank or to other corporations such as the Electrical Power Corporation."*

In terms of the bank's loan applications, a senior officer explained that they have established relationships with the major suppliers such as Electrical Power Corporation and Samoa Communications Limited, whom they have to telephone to find out if an applicant owes money to them.

Having no credit risk management system has also made it difficult for SMEs to apply for loans and for investors to invest in SMEs. A senior official of the Australia and New Zealand (ANZ) bank explained that they consider Samoan SMEs to be high-risk and high-cost borrowers because, in many cases, SMEs lack reliable financial information and collateral. This issue was supported at the United Nations Conference on Trade and Development 2001 meeting on the competitiveness of SMEs in developing countries (United Nations Development Program, 2001). To overcome this problem, the government has established an agency that provides assistance to SMEs in financial record keeping and preparing financial business cases when applying for loans.

This barrier reduces the ability of local SMEs and the general public to purchase goods over the Internet or conduct efficient B2C and B2B transactions. The only SMEs that have credit cards are those owned by people who used to live overseas.

Opportunities Presented by the Internet and E-Commerce

While the Internet is beginning to be adopted quickly in Samoa, e-commerce has not yet contributed to the economy of Samoa in a significant way. The Prime Minister stated:

> *"They [SMEs] form a very large part of Samoa's economy and we have recognized that fact, hence the reason why we have set up the Small Business and Enterprise Centre. In terms of the Internet and e-commerce, we are still working around developing a favorable electronic environment for SMEs to do business in."*

Although a number of SMEs now have websites, they are used mainly for advertising and information sharing purposes only. Our research with Samoan SMEs suggests that the key opportunities for e-commerce include:

1. Cheaper advertising
2. Effective and cheaper communication
3. Exposure to a much wider market
4. Easier access to information
5. The possibility of attracting multinational organizations

The participants in this study believed that the Internet has done wonders for their businesses. In the tourism industry, those that participated in this study but did not yet have a website said that the Samoa Visitors Bureau's website advertises their businesses together with their e-mail addresses (http://publicwww.pi.se/~orbit/samoa/info.html). Those who already have websites are enjoying the business they receive over the Internet, although they cannot make or receive payments online. As one motelier said:

> *"We are now building extra fales to cope with the demand. In fact, during the tattoo festival held here, we had guests that were willing to sleep in our kitchen. Through the Internet we found the tourists' needs that we were not aware of before and that is, they want to experience living the Samoan way. As a result, we have now started to build our second tourist accommodation using the traditional fales on the beach. As you know, there are now more European-styled houses in Samoa than Samoan traditional fales. IT means the Internet has given us a 'wakeup call' to preserve the Samoan traditional fales and way of life. This is our niche in the tourism market."*

In the manufacturing sector, use of the Internet has helped obtain new business from as far away as Germany, Canada, and the U.S. One manufacturer has had to open a second branch in order to cope with demand. Through their website, customers can now order online or through e-mail, although payments are still processed by the bank.

The consultancy firms who participated in this study stated that the Internet makes a big difference to the service they provide. The Internet has allowed them to compete with overseas consultancy firms for consultancy work required by the international organizations such as United Nations Development Program, World Bank, and the World Health Organization.

The participants from the retail sector stated that for them, the Internet is used mainly for e-mail and advertisements. However, the participants are enthusiastic about the fact that they can now order products from overseas vendors that are not available locally, although they still have to visit the bank to pay for the goods, using the bank's money transfer system or bank drafts. Retailers with websites now stock goods formerly not available but needed in Samoa, giving them a competitive advantage over those that have not yet adopted the Internet. One of the local manufacturers said:

> *"The good thing about the Internet is that we can now order raw products cheaply from overseas. Not only that, but we are buying goods not available in Samoa then advertising them. As more and more Samoan people living overseas move back here, we find that if we order the goods they used to use overseas but [that are] not available locally, then we have a leading edge in the competition."*

Comparison with Other Studies

The Internet and e-commerce issues in SMEs in Samoa are consistent with the studies conducted in other developing countries (Schmid, Stanoevska-Slabeva, & Tschammer, 2001; El-Nawawy & Ismail, 2000; Boalch & Bazaar, 1997). For example, El-Nawawy and Ismail (1999) in their study of e-commerce adoption by SMEs in Egypt found that the main factors contributing to the non-adoption of e-commerce in Egypt are:

- Awareness and education
- Market size
- E-commerce infrastructure
- Telecommunication infrastructure
- Financial infrastructure
- Legal system
- Government role
- Pricing structure
- Social and psychological factors

Schmid et al. (2001) suggest that the main e-commerce issues facing SMEs in Argentina are:

- Awareness
- Access to hardware
- Infrastructure
- Organizational culture
- Financial issues

A comparison of the two studies in Argentina and Egypt (both developing countries) suggests that the key factors of e-commerce adoption in developing countries are awareness, telecommunication infrastructure, and cost. It also suggests that SMEs in developing countries share similar issues.

SME studies of e-commerce issues in developed countries (Corbitt, Behrendorf, & Brown-Parker, 1997; Huff & Yoong, 2000; Mehrtens et al., 2002; Poon & Swatmann, 1999) indicate that e-commerce issues faced by SMEs in developed countries can be totally different from those experienced by SMEs in developing countries. The issues discussed previously indicate why this is so in the case of Samoa.

Using Diffusion of Innovation Theory

According to Rogers (1983), adoption is a decision to make full use of an innovation as the best course of action, whereas rejection is a decision not to adopt an available innovation. In this study, adoption is therefore defined as *the decision to make use of the Internet and e-commerce to conduct business or transactions with trading partners, customers, and families.*

There are two levels of adoption. Initially, innovation must be purchased, adopted, or acquired by an organization. Subsequently, it must be accepted by the ultimate users in that organization and/or community. In this study, it is proposed that several factors influence different levels of Internet and e-commerce adoption for the SMEs.

A number of factors interact to influence the diffusion of an innovation. The four major factors that influence the diffusion process are the innovation itself, how information about the innovation is communicated, time, and the nature of the social system into which the innovation is being introduced (Rogers, 1995). Diffusion research, in its simplest form, investigates how these major factors, and a multitude of other factors, interact to facilitate or impede the adoption of a specific product or practice among members of a particular adopter group. By better understanding the factors that influence adoption of innovations, Samoa will be better able to explain, predict, and account for the factors that impede or facilitate the diffusion of the Internet and e-commerce among SMEs.

The Innovation Decision Process

The innovation decision process (Rogers, 1995) states that diffusion is a process that occurs over time and can be seen as having five distinct stages. These five stages are: knowledge, persuasion, decision, implementation, and confirmation, which occur at different times.

In the context of this study, it was found that, after becoming aware of the Internet, SMEs immediately wanted to know more about this phenomenon. They attended Internet seminars that were run by the National University of Samoa and Samoa Communications Limited. According to the DOI theory, this is the process of developing *knowledge* about the innovation. Once the participants gained more knowledge about uses of the Internet, such as sending e-mails to families and friends overseas at a much cheaper rate, advertising their products cheaply, accessing customers from other countries, and gaining easy access to information, they *persuaded* themselves that the Internet was a very valuable tool. Not only that, but their families and friends overseas played a role in the persuasion process. At this stage, the SME owner managers made their *decision* to adopt the Internet. Once they decided to adopt, they contacted the ISPs to *implement* the Internet. Once they had the Internet installed, they began using it to communicate with families and friends overseas, which (among other uses) served to *confirm* their decision. In summary, then, the process that SMEs went through before they decided to adopt the Internet was:

- Knowledge. SMEs learned from families and friends overseas and attended seminars.

- Persuasion. SMEs believed that the Internet was a valuable tool to the business.

- Decision. SME owners/managers making up their mind to install the Internet.

- Implementation. SME owners/managers requesting the ISP to install the Internet.

- Confirmation. SMEs' actual use of the Internet and agreeing of the usefulness of the Internet.

The various points and time when each of the five stages occurs are explained in Table 4.

Other Observations

The SMEs found that there are things they had to learn once the technology was adopted. One such lesson was the need for staff to learn how to use search engines and other Internet methods, skills, and knowledge that did not exist before. Another lesson involved how to use the Internet to order goods cheaply from overseas, not available in Samoa. Retailers who order goods from overseas and stock them quickly find that the Internet has contributed to moving their businesses to the leading edge of the competition and can be the tool to sustain its competitive advantage. Because they were among the first adopters, they learned more than those SMEs that have not yet adopted the

Table 4: Five Stages of Diffusion Decision Process for Internet Adoption in Samoa

Knowledge	Occurred when SME owners were exposed to the Internet's existence and gain some understanding of how it functions through families and friends overseas and attending seminars. Key players in providing seminars are government, through the university, SBEC and ISPs.
Persuasion	Occurred when SME owners form a favourable or unfavourable attitude toward the Internet. This attitude was influenced by the Perceived attributes of the Internet.
Decision	Occurred when SMEs engage in activities that lead to a choice to adopt or reject the innovation such as talking to the ISPs which eventually led to **requesting** connection to the Internet and/or building a website.
Implementation	Occurred when SMEs paid the connection fee and had the ISP action the connection to the Internet and/or build the websites. Key factor is infrastructure.
Confirmation	Occurred when SME used the Internet and/or website thereby confirming what they learnt was what actually happened when using the Internet and/or website. None of the participants that had the Internet and/or website has reversed a previous decision to adopt the Internet. However, those that did not adopt are now looking to reverse their previous decision from reject the to adopt because they had not heard any conflicting messages about the perceived attributes of the Internet they learned earlier.

Internet. As they continue to use the Internet, they increase the knowledge base of their employees and their businesses.

The downside of this is the risk of losing staff with the new skills. Once other SMEs finally decide to build a website, they will look for people with skills to manage it. This is the point where the risk takers will experience problems if they are not prepared to provide incentives for employees with this new skill to stay. The most appropriate incentive experienced by some participants is a pay raise. From a social perspective, it was found that not only the businesses benefit from the Internet and e-commerce, staff who were trained received pay raises to encourage them to stay; and while more customers were acquired over the Internet, overtime was offered to meet the demand. The demand due to the increase in customers gradually led to staff receiving more money through overtime, thereby raising the standard of living. Discussions with the participants during the focus group meeting (held after all the individual interviews had been completed) led to most participants believing that Internet adoption in Samoa can be seen as evolutionary, because the causes of change lie in social conditions and in human aspirations for change and improvement. This is an interesting theory that needs further research in the future.

Conclusion

While the use of the Internet in Samoa is still at a very early stage in terms of numbers of connections and overall use, the promise it offers for increased productivity and enhanced economic growth in the future is significant. Most benefits are likely to come from business use of the Internet for both internal control and for dealing with business customers and suppliers, rather than from local consumer use, due to the unavailability of a credit card system. For example, global connections will be much enhanced by Samoa's liberalized access to international Internet gateways and to the use of fiber optic cables to replace the copper cable. This access alone could offer Samoan SMEs business opportunities that otherwise would flow to large corporations.

Unlike other developing countries of the South Pacific, the Samoan government began to encourage development and improvement of the telecommunication infrastructure, and the Internet more specifically, through various incentives. As the Prime Minister said:

> *"In fact my dream is that we lead the Pacific in terms of IT diffusion, the Internet, and e-commerce. So that is why I have taken over Telecommunication as my portfolio and forced the corporatization issue through Parliament, because I want to move things as fast as possible. I know from attending various conferences overseas that a country that rapidly adopts the Internet and e-commerce is the country that will quickly realize the benefits of information technology and will not be left behind."*

There is much to learn about the dynamics influencing Internet and e-commerce adoption by SMEs in developing countries. Although international organizations are developing initiatives to help developing countries maximize access to the Internet, such initiatives have focused largely on the more populous developing countries (Johnston & Acquaah-Gaisie, 2001). The relatively small population of the South Pacific makes it a less attractive proposition for investment. Further research focusing on such countries should help improve our understanding of the special barriers, threats, and opportunities they face as they try to utilize the Internet and e-commerce in furthering their development.

References

Boalch, G., & Bazaar, B. (1997). A preliminary model of Internet diffusion in developing countries. *Proceedings of the Third Australian World Wide Web Conference*, Southern Cross University, Australia (July 5-9).

Bright, J. (1997). Electronic commerce: The new global marketplace. *Telecommunications,* (January), 64-68.

Corbitt, B., & Thanasankit, T. (2000). Cultural context and its impact on requirements elicitation in Thailand. *The Electronic Journal on Information Systems in Developing Countries, 1*(January).

Corbitt, B., Behrendorf, G., & Brown-Parker, J. (1997). Small and medium-sized enterprises and electronic commerce. *The Australian Institute of Management, 14,* 204-222.

Davis, F.D., & Venkatesh, V. (1996). A critical assessment of potential measurement biases in the technology acceptance model: Three experiments. *International Journal of Human-Computer Studies*, *45*(1), 19-45.

El-Nawawy, M.A., & Ismail, M.M. (1999). Overcoming deterrents and impediments to electronic commerce in light of globalization: The case of Egypt. *Proceedings of the 9ᵗʰ Annual Conference of the Internet Society,* San Jose, California, USA (June 22-25).

Hofstede, G.H. (1980). *Culture's Consequences: International Differences in Work-Related Values.* Beverly Hills, CA: Sage Publications.

Huff, S., & Yoong, P. (2000). SMEs and e-commerce: Current issues and concerns. A preliminary report. *Proceedings of the International Conference on E-Commerce,* Kuala Lumpur, Malaysia (pp. 1-5).

Johnston, S., & Acquaah-Gaisie, G. (2001). Development via the Net in Oceania. *Proceedings of the 3ʳᵈ World Conference of the Global IT Management,* Dallas, Texas, USA (p. 31).

Kiggen, G. (2000). Accessed April 24, 2001 on the Web: http://www.electronicmarkets.org.

Klein, M. (1998). Small business grows online. *American Demographics, 20*(2), 30.

Kong, W.C. (1999). *Issues affecting the implementation of e-commerce in Singapore.* Unpublished thesis, University of Melbourne, Australia.

Licker, P., & Motts, N. (2000). Extending the benefits of e-commerce in Africa: Exploratory phase. *Proceedings of the 1ˢᵗ Annual Conference of the Global IT Management Association,* Memphis, Tennessee, USA (pp. 115-118).

Mehrtens, J., Cragg, P.B., & Mills, A.J. (2001). A model of Internet adoption by SMEs. *Information & Management, 39*(3.), 165-176.

Myers, M.D., & Tan, F.B. (2002). Beyond models of national culture in information systems research. *Journal of Global Information Management, 10*(1), 24-32.

OECD. (1998). SMEs and e-commerce. DSTI/CCP(98). Available on the Web: http://www.oecd.org/dsti/sti/it/-infosoc/prod/minitel.htm.

O'Keefe, R.M., O'Connor, G., & Kung, H. (1998). Early adopters of the Web as a retail medium: Small company winners and losers. *European Journal of Marketing, 32*(7/8), 629-643.

Poon, S., & Swatman, P. (1999). An exploratory study of small business Internet Commerce issues. *Information and Management, 35*(1), 9-18.

Rogers, E.M. (1983). *Diffusion of Innovation* (3ʳᵈ ed.). New York: The Free Press.

Rogers, E.M. (1995). *Diffusion of Innovations* (4ᵗʰ ed.). New York: The Free Press.

Rommel, K. (1997). Electronic commerce: A business opportunity. *AIC Conferences/EDI Over the Internet Conference,* Hong Kong (March 24-25).

Schmid, B., Stanoevska-Slabeva, K., & Tschammer, V. (2001). *Towards the e-society: E-commerce, e-business, e-government.* Zurich, Switzerland (October 13).

Swatman, P. (1998). Look Ma, no hands—Product delivery systems in the information economy. *Proceedings from South East Asia Regional Conference,* Darwin, Australia (July 8-10).

Tassabehji, R. (2000). E-commerce in Dubai: Realities and impediments. *10*(1/2), 144-145. Available on the Web: http://www.electronicmarkets.org.

United Nations Development Program. (2001). *Making new technologies work for human development, human development report.* New York. Available on the Web: http://www.undp.org/hdr2001/.

Yin, R.K. (1984). *Case Study Research: Design and Methods* (2nd ed.). Beverly Hills, CA: Sage Publications.

Appendix A

Interview Protocol

Information Required	Question
Organizational and Current IT Background 1. Nature of the business 2. Establish if it's an SME 3. Establish business process 4. Level of computer usage 5. Establish if findings an issue 6. Level of PC support 7. Frequency of service	**After Introductions:** Please explain the nature of your business. How many employees do you employ? Please give a brief explanation of the current process. Are you currently using a computer? What do you use the computer for? Do you have the Internet? What is your view on the cost of computers and Internet access? If your PC breaks down, whom do you call? How long do you usually wait until it is fixed? What is the estimate cost?
E-Commerce Awareness and Mode of Acceptance 1. Establish Internet access 2. Establish if Internet a future option 3. Establish knowledge of e-commerce 4. Access cost 5. Factors that influenced acceptance of the Internet	• Do you or have you had access to the Internet? • If yes, what did you use the Internet for? • Does your company have a website? • If no, why not? Do you plan to have the Internet in the future? • Would you develop a website? • Please explain what you know about e-commerce. • If not a lot, explain what it is all about. • What is your monthly cost to use the Internet? • How did you arrive at the decision to adopt the Internet? That is, what motivated you to buy into the Internet and develop a website? • What were the main factors that influenced your decision? • Explain where you first heard about the Internet and what you did about it.
Barriers 1. Identify the barriers 2. Establish ways to break the barriers	• What do you see as the main difficulties for you to do business on the Internet? • What do you think is the best way to eliminate these difficulties? • Who in Samoa do you think can help with eliminating these barriers?
Opportunities 1. Establish perception of e-commerce opportunities 2. Competition and e-commerce	• What do you think are the benefits of doing business over the Internet for your company? • What about it benefits you personally? Your family? • Who are your competitors? • What is different between your business and your competitors?
Threats 1. Find out what they perceive as threats	• What do you see as a negative impact of doing business over the Internet? • What about your family? Your community? • Do you think doing business over the Internet will impact your culture? How? • What would your company do to eliminate these threats?
Role of the Government 1. Establish government help	• Are you aware of any government programs to help small businesses like yours to buy PCs and develop a Webster for your business? • If yes, please explain the process.
Business Strategy 1. E-commerce plan	• In moving forward, would you consider adopting e-commerce? • If there were a government agency to help SMEs, would you consider their offer?
Focus Group	• Are you available for ½ day on_date_place for half a day? The documented analysis was sent to you on _date. Morning tea was provided.
Future Research	• Would you be happy to participate in future research?

Section V

Adoption and Diffusion Patterns of E-Commerce in SMEs

Chapter VII

Factors Influencing Electronic Commerce Adoption in Small and Medium Businesses: An Empirical Study in Thailand

Chalermsak Lertwongsatien, Ministry of Finance, Thailand

Nitaya Wongpinunwatana, Thammasat University, Thailand

Angsana Achakulwisut, University of Minnesota, USA

Abstract

This study examines the factors influencing the variations of e-commerce adoption decisions in small and medium businesses in Thailand. Based on the literature review, three groups of factors are identified, including organizational, technology, and environmental factors. Firms are classified into three main groups based on the extent to which an organization is relatively earlier to adopt e-commerce than others, namely adopters, prospectors, and laggards. Data was collected through a national survey in several provinces in Thailand. The statistical analysis results strongly support the hypotheses. The results are interpreted and the implications of this study are subsequently discussed.

Introduction

The adoption and use of IT innovation in an organization have been studied extensively for many years (Chau & Tam, 1997; Fichman & Kemerer, 1997; Grover & Goslar, 1993; Iacovou, Benbasat, & Dexter, 1995; Ravichandran, 2000). Grover and Goslar (1993), for example, studied the adoption and diffusion of telecommunications technologies in U.S. organizations. Chau and Tam (1997) examined the factors affecting the adoption of open systems. Iacovou et al. (1995) examined the adoption of Electronic Data Interchange (EDI) in small organizations. Though a large number of studies have explored various types of IT-related innovation adoption, few have studied specifically the adoption of an emerging IT-driven innovation, electronic commerce (e-commerce).

E-commerce is "the sharing of business information, maintaining business relationships, and conducting business transactions by means of telecommunication network" (Zwass, 1996). Currently, e-commerce pervasively and dramatically affects the ways firms think, operate, and compete in the market. Many innovative business models such as supply chain management, customer relationship management, and enterprise resource planning are also enabled by e-commerce. The adoption of e-commerce has brought new opportunities and challenges to business organizations.

The main purpose of this chapter is to examine the factors that influence the variations of e-commerce adoption behaviors of small and medium businesses in Thailand. Prior studies found that small businesses are slow in adopting technological innovations (Yap, Thong, & Raman, 1994). Since small and medium businesses constitute almost 90% of all businesses in many economies, the slowing rate of innovation adoption is a critical issue needed to be examined. Moreover, small and medium businesses are different from large businesses in many aspects. Organizational theories that are applicable to large businesses may not fit in small and medium business environments (Wesh & White, 1981). There is a need to examine whether models of IT innovation tested on the large organization context can be similarly applied to small and medium business environments.

While most prior studies in IT innovation have focused on traditional dichotomous variables (for example, use/non-use, adopt/non-adopt), they were criticized for inadequacy in completely capturing a complexity of the innovation and adoption behaviors (Ravichandran, 2000). In addition, most of them emphasized firms that already adopted an innovation. Few studies distinguished firms intending to adopt innovation in the near future from non-adopter firms. In response to this gap, we classify firms into three main groups based on the extent of e-commerce innovativeness (Roger, 1983), the extent to which an organization is relatively earlier to adopt e-commerce than others, namely *adopters*, *prospectors*, and *laggards*. First, adopters are firms that have already implemented and used e-commerce in their business activities. These firms are creative and innovative in applying leading-edge technologies, such as e-commerce, compared with their competitors. Second, prospectors are firms that have not yet implemented e-commerce, but they have a specific plan in the near future to adopt and implement e-commerce. Prospectors tend to avoid the immediate application of leading-edge technologies; however, after a certain period of time, they are ready to adopt innovations that have been proven effective. Finally, laggards are firms that have not implemented e-commerce, and have no plan or intention to adopt e-commerce in the near future. Laggards are typically slow in adopting new innovation; however, they may decide to adopt the technologies when forced by business competition.

Prior studies in the organization innovation, information technology use, and diffusion of information technology innovation suggest a set of variables that can be used as predictors of e-commerce adoption (Kimberly & Evanisko, 1981; Kwon & Zmud, 1987; Tornatzky & Fleischer, 1990). Based on the review of the literature, particularly the study by Tornatzky and Fleischer (1990), we identify three sets of predictors for e-commerce adoption: *organizational factors*, *technology factors*, and *environmental factors*. Since this study focuses on e-commerce adoption at an organizational level, individual characteristic variables, such as individual innovation perceptions, are not considered in this study. The sample frame includes small and medium businesses located in Thailand—an Asia-based country. Most of the IT innovation studies have been conducted in the U.S. However, Asian firms are different from U.S. firms in many respects, such as geographic, political, and cultural aspects. The research findings from this study can help in determining whether the organizational innovation theory can be generalized across other settings, particularly in Asian settings. In addition, newly industrializing and developing countries have been initiating government interventions to accelerate the use of IT within their countries. King et al. (Thong, 1999) suggested that the role of institutions such as governments must be considered as essential components in IT innovation adoption. The key factors found to be crucial from this study could be incorporated in governmental initiatives and could be used in developing the strategy for promoting e-commerce adoption among small and medium businesses in the region.

The outline of this chapter is as follows. First, the background of small and medium businesses, the e-commerce status in Thailand, and the theoretical background are discussed. Consequently, the hypothesis development, methodology, and the results of data analysis are explained. The final section discusses the implications of this study for research and practice.

Background

Small and Medium Businesses in Thailand

The definition of small and medium businesses in Thailand has gone through a series of modification and changes (Sevilla & Soonthornthada, 2000). In the past, many criteria had been used such as annual sales, net fixed assets, number of employees, and registered capital (Allal, 1999). While the size of small and medium businesses, reflected by the number of employees, has mutually been accepted to be fewer than 200, the asset value aspect has been periodically changed to reflect a more current economic condition. For example, in the early 1990s, it was reported that small businesses were defined as those having fixed assets less than 10 million baht, and medium businesses as those having between 10 and 50 million baht (one U.S. dollar approximately equals 43 baht, as of September 2002) (Thongpakde, Puppahavesa, & Pussarangsri, 1994). The Department of Industrial Promotion (DIP) defined small businesses as having invested capital less than 10 million baht, and from more than 10 million to 100 million baht for medium businesses. These classifications had been internally used within the Ministry of Industrial since 1987 (UNICO, 1995).

In 1998, the Cabinet approved a definition of small and medium businesses. This definition was derived through a meeting organized by the Ministry of Industry; representatives from other ministries, banks, agencies, and departments, and private sector and technical experts participated in the meeting. The definition (Table 1), which subsequently has been accepted by all government agencies, uses only the net fixed assets as the classification criteria. Based on this definition, small and medium businesses are classified into three sectors: (1) production sector (i.e., agricultural processing, manufacturing, and mining); (2) service sector; and (3) trading sector (i.e., wholesale and retail).

According to a survey in 1998, there were 311,518 small and medium businesses, accounting for 92% of the total business enterprises in Thailand. The majority of small and medium businesses were in the trading sector (43 %). The remainder were in manufacturing (29%) and service sectors (28%) (Sevilla & Soonthornthada, 2000).

E-Commerce Status in Thailand

Thailand has initiated and implemented a series of national plans and activities to promote diffusion of e-commerce in both public and private sectors. Several governmental agents have engaged in these activities. For example, the National Electronics and Computer Technology Center (NECTEC), the governmental agency responsible for the

Table 1: Definition of Small and Medium Businesses in Thailand (Total Assets Value in Million Baht)

Sector	Medium	Small
Production	Not more than 200	Not more than 50
Service	Not more than 200	Not more than 50
Trading		
- Wholesale	Not more than 100	Not more than 50
- Retail	Not more than 60	Not more than 30

development of information technology in Thailand, has initiated various projects and activities promoting the use of e-commerce in Thailand, such as developing the electronic commerce framework for Thailand, drafting IT laws facilitating the diffusion of e-commerce, and drafting technical specifications and recommendations and becoming a resource center to run awareness, information center, and human resource development programs on e-commerce (NECTEC, 2002). In January 1999, the cabinet approved a proposal by the Ministry of Science, Technology, and Environment to set up the Electronic Commerce Resource Center (ECRC) to ensure the smooth development of e-commerce in Thailand through awareness, training, and information (ECRC, 2002).

The Ministry of Commerce is also another key government agency that has initiated several projects to promote e-commerce, particularly for importers and exporters in Thailand. Such initiatives include ThaiEcommerce.net and exporter.org, a resource center for Thai's exporters. Several departments under the Ministry of Commerce—such as the Department of Export Promotion—are also key drivers of e-commerce development in Thailand. In the context of small and medium businesses, the Ministry of Industry is in a leading role in promoting the use of e-commerce for competitiveness. The Ministry of Industry, through the Department of Industrial Promotion, has developed a website (www.smethai.net) specifically for promoting small and medium businesses' products and services. The department also arranges a free homepage with URL and e-mail, and provides seminars and training programs for SMEs.

According to an e-commerce website survey conducted by the E-Commerce Resource Center/NECTEC, mid-2001, 12% of about 6,000 e-commerce websites (both .com and .co.th Thai companies) offered full-scaled e-commerce services, such as online catalogs, electronic ordering, and logistic services.

Theoretical Background and Development of the Research Model

Organizational innovation was adopted as a theoretical foundation for developing the research model. Organizational innovation can be defined as the development and implementation of ideas, systems, products, or technologies that are new to the organization adopting it (Rogers, 1983). Innovations are means of changing an organization, either as a response to changes in the external environment or as a preemptive action to influence the environment. The adoption of innovation is a process that includes the generation, development, and implementation of new ideas or behaviors (Rogers, 1983). Innovations can be categorized as a broad range of types, including new products or services, new process technologies, new organizational structures or administrative systems, or new plans or programming pertaining to organizational members (Poutsma, Van Uxem, & Walravens, 1987). Adoption of e-commerce, hence, can be regarded as one form of innovation adoption.

The innovation literature has identified various groups of variables that are possible determinants of organizational adoption of an innovation (Fichman & Kemerer, 1987; Kimberly & Evanisko, 1981; Tornatzky & Fleischer, 1990). Based on a synthesis of the organizational innovation literature, Kwon and Zmud (1987) identified five sets of factors that may influence IT innovation. These sets include user characteristics, task characteristics, innovation characteristics, organizational characteristics, and environmental characteristics. Kimberly and Evannisko (1981) proposed three clusters of predictors for innovation adoption: characteristics of organization, characteristics of leader, and characteristics of environment.

Recently a number of IT innovation studies (e.g., Boynton, Zmud, & Jacobs, 1994; Tornatzky & Fleischer, 1990) have adopted an emerging theory from the strategic management literature—absorptive capacity (Cohen & Levinthal, 1990)—to explain a firm's abilities in adopting and assimilating an innovation. Boynton et al. (1994), for example, argued that a firm's ability to effectively use IT is influenced by the development of an IT-related knowledge and processes that bind together the firm's IT managers and business managers. They pointed to the organizational climate as the key factor influencing the ability of firms to absorb new knowledge and technology. Fitchman and Kemerer (1990) found that organizations are more likely to initiate and sustain the assimilation of software process innovations when they have a more extensive existing knowledge in areas related to the focal innovation.

Drawing from these studies, we develop a research model for e-commerce adoption. It consists of seven variables representing three major groups: organizational factors, technology factors, and external factors. First, organizational factors have been the most widely used and tested as the key determinants of innovation (Grover & Goslar, 1993; Thong, 1999). In this study, we focus on three sets of variables: structural variable (size), process variable (top management support for e-commerce), and IT context variables (IT emphasis, and existence of IT department). Many studies have examined the effects of structural factors on innovation, such as size, specialization, and formalization (Grover & Goslar, 1993). Size is one of the most widely investigated variables for innovation adoption. The arguments for the impact of size on organizational innovation are mixed. Some argued that larger sizes promote innovation due to greater slack resources, while others argued that smaller sizes foster innovation due to the flexibility advantage (Utterback, 1974).

Process factors have also been frequently adopted as a key determinant of IT-related innovation adoption, especially by top management. The IT innovation literature generally reported a positive effect of senior management support on IT-related innovation (Orlikowski, 1993; Rai & Patnayakuni, 1996). The common rationales provided include influencing the allocation of slack resources, and generating enthusiasm and commitment toward changes among organizational members. This study examines the positive effect of top management support in the context of e-commerce innovation.

Finally, since e-commerce is largely a bundle of various IT components (i.e., hardware, software, networking), IT context factors could play an important role in determining e-commerce adoption. Two IT context factors are examined: IT emphasis, and existence of IT department. First, prior studies suggested the positive relationship between the roles of IT and IT-related innovation adoption (e.g., Premkumar & King, 1994; Ravichandran, 2000). Organizations that highly emphasize IT are more likely to try new technologies and ideas. This study examines the influence of IT emphasis, reflected by IT investment intensity, on e-commerce adoption. Second, evidence from the innovation literature recently suggests that the role of a firm's ability to absorb new knowledge related to innovation can play an important role in innovation adoption (Cohen & Lavinthal, 1990). Small and medium businesses that are familiar with IT skills and knowledge might find it easier to acquire additional knowledge necessary for adopting e-commerce. The IT department is a major source of IT skills and knowledge in organizations, and could be a main unit in acquiring and assimilating the knowledge necessary to adopt and implement e-commerce innovation. Hence, it is conceivable that the existence of an IT department in small and medium businesses could promote e-commerce adoption.

The second group of variables is technology factors. Specific factors related to innovation characteristics are frequently used as a key determinant of innovation adoption intention. Rogers (1983), for example, identified several attributes of an innovation that can influence innovation acceptance behaviors, such as relative advantage, complexity, compatibility, and observability. Tornatzky and Klein (1990) identified relative advantage, compatibility, and complexity as innovation characteristics that are salient to the attitude formation of innovation adoption. Though most of these factors are more pertinent to an individual perception, some attributes are applicable at an organization level (e.g., Chau & Tam, 1997; Thong, 1999). This study investigates the effects of two innovation characteristics: perceived compatibility and perceived benefits. Different organizations may face different innovation opportunities. Whether these opportunities can be exploited depends on the degree of match between the innovation's characteristics and the infrastructure currently available in the organization (Rogers, 1983). In addition, not all innovations are relevant to an organization. The degree of relevance depends on the potential benefits organizations received.

The third group of research variables is an external factor. Past studies have stressed the importance of environments. Environmental contingencies such as environmental uncertainty and heterogeneity have been found as facilitators of innovation (Grover & Goslar, 1993; Schroeder & Benbasat, 1975). When organizations face a complex and rapidly changing environment, innovation is both necessary and justified (Pfeffer & Leblebici, 1977). Environmental factors, especially market factors (i.e., competitiveness), cannot be controlled by organizations; rather, they affect the way firms conduct their businesses. Thus, it is conceivable that environmental factors create a need for firms to adopt IT-related innovation such as e-commerce. This study examines the effect of competitiveness on e-commerce adoption.

Table 2 summarizes the research variables used in this study. The variables included in the research model are not meant to be all-inclusive. Rather, they are selected based on the consensus in the innovation literature and empirical evidence as representing key theoretical factors affecting organizational innovation adoption. These variables reflect three elements—organizational, technological, and environmental elements—that influence the process by which innovations are adopted suggested by Tornatzky and Fleischer (1990).

Table 2: Examined Variables

Factors	Theoretical Representation	Variables
Organizational Factors	Organizational Structure	Size
	Organizational Process	Top Management Support for E-Commerce
	IT Context	IT Emphasis
		Existence of IT Department
Technology Factors	Technological Context	Perceived Benefits
		Perceived Compatibility
Environmental Factors	Organizational Environment	Competitiveness

Hypotheses

Organizational Factors

Size

Organizational size has been one of the most frequently examined factors in the study of organizational innovation (e.g., Rai & Patnayakuni, 1996; Thong, 1999). Prior studies reported that size has a positive impact on the likelihood of IS-related innovation adoption such as adoption of CASE tools (Rai & Patnayakuni, 1996), object oriented (Fitchman & Kemerer, 1997), and TQM (Ravichandran, 2000). Large-size firms are more likely to adopt innovation since they are capable of absorbing risk associated with innovation, and have sufficient resources and infrastructure to facilitate the implementation of innovation (Fitchman & Kemerer, 1997).

Small and medium businesses encounter barriers to innovation adoption by limited financial resources, insufficient technological expertise, and a shortage of management perspective (Wesh & White, 1981). Adoption and implementation of e-commerce demand a certain level of organizational resources. Larger organizations should be in a better position to support such demands. Moreover, larger organizations should have a higher potential to use e-commerce due to a larger scale of business operations (Lind, Zmud, & Fischer, 1989). Therefore, we expect that e-commerce adopters would have a larger size than prospectors and laggards.

Hypothesis 1: The three types of organizations significantly differ in their size.

Top Management Support for E-Commerce

It is well accepted that top management plays a critical role in acquisition and diffusion of innovation (Orlikowski, 1993; Rai & Patnayakuni, 1996; Wesh & White, 1981). Top management can stimulate change by communicating and reinforcing values through an articulated vision for the organization (Thong, 1999). Moreover, top management can ensure that resources and capabilities required for adopting and implementing innovation will be readily available when they are needed (Rai & Patnayakuni, 1996). Empirical studies in IT innovation suggested a positive effect of leadership support on innovation adoption. Rai and Patnayakuni (1996), for example, found that top management support has a positive effect on CASE tools adoption behavior in IS departments.

Adopting and implementing e-commerce requires resources extensively that are forthcoming only with the active support from top management. In addition, top management support for e-commerce would also send a strong signal to get line management to actively participate in proposing and developing an e-commerce initiative. Therefore, we expect that e-commerce adopters would have a higher level of top management support for e-commerce than prospectors and laggards.

Hypothesis 2: The three types of organizations significantly differ in the extent of top management support for e-commerce.

IT Emphasis

Firms significantly differ in their level of IT emphasis. Case studies that highlight strategic IT applications (e.g., Reich & Benbasat, 1990) also suggest that firms in service industries are more conductive to the use of IT for their business operations. Jarvenpaa and Ives (1991) found that top management's interest in IT, as an indirect measure of the importance of IT, was lower for firms in the petroleum industry compared to firms in banking.

IT emphasis is defined as the level of importance the firms have placed on IT. In this study, we use the intensity of IT investment as a surrogate measurement of this variable. Differences in the level of IT emphasis are expected to significantly influence the adoption action of IT-related innovation such as e-commerce. Prior studies suggested that organizations that put more emphasis on IT tend to be more aggressive in seeking and trying new technologies and ideas. For example, Premkumar and King (1994) found that firms in service industries, which place more emphasis on IT, are more likely to adopt IS planning. Orlikowski (1993) found that adoption and implementation of CASE tools were influenced by the roles of IT in the firms. Ravichandran (2000) also found that firms where IS plays a strategic role are more likely to adopt TQM in information systems development. Based on these cumulative evidences, we expected that e-commerce adopters would have a higher level of IT emphasis than prospectors and laggards. This leads to the following hypothesis:

Hypothesis 3: The three types of organizations significantly differ in the level of IT emphasis.

Existence of IT Department

Absorptive capacity theory (Cohen & Levinthal, 1990) asserts that a firm's ability to appreciate an innovation, to assimilate it, and apply it to new ends is largely a result of the firm's preexisting knowledge in areas related to the focal innovation. This prior related knowledge makes it easier for organizations to acquire and retain new knowledge for innovation adoption. Complementary to this perspective, it was found that the technology assimilation is best characterized as a process of organizational learning, wherein individuals and the organization as a whole acquire the knowledge and skills necessary to effectively acquire and apply the new technology (Boynton et al., 1994). Prior empirical studies in IT innovation also point to prior knowledge as a key determinant of IT innovation adoption (Fitchman & Kemerer, 1997).

Adopting and implementing e-commerce innovation requires organizations to posses a bundle of IT-related skills and knowledge (Turban, King, Lee, Warkentin, & Chung, 2002) such as telecommunication knowledge (i.e., TCP/IP, HTTP protocol), security management knowledge (i.e., SSL, Public Key Infrastructure), and Internet application environment (i.e., HTML coding, Java technology). Though many small firms may adopt an outsourcing strategy for e-commerce operation, they still need some basic knowledge for selecting appropriated service providers, and, in many cases, they need these IT skills and knowledge to control and monitor the operation of e-commerce.

The IT department can be viewed as a source of IT-related skills and knowledge within organizations. Most small businesses do not have any formal, or even informal IT department, and routine IT services are usually performed by accounting or administrative units. Small businesses that have an IT department should be in a better position to acquire some IT-related skills and knowledge, which make it easier for them to acquire new knowledge for adopting e-commerce. Therefore, we expect that e-commerce adopters are more likely to have a formal IT department within organizations than prospectors and laggards.

Hypothesis 4: The three types of organizations significantly differ in the existence of an IT department.

Technology Factors

Perceived Benefits

Perceived benefits refer to the extent of management recognition of the relative advantage that e-commerce can provide to the firms. Perceived benefits are regarded as an important factor in determining adoption of new innovations (Iacovou et al., 1995; Rogers, 1983). For example, Iacovou et al. (1995) found that perceived benefits have a positive effect on the likelihood of EDI adoption in small businesses.

The higher the level of management understanding on the relative advantage of e-commerce, the more the likelihood of the allocation of the managerial, financial, and technological resources necessary to adopt and implement e-commerce. This positive perception of the benefits of e-commerce should provide an incentive for the small and medium businesses to adopt the innovation. Therefore, we expect that adopters of e-commerce would have a higher level of perceived benefits than those of prospectors and laggards.

Hypothesis 5: The three types of organizations significantly differ in the extent of perceived benefits.

Perceived Compatibility

Perceived compatibility is defined as the extent to which an innovation is perceived as being consistent with the existing needs, values, and technological infrastructure of potential adopters (Rogers, 1983). Adopting e-commerce entails the selection and implementation of a suite of technologies (i.e., hardware, software, communication networking). If the innovation is compatible with existing work practices, environments, and overall objectives, firms will be more likely to adopt them. Therefore, we expect that adopters of e-commerce would have a higher level of perceived compatibility than that of prospectors and laggards.

Hypothesis 6: The three types of organizations significantly differ in the extent of perceived compatibility.

Environmental Factors

Industry Competitiveness

Innovation literature widely recognizes the influences of environmental contingencies. The environment creates contingencies to which firms have to respond typically through product and process of innovation (Duncan, 1972). Moreover, firms have to be compatible with their environment, which is essential for their long-term survival and growth (Thomson, 1967).

Competitiveness reflects the intensity level of competition within the industry where the firms operate. In a competitive environment, businesses are pushed to be innovative by the rivalry (Pfeffer & Leblebici, 1977). Firms respond to competition by offering innovative services and products. Past studies in IT innovation suggest that, in a competitive environment, firms have a greater need to adopt IT-related innovation for competitive advantage (Grover & Goslar, 1993; Ravichandran, 2000; Thong, 1999). For example, Iacovou et al. (1995) found a strong relationship between external pressure and EDI adoption behavior. Therefore, firms in a highly competitive environment are pressured to adopt e-commerce to respond to the competition. E-commerce can be used as a strategic tool to implement an organization's chosen strategy and to respond to competitors. Therefore, we expect that e-commerce adopters would face a higher level of competitiveness than prospectors and laggards.

Hypothesis 7: The three types of organizations significantly differ in the extent of competitiveness.

Research Methodology

Data Collection

Survey was the primary research methodology of this study. Prior to the full-scale data collection phase, questionnaires were sent to a number of reviewers who were qualified to evaluate the content and appropriateness of the questions. Reviewers were asked to examine the document for question clarity, interest, and mechanical considerations, as well as the length of time necessary to complete the questionnaire.

Data for testing the hypotheses were collected through a national survey in several major provinces in Thailand including Chiang-Mai (northern province), Songkla (southern province), Khon-Kaen (north-eastern province), and Bangkok (the capital city). Based on the definition generally accepted in Thailand, we define small and medium businesses as those which have less than 200 full-time employees, and have overall asset values less than or equal to 200 million baht for manufacturing and service firms, 100 million baht for wholesalers, and 60 million baht for retailers. Respondents were those who influenced or were part of a decision-making process of e-commerce adoption. Data were collected through several approaches, such as a direct-mail-based survey, questionnaire distribution during small and medium-sized enterprise (SME) seminars, and individual interviews. In total, 1,200 questionnaires were distributed and 452 were returned. Sixty-six questionnaires were unusable. The total response rate of this study is 32%, which is very high compared to the typical response rate of survey studies in North America. Table 3 presents the response rate of this study. From the total 386 responses, 108 (28%) were manufacturers, 111 (29%) were firms in the service industry, 92 (24%) were retailers, and 75 (19%) were wholesalers. Table 4 presents the profile of responses by industry.

Organization Types

Respondent firms were subsequently classified based on their e-commerce adoption action. The questionnaire asked respondents whether their organizations had already

Table 3: Response Rate

Provinces	Number of Questionnaires				Response Rate
	Sent	Received	Discarded	Total	
Bangkok (Capital)	500	210	35	175	35.0%
Outside Bangkok	700	242	31	211	30.14%
Total	*1200*	*452*	*66*	*386*	*32.16%*

adopted e-commerce. If respondents answered no, they had to specify the plan of e-commerce adoption, ranging from adoption within three months, six months, one year, no specific plan, or no intention of adoption. Firms were classified as *adopters* if they had already adopted e-commerce; as *prospectors* if they had not adopted e-commerce, but had a specific plan to adopt e-commerce within one year; and as *laggards* if they neither had a specific plan nor intended to adopt e-commerce. From the total 386 responses, 107 firms (28%) were classified as adopters, 52 firms (13%) as prospectors, and 227 firms (59%) as laggards. Table 5 summarizes this information.

Measure

The target respondents were small and medium businesses in Thailand; therefore, all questions were originally composed in Thai language. (The English version of the questions is provided in the Appendix.)

Organization size was determined by the number of full-time employees. Respondents were asked to specify the number of employees: less than 10, 10-30, 31-50, 51-100, and more than 100. Top management support was measured by a three-item scale assessing top management's interests and understanding in e-commerce, and perceptions of top

Table 4: Responses by Industry

Industry	Number	Percentage
Manufacturers	108	27.97
Services	111	28.75
Retailers	92	23.8
Wholesalers	75	19.4
Total	*386*	*100*

Table 5: Distribution of the Three Organization Types

Organization Type	Number	Percentage
Adopters	107	27.72
Prospectors	52	13.47
Laggards	227	58.8
Total	*386*	*100*

management towards e-commerce. IT emphasis was assessed by using a surrogate measurement of IT investment intensity. Respondents were asked to specify the proportion of IT investment on the total annual budget. Answers ranged from no budget for IT investment, less than 2.5%, 2.5-5%, >5-7.5%, >7.5-10%, to more than 10%.

Existence of an IT department was measured by asking respondents whether they formally had an IT department within their organization. The answers were coded to "0" for having an IT department and "1" for not having an IT department. A score for each organization type was calculated by dividing the total score with the number of firms in each type. Therefore, the lower the average score, the more the organization type had an IT department.

Perceived compatibility is assessed by a three-item scale, perceived benefit by a five-item scale. These two scales were developed based on prior studies' scales (Thong, 1999). Finally, we used a three-item scale to assess industry competitiveness, measuring the number of competitors adopting e-commerce, and the success and failure of the competitors in adopting e-commerce.

Analysis

Since the main objective of the hypotheses is to test the differences among the three organization types based on the identified factors, Analysis of Variances (ANOVA) was employed to analyze a mean difference among the three groups. A post-hoc multiple comparison (Scheffee's) was subsequently employed to perform a pair-wise comparison of the mean difference among the three organization types. Results from ANOVA analysis supported all of the seven hypotheses. In particular, analysis results strongly support hypotheses 2-6 ($p < 0.001$), support hypothesis 1 ($p < 0.01$), and moderately support hypothesis 7 ($p < 0.05$). Table 6 presents the statistical analysis results.

Furthermore, pair-wise analysis was performed to determine the mean difference among the three organization types (Table 7). The results suggest that adopters and laggards

Table 6: Statistical Analysis Result

Variables	F Statistic	Adopters		Prospectors		Laggards	
		Mean	SD	Mean	SD	Mean	SD
Size	4.73**	2.56	1.72	1.82	1.22	2.12	1.48
Top management support for e-commerce	26.39***	4.03	0.81	3.90	.130	3.33	.06
IT emphasis	34.00***	3.15	1.37	2.60	1.29	1.96	1.08
Existence of IT department	33.73***	1.49	.50	1.80	.404	1.87	.34
Perceived benefits	10.203***	3.62	.80	3.69	.870	3.20	1.00
Perceived compatibility	30.57***	3.75	.69	3.59	.840	3.01	.92
Industry competitiveness	3.89*	4.00	.10	3.66	.154	3.66	.70

$*p < 0.05; **p < 0.01; ***p<0.001$

Table 7: Pair-Wise Analysis of the Mean Difference Among the Three Organization Types

Variables	Mean Difference Between Adopters and Laggards	Mean Difference Between Adopters and Prospectors	Mean Difference Between Prospectors and Laggards
Size	Significant*	Significant*	Not Significant
Top management support for e-commerce	Significant***	Not Significant	Not Significant
IT emphasis	Significant***	Significant*	Significant**
Existence of IT department	Significant***	Significant***	Not Significant
Perceived benefits	Significant**	Not Significant	Significant*
Perceived compatibility	Significant***	Not Significant	Significant***
Industry competitiveness	Significant**	Not Significant	Not Significant

$*p < 0.05; **p < 0.01; ***p<0.001$

were significantly different in all variables. However, the results of the mean difference between adopters and prospectors, and between prospectors and laggards are mixed. In particular, adopters and prospectors are significantly different in size, IT emphasis, and existence of IT department. Prospectors and laggards are significantly different in IT emphasis, perceived benefits, and perceived compatibility. Table 7 shows the result of pair-wise analysis.

Discussion and Conclusion

It is unarguable that e-commerce is becoming one of the key technologies driving businesses in the current dynamic environment. A study of e-commerce would expand our understanding on the rationale underlying the thinking logic of firms in adopting the technology.

Results from our statistical analysis reveal insides on key factors that influence adoption decision of small and medium businesses in Thailand. Overall, the results strongly support the hypotheses, which is consistent with prior studies of IT innovation in other Asian countries (e.g., Thong, 1999), reinforcing that key variables identified from the organization innovation theory are applicable in the context of Asian settings, and in the context of e-commerce innovation. In particular, we found that adopters significantly differ from laggards in all key variables. While prospectors are significantly different from adopters in size, IT emphasis, and existence of IT department, they are significantly different from laggards in IT emphasis, perceived benefits, and perceived compatibility.

A number of conclusions can be drawn based on these results. First, the amount of strategic emphasis firms give to IT (i.e., IT-related knowledge, resources, and capabilities) has an impact on e-commerce adoption intention. Firms that strongly support the use of information technology, by formally establishing an IT department and making a significant amount of IT investment, are more likely to adopt e-commerce earlier than firms with less IT support. Firms that have IT assets readily in place should be in a better position to adopt and implement e-commerce than firms that need to build technology knowledge and infrastructure required for e-commerce adoption.

Second, we found that prospectors significantly differ from laggards in technology factors—perceived benefits and perceived compatibility—whereas there is no difference between prospectors and adopters in the technology factors. These results imply that technology factors do have an influence on attitudes toward e-commerce [i.e., changing from unfavorable (laggards) to favorable tendency (prospectors)], but have no influence on a relative earliness of adoption stage (i.e., no change from prospectors to adopters). This finding is consistent with the model of the innovation-decision process (Rogers, 1995) on the point that perceived characteristics of the innovation play a major role during the persuasion stage. One explanation to this phenomenon is the cost-benefits justification. Due to limited resources, laggards may hesitate to invest in new technologies because they are uncertain about the benefits of e-commerce, and the compatibility of the technology with their existing culture and business environment. On the other hand, adopters and prospectors are more willing to take a risk of e-commerce adoption since they perceive a more perceptible contribution of e-commerce to their business, and are more certain on the compatibility of the technology with their organizations.

Third, e-commerce adopters are more likely to operate in a more competitive environment, compared with the other two organization types. This result is consistent with prior studies that point to the environmental factors as the key factors influencing small and medium businesses' decision to adopt innovation (e.g., Iacovou et al., 1995). This also implies that small and medium businesses operating in a competitive environment are constantly scanning and implementing new technologies such as e-commerce.

Limitations

It is appropriate to mention the limitations of this study before discussing the implications. First, the data used in this study was collected in 1999. At that time, diffusion of e-commerce in Thailand was still in an infant stage. From our survey, only 20% of respondents were e-commerce adopters. This adoption profile will be unlikely if the survey is conducted today. Nevertheless, we believe that the results from this study would be valid even if tested with the more current sample. Second, due to the nature of our hypotheses formulating, it does not allow comparison testing on the effect of the independent variables. This limitation restricts an ability to determine the predicting power of independent variables for e-commerce adoption. Third, the focus of the research model has been on the relationships among constructs identified in this study. The variables included in the research model are not meant to be all-inclusive. They are selected as representing key theoretical factors potentially affecting organizations' adoption decision. The findings should be viewed with caution in so far as other potentially important factors have been excluded. Finally, this study used single-respondent perceptual measures for various constructs. The use of single respondents helped in obtaining the necessary response rate; however, the results would have been more rigorous if multiple respondents had been used to measure the research constructs.

Implications

This study has implications for both research and practice. For research, this study is one among a few which empirically test the organizational innovation model in the context of Thailand. The results of this study can be used as a guideline for future research that wishes to examine the phenomenon in other Asian settings. This study also reaffirms that the innovation adoption theory, widely applied in North America or European countries, is applicable in the Asian context. For future research, while this study incorporates a number of key variables identified from the literature, future studies may expand the research model by incorporating a range of variables to cover more comprehensive aspects of the phenomenon, such as variables reflecting key aspects of e-commerce, variables reflecting small and medium business context, and variables representing a gap between Asian and Western cultures.

In addition, this study examines only one aspect of e-commerce adoption—the extent to which an organization is relatively earlier to adopt e-commerce than others. A future study may attempt to test other aspects of e-commerce adoption. The diffusion of innovation literature can be used as a foundation to develop dependent variables. Fitchman (2001), for example, identified a number of measures of organizational innovation such as earliness of adoption, infusion, and assimilation. While these variables are widely used specifically in the context of information technology, they can be applied in the context of e-commerce. For instance, future study may develop a research model to test the infusion of e-commerce in small and medium businesses (i.e., the extent to which e-commerce is used in a complete and sophisticated way). By adopting a more sophisticated measure, future study might apply a more sophisticated technique in testing the relationships in the research model, such as linear regression and structural equation modeling techniques (i.e., LISREL, PLS).

For practitioners, our study highlights the importance of IT skills and knowledge in influencing e-commerce adoption. This study shows that a knowledge base about IT plays a major role in influencing a firm's adoption decision. Small and medium businesses that strongly support IT deployment (i.e., high level of IT investment, existence of IT department) are more likely to adopt e-commerce earlier than those with less IT support. Since e-commerce is a key technology driving businesses in a current competitive environment, the earlier the firms adopt e-commerce, the faster the firms can extend their reach to customers and secure their share in the market by using a market access capability of e-commerce. However, knowledge-based skills and technologies required to adopt e-commerce cannot be acquired overnight. It takes time to accumulate. Hence, small and medium businesses should cultivate and develop their own IT skills and knowledge to be readily in place so that they can adopt and implement e-commerce to respond to competition in a timely manner.

References

Allal, M. (1999). Micro and small enterprises (MSEs) in Thailand—definitions and contributions. In G. Finnegan (Series Ed.), *Micro and Small Enterprise Development & Poverty Alleviation in Thailand (working paper 6)*, Project ILO/UNDP: THA/99/003.

Boynton, A.C., Zmud, R.W., & Jacobs, G.C. (1994). The influence of IT management practice on IT use in large organizations. *MIS Quarterly*, (September), 299-318.

Cash, J.I., & McLeod, P.L. (1985). Managing the introduction of information systems technology in strategically dependent companies. *Journal of Management Information Systems*, *1*(4), 5-23.

Chau, P.Y.K., & Tam, K.Y. (1997). Factors affecting the adoption of open systems: An exploratory study. *MIS Quarterly*, *21*(1), 1-25.

Cohen, W., & Levinthal, D. (1990). Absorptive capacity: A new perspective on learning and innovation. *Administrative Science Quarterly*, 128-152.

Duncan, R. (1972). Characteristics of organizational environment and perceived environmental uncertainty. *Administrative Science Quarterly*, *17*(3), 312-327.

ECRC. (2002). *Electronic Commerce Resource Center*. Available on the Web: http://www.ecommerce.or.th.

Fichman, R., & Kemerer, C.F. (1997). The assimilation of software process innovations: An organizational learning perspective. *Management Science*, *43*(10), 1345-1363.

Fitchman, R. (2001). The role of aggregation in the measurement of IT-related organizational innovation. *MIS Quarterly*, *25*(4).

Grover, V., & Goslar, M. (1993). The initiation, adoption, and implementation of telecommunications technologies in U.S. organizations. *Journal of Management Information Systems*, *10*(1), 141-163.

Iacovou, C., Benbasat, I., & Dexter, A. (1995). Electronic data interchange and small organizations: Adoption and impact technology. *MIS Quarterly*, (December), 465-485.

Jarvenpaa, S.L., & Ives, B. (1991). Executive involvement and participation in the management of information technology. *MIS Quarterly*, (June), 204-227.

Kimberly, J.R., & Evanisko, M.J. (1981). Organizational innovation: The influence of individual, organizational, and contextual factors on hospital adoption of technological and administrative innovations. *Academy of Management Journal*, *24*(4), 689-713.

Kwon, T.H., & Zmud, R.W. (1987). Unifying the fragmented models of information systems implementation. In R.J. Boland, Jr., & R.A. Hirschheim (Eds.), *Critical Issues in Information Systems Research* (pp. 227-251). New York: John Wiley & Sons.

Lind, M., Zmud, R., & Fischer, W. (1989). Microcomputer adoption—the impact of organizational size and structure. *Information & Management*, *16*(3), 157-162.

NECTEC. (2002). *National Electronics and Computer Technology Center*. Available on the Web: http://www.nectec.or.th/home.

Orlikowski, W.J. (1993). CASE tools as organizational change: Investigating incremental and radical changes in systems development. *MIS Quarterly*, *17*(3), 309-340.

Pfeffer, J., & Leblebici, H. (1977). Information technology and organizational structure. *Pacific Sociological Review*, *20*(2), 241-261.

Poutsma, E.F., Van Uxem, F.W., & Walravens, A.H.C.M. (1987). *Process Innovation and Automation in Small and Medium Sized Business*. Delft, The Netherlands: Delft University.

Premkumar, G., & King, W.R. (1994). Organizational characteristics and information systems planning: An empirical study. *Information Systems Research*, *5*(2), 75-109.

Rai, A., & Patnayakuni, R. (1996). A structural model for CASE adoption behavior. *Journal of Management Information Systems*, *13*(2), 205-234.

Ravichandran, T. (2000). Swiftness and intensity of administrative innovation adoption: An empirical investigation of TQM in information systems. *Decision Sciences*, *31*(3), 1-30.

Reich, B.H., & Benbasat, I. (1990). An empirical investigation of the factors influencing the implementation of customer oriented strategic systems. *Information Systems Research*, *1*(3), 325-347.

Rogers, E.M. (1983). *Diffusion of innovation*. New York: The Free Press.

Schroeder, R.G., & Benbasat, I. (1975). An experimental evaluation of the relationship of uncertainty in the environment to information used by decision makers. *Decision Sciences*, *6*(3), 556-567.

Sevilla, R.C., & Soonthornthada (2000). *SME Policy in Thailand: Vision and Challenges*. Mahidol University, Thailand: Institute for Population and Social Research.

Thomson, J. (1967). *Organizations in Action.* New York: McGraw Hill.

Thong, J. (1999). An integrated model of information systems in small businesses. *Journal of Management Information Systems*, *15*(4), 187-214.

Thongpakde, N., Puppahavesa, W., & Pussarangsri, B. (1994). In S.D. Meyanathan (Ed.), *Industrial Structures and the Development of Small and Medium Enterprises Linkages* (EDI Seminar Series). Washington, DC: The World Bank.

Tornatzky, L.G., & Fleischer, M. (1990). *The Process of Technological Innovation.* Kexington, MA: Lexington Books.

Turban, E., King, D., Lee, J., Warkentin, M., & Chung, H.M. (2002). *Electronic Commerce: A Managerial Perspective.* Prentice-Hall.

UNICO International Corporation. (1995). *The study on industrial sector development, supporting industries in the kingdom of Thailand* (Draft final report). Tokyo, Japan: UNICO.

Utterback, J.M. (1974). Innovation in industry and the diffusion of technology. *Science*, *183*, 620-626.

Wesh, J., & White, J. (1981). A small business is not a little big business. *Harvard Business Review*, *59*(4), 213-223.

Yap, C.S., Thong, J.Y.L., & Raman, K.S. (1994). Effect of government incentives on computerization in small business. *European Journal of Information Systems*, *3*(3), 191-206.

Zmud, R.W. (1984). An examination of "push-pull" theory applied to process innovation and knowledge work. *Management Science*, *30*(6), 727-738.

Zwass, V. (1996). Electronic commerce: structures and issues. *International Journal of Electronic Commerce*, *1*(1), 3-23.

Appendix

Outline of the Survey Instrument

Questions are originally composed in Thai language. All items solicit responses on a five-point Likert scale with the following anchors: 1 = Strongly disagree, 3 = Neutral, 5 = Strongly agree.

1. *Top Management Support for E-Commerce*
a. Our management is interested in the use of e-commerce.
b. Our management is supportive of the use of e-commerce in business operations.
c. Our management well understands the potential benefits of e-commerce.

2. *Perceived Benefits*
a. E-commerce can help increase our sales.
b. E-commerce can help our market expansion.
c. E-commerce can help create new business opportunities for our organization.
d. E-commerce can help improve our customer service.
e. E-commerce can help expand our marketing and advertising channels.

3. *Perceived Compatibility*
a. E-commerce fits well with our organizational beliefs and practices.
b. E-commerce fits well with our existing technology infrastructure.
c. Our organization has a positive attitude towards e-commerce.

4. *Competitiveness*
a. We are in a very competitive industry.
b. In our industry, we are competing in the quality of new services and products.
c. In our industry, the number of competitors is increasing.

Chapter VIII

Mapping the Diffusion of the Internet Technology Cluster: An Examination of Irish SMEs

James Griffin, Tipperary Institute, Ireland

Abstract

This chapter adopts a 'technology cluster' perspective in examining Internet usage within SMEs, analyzing Internet usage in terms of three distinct Internet technology groupings. Specific attention is paid to identifying and categorizing the diffusion pattern of website development among the SME sector on the basis of the theory of mimetic IT adoption patterns. Two potential hybrid diffusion patterns are identified, and their implications for policy makers and development agencies in the SME sector are discussed.

Introduction

Electronic commerce (e-commerce) has been recognized as a source of fundamental, pan-sectoral change to the conduct of business (Malone, Yates, & Benjamin, 1989; Quelch & Klein, 1996; Benjamin & Wigand, 1995). Chan and Swatman (2000) use the term, 'a new paradigm for doing business'. Other authors have gone further, viewing modern IT developments as the latter part of a period starting in the mid-1970s that represents a transition to nothing less than a new phase of capitalist development (Amin, 1994). Benjamin, Rockhart, Scott Morton, and Wyman (1983) also suggest that the world economy has been fundamentally altered by the globalization of competition, which has largely been caused by the declining cost and consequent increasing spread of IT developments.

The resulting shift in business practices as businesses attempt to exploit these new opportunities will necessitate wide-scale adoption of new processes and technologies. Elliot and Loebbecke (2000) suggest that this requires new thinking on how organizations adopt innovations and the revision of theoretical models of adoption. Bamfield (1994) identifies innovation theory as an appropriate framework for understanding IT adoption processes. La Rovere (1998) concurs, stating that the diffusion of innovations in information technology (IT) is becoming an increasingly important area of study.

Furthermore, any overview of recent Internet-related literature will identify that the issue of mapping diffusion patterns is being increasingly effected by the range and variety of technologies that are drawn into the e-business platform. In terms of understanding the nature of Internet usage and diffusion within SMEs, it is necessary therefore to measure individually the extent to which the different elements—of what essentially comprise an Internet Technology Cluster—are used among adopting firms.

This necessitates a definition of the different elements of the Internet Technology Cluster. This can be accomplished through the analysis of past surveys and technical articles written in the field of Internet research. Three basic elements are identifiable. Firstly, several studies have identified e-mail as the most common Internet application used in business (Howe, 2001; Everett, 1998; Feher & Towell, 1997).

Secondly, many of the most common Internet technologies and applications center around the Internet browser. Graphics, audio, HTML, and HTTP technologies are all involved in the presentation of websites to the viewer via the browser, while research and communications applications such as search engines, newsgroups, and discussion groups and online journals are viewed via the browser (Enterprise Ireland, 2001; Bina & Andresson, 2001; Winder, 1995; Turban, Lee, King, & Chung, 1999; Engle, 1998; NCSA, 1997; Ellsworth, 1995). These elements can be combined together under the banner of Internet browser usages.

Finally, more complex technologies based around back-end activities and remote access to Internet services (through FTP, WAP, and Telnet) can be grouped together to give an indication of the extent of usage of more advanced Internet applications.

Examining IT/IS Diffusion Pattern Theory

The usefulness of adopting an Internet Technology Cluster approach is in its application to the mapping of Internet diffusion patterns among firm populations. Let us take a moment to review some particularly relevant concepts in diffusion theory. Abrahamson and Rosenkopf (1993) describe innovations that create *'Bandwagon Effects'*. These Bandwagon Effects are self-reinforcing diffusion patterns that effectively dismiss the technical attributes or properties of an innovation, its level of adoption instead being a factor of the number of adoptions that have already taken place (Abrahamson & Rosenkopf, 1993).

Support for the importance of examining adoption patterns at what Abrahamson and Rosenkopf term the 'macro-cultural' level can be found in the work of DiMaggio and Powell (1983), who describe innovation diffusion in a firm's network of customers, suppliers, and competitors (the macro-culture) as being 'mimetic'. They describe this mimicry of innovation adoption in very similar terms to Abrahamson and Rosenkopf's Bandwagon Effect:

> *"A high proportion of firms adopting the change do so because other organizations have adopted it and because stakeholders define the change as accepted practice... One criterion that organizations use to evaluate adoptions is the adoption behavior of other firms." (DiMaggio & Powell, 1983, p. 149)*

O'Neill, Pouder, and Buchholtz (1998) draw attention to the problems associated with such behavior:

> *"[I]n bandwagons triggered by competitive pressures, firms may adopt inefficient innovations based on their fear that other firms will use them successfully. Also, firms may conclude that the cost of adopting an inefficient innovation is less than the cost of not adopting it." (O'Neill et al., 1998, p. 4)*

O'Neil et al. (1998) are drawing attention to the fact that many adoptions prompted by Bandwagon Effects are inefficient. This is an issue of major concern when examining website development among SMEs, considering the often superficial nature of general Internet adoptions among this population.

In these types of patterns, small numbers of enterprising 'IT initiators' pave the way for a somewhat larger group of 'Early Adopters', then, with the growing *'Reputation Effect'* of the innovation in question, a sharp increase in uptake gives rise to the 'Early Majority' and 'Late Majority' of adopters.

In the examination of diffusion pattern theory, it is helpful at this point to review the main characteristics of mimetic adoption patterns. A review of relevant diffusion theory highlights two key characteristics.

Firstly, generally higher benefits for early adopters/entrants are evident in these types of patterns. Many authors, through the examination of the EDI adoption experience in SMEs, have identified a key characteristic of mimetic adoptions to be a reduction in benefit among organizations partaking in reactionary and later adoptions vis-à-vis firms engaging in earlier, more strategic adoptions (see O'Neil et al., 1998; Cash, 1985; Friedman, 1998; Raymond, Julien, Carrier, & Lachance 1996; Clemons, 1986; Benjamin, deLong, & Scott Morton, 1990; Swatman & Swatman, 1992).

Secondly, a feature of mimetic adoption patterns is that many firms, during the adoption decision process, feel increasing levels of pressure from their external environment. Authors such as Cash (1985), Friedman (1998), Raymond et al. (1996), DiMaggio and Powell (1983), Ettlie (1983), and Pierce and Delbecq (1977) identified pressure from many elements of the multi-participant environment as creating a considerable impetus among later adopters to acquire the IT innovation in question.

Fried-Cassorta (1995), Haynes, Becherer, and Helms (1998), and Vassos (1996) all suggest that many firms' adoption decision processes stem from a perceived need to adopt an innovation as a reactionary strategy in an uncertain environment, suggesting a decreasing level of what Moore and Benbasat (1991) termed 'voluntariness' among later, 'me-too' adopters.

An analysis of the empirical research undertaken by this author is now presented that applies, combines, and synthesizes these various theoretical issues

Research Design and Methodology

During the summer of 2001, the author conducted a detailed survey of SMEs in six distinct geographical regions of the Republic of Ireland (three urban and three rural). The survey examined current Internet usage levels, the factors influencing the adoption decision process, and the actual benefits achieved by SMEs that have adopted the Internet.

Ireland is an interesting survey population, as a significant nationwide program designed to increase awareness of the Internet (involving both the government and the private sector), especially aimed at small- and medium-sized firms, has been undertaken over the past five years (see, for example, Institute of National Trade of Ireland, 2002; SEISS, 2001; Regional Programme of Innovative Actions, 2002). A high level of connectivity could therefore be expected in both the urban and rural regions surveyed, thereby increasing the predictive validity of the findings and allowing for an analysis of the relative success or failure of such broad awareness-building programs.

This chapter focuses on data gathered from the study described above in two main areas. Firstly, the overall level and nature of Internet usage in SMEs in Ireland is analyzed through the lens of a *'cluster-based'* definition of Internet technology. Secondly, the specific issue of website ownership and development is examined with the intent of mapping the diffusion of this particular element of the *'Internet Technology Cluster'* among the population of SMEs examined.

The unit of measurement for this research is best described as the SME in Ireland. In the case of Ireland, this includes firms that employ up to 250 employees (Task Force on Small Business, 1994). It is worth noting that the vast majority of SMEs in Ireland fall into the 'small firm' category, the accepted Irish definition of which is firms with under 50 employees and with a turnover not in excess of 3 million Irish Pounds or 3.78 million Euro approximately (Garavan, O'Cinneide, Garavan, Hynes, & Walsh, 1997). The respondent breakdown provided in Table 1 supports this point. For the purpose of international readers, therefore, this chapter would probably be most accurately viewed as an examination of small firms specifically.

Table 1: Respondent Breakdown by Employee Size and Industrial Sector

No. of employees	N	% of sample	Industrial Sector	N	% of sample
1-5	63	41.2	Agriculture	13	8.5
6-10	29	19.0	Manufacturing	33	21.6
11-15	9	5.9	Construction	9	5.9
16-20	15	9.8	Wholesale/Retail	9	5.9
21-25	7	4.6	Transport/Communications	7	4.6
26-30	10	6.5	Business Services	58	37.9
31-35	6	3.9	Education/Training	5	3.3
36-40	2	1.3	Health	3	2.0
41-45	4	2.6	Cultural/Tourism	16	10.5
46-50	1	0.7			
50+	7	4.6			
Total	**153**	**100**	**Total**	**153**	**100**

A stratified sample frame of 700 companies was chosen from the population of 3,500 SMEs (identified through SME support agency lists and the Kompass Ireland Business Directory, 2001). With 46 *'ineligible units'* identified after mail-out, the final sample frame for this research can be considered to be 654 firms for the purposes of calculating an accurate response rate. A total usable response rate of 153 responses was achieved. Considering the readjustments to the sample frame size, the overall response rate for the survey therefore stands at 23.4%.

This response rate is comparable to response rates achieved by many other key mail surveys in the field of Internet usage studies (for example, Enterprise Ireland, 2001—21%; Germain & Dröge, 1995—22.7%; Geiger & Martin, 1999—23%; Drennan & Kennedy, 1999—24%; Feher & Towell, 1997—29%; Proudlock, Phelps, & Gamble, 1999—33%).

Table 1 provides respondent breakdowns by employee size and by industrial sector [as defined by the ILO's (2001) International Standard Industrial Classification (ISIC) system].

Both a wave analysis and a respondent/non-respondent analysis were undertaken and identified no significant non-response bias within the respondent group. Table 1

Table 2: Key Findings Related to the Extent of Internet Usage in Irish SMEs

	Yes		No	
Does your firm currently have Internet access? (n = 153)	90.8% (n = 139)		9.2% (n = 14)	
Does your firm currently have a website? (n = 139)	52.5% (n = 73)		47.5% (n = 66)	
	ISDN	**LAN**	**Dial-up**	**Unsure**
Type of Connection (n = 139)	23% (n = 32)	8% (n = 11)	62% (n = 86)	7% (n = 10)

therefore highlights both the nature of the firms surveyed and adequately indicates the population being described in the findings that are outlined in the following sections.

Analyzing the Internet Technology Cluster

As highlighted in Table 2, the current level of Internet connectivity within Irish SMEs is very high (more than 90% of firms). This is no doubt a function of the high level of awareness that has been created over recent years. However, problems arise when the nature of this connectivity is examined in more detail.

Only 52.5% of firms with Internet connections have a website of their own; this is lower than would have been expected for a 90% rate of connectivity. The type of physical Internet connection is generally a simple dial-up (62%), with few firms engaging in higher speed connections. A worrying 8% of owner managers could not even describe their connection type, suggesting a lack of understanding of, or degree of separation from, Internet applications in their organizations.

To further examine the apparently 'superficial' nature of many Internet adoptions within the sample, the cluster-based definition of the Internet, described earlier, has been adopted in the research instrument.

The 90.8% of respondents with Internet access were therefore asked to rate the extent to which they used these three separate elements of Internet technologies. Rating of each element was on a five-point Likert scale.

In accordance with previous literature, e-mail was the most used Internet application with an average usage rating of 3.43. Internet Browsers received an average rating of 2.82, while the 'Advanced Applications' category received an average usage rating of 1.43 (see Figure 1).

Figure 1: Nature of Internet Usage, Applying Technology Cluster Theory

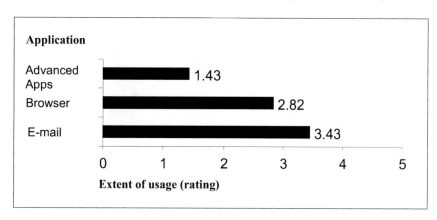

These findings are certainly in keeping with the literature regarding the extent of usage of different Internet technologies in firms in the U.S. (Feher & Towell, 1997; Howe, 2001; Turban et al., 1999). E-mail is considerably more widely used than other technologies, while advanced applications like WAP and FTP are not used extensively in the sample.

From the exploratory findings described here, a snapshot of Internet usage among Irish SMEs is developing. A high level of Internet connectivity is obvious. However, a low usage rate of advanced technologies and applications (even a relatively low use of Internet browser technology), coupled with a level of website ownership that is also lower than expected, suggests that the nature of Internet usage in the sample is underdeveloped.

Explanations for this need to be identified and analyzed. Of particular concern from the above analysis is the relatively low rate of advanced website development among the sample arising from the 'underdeveloped' or 'superficial' nature of Internet usage. Website development represents one of the key potential sources of competitive advantage for SMEs engaging in Internet adoptions. An understanding of the issues surrounding this point therefore needs to be developed as a matter of some urgency. A suitable framework for this is the wider body of diffusion theory; this forms the basis for the following section.

A Suggested Diffusion Pattern of Website Development

To further examine the diffusion and uptake patterns of website technology, respondents were asked about the age of their websites. Responses to this particular open question gave an exact indication of the rate of diffusion of this specific Internet technology element throughout the population of SMEs.

Figure 2: Diffusion Pattern of Website Development

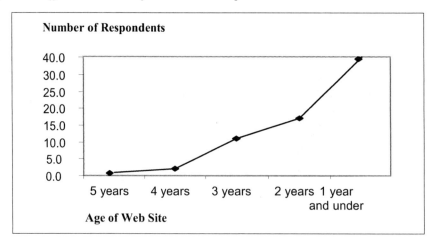

Of those respondents without a website, 67% did express an intention to set one up within the next 12 months. This fact, coupled with the steadily increasing website adoption rate depicted in Figure 2, is strongly reminiscent of the types of mimetic and bandwagon diffusion patterns described by Abrahamson and Rosenkopf (1993), DiMaggio and Powell (1983), and O'Neil et al. (1998).

Given the coverage and attention that the Internet has received in media, commercial, and academic circles over the past five years in Ireland, it is unsurprising that a bandwagon type of diffusion pattern is evident among SMEs in Ireland. However, more evidence needs to be accumulated to support this initial evidence, and indeed in the examination to follow some issues regarding the likely future pattern that Web technology diffusion will take give cause for concern.

Examining the Mimetic Nature of Website Development

To explore the supposition that Internet technology diffusion in SMEs in Ireland may be following a mimetic pattern, it is necessary to compare the characteristic elements that make up a mimetic pattern against the findings of this study.

Generally Higher Benefits for Early Adopters/Entrants

If the Web technology diffusion pattern identified through this research is indeed based on bandwagon-type behavior, it should be possible therefore to identify differences in benefits achieved among earlier and later adopters of websites. To this end, the 52.5% of respondents with a Web presence were asked to rate how useful these sites had been in terms of six key business characteristics. These are listed in Figure 3.

Figure 3: Benefits Experienced from Websites

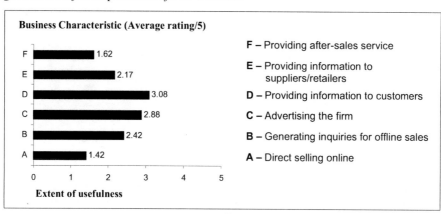

Each characteristic was rated separately on a five-point scale, with the *'provision of information to customers'* receiving the highest average rating (3.08) and *'direct online selling'* receiving the lowest rating (1.42). This finding supports the view expressed by many respondents that the Internet was not ready for full e-commerce activity in their sector.

To identify any significant differences between early and late adopters, the average age of these websites was first calculated. The average age of websites in the sample was one and a half years. Table 3 now facilitates comparison between respondents with older and newer websites and average website usefulness ratings.

Respondents with websites older than the average one and a half years differed in their rated usefulness from newer sites mainly in the areas of greater benefits arising in *'generating offline inquiries'* and *'advertising the firm'*. Both of these uses could be seen as benefits that accrue from a continued Web presence. While earlier adopters of Web technologies achieved higher-than-average ratings in every category of business benefit, later adopters reported lower-than-average ratings in three of the five categories.

It would appear, therefore, that evidence exists to suggest that later adopters are experiencing lower benefits than earlier adopters, thereby suggesting a more reactive, less innovative adoption, supporting a broadly mimetic pattern in the diffusion of website technologies.

More evidence that the diffusion of Web technologies is currently following a mimetic pattern can be found when the updating behavior of website owners is examined. Earlier adopters of websites had an average updating rate of 1.06 updates per month, while later adopters had a lower updating rate of 0.8 updates per month. As regular updating has been described as a feature of a more integrated and planned Internet strategy (McCue, 1999; Howcroft & Mitev, 2000), this finding suggests that the more proactive adopters tended to adopt earlier in the diffusion process. These adopters, with websites more than one and a half years in existence, most likely represent the 'IT initiators' group mentioned earlier. This is exactly the type of finding that one would expect when examining a bandwagon or mimetic diffusion process.

It should be noted, however, that differences between early and late adopters in terms of benefit accrued through website adoption are surprisingly small. To aid in this

Table 3: Business Benefits Received Compared to Website Age

	Website usefulness factor					
	A	**B**	**C**	**D**	**E**	**F**
	Direct selling	Inquiries for offline sales	Advertising the firm	Information to customers	Informing suppliers/ retailers	Providing after-sales service
Ratings for sites more than 1.5 years in existence	1.5	2.7	3.1	3.0	2.2	1.7
Ratings for sites 1.5 years and less in existence	1.4	2.1	2.7	3.1	2.2	1.4
Overall Average Ratings (as per Figure 3)	1.42	2.42	2.88	3.08	2.17	1.62

comparison, Figures 4(a) and 4(b) present the same data from Table 3 in radar graph form; the similarity in the shapes of these radar graphs accentuates this finding.

It can be clearly seen from Figures 4(a) and 4(b) that both sets of ratings are a similar shape and definitely tending towards the lower end of the scales.

This finding highlights a major issue for the diffusion of Web technologies, namely, that with low benefits accruing to many early adopters in a majority of business categories, the subsequent poor results of adoptions in these firms will represent a significant weakening of the vital *'Reputation Effect'* that sustains the mimetic or bandwagon patterns described earlier. The result of this reduction in the reputation effect may well be that the sharp increase in uptake that normally gives rise to the early and late majorities in other mimetic adoption patterns may not occur in the case of the Internet and specifically in the case of website technologies.

Increasing External Pressure on Later Adopters

It is with the comparison of the perceived influence of external pressure between early, late, and non-adopters among the sample that difficulties begin to arise with the description of the Internet diffusion pattern as wholly mimetic. These comparisons are now outlined and the difficulties identified.

The research instrument examined this issue of external pressure by asking respondents to rate six separate sources of pressure (listed in Table 4) on a five-point scale ranging from *'no influence'* to *'very high influence'*. These six factors were derived from the literature reviewed above, with specific reference to the work of Drennan and Kennedy (1999), who studied this issue in detail in their work on Australian SMEs in the medical sector.

Figure 4(a): Average Benefit Ratings for Sites more than 1.5 Years Old

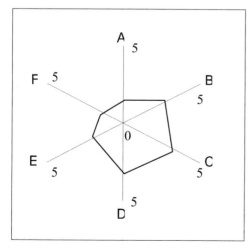

Figure 4(b): Average Benefit Ratings for Sites less than 1.5 Years Old

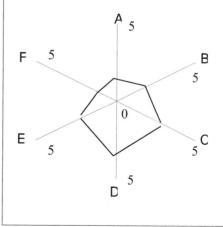

Table 4: External Pressure Felt by Respondents (Grouped by Time Taken to Adopt the Internet)

	Areas of External Pressure						
Time to Adoption	Use by competitors	Desire for relative advantage	Trading partners	Increasing user rates	Increasing media coverage	Government programme	**Overall average**
Connected at Start-up	2.70	3.52	2.85	3.03	2.82	1.64	**2.76**
1-2 months	2.29	3.07	2.71	3.57	3.00	1.62	**2.71**
3-4 months	2.50	3.88	2.38	3.88	3.38	2.13	**3.02**
4-5 months	2.67	3.67	3.67	3.33	2.67	1.67	**2.94**
6-12 months	2.50	3.63	3.06	3.63	3.06	1.71	**2.93**
1+ years	2.32	3.12	2.48	3.18	2.70	1.46	**2.54**
NO ACCESS	3.13	3.50	2.88	3.25	3.38	1.75	**2.98**

Table 4 depicts the comparison of average ratings for each area of external pressure vis-à-vis time taken to consider the adoption of the Internet. Figure 5 then graphs the overall average ratings for each cohort in a format similar to Figure 2 previously (overall averages can be used here due to the high Cronbach's Alpha coefficient of this set of variables).

According to the literature discussed above, one would expect to find the level of external pressure increasing the longer a respondent takes to decide to adopt (indicating a reduction in voluntariness over time as the reputation of the innovation grows). It is evident from Figure 5, however, that the level of external pressure felt by respondents does not closely follow such a pattern. Specifically, two interesting findings arise from the figure that merit deeper examination.

Firstly, considerably high external pressure to adopt the Internet was reported by respondents with no Internet connectivity at all, suggesting that despite such pressure, others factors are strong enough to overcome the pressure.

Secondly, 'slow adopters' (i.e., respondents who considered their adoption for over a year) exhibited a major drop in perceived external pressure; this is very evident from Figure 5.

Figure 5: External Pressure Felt by Respondents (Grouped by Time Taken to Adopt)

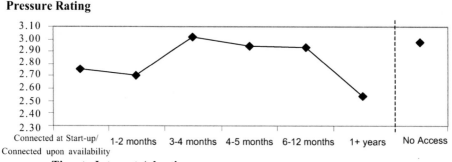

Figure 6, which compares external pressure ratings among early adopters of websites vis-à-vis later adopters, further highlights the drop in external pressure among later adopters. Indeed, external pressure from five of the six sources is actually shown to be higher among earlier or 'faster adopters'.

These results suggest that the influence of peer networks and the pressures they bring to bear in relation to the Internet adoption decision process are decreasing over time, most likely due to low levels of benefits accruing to the adopting firms. This represents a significant shortening of what Thorelli (1986) termed 'innovation poles', described as the influence of peer networks (or 'macro-cultural' pressure) elsewhere in e-business literature. This is indicative of the reduction in the reputation effect of Internet technologies posited earlier and strongly suggests that the effect has essentially reached its peak and is now beginning to decline, rather than increase over time. This is in opposition to what we would expect to see in a classic mimetic pattern and may well prove to be a characteristic feature of Internet diffusion patterns.

Forecasting the Diffusion Pattern of Internet Technologies

Consideration of the findings presented regarding the generally higher benefits accruing to earlier adopters and the increasing level of uptake of website technology suggests an Internet diffusion pattern displaying an initially mimetic pattern.

Difficulties arise, however, when we consider how that diffusion pattern is likely to develop in the future. With the evident reduction in the reputation effect of the Internet, it is unlikely that a high rate of mimicry will continue. With this in mind, different potential diffusion patterns become apparent. These potential patterns center on the questions:

Figure 6: External Pressure Felt by Respondents (Grouped by Website Age)

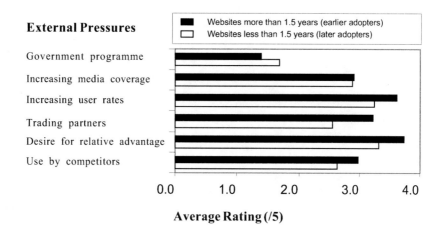

'When will the late majority arrive?' and 'Will there be a late majority?' One conclusion from these findings may be that we may have arrived (or are arriving) at the diffusion 'plateau' described by authors such as Cooper and Zmud (1990) and Kautz and Larsen (2000) in traditional IT/IS innovation diffusions.

If so, the reduction in the reputation effect of the Internet and the low levels of benefits accruing to firms currently may well create a long hiatus before the 'late majority' of adopters arrive. This long hiatus represents a period where policy makers and development agencies will struggle to improve the strategic nature of current Internet adoptions within SMEs. This could be termed a *'Delayed Reputation Effect'* and will give rise to an *'Elongated Diffusion Pattern'*. Furthermore, if we take into consideration the extremely high connectivity rates that currently exist at this stage of the diffusion process, this makes the potential numbers for a late majority much smaller than that of the early majority. This fact, combined with the fact that a declining reputation effect will further reduce the number of later adopters, suggests that it may be more accurate to apply the term *'Late Minority'* to any further adopters of Internet technologies. This possible diffusion pattern, derived from the above discussion, is presented in Figure 7(a).

Another conclusion that can be reached from these findings is that we may be about to experience what can best be termed a *'Dipping Diffusion Model'* (shown in Figure 7(b)).

If policy makers and development agencies fail to improve the strategic nature of Internet adoptions among SMEs (from generally superficial connections to more integrated and complex forms), then the benefits of website ownership actually experienced will remain low among adopters. If this remains the case, it is likely that firms will become disillusioned with the entire cluster of Internet technologies. This will result in an increase in *'Internet Disconnections'*.

In such a pattern, the late majority of adopters will never arrive, and disconnections from the Internet actually begin to result in a reduction in overall numbers of adopters over time.

Figure 7(a): The Elongated Diffusion Pattern

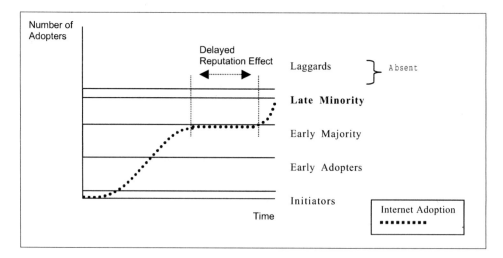

Figure 7(b): Dipping Diffusion Model

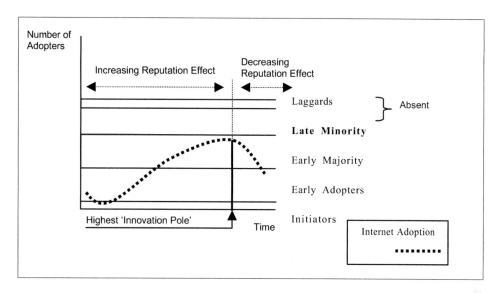

Some anecdotal evidence for this can be found in the comments of several respondents who have had experience with Internet adoptions.

"Value of Internet, Web, e-commerce hugely overrated."

"Follow-up customer service…appalling. Frustration with call-centers and security will detract from Internet dominance."

"How will our website be found now that everybody seems to have a website?"

"Website out of use since July 2000."

"Internet is too hyped."

"We find selling requires building a relationship with client, hard to apply online."

These frank responses were facilitated by the final, open question of the research instrument. While there is no claim by this positivist researcher that these comments have undergone any rigorous coding or analysis from a qualitative methodology, they clearly exhibit the reduction in the reputation effect of the Internet that has been evidenced by quantitative analysis already in this chapter.

It is important to note that Figures 7(a) and 7(b) are indicative models only and are an attempt, based on the analysis of these research findings, to identify the most likely Internet diffusion pattern that will be experienced among SMEs in Ireland in the future. Much will depend on the behavior of policy makers and development agencies, and their ability to repair the damaged reputation of the Internet as a useful facilitation tool for small businesses.

The reality of which, if any, of these Internet diffusion patterns will actually be experienced by SMEs in Ireland can only be tested over time. As such these findings create the basis for further extensive longitudinal research in this area.

Conclusion

A significant feature of this chapter is the presentation of the concept of the Internet as a cluster of technologies. The absence of this approach to date has led to much confusion in the interpretation of empirical findings. The application of the concept of an *'Internet Technology Cluster'* in further research, where technologies such as e-mail, browser, and more advanced uses are examined individually, should ensure greater accuracy in the reporting and analysis of Internet adoption and usage rates in the future.

With this issue in mind, the presentation of the Internet Usage findings of this empirical research among Irish SMEs provides a strong basis for comparative studies in this field.

While uptake is high in terms of connectivity, the nature of usage is not advanced. It is this *'low-end-only'* use of Internet technologies in the SME sector that has limited the benefits being derived by these firms. Consequently, firms are becoming 'disenchanted' with their Internet experience, leading to a potentially high and damaging 'disconnection rate' and a tendency for later adopters to postpone their adoption process.

This finding has obvious policy and infrastructural implications for the development of Internet usage in Ireland. SMEs in all sectors of the economy must have access to the *sector-specific* training and support necessary for them to climb the learning curve involved in moving from basic Internet usage to the use of more advanced Internet technologies. Evidence supporting the existence of such needs is found in the comments made by many respondents to this survey:

"The Internet will be a new experience and learning curve."

"A big problem is getting and maintaining the Internet/e-mail connection."

"ISDN charges are too high. Help is needed for people to use the Internet as a daily tool."

"We would like to develop our Internet presence, but we are unable to keep up with current demand."

These comments highlight the substantial training needs, telecommunications access needs, and financial support that SMEs have regarding advanced Internet usage. If these needs are not made readily available to SMEs, usage will remain basic and benefits limited, leading to the types of problematic diffusion models predicted above.

References

Abrahamson, E., & Rosenkopf, L. (1993). Institutional and competitive bandwagons: Using mathematical modeling as a tool to explore innovation diffusion. *Academy of Management Review, 18,* 487-517.

Amin, A. (1994). *Post-Fordism, A Reader.* Oxford: Blackwell.

Bamfield, J. (1994). Technology management learning: The adoption of EDI by retailers. *International Journal of Retail and Distribution Management, 22*(2), 3-11.

Benjamin, R., & Wigand, R. (1995). Electronic markets and virtual chains on the information superhighway. *Sloan Management Review*, (Winter), 62-72.

Benjamin, R., deLong, D.W., & Scott Morton, M.S. (1990). EDI: How much competitive advantage? *Long Range Planning, 23*(1), 3-11.

Benjamin, R.I., Rockhart, J.F., Scott Morton, M.C., & Wyman, J. (1983). Information technology: A strategic opportunity. *Sloan Management Review*, (Winter).

Bina, E., & Andresson, M. (2001). *Internet browser technology.* Retrieved January 20, 2001 from the Web: www.web.mit.edu/invent/www/inventorsA-H/andreesen=bina.html.

Cash, J.I (1985). Interorganisational systems: An information society opportunity or threat? *The Information Society, 3*(3), 199-228.

Chan, C., & Swatman, P.M.C. (2000). From EDI to Internet commerce: The BHP steel experience. *Internet Research, 10*(1), 72-82.

Clemons, E.K. (1986). Information systems for sustainable competitive advantage. *Information and Management*, (November), 131-136.

Cooper, R.B., & Zmud, R.W. (1990). Information technology implementation research: A technological diffusion approach. *Management Science, 36*(2), 123-139.

DiMaggio, P., & Powell, W. (1983). The iron cage revisited: Institutional isomorphism and collective rationality in organizational fields. *American Sociological Review, 48,* 147-160.

Drennan, J., & Kennedy, J. (1999). Internet use factors for small business. In G. Capaldo & M. Raffa (Eds.), *Proceedings of the 44th ICSB World Conference*, Turin: Edizioni Scientifiche Italiane. Retrieved March 16, 2001 from ICSB software ICSB 064.

Elliot, S., & Loebbecke, C. (2000). Interactive, inter-organisational innovations in electronic commerce. *Information Technology and People, 13*(1), 46-66.

Ellsworth, J.H. (1995). *The Internet Business Book.* New York: John Wiley & Sons.

Engle, M. (1998). *World Wide Web terms and acronyms.* Retrieved February 4, 2002 from the Web: http://www.library.cornell.edu/okuref/research/glossary.html.

Enterprise Ireland. (2001). *Internet Usage Survey, 2000/2001.* Retrieved November 12, 2001 from the Web: http://www.enterprise-ireland.ie/surveys.html.

Ettlie, J.E. (1983). Organisational policy and innovation among suppliers to the food processing sector. *Academy of Management Journal, 26*(1), 27-44.

Everett, J. (1998). Internet security. *Employee Benefits Journal*, (September), 14-18.

Feher, A., & Towell, E. (1997). Business use of the Internet. *Internet Research, 7*(3), 195-200.

Fried-Cassorta, A. (1995). Successful marketing on the Internet: A user's guide. *Direct Marketing, 57*(11), 39-42.

Friedman, L. (1998). Technology acquisition decision making revisited: Lessons learned in an age of environmental uncertainty. *International Journal of Technology Management, 15*(5), 222-237.

Garavan, T.N., O'Cinneide, B., Garavan, M., Hynes, B., & Walsh, F. (1997). *Entrepreneurship and Business Start-Ups in Ireland [volume 2: cases].* Dublin: Oak Tree Press.

Geiger, S., & Martin, M. (1999). The Internet as a relationship marketing tool—some evidence from Irish companies. *Irish Marketing Review, 12*(2), 24-36.

Germain, R., & Dröge, C. (1995). Just-in-time and context: Predictors of EDI technology adoption. *International Journal of Physical Distribution & Logistics Management, 25*(1), 18-33.

Haynes, P.J., Becherer, R.C., & Helms, M.M. (1998). Small and mid-sized businesses and Internet use: Unrealized potential? *Internet Research, 8*(3), 229-235.

Howcroft, D., & Mitev, N. (2000). An empirical study of Internet usage and difficulties among medical practice management in the UK. *Internet Research, 10*(2), 170-181.

Howe, W. (n.d.). *A brief history of the Net.* Retrieved November 16, 2000 from the Web: http://www.walthowe.com/navnet/history.html.

Institute of National Trade of Ireland. (2002). *Profile and Assessment of the Current and Future E-Business ICT Requirements of Exporters in the Republic of Ireland.* Dublin: UCD.

International Labour Organisation Homepage. (2001). Retrieved June 25, 2001 from the Web: http://www.ilo.com.

Kautz, K., & Larsen, E.A. (2000). Diffusion theory and practice: Disseminating quality management and software process improvement innovations. *Information Technology and People, 13*(1), 11-26.

Kompass. (2001). *Register of Irish Industry and Commerce 2001.* Dublin: Kompass Ireland.

La Rovere, R.L. (1998). Diffusion of information technologies and changes in the telecommunications sector: The case of Brazilian small- and medium-sized enterprises. *Information Technology and People, 11*(3), 194-206.

Malone, T.W., Yates, J., & Benjamin, R.I. (1989). The logic of electronic markets. *Harvard Business Review,* (May-June), 166-171.

McCue, S. (1999). Small firms and the Internet: Force or farce? *International Trade Forum, 1,* 27-31.

Moore, M., & Benbasat, I. (1991). Development of an instrument to measure the perceptions of adopting an information technology. *Information Systems Research, 2*(3), 192-222.

National Center for Supercomputing Applications. (1997). *A glossary of World Wide Web terms and acronyms.* Retrieved August 14, 2000 from the Web: http://www.ncsa.uiuc.edu/SDG/Software/Mosaic/Glossary/.

O'Neill, M.H., Pouder, R.W., & Buchholtz, A.K. (1998). Patterns in the diffusion of strategies across organizations: Insights from the innovation diffusion literature. *The Academy of Management Review,* (January), 17-24.

Pierce, J.L., & Delbecq, A.L. (1977). Organisational structure, individual attitudes and innovation. *Academy of Management Journal, 2*(1), 27-37.

Proudlock, M., Phelps, B., & Gamble, P. (1999). IT adoption strategies: Best practice guidelines for IT professionals. *Journal of Small Business and Enterprise Development*, (June), 240-252.

Quelch, J.A., & Klein, L.R. (1996). The Internet and international marketing. *Sloan Management Review,* (Spring), 60-75.

Raymond, I., Julien P.-A., Carrier, J.-B., & Lachance, R. (1996). Managing technological change in manufacturing SMEs: A multiple case analysis. *International Journal of Technology Management, 11*(3), 270.

Regional Programme of Innovative Actions. (2002). *Call for proposals: Innovative transfer of knowledge from higher educational sector to rural SMEs, March, 2002.* Waterford: South-East Regional Authority.

SEISS. (2001). *South-East Regional Information Society Strategy & Action Plan, September 2001.* Waterford: South-East Regional Authority.

Swatman, P.M.C., & Swatman, P.A. (1992). EDI system integration: A definition and literature survey. *The Information Society, 8*, 169-205.

Task Force on Small Business. (1994). *Task Force on Small Business Report.* Dublin: Government Stationary Office.

Thorelli, H.B. (1986). Networks: Between markets and hierarchies. *Strategic Management Journal, 7*(1), 32-45.

Turban, K., Lee, D., King, L., & Chung, C. (1999). *Electronic Commerce—A Managerial Perspective.* London: Prentice-Hall.

Vassos, T. (1996). *Strategic Internet Marketing.* Canada: Que Books.

Winder, D. (1995). *All You Need to Know About the World Wide Web.* Bath: Future Publishing.

Chapter IX

SMEs Adoption and Implementation Process of Websites in the Presence of Change Agents

Zakia A. Elsammani, Manchester Metropolitan University, UK

Ray Hackney, Manchester Metropolitan University, UK

Phil Scown, Manchester Metropolitan University, UK

Abstract

E-business, through the exploitation of Internet technologies, is frequently associated in the literature with improvements in business performance and service delivery enhancements particularly apparent for the potential competitive advantage of small to medium-sized enterprises (SMEs). Recent research has focused on the benefits gained from adoption and barriers to adoption. This chapter considers a similar aspect, but identifies a gap in the literature, namely, SME implementation practices of a Web presence in the Northwest of the United Kingdom, and the role of perceived change agents in the overall adoption process. It also provides a comparison between the adoption practices of two groups of SMEs: Need Pull SMEs that identified a need to adopt a Web presence, and Technology Push SMEs that are mainly pushed into adoption due to the change agents' efforts. It is argued that this approach is unique within e-business activities, and provides a valuable contribution to best practice and further research efforts to improve SME performance.

Introduction

On the Internet, the website is the medium of communication between companies and their prospective consumers. A Web presence does not only include the hardware and software through which the two parties communicate, but also involves the cognitive and emotional aspects of the user's experience and expectations (Laurel, 1995). Web design and development is a complex process and does not stop at defining objectives for the website. It involves defining objectives for usability, development, testing, and ongoing maintenance. However, the plethora of Web development tools (Fraternali, 1998), and the ease by which a Web presence is developed, has encouraged many companies to develop their own Web presence without following any methodological approach. In the case of SMEs, the lack of application of methodology stems from (1) ignorance of the existence of methodologies, and (2) lack of sufficient staff and technical resources to follow a methodology should they be aware of the benefits of adoption. The ease of use of Web development tools makes it easy to make rapid progress. However, the quality of the results of this approach is questionable.

In a commercial environment, where many or most e-commerce sites have design or maintenance flaws, there is a competitive advantage by owning a quality site. Thus, for two companies selling the same product, we would expect the one with the better site to be more competitive and thus more profitable. The problem for many businesses is not only knowing that a well-designed site is an asset, but knowing how to produce one. Designing effective Web pages is therefore a strategic competitive edge and forms a new challenge, as the Web pages refer to the company's position on consumer minds (Angelides, 1997). This chapter will start by stating the problem of SMEs and Web presence adoption. It then discusses diffusion of new technologies and Web design, followed by the methodology used in capturing primary data using triangulation of both quantitative and qualitative approaches. The findings provide a comparison in implementation practices between the two main groups of SMEs identified in this research: Need Pull (NP) SMEs that have their own initiative in developing their Web presence, and Technology Push (TP) SMEs that were mainly influenced by efforts of a change agent.

SMEs and Web Presence

This research defines SMEs as small to medium-sized enterprises, from small traders with no employees, to those enterprises with 249 employees. The Department of Trade and

Industry (DTI) UK (1999, 2001) further classifies these businesses into small (0 to 49 employees) and medium (50 to 249 employees). The DTI statistical findings show 3.7 million active businesses in the UK of which less than 28,000 were medium-sized (50 to 249 employees) and less than 7,000 were large (250 employees and more). The remaining 99% of businesses were small enterprises, including those without employees (micro-SMEs). Generally, small SMEs account for 43% of non-government employment and 31% of turnover. In contrast the 7,000 largest businesses accounted for 45% of non-government employment and 55% of turnover.

Survey results show that 67.3% of business sites belong to companies that employ fewer than 50 employees (Hooi-Im Ng et al., 1998). Many websites developed by smaller companies are designed in an ad-hoc manner and contain many design mistakes (Nielsen, 1999). These websites suffer from a number of usability problems from a consumer's perspective, hereby driving the consumer to look for other websites (De Troyer & Leune, 1998). Such problems can include poor layout, inconsistent information, and out-of-date information. Furthermore, companies develop a Web presence without foreseeing the effort that goes into maintaining the site and attracting consumers (Loebbecke et al., 1999). It is reasonable to conclude that these practices have a negative effect on a consumer's acceptance of a particular website. In addition, consumers' negative recognition of the website can affect a company's perception of the advantages of adopting a Web presence.

The diffusion and adoption of e-commerce, and hence e-business, by SMEs has been of concern for researchers, practitioners, and government agencies. The majority of research in the area of SMEs' adoption of Internet and EC is focusing on the benefits gained by SMEs, and the barriers and the factors influencing the adoption of EC (Fink, 1999; Poon & Storm, 1997; Poon & Swatman, 1997a; Riemenschneider & McKinney, 1999; Sillince, MacDonald, Lefang, & Frost, 1998; Webb & Sayer, 1998). Research into SMEs' adoption and usage of the Internet has been focused on the business context of Internet usage and how to develop business strategy (Poon & Swatman, 1997b). The present research into SMEs' Web presence looks at classification of the types of website, structure of websites, and usage of websites by different groups of SMEs (Huizingh, 2000). The research community has strongly and repeatedly stressed the importance of adopting Internet technology as the driving force for competition and the importance of strategic planning to achieve a competitive edge, ignoring the fact that the SME manager plays a number of roles in the organization from manager, accountant, IT person (Paliva, 1996), to the actual developer of the Web presence. This new role for the SME manager has been encouraged by media attention, peer competition, the fear of being left behind, and the plethora of Web editing tools and ease by which a Web presence can be developed. Thus, a majority of SMEs now own a Web presence. SME websites are often strongly criticized for their simplicity and lack of business objective and planning. Research so far has yet to pay attention to the process of EC implementation (Chan & Swatman, 1999).

There is a lack of research into the actual implementation and management process of Web presence and the factors that positively or negatively affect the successful adoption of EC by SMEs. SMEs are known to suffer from time, financial, expertise constraints, and they seek external assistance to overcome the knowledge gap within the company (Thong & Yap, 1997). Nonetheless, there is still a lack of knowledge about the nature and the extent of SME support, needs, and the mechanisms for delivering these needs effectively (Hoffman et al., 1998). Limited research has been performed into the actual development and management process of a Web presence, from the initial stage of setting criteria and objectives for the website, to development and testing, to its continuous management. To ensure the inclusion of the majority of adopters of Web presence, both able and less able SMEs, the definition used in this research is similar to the one proposed by Hoffman et al. (1995) where Internet presence can take the form or flat ads (single documents), image sites (emotional customer appeal), or detailed information sites. This set of definitions acts as a basic starting point and not as a limiting factor. This definition broadens the scope of the research and does not limit it to the more successful and more able SMEs with complex websites.

Web Design

Web design describes the process of creating appealing and usable websites. Nielsen (2000) states that there are mainly two basic approaches to design: *"the artistic ideal of expressing yourself or the engineering ideal of solving a problem for a customer."* Web publishing is a more appropriate term for describing the overall process of planning and putting together a website, particularly when some degree of forethought, skill, and artistry is employed (Powell et al., 1998). Traditional Web publishing focuses on websites as online marketing pieces with a minor amount of interactivity and technology. This way of thinking about a website might be appropriate for some promotional purposes, but as the size of content and amount of information on the website grows, a more rigorous software-centered approach to Web design is required. Similarly, Lawe and Hall (1999) argue that development and usage of a Web application is influenced by the size of the application. A disciplined approach becomes critical with large-scale applications. For small-scale applications it is often satisfactory to have an awareness of the design issues and develop the application in an ad-hoc approach (Lawe & Hall, 1999). Furthermore, Nielsen (2000) argues that Web pages and sites turn out to be useless if they are built from an understanding of HTML and graphics without corresponding understanding of Web design and user needs.

By applying software engineering practices and combining them with Web publishing ideas, a next-generation hybrid process called website engineering is born (Powell et al., 1998). Nielsen (2000) suggests that treating a Web project as a software development project will make it easier to meet schedules and to ensure the quality of the site. In particular, pervasive application of usability engineering methodology throughout the Web project will lead to continuous improvement of the site, both with respect to the initial design and subsequent designs. Nonetheless, Huizingh (2000) argues that lack of Web methodologies is listed as an extremely important factor in the design of websites.

Web design and development is a complex process. However, the factors discussed above have encouraged many companies to develop their own Web presence using ad-hoc design approaches without following any methodological approach. As discussed previously, in the case of SMEs the lack of application of methodology stems from ignorance of the existing methodologies and lack of sufficient staff and technical resources to follow a methodology. Thus SMEs' Web development practices include a minimum of four generic stages: (1) set objectives and criteria for the website, (2) design and develop the site, (3) test the site before going online, and (4) continuous update and management. These proposed stages are not exclusive and may overlap in some cases.

Methodology

The methodology used in conducting this research is a combination of quantitative and qualitative methods (Poon & Swatman, 1999). The quantitative approach (a survey) was essential to capture a cross-sectional picture of SMEs' implementation practices from a diverse and widely spread population (Fitzgerald et al., 1999). The qualitative approach was used to develop an in-depth understanding of SMEs' experience in website development in the presence of change agents, and to validate the findings of the quantitative analysis. Each part of the research yielded data on a different part of the phenomena. A two-stage design enhances the validity of overall analysis by producing data on different aspects of the research area to build up a rounded and credible overall picture.

The sample of SMEs was selected from a Web directory aimed at SMEs using systematic random sampling (Elsammani & Scown, 2000). Of the total 600 questionnaires sent, 192 were included in the analysis of the survey (32% response rate). The questionnaire consisted of four main sections: company information; Web presence information; development, testing, and maintenance; and benefits gained from Web presence. Ten companies participated in the semi-structured interviews; these were selected from the respondents to the survey study. The criteria for selecting these SMEs for the semi-structured interviews were: (1) SMEs having been influenced by the same change agent, (2) within the same geographic area, (3) their decision to adopt was at the same time, and (4) their willingness to participate. A series of questions was prepared and each manager was personally interviewed using a semi-structured interview format. Semi-structured interviewing calls for a specific list of questions given in a specific order. It permits the interviewer to ask optional questions, pass on others, and depart briefly to follow unexpected paths (Lindlof, 1995). Each interview lasted an hour. Interviews were both noted and tape-recorded and then transcribed. Understanding of the problems and conceptualization improved as more companies were interviewed. The survey was conducted in April 1999 and semi-structured interviews in June 2000. The study encompasses triangulation of methods, and the analysis presented of each phase is complementary to one another and equal weight is given to both data sets to produce an enhanced understanding of the adoption and implementation process in the particular sample.

Demographics of SMEs Participating in the Survey and Case Study

Participants to the survey share a number of attributes. The most obvious attribute is their size, companies with less than 250 employees. Secondly, each company has a Web presence hosted by the same Web directory, MerseyWorld Site (currently renamed to MerseyWideWeb). MerseyWorld Site is a local authority-led initiative established in 1997 to improve access to technology in the Merseyside, in the Northwest of the UK (Charlton et al., 1998a). It is part of a European-funded project, managed by Connect Centre, the Internet Centre for Merseyside Businesses, based at the Department of Computer Science at the University of Liverpool. Connect was established in December 1994, with a mission of helping Merseyside SMEs make best use of the Internet. Connect, a diffusion agent, is responsible for the diffusion of Internet awareness and skills to small businesses and the local communities in Merseyside, UK (Charlton et al., 1997a). Connect is primarily concerned with providing businesses with the necessary Internet know-how to effectively exploit the technology and bring businesses onto the Internet (Charlton et al., 1998b). This was performed through Awareness Days, Short Course Programs, The MerseyWorld Site, and its Work Experience and Work Placement programs. Awareness days are designed to give businesses a brief introduction through lectures and hands-on experience to those aspects of the Internet they could usefully employ in daily practice: e-mail, WWW, Usenet, file transfer, local area networks, and security.

Connect also acts as a "cybermediary" through the MerseyWorld site (Charlton et al., 1998). This site is aimed at marketing the electronic potential of the Merseyside region. A Web presence is developed for businesses based on information submitted in any format (Charlton et al., 1997b). Connect employs programmers, designers, and system specialists to develop the websites. Any company can join MerseyWorld whether it has an existing Web presence or not. The first 12 months are free, irrespective of the level of service the company chooses. Starting from the second year, charges are incurred depending on the type of service selected. The following services are provided: link service, basic service, full service, domain name registration, mailing lists, CGI scripts, quickstart site creation, larger sites. Furthermore, through the training provided by the Short Course Program, businesses can gradually become responsible for managing their Web presence.

The roles played by Connect and MerseyWorld in the diffusion of the technology in the Merseyside region are both inter-winding and different. Though MerseyWorld is run by Connect, MerseyWorld is more an Internet service provider "Cybermediary" and a professional Web design agency that charges fees for its services at some stage. This difference led us to the hypothesis that there are two different categories of companies in the MerseyWorld directory:

1. *Technology Push (TP)*. SMEs that are being influenced by the awareness days and training developed by Connect to adopt the technology. These companies had their websites developed by Connect free of charge.

2.   *Need Pull (NP)*. SMEs that were already technology aware and had the initiative to adopt the technology. These companies developed their sites either within the company by in-house staff or through an external body, i.e., any Web design agency, including MerseyWorld.

Though we reached this hypothesis, at the time of conducting the survey we were not in a position of strictly stating that the technology pull companies had not been influenced by Connect at an earlier stage (Elsammani & Scown, 2000). However, after conducting the semi-structured interview in the second phase of the research, these hypotheses were validated. Although selecting a sample from MerseyWorld possibly created an unintentional bias in that they may have had a common influence on all their clients, the approach was deemed appropriate as it allows comparison between patterns of adoption by technology push and need pull SMEs.

Survey Findings

Characteristics of SMEs

The main characteristic of SMEs is size: micro, small, and medium. SMEs also differ by business activity, trade sector, and age of company. These attributes were included in the design of the questionnaire for the purpose of control. The majority of respondents were micro-SMEs (60.9%), followed by 28.1% of small enterprises and 10.9% of medium enterprises. Respondents consist of more enterprises in the business-to-business activity than business-to-consumer activity (56.3% and 43.8% respectively). This is in line with the expected growth and faster adoption of EC in business-to-business companies (Hooi-Im Ng et al., 1998). Nearly half of the respondents (48.1%) can be regarded as relatively young companies, established between 1990-1999. The majority of the participating companies belong to the wholesale, retail, and repairs industry (20.8%) and manufacturing industry (19.8%). SMEs form smaller percentages in the community, social, and personal industry (9.9%); construction (6.3%); real estate, renting, and business activities (6.3%); and "others" (16.7%). The rest of the companies (20.3%) belong to the remaining industry sectors, with each presenting less than 5%. SMEs belonging to the electricity, gas, and water supply industry form the smallest percentage of 0.5%. There are no companies from the mining and quarrying industry.

The final characteristic of the sample was ownership of Web presence. The majority of companies (57.1%) had a Web presence for "one to three years" followed by companies that had a Web presence for "less than a year" (34.0%). A minority of SMEs (7.9%) had a Web presence for "three to six years" and only two companies (1.0%) had a Web presence for "more than six years." The last two categories ("three to six years" and "more than six years") were grouped into one group "more than three years" (8.9%). Further details are presented in Table 1.

Table 1: SMEs' Characteristics and Experience with Web Presence

Characteristics	Number of Companies	Percentage
Company Size		
Micro 0-9	117	60.9
Small 10-49	54	28.1
Medium 50-49	21	10.9
Business Activity		
Business-to-business	84	43.8
Business-to-consumer	108	56.3
Company Established		
Before 1969	31	16.9
1970-1979	19	10.4
1980-1989	45	24.6
1990-1999	88	48.1
Industry Sector		
Agriculture, Forestry and Fishing	4	2.1
Manufacturing	38	19.8
Electricity, Gas and Water Supply	1	0.5
Construction	12	6.3
Wholesale, Retail and Repairs	40	20.8
Hotels and Restaurants	4	2.1
Transport, Storage and Communication	8	4.2
Financial	7	3.6
Real Estate, Renting and Business Activities	12	6.3
Education	7	3.6
Health/Social Work	8	4.2
Other Community, Social/Personal	19	9.9
Others	32	16.7
Experience with Web Presence		
Less than a year	65	34.0
Between 1-3 years	109	57.1
More than 3 years	17	8.9

Need Pull and Technology Push SMEs

Survey findings indicated the presence of a new attribute for SMEs, Need Pull, and Technology Push SMEs (Figure 1). Need Pull SMEs are SMEs that had the initiative to develop their Web presence in-house or approached an independent Web design bureau. These SMEs developed their own website using internal resources in the form of employed staff or outsourced their website development to a Web design bureau. Technology Push SMEs are SMEs that owned a Web presence mainly due to change agents' efforts and incentives. Their website was developed by Connect or by a service

Figure 1: Where was the Website Developed? (The three different categorizations are used within this research.)

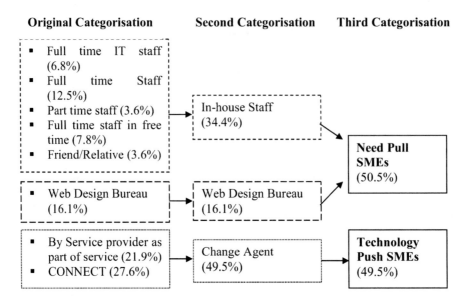

Table 2: Chi-Square of NP and TP Attributes and SMEs' Characteristics

SMEs Characteristics	Pearson Chi-Square	df	Significance
Number of Employees	4.014	2	0.134
Business Activity	1.000	1	0.317
Company Established	9.055	3	0.029**
Internet/Web Experience	13.738	2	0.001***

*/**/*** Significantly different from zero at 0.10/0.05/0.01 level of significance*

provider, whether that service provider was MerseyWorld or some other. These findings prove the presence of these two distinctive groups of SMEs. Pearson Chi-square tests (in Table 2) were performed to establish if associations exist between NP and TP attributes and SMEs' general characteristics (size, business activity, age of company, and experience with Web Presence). These tests reflected highly significant associations with only two variables: age of company (p=0.029) and experience with Web presence (p=0.001).

Description of SME Web Presence

Features and functions on the Web presence were classified based on the topology used by Cockburn and Wilson (1995) and Hooi-Im Ng et al. (1998). The topology was adopted to develop a list of features present in the website. One extra category—"quality standard and assurance certification"—was added, as it is an important factor in building trust with the consumers or visitors to the website. This question was a multiple response question where respondents were allowed to select any number of relevant features present in their Web presence. Thus, each feature (variable) of the question is a nominal variable (dichotomous) (Fink, 1995). To analyze this question, each variable was regarded as having a "yes" or "no" answer.

As reflected in Table 3, the majority of SMEs have websites with basic company information (96.4%) and information about product and service (86.5%). A smaller percentage of companies provide price information of products and services (32.8%). Nearly half of the SMEs (47.4%) provide conventional purchasing facilities, and a smaller percentage allows ordering of goods by e-mail and paying with conventional means (36.5%). Only 9.9% of SMEs can cope with online ordering and payment, and 2.6% allow pre-registration of credit card. A minority of 14.6% provides proof of quality of standards and assurance certification, and 6.3% provide free software, products, or service. These findings are in line with Angehrn's (1997) definition of the first phase of Internet development. Angehrn (1997) describes the initial Virtual Information Space as "Internet-based channels through which economic agents can display information about themselves and the products and services they offer."

Generally speaking, the respondent SMEs seem to own basic websites with minimum functionality. However, it seems that TP SMEs have more basic websites, similar to billboards. NP SMEs seem to have websites with higher functionality: facilitate online ordering and payment (14 SMEs) and pre-registration of credit card (four SMEs), than TP SMEs (five and one SMEs respectively). However, this number of NP SMEs is too small to indicate any significant difference.

Table 3: Frequency Table of Features on SMEs' Web Presence by NP and TP Attribute of SMEs

Features on the Web Presence	SMEs		No. Websites	% Web-sites
	NP (97)	*TP (95)*		
▪ Information about the company	93	92	185	96.4
▪ Information about products or services	90	26	166	86.5
▪ Price information of products and services	34	29	63	32.8
▪ Facilities for conventional purchasing, e.g., post, telephone and fax	46	45	91	47.4
▪ Facilities to order products or services by e-mail and pay by conventional means	37	33	70	36.5
▪ Ability to cope with online ordering and payment	14	5	19	9.9
▪ Pre-registration of credit card	4	1	4	2.6
▪ Quality Standards and assurance certification	14	14	28	14.6
▪ Provide free software, products or services	9	3	12	6.3
▪ Others	6	1	7	3.6

Implementation of SMEs' Web Presence

SMEs' implementation practices involve a sequence of steps: criteria selection, developing the Web presence, testing the Web presence, and continuous maintenance. Due to lack of competent internal SME resources, SMEs are known to seek external assistance and perform ad-hoc allocation of financial resources for the implementation of their IT infrastructure. Similar behavior can be expected at Web presence development and management of Web presence. Each of the above points was a contingency question in the survey, and each section was inspected at a detailed level. This section presents an abstract of these findings (Table 4).

- *Seeking external assistance:* Of the total 192 respondents, 157 SMEs sought external assistance and advice before implementing their Web presence. The majority of these SMEs were TP SMEs (87 TP and 70 NP). The main reasons for seeking assistance include the cost of setting up a site, content and design issues, and lack of expertise within the company. TP SMEs mainly approached Connect (48), Business Links (31), and TEC/LEC (24). NP SMEs mainly approached business links (21), specialist computer agency (18), and finally Connect (15). As indicated, more TP SMEs approached the change agent than NP SMEs.

- *Setting a budget for implementation:* Only 43 SMEs of the total respondents set a budget for implementing their Web presence. The majority of TP SMEs did not set a budget for implementation, as their site was developed by Connect as part of the awareness creation program. Sixty-nine NP SMEs did not set a budget, as they have developed their website using their own resources.

- *Objectives and criteria:* The majority of SMEs (108) have set criteria and objectives for their site before implementing it. This reflects some level of awareness of the benefits of acquiring a Web presence. Nonetheless, a substantial number of SME managers, both TP (46) and NP (38), have not set any objectives or criteria, reflecting lack of awareness or lack of interest in the benefits and risks associated with adoption of Web presence.

- *Problems during development:* Only 44 SME managers know of problems faced during developing the website. The majority of these were NP SMEs that developed their website in-house. These SME managers either developed the site themselves or were working closely with the designer. Only 11 TP SMEs were aware of problems during development, and these problems were mainly due to difficulty or lack of communication with the designer. The majority of problems reflected by both groups were related to lack of time and technical resources in the form of lack of awareness of the limitation of the technology (Elsammani, Scown, & Hackney, 2001).

- *Website testing:* The majority of SMEs (121) had their website tested before going live online, though only a few (44) knew of problems faced while developing the Web presence. This can indicate the minimum involvement of SME management in the implementation process of their website, especially if the Web presence development was outsourced to third parties or if management was not directly involved in the development.

Table 4: Frequency Table of NP and TP SMEs' Implementation Practices and Chi-Square Tests

Response	Seek external assistance before implementation			Set budget for implementing site			Objectives for website			Problems during development			Website testing			Set budget for maintenance		
	TP	NP	Total	TP	NP	Total	TP	NP	Total	TP	NP	Total	TP	NP	Total	TP	NP	Total
Yes	87	70	157	15	28	43	49	59	108	11	33	44	53	68	121	28	25	53
No	8	27	35	80	69	149	46	38	84	51	51	102	11	13	24	67	72	139
Do not know	—	—	—	—	—	—	—	—	—	33	13	46	31	16	47	—	—	—
Total	95	97	192	95	97	192	95	97	192	95	97	192	95	97	192	95	97	192
Chi-Square Test	$\chi^2 = 12.136$; df = 1; p = 0.000***			$\chi^2 = 4.722$; df = 1; p = 0.030**			$\chi^2 = 1.667$; df = 1; p = 0.197			$\chi^2 = 19.677$; df = 2; p = 0.000***			$\chi^2 = 6.793$; df = 2; p = 0.033**			$\chi^2 = 0.329$; df = 1; p = 0.566		

*/**/*** Significantly different from zero at 0.1/0.5/0.01 level of significance.

- *Setting a budget for update and maintenance:* Only 53 SMEs (28 TP and 25 NP SMEs) have set a budget for ongoing maintenance and update of the site. The majority of SMEs (139) have not set a budget for maintenance and update. This is influenced by a number of factors: 65 SMEs have owned a Web presence for less than a year, MerseyWorld provides maintenance services for the first year, and NP SMEs are using their internal resources for site maintenance.

Pearson Chi-square tests were conducted to identify association between SMEs' characteristics and implementation practices. These tests reflect significant association between the NP and TP attributes of SMEs and their implementation practices (Table 4). Two highly significant associations have been established between: (1) seeking external assistance before developing the Web presence (p=0.000), and (2) knowledge of problems faced during developing their Web presence (p=0.000). Additionally, two significant associations are established between: (1) setting a budget before developing the Web presence (p=0.030), and (2) between testing the website before going online (p=0.033). However, no association was established between setting criteria and objectives and setting budget for keeping the site up to date. No systematic or coherent pattern is evident within any group of SMEs.

Further Chi-square tests were performed to establish if there is an association between implementation practices and SME general characteristics. These tests did not reflect any significant associations. The absence of any association between SMEs' general characteristics and the implementation process, and the presence of strong associations between the implementation process and NP and TP attributes, reflects the importance of where the Web presence is initially developed as a crucial factor influencing the implementation process, and hence the overall adoption and implementation of Web presence. These findings necessitated the importance of interviewing SMEs from within the same sample to develop a further understanding of factors that influence this implementation pattern, particularly the role of the change agent in the implementation process.

Interview Findings: Web Presence Adoption and Role of Change Agent

Huberman and Miles (1994) argue that there is no one or two central approaches to the conclusion drawing and verification of qualitative data; rather, there are multiple iterative sets of tactics that can be use. The analysis of the semi-structured interviews took the form of hierarchical coding using template analysis as described by King (1998). Hierarchical coding enables the analysis of text at varying levels of specificity. Themes in the interviews were coded and grouped by similar codes clustered together to produce more general, higher order codes. Broad higher codes give an overview of the general direction of the interview, while detailed lower order codes allow for the fine distinctions both within cases and between cases. Interviews were grouped into NP and TP companies, thus enabling a within and between groups comparison.

The analysis was performed with the aid of the *QSR Nvivo* software package for qualitative analysis. The main themes or codes were predefined based on the interview questions and Innovation Decision Process model, which describes the five stages an individual adopter undergoes to adopt and implement any new technology (Rogers, 1983). Stages in the IDP model include: *knowledge* stage of acquiring information about the innovation, *persuasion* stage of being persuaded to adopt the innovation, *decision* stage of deciding to adopt, *implementation* stage of implementing the innovation and using it, and finally *confirmation* stage of evaluating the actual outcome with expectations. A description of the 10 SMEs that participated in the interviews is presented in Table 5.

Table 5: SMEs Participating in the Semi-Structured Interview

Company	Size	Business Activity	Business Industry	Push/Pull SME
Case1	Micro	BC	Manufacturing	Technology Push
Case2	Small	BB and BC	Service	Technology Push
Case3	Small	BC	Manufacturing	Technology Push
Case4	Small	BB	Service	Need Pull
Case5	Small	BB	Service	Need Pull
Case6	Medium	BC	Service	Technology Push
Case7	Micro	BC	Manufacturing	Technology Push
Case8	Micro	BC	Service	Technology Push
Case9	Micro	BC	Service	Need Pull
Case10	Medium	BC	Publishing	Need Pull

- *Knowledge and Persuasion.* Word of mouth and the public media influence initial awareness about Internet and Web presence. Though the change agent had an influential role in the TP SMEs' awareness creation, this was not the case for the NP SMEs. They merely approached the change agent to gain more detailed information about the technology. The behavior of champions and change agents can accelerate the adoption of an innovation. The change agent played an influential role in awareness creation and hands-on experience on website adoption. The training provided was viewed differently by both groups of SMEs. TP SMEs found the awareness courses and training influential in their decision to adopt a website. However, NP SMEs thought the awareness courses were removed from the SME reality and the training as being very basic and not addressing the whole complexity of Web design. One NP viewed these courses as *"waste of time and too generalized,"* and another reported that *"it was removed from the SME reality as they were showing Sainsbury's website and the White House."*

- *Decision to Adopt.* The decision to develop a Web presence was accelerated by the incentives provided by the change agent via the Web directory. The change agent provided free services for the first 12 months. These services included free hosting of website, submission to search engines, and feedback on traffic activity on the site. TP SMEs reported that *"free Web design was the main incentive in adopting a Web presence at the time,"* as they discovered *"the complexity of Web design and development while attending the awareness courses."* NP SMEs reported that they had developed a website before approaching the change agent; however, they found the services offered, *"especially submission to search engines was attractive"* and encouraged them to host their site in the Web directory.

- *Implementation Process.* All SMEs reported that their first website was a presentational website containing company, product, price, and contacts (including e-mail). NP SMEs developed their website depending on personal efforts in learning HTML and Web design. Though they approached the change agent to acquire more information and a better understanding of website development, they found that the courses were too basic. TP SMEs mainly depended on the change agent to develop their website, as they realized the complexity of Web design in the courses. TP SMEs set criteria for their website and had minimum involvement in the actual development process. Both groups of SMEs faced problems when developing their initial website. However, these problems varied. TP SMEs reported lack of support and communication with designer of the website, whereas NP SMEs reported limited technical resources, knowledge of Web design issues, and lack of awareness of the limitations of the technology (Elsammani et al., 2001).

- *Continuous Adoption.* All SMEs agreed that, though they have adopted a Web presence for the last four years, they still view the Web presence as a low-budget promotional means rather than a serious business tool. All SMEs reported a limited increase in turnover (less than 5%) from business activity via the website. However, two SMEs reported doing business with international clients, *"though limited to less than 1% per year."* Customers, both national and international, mainly visit the website to check product information, use e-mail for an initial enquiry, and finalize the majority of enquiries and contracts via the phone. Some SMEs discovered alternative ways of conducting business activity over the Internet. One SME reported that the *"majority of sales are made via a portal website, where most of the products are advertised."* Another SME performs most *"online transactions through an auction site like e-Bay."* This reflects a confirmation of general use of the Internet, but not the Web presence as a business tool.

Management enthusiasm and optimism towards future business activity through the website are the main driving forces for the confirmation stage of adoption and management of a website. All SMEs have developed a second website from the one originally developed. Nonetheless, SMEs suffer from the same problems at successive website development stages as in the initial stage: lack of time, technical and financial resources, lack of awareness of the limitations of the technology, and legal issues (Elsammani et al., 2001). They find it difficult to keep track with a fast-evolving technology. SMEs reported the need for some support mechanism where the website can be analyzed and tested, and improvements suggested. One SME found *"no support mechanism; we moved our site from Merseyworld."*

Looking at the current websites owned by SMEs, we find that websites owned by NP SMEs are more professional, while websites owned by TP SMEs suffer from usability problems (e.g., dead links and incomplete websites) that might reflect negatively on a customer's perception of the company. All SMEs have acknowledged the competition created by competitor websites; nonetheless, none of the SMEs interviewed have any intention of taking the Web presence a step further from being a presentational website and incorporating the website in their business strategy. Furthermore, no SME reported the need for external assistance or employing extra staff to manage the website. SMEs are generally hesitant to seek alternative professional Web design or consultancy due to their lack of trust of external assistance and the extra cost.

Conclusion

Benefits of adopting e-commerce have been frequently stressed in literature. Nonetheless, findings in this chapter indicate that e-commerce benefits cannot be gained unless successful implementation and adoption is achieved first. This chapter identified two groups of SMEs: Technology Push (TP) and Need Pull (NP) SMEs. TP SMEs are those companies that have been brought to the technology by some external agency. Typically the government funds a specialist agency or technical group to introduce a new technology or process to potential users. The effect of this on SMEs is to provide free training in technologies that they are not necessarily highly motivated to take up or adopt. Thus, effects tend to be less enduring. NP SMEs are motivated to adopt a technology for various reasons (e.g., to remain competitive or to expand), but don't have the know-how to do so. They appreciate the benefits and may have done considerable research before working with an external agency to acquire the necessary knowledge.

Thus, NP SMEs are more likely to follow through on suggestions where they can see obvious benefits in the medium term.

Change agents play a significant role in the adoption and implementation process. In this study, the role of change agents was discussed in relation to implementation of websites and affects the specific sample only. However, the role of change agents is not only limited to start-up companies or first-time adapters of new technology. Interview findings indicate that SMEs that had initially developed their own Web presence approached the change agent only to gain more knowledge and bridge the gap in their knowledge of Web development and adoption. Results indicate that management enthusiasm is the driving force for adoption in both groups of SMEs (Need Pull and Technology Push), though the implementation process differs significantly. Lack of internal technical resources is one of the main factors inhibiting the implementation process. Nonetheless, the implementation process and website developed was influenced by external factors in the form of change agent support, SME training, and consultant understanding of the SME business environment. Results also reflect on the role of a change agent in training, and transferring adequate skills and support provided by government initiatives, practitioners, and vendors for continuous adoption of Web presence. Results show that, for most SMEs, the implementation stage was followed by either reinvention of their use of the Internet as a marketing medium or discontinuing their Web presence rather than confirmation of adoption.

References

Angelides, M.C. (1997). Implementing the Internet for business: A global marketing opportunity. *International Journal of Information Management, 17*(6), 405-419.

Chan, E., & Swatman, P.M.C. (1999). Electronic commerce: A component model. Paper presented at *CollECTeR'99—3rd Annual CollECTeR (Collaborative Electronic Commerce Technology and Research) Conference on Electronic Commerce,* Wellington, New Zealand (November 29).

Charlton, C., Gittings, C., Leng, P., Little, J., & Neilson, I. (1997a). Diffusion of the Internet: A local perspective on an international issue. Paper presented at the *IFIP TC8 WG8.6 International Working Conference on Diffusion, Adoption and Implementation of Information Technology,* Ambleside, Cumbria, UK (June 25-27).

Charlton, C., Gittings, C., Leng, P., Little, J., & Neilson, I. (1997b). The impact of the new connectivity: Transferring technological skills to the small business community. *Proceedings of the 1997 ACM SIGCPR Conference,* San Francisco California, USA.

Charlton, C., Gittings, C., Leng, P., Little, J., & Neilson, I. (1998a). Diffusion of technological innovations: Bringing businesses onto the Internet. In T.J. Larsen & E. McGuire (Eds.), *Information Systems Innovation and Diffusion: Issues and Directions* (pp. 251-296). Hershey, PA: Idea Group Publishing.

Charlton, C., Grant, S., Leng, P., & Neilson, I. (1998b). *Promotion of electronic commerce by a regional centre.* Retrieved December 12, 2000 from the Web: http://www.electronic-markets.org/netacademy/publications.nef/all-pk/958.

Cockburn, C., & Wilson, T.D. (1995). *Business use of the World-Wide Web.* Retrieved August 9/September 8, 1999 from the Web: De Troyer, O.M.F., & Leune, C.J. (1998). WSDM: A user centered design method for websites. *Computer Networks and ISDN Systems, 30,* 85-94.

Elsammani, Z., & Scown, P. (2000). How SMEs perceive and develop their Web presence. *Journal of New Product Development and Innovation Management,* (March/April), 71-86.

Elsammani, Z., Scown, P., & Hackney, R. (2001, April 18-20). A case study of the impact of a diffusion agent on SMEs adoption of Web presence. Paper presented at *UKAIS 2001, United Kingdom Academy of Information Systems,* Portsmouth, UK.

Fink, A. (1995). *How to Analyze Survey Data.* Sage Publications.

Fink, D. (1999). Guidelines for the successful adoption of information technology in small and medium enterprises. *International Journal of Information Management, 18*(4), 243-253.

Fitzgerald, G., Philippides, A., & Probert, S. (1999). Information systems development, maintenance and enhancement: Findings from a UK study. *International Journal of Information Management, 19,* 319-328.

Fraternali, P. (1998). Web development tools: A survey. *Computer Networks and ISDN Systems, 30,* 631-633.

Hoffman, D. L., Novak, T. P. & Chatterjee, P. (1995). Commercial scenarios for the Web: Opportunities and challenges. *Journal of Computer Mediated Communication, 1*(3), December.

Hoffman, K., Parejo, M., Bessant, J., & Perren, L. (1998). Small firms, R&D, technology and innovation in the UK: A literature review. *Technovation, 18*(1), 39-55.

Hooi-Im Ng, Pan, Y.J., & Wilson, T.D. (1998). Business use of the World Wide Web: A report on further investigations. *International Journal of Information Management, 18*(5), 291-314.

Huizingh, E. (2000). The content and design of websites: An empirical study. *Information & Management, 37,* 123-134.

Laurel, B. (1995). *The Art of Human Computer Interface Design.* Addison-Wesley.

Lawe, D., & Hall, W. (1999). *Hypermedia & the Web: An Engineering Approach.* New York: John Wiley & Sons.

Lindlof, T.R. (1995). *Qualitative Communication Research Methods.* Thousand Oaks, CA: Sage Publications.

Loebbecke, C., Powell, P., & Gallagher, C. (1999). Buy the book: Electronic commerce in the book trade. *Journal of Information Technology, 14,* 295-301.

Nielsen, J. (1999). The top ten mistakes of Web design. 8/2/1999—

Paliva, P.C. (1996). A model and instrument for measuring small business user satisfaction with information technology. *Information and Management, 31,* 151-163.

Poon, S., & Storm, J. (1997a). Small business' use of the Internet: Some realities. Paper presented at *INET 97, The Internet: The Global Frontier, The Seventh Annual Conference of the Internet Society* (June 24-27).

Poon, S., & Swatman, P.M.C. (1997b). Internet-based small business communication: Seven Australian cases. *EM—Electronic Markets, 7*(2), 15-21.

Poon, S., & Swatman, P.M.C. (1999). An exploratory study of small business Internet commerce issues. *Information & Management, 35,* 9-18.

Powell, T.A., Jones, D.L., & Cutts, D.C. (1998). *Website Engineering: Beyond Web Page Design.* Prentice-Hall.

Riemenschneider, C.K., & McKinney, V.R. (1999). Assessing the adoption of Web-based e-commerce for business: A research proposal and preliminary findings. *Electronic Markets, 9*(1/2), 9-13.

Rogers, E.M. (1983). *Diffusion of Innovations* (4th ed.). New York: The Free Press.

Sillince, J.A.A., MacDonald, S., Lefang, B., & Frost, B. (1998). Email adoption, diffusion, use and impact within small firms: A survey of UK companies. *International Journal of Information Management, 18*(4), 231-242.

Thong, J.Y.L., & Yap, C.S. (1997). Effects of resource constraints on information technology implementation in small business. Paper presented at the *Facilitating Technology Transfer Through Partnership, Learning from Practice and Research. IFIP TC8 WG8.6 International Working Conference on Diffusion, Adoption and Implementation of Information Technology,* Ambleside, Cumbria, UK (June 25-27).

Webb, B., & Sayer, R. (1998). Benchmarking small companies on the Internet. *Long Range Planning, 31*(6), 815-827.

Section VI

Successful SMEs in
E-Commerce

Chapter X

Traits of Successfully E-Enabled Irish SMEs

William Golden, National University of Ireland Galway, Ireland

Martin Hughes, National University of Ireland Galway, Ireland

Lucy Ruane, National University of Ireland Galway, Ireland

Abstract

This chapter investigates the factors that have contributed to successful e-enablement within Irish SMEs. These factors are categorized as organizational, management, and implementation factors. The organizational factors that contribute to such success include previous organizational IT expertise, previous experience with logistics, and the suitability of the product for sale on the Web. The management factors that have a positive influence on success include the existence of a champion, having an e-commerce strategy, and integrating the Web presence into the existing business. The implementation issues that contribute to success include planning the Web presence, usability of the website, the existence of security features on the website, outsourcing elements of the e-commerce project, and website marketing. The authors purposefully chose to study recognized successful e-enabled SMEs so as to identify the salient factors and explore how these factors contributed to the success of the SMEs e-commerce initiative.

Introduction

The advent of the World Wide Web has provided an easily accessible means through which firms can conduct commerce electronically and has been successfully exploited by Irish SMEs since the mid 1990s (Golden, 1996). It has been hailed as a revolution in commerce (Hof, 1999) that will enable "friction free capitalism" (Palmer & Griffith, 1998, p. 46). The predictions are particularly relevant to SMEs, as it has been argued that e-commerce presents a unique opportunity for such firms due to the absence of barriers to entry for the new medium (O'Connor & O'Keefe, 1997; Poon & Swatman, 1998). In addition it provides SMEs with a global market (Quelch & Klein, 1996; O'Keefe & McEachern, 1998), which negates geographic boundaries (Cairncross, 1997). Web-based e-commerce enables SMEs to compete effectively against large companies (Watson, Akselsen, & Leylan, 1998).

Background

To date, existing empirical research focusing on the success factors of websites is mainly anecdotal and exploratory in nature (Liu & Arnett, 2000). Thus, while there should be a considerable number and variety of factors associated with the success of websites, little knowledge exists about the combination of these factors (Liu & Arnett, 2000). The primary motive for this research is to provide an empirical analysis of successful Irish SMEs engaging in e-commerce and to find out the most successful combination of factors that attribute to success on the Web.

The focus of this chapter is on small to medium-sized enterprises (SMEs) operating in Ireland. An SME is defined in this research in accordance with the EU definition as firms with less than 250 full-time employees. The growth of SMEs plays a significant role in the economic vitality of a nation (Haynes, Becherer, & Helms, 1998). The SME sector is vital to the economic success of the Irish nation, given the contribution of small business to economic growth and job creation. Businesses with fewer than 50 employees account for 98% of the country's businesses, and more than 90% of Irish businesses employ fewer than 10 people. Today's small businesses face an increasingly unstable marketplace rife with change. Perhaps no single aspect of these changes has reverberated as clearly as the growth of the Internet. This growth raises issues which concern not only how the Internet is currently being used, but also which areas of Internet use may offer additional resources for SMEs (Guthrie & Austin, 1996).

The primary objective of this research is to determine what factors contribute to a successful e-commerce project within an SME. Various studies have investigated website success from different perspectives. Liu and Arnett (2000) investigate website success on the basis of outcome variables such as attractive, dependable, reliable, trustworthy, meeting demand, and pleasing customers. O'Keefe and McEachern (1998) investigated success on the basis of number of hits, visits, and orders. This study investigates specific success factors within the categories of organizational character-istics, management issues, and implementation issues.

The research model is presented in Figure 1. Certain organizational characteristics have been identified as contributing to the success of an e-commerce project as identified in the figure. The existence of IT expertise has a positive impact on the success of a project (Hamill & Gregory, 1997) and is something that is often deficient in SMEs (Pollard & Hayne, 1998). The second organizational trait, previous experience with logistics, is important, as logistics are often the difference between e-commerce success and failure (Wilson, 1999). Improvements in logistics was one of the major factors contributing to the first quarterly profit report by Amazon.com (Hof, 2002). The Internet and the World Wide Web will change distribution like no other environmental force since the industrial revolution (Pitt, 1999), as it can help to reduce the need for high inventories through better information, reduce delivery costs, and provide instant delivery of products and services (Kiang, Raghu, & Shang, 2000). The third organizational factor—the traits of a product—arises due to the fact that the Internet is effective for the distribution of symbolic, informational, or knowledge services, but it is extremely ineffective for the distribution of matter dependent on physically embodied services (Berthon, Pitt, Katsikeas, & Berthon, 1999). In addition, the Internet can realistically reproduce only two of our five senses, namely, sight and sound. This limitation restricts the kind of products that are sellable on the Internet (Kiang et al., 2000).

The successful completion of an e-commerce project requires management input. The first management issue is the need for a champion. Poon and Swatman (1997) found in their research that management enthusiasm for Internet adoption was common among SMEs. They found that often the director or a senior partner could see the potential the Internet offers to his/her business and plays an active role in adopting the technology. Such managers play a similar role to that of product champion, illustrated by Runge and Earl (1988). A second management issue of primary importance is the need for a formal e-commerce strategy. DeCovny (1998), Teubner and Klein (1998), and Williams (1999) have all commented that many companies have failed to succeed on the Internet due to the lack of a thought-through e-commerce strategy. They may be aware of the importance

Figure 1: Research Model

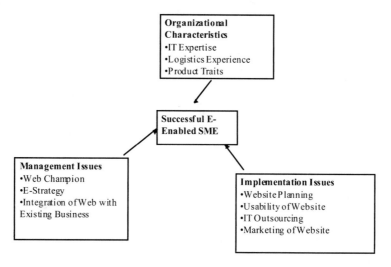

of IT, but do not realize the full range of benefits that Internet strategies can provide (Dandridge & Levenburg, 2000). They do not foresee the effort that goes into maintaining a website, the increased competition from exposure to a 'global market', and the impact a website will have on the existing business (Loebbecke, Powell, & Gallagher, 1999). The third management issue is the need to integrate business and Web-based activities. IS and business integration is seen as a critical success factor in ensuring the potential of IT is delivered to an organization (Earl, 1989; Ward & Griffiths, 1996). This integration enables IS to support business strategies more effectively (Teo & King, 1997). The necessity for integration of IS systems and their alignment with corporate strategies has been acknowledged as applicable to Internet activities (Elliot, 2000).

The third set of factors identified in the research model are implementation issues. The first of these is the need to plan the website. Competitors who spend the time and effort designing well-thought-out websites will most likely gain from the mistakes made by businesses that proceed without planning (Van Doren, Fechner, & Green-Adelsberger, 2000). Indeed, the difference between Web success and Web failure often hinges on how carefully people sift through details and fine tune trivial plans (Brown & Fox, 1999).

The second implementation issue is website usability. Usability consists of the issues of whether Web pages are easy to read, easy to browse, and subjectively pleasing (Nielsen, 1995, 2000). The promise of electronic commerce and online shopping depends to a great extent on user interfaces and how people interact with computers (Hoque & Lohse, 1999). Increasing customer demands, intensive competition, the speed at which Web technology is occurring, and the rapid increase in the numbers of users are all augmenting the challenges for designing usable and useful commercial websites (Vassilopoulou, Keeling, Macaulay, & McGoldrick, 2000). In addition to usability, the website needs to demonstrate to users that it is secure. The lack of such site security features prevents the conducting of commerce online (Hoffman, Novak, & Peralta, 1999).

SMEs usually do not have the capacity to develop and manage their own system and must therefore rely heavily on outsourcing (Ballintine, Levy, & Powell, 1998; Blili & Raymond, 1993). This lack of control over their informational resources increases the level of risk, especially where these resources are used for both operational and strategic purposes (Blili & Raymond, 1993) as they are in e-commerce-based systems.

A clear promotional strategy is critical in justifying a website (Van Doren et al., 2000). A site needs to be marketed properly in order to ensue high access. This can be done in various ways, including registering the site with all online search engines, establishing reciprocal cross-linkages to other sites, and ensuring the URL address is used in all company correspondence (Hamill & Gregory, 1997; Zarowin, 2000; Thelwell, 2000).

Success Factors for E-Enabled SMEs

The objective of the research is to investigate the factors that influence the degree of success of an e-commerce project. A purposive or judgmental sampling technique was used in which examples of best-practice projects were sought. In order to be eligible for inclusion in this study, the company had to be accredited for their use of the Internet in their businesses. Such accreditation was deemed to have been given if the company was nominated for an award for excellence in Web design or e-commerce implementation. In Ireland, a number of sources provide such awards—the government enterprise development agency, an Internet directory company, and the business and technical press. In addition, most of these awards have a specific category for SMEs. From these lists an initial prospective sample of 55 companies was compiled.

However, given that the purpose of the research was to investigate the implementation success factors for best-practice companies, further refinement of the sampling frame was carried out. This refinement involved reviewing and assessing the Web presence of each of the 55 companies on the basis of predefined criteria set down in a structured evaluation form. The purpose of this appraisal was to investigate and rank the extent, scope, and comprehensiveness of the online offering of each company. The main criteria used in the assessment were usability and design, the extent of the content provided, and the degree of interactivity and personalization on the website. The total aggregate score for each of the individual websites was then used to rank the companies and to guide the selection of companies for the research.

In-depth interviews were conducted with the person deemed to be most knowledgeable on the e-commerce developments within the 25 selected companies. On average, the interviews lasted one hour and were recorded using a Dictaphone. These interviews were conducted using a semi-structured questionnaire. Two of the questions obtained data on the average number of site visits per week and the average turnover generated from the website. These two measures were then used as success measures to allow comparisons between the 25 companies interviewed.

The companies operate in a variety of different sectors: eight computer-related services/software development, eight professional services and consulting, seven retail, and two distribution/wholesaler. All were SMEs, with the average number of employees being 18; 64% were traditional companies who had established a Web presence, the remainder were start-ups that have come into existence due to the opportunities presented by the Internet. Sixty percent are business-to-consumer and the remainder are business-to-business.

None of the companies have less than 500 visits to their Web pages per week: 28% had between 501 and 2,000, and the remaining 72% had greater than 5,000. Seventy-six percent have an average monthly turnover (directly related to the website) in excess of € 6,350, 8% have between € 1,271-€ 6,349, and 16% between € 0-€ 1,270. The main strategic thrust of the Web presence of the companies, as categorized by Timmers (1998), is presented in Figure 2.

Organizational Characteristics

The research found that organizational characteristics, as identified in Table 1, have a positive impact on the success of the e-commerce project. The table presents the mean and standard deviation for the number (n) of companies that answered each particular question. Some of the 25 companies interviewed did not answer specific questions, because the particular characteristic or issue was not applicable to them.

Figure 2: E-Commerce Strategies of Companies

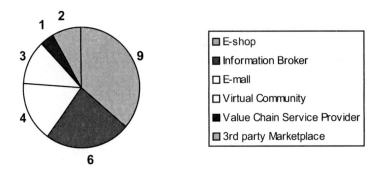

All of the companies believe that their product offerings have a positive impact on the success of their e-business. The traits of such products, as identified by the companies, are that they are: information rich (56%), customizable (32%), tangible (28%), unique (no competing product) (24%), Web-based (20%), and digitally based (20%) products. Companies with information-rich products are using the Web to make searching for their products online easier. Customizable products and tangible products do extremely well, as the Web provides a global market for these products that was prohibitively expensive to market to, prior to the advent of the Internet as a marketing channel. Digitally based products capitalize on the new medium of the Web, as they can be updated quickly, delivered promptly, and paid for instantly.

Previous exposure to technology was only applicable to 16 of the participating companies; the other nine had come into existence as a result of the opportunities presented by the Internet. Fourteen of these 16 described themselves as technologically competent. The positive benefits of this competency included the ability to introduce e-commerce more easily into the business and the ability to utilize the Web to a greater capacity.

Only nine companies had a remote order and delivery service prior to their Web presence. Previous experience with logistics was deemed to have a positive effect on the success of the website. In particular, such prior experience enables companies to be more efficient in their delivery mechanisms, as they had learned from their past experience that customers wanted an efficient service with speedy delivery, the next day if possible. As these companies moved onto the Web, they sought to convert their existing delivery

Table 1: Organizational Characteristics

Organizational Characteristics	Mean*	S.D.	n
Suitability of product for sale on the WWW	1.12	.33	25
Previous IT Expertise	1.43	.65	14
Previous experience with Logistics	1.33	.71	9

*Had a positive impact on your firms success on the Web

1=Strongly Agree, 2=Agree, 3=Neutral, 4= Disagree, 5=Strongly Disagree

Table 2: Management Issues

Management Issues	Mean*	S.D.	n
Presence of a Web champion	1.22	.33	23
Existence of an E-business strategy	1.39	.98	18
Integration of business and web activities	1.14	.36	21

*Had a positive impact on your firms success on the Web

1=Strongly Agree, 2=Agree, 3=Neutral, 4= Disagree, 5=Strongly Disagree

mechanisms to be Web enabled. In so doing, they made these systems more efficient by reducing labor costs and also reducing the amount of time to fulfill customer orders. This is achieved by using online order forms—which means that in effect the customer does the data entry. For existing retail outlets that already exported globally through mail order, their Web presence made them more efficient by replacing communication mechanisms like telephone, fax, and conventional post.

Management Issues

The importance of management in a successful e-business was reiterated in this research. The management issues identified in Table 2 were all found to have a positive impact on the success of the e-commerce project.

Ninety-two percent had a designated person in charge of the development of the website, with the other 8% preferring a team-based approach. The most important trait of the Web champion, as identified by 76% of companies, was that he/she conceived and drove the idea for the site. The rationale for this was typified by one manager as: "Having somebody in charge of the site made a big difference in terms of our commercial success, as he was driving the site and looking at it as a business in itself." As well as driving the project, the Web champions were seen to be working hard to bring the project to fruition, and this had a positive impact on the perceived importance of the project. In addition to being the torchbearer for the site, the Web champions performed other tasks that were deemed important contributions to the success of the site. At a project management level, they set deadlines and targets, and created the specification for the project if it was going to be outsourced. In addition, 16% of companies identified the importance of the role of the Web champion in promoting the website internally. While this only represents four companies, it is still noteworthy given that the average size of these companies was 18 employees. Thus, even within small companies where communication is normally more fluid, the need to communicate new projects remains important.

Seventy-six percent of the companies had a formal e-commerce strategy and believe that the presence of such a strategy has a positive impact on the success of their Web presence. The remainder had no formal e-commerce strategy in place and consequently were not asked to rate the impact on the success of their websites. A formal strategy was more common among the pure-player Internet companies. Accordingly, the formal e-commerce plan would also be the business plan. Within these plans, specific strategic objectives were outlined. One example of this, identified by 24% of the companies, was the desire to become the number one site for a certain market segment.

The common view of those companies that did not have a formal e-commerce strategy was that such a prescribed strategy is not worth documenting due to the fluid nature of the environment. However, these companies have an e-commerce strategy that is emergent and responsive to the successes and problems encountered. The initial objective for the majority was to establish a brochure-ware site through which it was possible to provide low-cost and speedy communication with customers, and to gain access to an increased number of customers. Having "tested the waters of e-commerce" and being successful, most have evolved their sites to include more interactive elements and, as a result of this, evolved into online sales. This evolutionary strategic process is ongoing, according to one manager: "We are constantly changing what our objectives are. The Web is moving so fast, customers dictate what you do going forward, so it's really just dictated by what they want."

The majority agreed that the integration of their business and Web activities contributed to their success. Seventy-six percent were thoroughly integrated, while 8% were somewhat integrated. For the remaining 16%, the concept of integration did not apply, as they were totally online businesses. The importance of integration is summed up by the manager of a third-party marketplace who felt that it was "…essential, I couldn't over emphasize that. The Web is only as strong as the back up you have behind it."

The benefits that such integration brought include: increased efficiency (40%), better use of customer information (20%), and the ability to better "exploit the potential" of e-commerce (20%). Efficiency manifested itself in the ability to run the business more cost effectively due to the seamless transfer of data through all functions of the organization. Better use of customer information included analyzing such information as site statistics, e-mail, and customer feedback forms.

Implementation Issues

Attention to detail in the planning, design, and ongoing maintenance of the e-business project are important characteristics of best practice (Liu & Arnett, 2000). The implementation issues featured in Table 3 were identified by companies as contributing positively to the success of their e-commerce project.

Ninety-two percent believe that planning the website had a positive impact on success. The key benefits that such planning brought about were the ability to better serve the intended website audience—the customer—and a more focused approach. In terms of meeting the needs of the intended audience, companies felt that planning had meant they had a site that had a purpose to it and was not just keeping up with the times. Planning resulted in a more focused approach being adopted in a number of areas: firstly, companies gained competitive intelligence and ideas by investigating other companies' websites; secondly, the planning process provided a "roadmap to proceed"; and thirdly, it enabled them to better exploit e-commerce. An example of gaining competitive intelligence was given by a travel company that found out as a result of their research that 80% of tourists came from four to five different markets. As a result of this, the

Table 3: Implementation Issues

Implementation Issues	Mean*	S.D.	n
Website planning	1.13	.34	24
Ease of use of the website	1.00	.00	25
Security on the website	1.78	.85	23
Outsourcing of tasks specific to the website	1.96	1.16	24
Marketing of the website			
• Registration with search engines	1.72	1.06	25
• Linking with other sites	1.60	.94	20
• Publication of URL on promotional material	1.20	.50	25

Had a positive impact on your firm's success on the Web 1=Strongly Agree, 2=Agree, 3=Neutral, 4= Disagree, 5=Strongly Disagree

company set up individual sites for these markets, and thus opened up new markets and increased their market share. The planning process provided a roadmap in the sense that companies felt that after the planning process, they knew what to do and had learned from the experience of planning.

All the interviewees strongly agreed that the ease of use of the site positively impacted on their success on the Web. Indeed, usability is perceived among them as being more important than the actual presentation of the site. The key components of good site design include ease of use, speed of access, information content, and site interactivity.

Ease of use was created and measured in different ways: by adhering to the three-click rule, by using customer feedback to elicit improvements to the site, by formal usability techniques, and by informal usability tests among employees. Companies improved speed of access by avoiding the use of flash techniques and heavy graphics. Information content was a critical component in the implementation of site design. The commercial director of one company went so far as to say, "The information itself is more important than the design of the site." Forty percent of companies indicated that they wanted the site to project a certain image of the company and, in particular, 12% wanted the site to emphasize that there was a real business "behind the site, with real people involved in order to project a favorable image." The owner-manager of an e-mall claimed that, when people log onto their site, they "identify your company with the Web page; it's a portrayal of your company, so it's extremely important, obviously, to have it looking brilliant." Information content was also dependent on the type of business. For sites that have a large level of content, like e-malls and information brokers, searchable features such as keywords were important. Meanwhile, sites that ask customers for personal information identified trustworthiness as an important feature of site design. Twelve percent of companies sought to create a particular image for the site that was in keeping with the niche target market they were serving—for example invoking an "Irish theme" to their site, by the use of green and white.

All of the sites provided security features. Sixty-eight percent believe that site security positively impacts on their success, while 32% felt it made no difference to their success. Forty percent of the companies, however, believe that security was a prerequisite because customers expected it to be there. The companies participating in this research felt that this requirement was even more pronounced for them as they had all been cited as e-commerce success stories. Twenty-four percent were adamant that security was crucial. These were companies that either carried out transactions or required visitors to divulge a lot of personal details. For them, it was imperative to have secure features displayed in order to ensure that visitors would go on to conduct business with them. For example, the owner-manager of an online retailer claimed that "people will not give their credit card details unless they see the padlock at end of the page." Another reason why security is crucial is to minimize the risk of losing a customer: the manager of a third-party marketplace pointed out that if a security breach occurred, "you will never get your customer back."

The outsourcing of IT capabilities is becoming increasingly popular due to the anticipated benefits of reduced operating costs, improved efficiency, access to IT expertise, and the achievement of flexibility in managing IT resources (Jurison, 1995). Sixty-eight percent of the participating companies thought that outsourcing had a positive impact on their success, while 12% felt it made no impact, and 6% didn't think it had a positive impact. The extent of outsourcing varied depending on the task: 88% outsourced hosting, 48% outsourced design, 36% outsourced maintenance. There seems to be a trend to take some aspects back in-house as the website matures, e.g., 16% of companies have elected to take back design and 12% electing to take back maintenance. This was not because they had experienced any problems with outsourcing, but rather their website became such an integral part of their business that they had to take on someone full time or train an employee in-house to manage it.

Companies chose to outsource hosting because it provided access to expertise, was more cost effective, and benefited from the support and reliability of the outsourcing company. The decision to outsource design and maintenance was taken by 28% of companies simply because they had no in-house expertise in the area. This, however, was not seen as a problem for companies; rather they used the requirement to acquire expert advice. The owner of a software company said, "When you are aiming to be the best in the world, you [have] got to have that brainpower and that expertise. We decided to go to world-class designers who had extensive Web experience and use those to put an international level of design on the site, and that strategy has proven to be effective." For 12%, speed to market was their main reason for outsourcing.

All of the companies have a good working relationship with their outsourcing partner. For some this has been achieved by changing the outsourcing partner, as they were not happy with the sites they were producing. Although outsourcing may have been expensive, these companies felt it was cheaper in the long run, because it was less expensive in comparison with the cost of training someone in-house or ending up making costly mistakes by trying to build the site in-house initially.

An important part of any Web implementation is the marketing of the website once it is established. This research investigates the impact of three promotion techniques: registration with search engines, linking with other websites, and publication of the site's URL. Seventy-two percent of the participating companies believe that registration with search engines enhanced their success, 20% felt it made no impact, and 8% disagreed. The key reason for being listed on the search engines is visibility. The owner of one e-shop remarked, "You have to be on that list; if you are not on that list, somebody else will be there." The perceived importance of listings on search engines was more pronounced in total e-commerce businesses, compared to clicks-and-bricks businesses. Those who believe that search engine listings do not positively influence success were predominantly clicks-and-bricks businesses that used alternative means such as trade shows or advertisements in industry magazines to promote their URLs.

Eighty percent use external links, while 20% do not. Of the companies that agreed that linking had a positive impact on their success, 36% felt they had benefited because linking gave them greater access to their target audience. This was because they felt they were benefiting from having additional entrances to their site. Thirty-two percent thought that the links gave them greater credibility, for example in linking them to high-profile sites. The third benefit of external links was by providing relevant content for customers. The companies that were more inclined to link included virtual communities, information brokers, e-malls, and third-party marketplaces. In contrast, there are those who make a conscious effort not to link to other sites. This was prominent among the e-shops, which didn't want their customers going into another site where they might be likely to purchase something. They were also the sites that mentioned "trustworthiness" as an important feature of site design. They believed that the absence of external links kept their site more authentic and trustworthy.

Ninety-six percent of the interviewees agreed that publicizing their URLs contributed to their success. Companies use a variety of promotional techniques to publicize their URLs—press releases, company stationery, trade shows, and radio/TV advertising. In fact, 20% of the participating businesses believe that traditional media is better than online promotional means.

Conclusion

This research had, as its sampling frame, companies that have created successful websites. The firms investigated included both existing companies and newly formed Internet companies, all of whom were successfully e-enabled, customer-focused SMEs utilizing the Web to deliver their products or services more efficiently and effectively. All made extensive use of planning at both the strategic and implementation levels in order to ensure the success of their project. At a strategic level, there was a clear emphasis on integrating the Web activities into the main business activities. This took either the form of a formalized e-commerce strategy or a more fluid, organic strategy. In planning their e-projects, all had either a single person or a team of people who had responsibility for the project.

For the pre-existing participating companies, IT expertise and knowledge of logistics was an additional factor for ensuring success. Most often, previous IT-expertise-provided knowledge was used in formulating and developing the proposed e-business project, but not necessarily in developing the system in-house. In common with other studies on SMEs, a deficiency in IT expertise was found to prevent the companies implementing e-commerce solutions without external assistance. This shortfall, however, was not seen as a negative; rather it provided the possibility for these companies to strategically outsource components of their website design and development. Having the right product—one that suited the Internet—was critical to success. All devoted considerable time, energy, and commitment to creating and implementing websites that would meet their stated objectives. Achieving this involved careful planning of the website, ensuring that the site was not only easy to use but also provided security features, and was promoted via electronic and traditional means.

This research emphasizes the need for future empirical research on the factors that contribute to Web success for SMEs. Although this research was empirical in nature, it was limited to 25 purposefully chosen case studies and as such, further research is required to test the generalizability of the results. This research primarily investigated the use of the Web as a new marketing channel by SMEs, whereas future research could adopt a broader perspective.

References

Ballintine, J., Levy, M., & Powell, P. (1998). Evaluating information systems in small and medium-sized enterprises: Issues and evidence. *European Journal of Information Systems, 7*(4), 241-251.

Berthon, P., Pitt, L., Katsikeas, C.S., & Berthon, J.P. (1999). Executive insights: Virtual services go international: International services in the marketspace. *Journal of International Marketing, 7*(3), 84-105.

Blili, S., & Raymond, L. (1993). Information technology: Threats and opportunities for small and medium sized enterprises. *International Journal of Information Management, 13,* 439-448.

Brown, E., & Fox, J. (1999). 9 ways to win on the web. *Fortune, 139*(10), 112-125.

Cairncross, F. (1997). *The Death of Distance: How the Communications Revolution will Change Our Lives* (1st ed.). Boston, MA: Harvard Business School Press.

Dandridge, T., & Levenburg, N.M. (2000). High-tech potential? An exploratory study of very small firms' usage of the Internet. *International Small Business Journal, 18*(2), 81-91.

DeConvy, S. (1998). Electronic commerce comes of age. *The Journal of Business Strategy, 19*(6), 38-44.

Earl, M.J. (1989). *Management Strategies for Information Technology.* London: Prentice-Hall International.

Elliot, S.R. (2000). Towards a framework for evaluation of commercial websites. *Proceedings of the 13th International Bled Electronic Commerce Conference,* Bled, Slovenia (June 19-21).

Golden, W. (1996). E-commerce @ work: Kennys Bookshop & Art Galleries, Galway Ireland: E-commerce for trade efficiency and effectiveness. *Proceedings of the 9th International Conference on EDI-IOS,* Bled, Slovenia (June 10-12, pp. 291-303).

Guthrie, R., & Austin, L. (1996). Competitive implications of the Internet. *Information Systems Management, 13*(3), 90-92.

Hamill, J., & Gregory, K. (1997). Internet marketing in the internationalisation of UK SMEs. *Journal of Marketing Management, 13,* 9-28.

Haynes, P.J., Becherer, R.C., & Helms, M.M. (1998). Small and mid-sized businesses and Internet use: Unrealized potential? *Internet Research, 8*(3), 229-235.

Hof, R.D. (1999). What every CEO needs to know about electronic business. *Business Week, 3631*(March 22).

Hof, R.D. (2002). How Amazon cleared that hurdle. *Business Week, 3768*(February 4).

Hoffman, D.L., Novak, T.P., & Peralta, M. (1999). Building consumer trust online. *Communications of the ACM, 42*(4), 80-85.

Hoque, A.Y., & Lohse, G.L. (1999). An information search cost perspective for designing interfaces for electronic commerce. *Journal of Marketing Research, 36*(3), 387-394.

Jurison, J. (1995). The role of risk and return in information technology outsourcing decisions. *Journal of Information Technology, 10*(4), 239-247.

Kiang, M.Y., Raghu, T.S., & Shang, K.H.-M. (2000). Marketing on the Internet: Who can benefit from an online marketing approach? *Decision Support Systems, 27*(4), 383-394.

Liu, C., & Arnett, K.P. (2000). Exploring the factors associated with website success in the context of electronic commerce. *Information and Management, 38*(1), 23-33.

Loebbecke, C., Powell, P., & Gallagher, C. (1999). Buy the book: Electronic commerce in the book trade. *Journal of Information Technology, 14*(3), 295-301.

Nielsen, J. (1995). *Multimedia and Hypertext: The Internet and Beyond.* Boston, MA: AP Professional.

Nielsen, J. (2000). *Designing Web Usability.* Indianapolis, IN: New Riders.

O'Connor, G.C., & O'Keefe, B. (1997). Viewing the Web as a marketplace: The case of small companies. *Decision Support Systems, 21*(3), 171-183.

O'Keefe, R.M., & McEachern, T. (1998). Web-based customer decision support systems. *Communications of the ACM, 41*(3), 71-78.

Palmer, J.W., & Griffith, D.A. (1998). An emerging model of website design for marketing. *Communications of the ACM, 41*(3), 44-51.

Pitt, L., Berthon, P., & Berthon, J.-P. (1999). Changing channels: The impact of the Internet on distribution strategy. *Business Horizons,* (March/April).

Pollard, C.E., & Hayne, S.C. (1998). The changing face of information system issues in small firms. *International Small Business Journal, 16*(3), 70-85.

Poon, S., & Swatman, P.M.C. (1997). Small business use of the Internet. *International Marketing Review, 14*(5), 385-402.

Poon, S., & Swatman, P.M.C. (1998). A combined-method study of small business Internet commerce. *International Journal of Electronic Commerce, 2*(3), 31-46.

Quelch, J., & Klein, L.R. (1996). The Internet and international marketing. *Sloan Management Review, 37*(3), 60-75.

Runge, D.A., & Earl, M.J. (1988). Gaining competitive advantage from telecommunications. In M.J. Earl (Ed.), *Information Management: A Strategic Perspective.* Oxford: Oxford University Press.

Teo, T.S.H., & King, W.R. (1997). Integration between business planning and information systems planning: An evolutionary-contingency perspective. *Journal of Management Information Systems, 14*(1), 185-214.

Teubner, R.A., & Klein, S. (1998). Planning and designing Web-based electronic commerce: A case study in the insurance industry. *Australian Journal of Information Systems*, (November), 86-96.

Thelwall, M. (2000). Effective websites for small and medium-sized enterprises. *Journal of Small Business and Enterprise Development, 7*(2), 149-160.

Timmers, P. (1998). Business models for electronic markets. *Electronic Markets, 8*(2), 3-8.

Van Doren, D.C., Fechner, D.L., & Green-Adelsberger, K. (2000). Promotional strategies on the World Wide Web. *Journal of Marketing Communications, 6*(1), 21-36.

Vassilopoulou, K., Keeling, K., Macaulay, L.A., & McGoldrick, P. (2000). Identifying a usability evaluation technique by following an SME-centred approach. *Proceedings of the 13th International Bled Electronic Commerce Conference,* Bled, Slovenia (June 19-21).

Ward, J., & Griffiths, P. (1996). *Strategic Planning for Information Systems* (2nd ed.). Chichester, UK: John Wiley & Sons.

Watson, R.T., Akselsen, S., & Leylan, F.P. (1998). Attractors: Building mountains in the flat landscape of the World Wide Web. *California Management Review, 40*(2), 37-56.

Williams, J. (1999). E-commerce and the inevitability of failure. *Information Technology Management, 3*(3), 95-100.

Wilson, T. (1999). Shippers repackeged as e-providers. *Information Week*, (758), 65-83.

Zarowin, S. (2000). How to make your debut on the Internet. *Journal of Accountancy,* 23-26.

Section VII

E-Commerce in the Supply Chain in SMEs

Chapter XI

Assessing the Impact of E-Commerce on SMEs in Value Chains: A Qualitative Approach

Judith Jeffcoate, University of Buckingham, UK

Caroline Chappell, The Trefoyle Partnership, UK

Sylvie Feindt, SFC, Germany

Abstract

This chapter is intended as a contribution to the establishment of a theoretical foundation for the e-commerce field. Our specific contribution to methodology is through the description of a qualitative approach based on multiple case studies across industry and country boundaries. This has enabled us to propose an analytical framework that will identify the triggers for value chain transformation that will encourage SMEs to adopt e-commerce. The chapter describes seven elements that make up this framework, including the automation of value activity interactions between partners in the value chain. These elements form the basis for a discussion of future trends.

Introduction

Knowledge Information Transfer Systems (KITS) was designed as a support action for small and medium-sized enterprises (SMEs) in Europe and funded by the European Commission. It included a research program whose aim was to analyze the activities of SMEs engaged in industry value chain relationships with suppliers and customers in order to establish best practice. An SME in this context is a company that employs fewer than 250 people. The research program for KITS included two main work packages: the first looked at individual companies, while the second looked at evaluation across the value chain. This chapter, which is based on the first of these packages, proposes an analytical framework that is designed to identify the triggers for value chain transformation that will encourage SMEs to adopt e-commerce.

The analytical framework draws on key concepts proposed by a number of authors. It consists of the following elements:

- Type of industry value chain, based on four types proposed by Baldock (1999): customer-centric, seller-driven, buyer-driven, or fragmented

- Stability of position within industry value chain, based on the number and type of customers/suppliers and customer/supplier churn (Yli-Renko & Autio, 1998)

- Level of penetration of electronic links with customers and suppliers, covering network connections, support for information exchange, the use of applications, and external services

- Complexity of automation of the internal IT environment, based on a classification proposed by Lockett and Brown (2001)

- Key value activities (Porter, 1984; Chu, 1995), extended to cover interactions between value activities

- Complexity of automation of value activity interactions, extending the Lockett and Brown classification to e-commerce solutions deployed in the industry value chain

- Level of achievable impact on the industry value chain, using a new four-level impact model

This chapter describes our findings under each of these headings and draws some conclusions about future trends.

Background

Our research was based on multiple case studies, using semi-structured interview guides. Case studies have been identified as a suitable strategy for research when a 'how' or 'why' question is being asked about a contemporary set of events over which the investigator has little or no control (Yin, 1994). They have been used extensively in social science research. However, they are also popular in other areas, including information systems (IS). There are three reasons to use a strategy based on case research in this context. Firstly, it allows us to study IS in a natural setting, learn the state of the art, and generate theories from practice. Secondly, we can answer the questions that lead to understanding the nature and complexity of the processes taking place. Finally, it is an appropriate way to research a previously little-studied area. Each of these reasons is applicable to the research program described in this chapter. Indeed, one of the areas in which case research is most useful is the relationship between information technology and corporate strategy—precisely the area that is crucial to the development of e-commerce.

A number of researchers have already adopted multiple cases for studies of SMEs in e-commerce or related areas. For example, Poon and Swatman (1997) studied 23 small businesses in Australia that were active Internet users in order to establish the pre-conditions for success and the strategic effects from its use. Multiple case studies were created based on interviews and site visits. Each interview lasted about an hour and was carried out by using a set of open-ended questions as a guide to avoid drifting from research fact. These authors draw a clear distinction between surveys designed to capture quantitative data, which are ideal for identifying the attitudes and activities of larger samples, and a qualitative case study approach that would help to understand the current and future activities of the SME sector. They note that case studies are suitable for areas in which research and theory are at their early formative stages and for sticky practice-based problems where the experiences of the actors are important and the context of action is critical. Furthermore, they report that the majority of researchers undertaking analysis of inter-organizational systems (IOSs) make use of single- or multiple-case studies, using interviews to gather data.

Other researchers in this area have relied on much smaller numbers of case studies, typically fewer than 10. Iacovou, Benbasat, and Dexter (1995) carried out interviews on the adoption of electronic data interchange (EDI) with the managers of seven SMEs that were suppliers to the British Columbia government. They used structured interview guides to ensure consistency and reliability. These guides included several open format questions to allow the participants flexibility in their responses. Another study of the effect of EDI on a sample of eight small businesses in the UK (Chen & Williams, 1998) was based on in-depth interviews with key personnel.

In contrast, our research was to be applicable across national and sectoral boundaries. This made it necessary to adopt a larger sample (43) than those of the qualitative studies described above. Telephone interviews were therefore used, rather than field visits. In all other ways, the approach adopted was consistent with previous practice in this area. Senior analysts, each of whom had many years' experience of such techniques as well as substantial domain knowledge, carried out the interviews. However, this imposed some limitations on the study: interviews were mainly restricted to the home countries of the interviewers (e.g., Germany, Italy, and the UK) so that they could be carried out in the native language of the interviewer and respondent as much as possible.

The sample consisted of European SMEs that are actively involved in business-to-business (B2B) e-commerce. The research focused primarily on traditional SMEs with some level of automation, with a secondary focus on e-commerce start-ups (the 'dot.coms'). The following criteria were important in selecting industry sectors:

Table 1: Companies by Sector and Country

	Manufacturing	Transport and logistics	Retail/wholesale	Business services	Total
Germany	7	3	1	3	14
Austria		1			1
Switzerland				1	1
Belgium			1		1
Italy	12	1	1		14
Sweden	1				1
UK	5	1	3	2	11
Total	**25**	**6**	**6**	**6**	**43**

- Size (in terms of value of production)
- Structure characterized by the presence of a relatively high number of SMEs
- Type of relationships with suppliers, subcontractors, distributors, and/or final customers

Companies were classified into three groups: micro (one to nine employees), small (10-99 employees), and medium (100-249 employees). We adopted the four sectors shown in Table 1, all of which have high numbers of SMEs and are potentially sensitive to value chain transformation.

The interview program was carried out between September 2000 and January 2001. All of the respondents had board-level responsibility. They varied from managing directors in the smaller companies to IT, operations, and marketing directors in the larger organizations. It was felt that, in an SME, only one point of view is necessary, providing it is at a high enough level within the organization.

The interviews were conducted using a semi-structured questionnaire that included both open and closed questions. The initial conceptual framework was adapted from one proposed by Ward and Griffiths (1996) for determining the strategic potential of information systems and establishing priorities for investment. Their framework takes a structured analytical route through the upper levels of the organization. It is closely linked to the industry value chain as well as to the organizational value chain, and was thus particularly appropriate for KITS. The following topics were covered: company background; strategy, objectives, and critical success factors; value chain partnerships and activities; use of technology.

The Analytical Framework

A value chain is defined by Porter (1984) as a collection of activities that are performed by a company to design, produce, market, deliver, and support its product. Other authors refer to this as the internal value chain of a company or organizational value chain, in contrast to the industry value chain. The latter consists of the organizational value chain, together with the value chains of the organization's competitors, suppliers, and customers. It represents the movement of goods and services from the source of raw materials through to the final customer (Benjamin & Wigand, 1995).

Type of Value Chain

An SME's perception of its value chain is important because it influences the company's strategy and therefore its e-commerce strategy. As a starting point for our analysis, we therefore classified the companies in the sample as participating in one of four types of value chains defined by Baldock (1999):

- *Customer-centric value chain:* The seller tailors its products to meet fast-changing consumer needs.

- *Seller-driven value chain:* The seller presumes to know what the market might want to buy.

- *Buyer-driven value chain:* The customer states what he or she wants, and sets out the terms and conditions that the supplier should meet.

- *Fragmented value chain:* Neither the buyer nor the seller business model dominates.

We identified 25 companies in the sample as being in customer-centric value chains. The majority of these believe that they need to become more customer-focused to meet the needs of such a value chain. They want to understand customers' needs better and more quickly, and, if possible, be proactive in meeting them. Such SMEs come from a variety of sectors, many of which—automotive, electronics, home furnishings, and tourism—serve fast-moving consumer markets. Others, for example in industrial automation and office automation, are becoming increasingly competitive, emphasizing the need for customer service. All the logistics companies in the sample were strongly customer-driven. They also perceived the need to respond to customer demand for new services.

Only three companies in the sample were in seller-driven value chains. One was a German association in the food-processing sector. The other two SMEs were in the medical sector. Their (indirect) customers are hospitals and health services, which are typically strongly price conscious. They do not specify the products they will buy, but are led by the products on offer, usually from multinational pharmaceutical companies. These two small biotech manufacturers are therefore relatively unusual in the sector and heavily dependent on powerful distributors—national wholesalers of medical supplies. Both are employing e-commerce to maintain these relationships: their focus is arguably customer-centric, even if the whole value chain is not.

The sole example of a buyer-driven chain was an SME that serves the construction industry. In its market, customers are king: they dictate the terms and conditions and prices that they will pay, and small suppliers either accept them or leave them. The strength of buyers is increasing and the SME is finding that geographical proximity to work is no longer an advantage as customers centralize procurement to drive prices down. A feature of buyer-driven value chains is that they require alliances between value chain partners that bring complementary capabilities, product sets, or geographic coverage, to meet buyers' needs.

Around a third of the sample (14) were in fragmented value chains, including textile manufacturers. Here, energetic groups of SMEs, such as an Italian association of knitwear producers, can gain economies of scale by working together, and win some influence with customers as a result of presenting a 'larger' interface than the companies would individually.

Stability of Position Within Value Chain

Partnerships form the backbone of the KITS research. Our questions focused on the upstream and downstream links that SMEs have with their business partners in the industry value chain. The objectives were to discover how many of these links each company had and why they were of significance. The strength, intensity, and permanence of these links are important in determining how deeply these SMEs are embedded in their networks (Yli-Renko & Autio, 1998).

Relationships with Customers

The majority of the SMEs in the KITS value chains reported stable relationships with customers that had lasted for a number of years. Among the less stable exceptions are e-marketplaces, which are in the process of building up customer and supplier bases. Other examples included SMEs in the Italian textile industry, which has a high 'churn' (turnover) rate of customers and suppliers due to the demands of high fashion, an Italian packaging supplier, and an Italian electronics component supplier. The latter two companies have particularly low levels of turnover among suppliers and customers. The medium-sized packaging supplier has a respectable-sized customer base (800), but claims that less than 2% regularly repeat their orders. Of its 200 suppliers, only 10% are regular.

Ten companies in the sample claim to have 1,000 customers or more, with an Italian office automation wholesaler claiming to have the highest number (6,000), although it is not clear whether these are all retail customers (resellers) or a total number of end-customers. An Italian salami company serves 5,000 retail outlets. Three of the logistics companies serve 1,000-2,000 customers, but one of these, an Austrian fuel transporter that complains of "fierce competition" in its market, only retains 30% of its customers on a regular basis. Six companies in this category claim that either all or the 'majority' of customers do repeat business with them, although the elapsed time between orders can vary from a few days, a few months, to a couple of years, depending on the product/service sold.

Sixteen companies in the sample had fewer than 100 customers. These are micro/small companies, all of which said that all or a large majority of relationships with customers were regular. This suggests that such companies currently have more stable customer bases than SMEs serving larger numbers of customers.

Relationships with Suppliers

The SMEs in the sample support similarly stable relationships with suppliers. However, they typically have far fewer suppliers than customers. Only two companies have more than 1,000 suppliers, an Italian pneumatics products manufacturer and the German association of farmers, which has 1,000 owner/member/suppliers. Sixty percent of the sample (26 companies) has fewer than 50 suppliers.

Most of the SMEs in the sample are highly loyal to their supplier base. While only 17 companies in the sample said that all their customers were regular buyers, 60% said that all their suppliers were regular. Italian companies again had the least stable supply chains, with two of the textile companies, the packaging supplier, and the electronics component manufacturer reporting supplier retention rates of less than 30%. The Italian wholesaler also retained only 17% of its suppliers on a regular basis.

A number of companies said they stayed with their suppliers because they could trust the quality of their products. In other cases, fear of losing control over the quality of supply was given as a reason for not implementing e-commerce with suppliers. Companies either did not feel the need to gain a wider choice of suppliers by changing procurement processes, or they wanted to check the quality of suppliers' goods in person before they would accept them. E-commerce-enabled just-in-time delivery or vendor-managed inventory was of little interest to such SMEs.

Level of Penetration of Electronic Links

We wanted to discover how the SME uses technologies to support the links with its business partners, and to what extent its success in the industry value chain depends on the technologies that it uses or adopts over time. Our questions covered network connections, support for information exchange, the use of applications (e.g., messaging, marketing), and of external services (e.g., value-added network service suppliers, application service providers, or Web hosting companies).

At present, the penetration of electronic links into the supplier and customer bases of these companies is low. Where such links exist, they are typically with a fraction of an SME's customer base: with key resellers or distribution partners, with one or two IT-literate customers. The electronic links are also typically being developed to secure and strengthen these relationships. As they proliferate through the customer and supplier base, however, the opposite effect may be achieved and more *ad hoc* relationships with value chain partners may develop.

Table 2: Electronic Links with Partners

Type of link	Number of companies
Suppliers only	4
Customers only	14
Both	10
None	15
Total	43

Electronic links with customers are more common and more extensive than electronic links with suppliers (Table 2), confirming that, in most cases, customers of these SMEs are larger and more e-commerce literate than suppliers. It is also consistent with the experience of larger companies that are automating their value chain activities. Fawcett and Magan (2001) report that most large U.S. companies surveyed are dedicating more resources to building strong customer relationships than to selecting and developing a world-class supply base.

Of the five SMEs with the highest customer churn rates (less than 50% of customers regularly re-order), only one has any electronic links with customers, and this is an Italian manufacturer which has links with 25 key distributors, out of 800 customers.

Complexity of Automation of IT Environment

It is widely agreed that SMEs are being held back from participating in B2B e-commerce by the fact that they lack suitable IT infrastructures to support it (Lockett & Brown, 2001). They may have Internet access for e-mail and hosted websites, but it is thought that few SMEs engage beyond this in B2B e-commerce and other more complex applications.

We assessed the complexity of the IT environment in each company, based on a classification system developed by Lockett and Brown (Table 3).

The assessment took into account:

- The type of applications and IT infrastructure the SME had in place, including legacy applications and network environment
- Whether applications were packages or proprietary developments
- The level of application complexity (as defined by Lockett and Brown)
- The nature of the links between applications (e-mail, intranet, extranet)

Table 3: Classification of E-Business Application Complexity

Proposed classification	Examples	Complexity
Communication	E-mail, Web access	Very low
Marketing	Website	Low
Productivity	MS Office, Intranet	Low
E-commerce	Buying and selling online	Medium
Collaborative	Extranet	Medium
Enterprise	Financials, SFA (sales force automation), vertical applications	High
Marketplace	e-marketplaces	High
Collaborative enterprise	eSCM (supply chain management), eCRM (customer relationship management)	Very high
Collaborative platform	Emerging platforms	Very high

More than a third of the sample (15 SMEs) does conform to the general perception that the lack of IT infrastructure is a barrier to SME e-commerce, with a complexity rating of "Very low." Eleven of these companies are among the 15 SMEs that do not have any electronic links with customers or suppliers (Table 2). The SMEs in this category have hosted websites for sales and marketing, but their internal IT infrastructure is not conducive to developing support for B2B e-commerce.

Another 10 companies, or nearly a third of the sample, have a complexity ranking of "Low." These companies do not necessarily automate more activities, but there is generally more integration between their activities: seven of these companies have an intranet, for example. In this category, activities are supported by small to mid-tier business packages or, in a number of cases, by proprietary systems, developed and extended in-house over a number of years.

Six of the companies in the KITS sample have a complexity rating of "Medium." Three of the logistics companies are in this category. Although two of them are likely to have advanced, Web-enabled IT systems, we have erred on the side of caution in classifying them, because it is difficult to verify that these in-house systems have been developed with the robustness of a commercial package. Other studies confirm that companies enjoying striking success with e-commerce have often developed their own solutions. Hawkins (2001) points out that "home-made systems appear not to damage the e-commerce prospects of firms and may even improve them by ensuring that technology investment and roll-out is linked to actual signals from the market."

Nine companies in the sample have a "High" complexity rating. The seven manufacturing companies in this category are using standard enterprise resource planning systems such as those supplied by SAP, or vertical applications, such as supply chain manage-ment or product data management, that are, or have the potential to be, Web enabled to support complex e-commerce. They are, with one exception, medium-sized companies.

The exception is the start-up Scandinavian manufacturer that, as a greenfield site, has been able to invest in an advanced IT infrastructure.

At least a third of the KITS sample has an IT infrastructure that can support relatively complex B2B e-commerce. A number of companies with lower complexity rankings are moving quickly towards this position.

Key Value Activities and Value Activity Interactions

The electronic links discussed above can link critical value activities internally and between value chain partners. A value activity is a physically and technologically distinct activity that the company performs and that adds value to a product or service (Porter, 1984). Critical value activities are those activities that an organization must execute satisfactorily to ensure successful performance (Chu, 1995). We wanted to establish the relative importance of these activities to the SMEs in our sample, using Porter's nine categories (Figure 1).

Respondents were asked to rank each activity on a scale from 1 to 5, where 1 was *unimportant* and 5 was *critical to the success of the company*. They were then asked whether the value activities that were rated 4 or 5 were automated in any way, for example, by an application running on a computer (Figure 2). They were also asked whether the activity was linked to other activities via an electronic network and, if so, whether these links were internal, external, or both.

We assumed that if an SME ranks a value activity as critical, then inputs and/or outputs to this activity which involve value chain partners will be a priority for automation. We therefore probed for e-commerce solutions that automate value activity interactions

Figure 1: The Value Chain

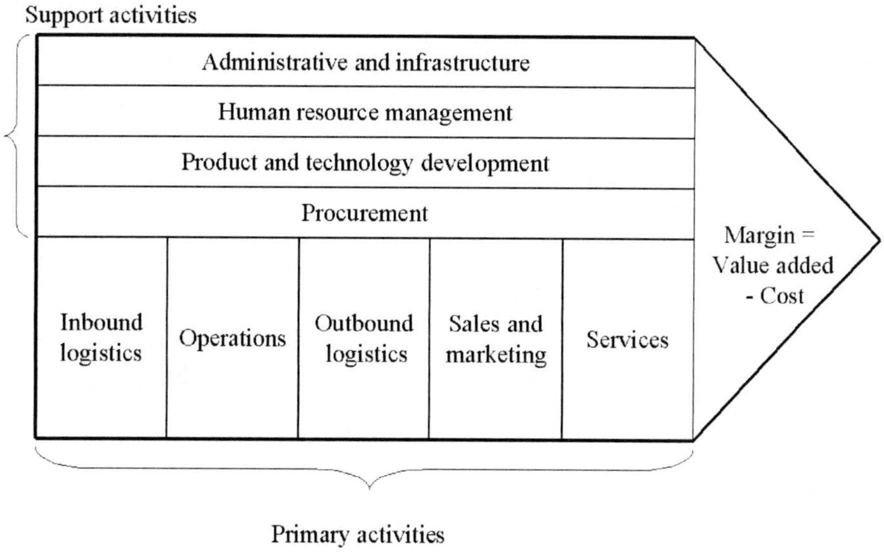

Support activities

Administrative and infrastructure	Margin = Value added - Cost
Human resource management	
Product and technology development	
Procurement	
Inbound logistics · Operations · Outbound logistics · Sales and marketing · Services	

Primary activities

(VAIs) between value chain partners—each SME's customers and suppliers. Most of the VAIs being supported with e-commerce solutions link SME primary value activities with customer/supplier primary activities.

By far the most widely supported value activity interaction is *Sales and marketing to Procurement.* All the SMEs in the sample have implemented a website with details of the company and its products. The majority of companies have such websites hosted for them by Internet service providers or Web design companies. Yet given the stability of most of the SMEs' value chains, and how few companies ranked sales and marketing as highly critical (16 SMEs), it is unclear how much value they are gaining from this e-commerce solution.

The second most supported VAI is *Outbound logistics to (customer) Procurement. Outbound logistics* was not, overall, rated quite as highly as *Operations.* However, the fact that so many companies have implemented online order processing suggests that they perceive this VAI to be important to customers, and that they will be better regarded by customers if they invest in it.

Inbound logistics is rated almost as highly as *Outbound logistics* [ratings tended to be critical (4), rather than highly critical (5) in more cases]. Furthermore, it is one of the most widely automated value activities in the sample, yet only four companies appear to be putting e-commerce solutions in place to support value activity interactions. This small number is, however, consistent with the SMEs' attitude towards and relationship with their suppliers.

The *Services* value activity is ranked highly by four of the five logistics companies in their customer-centric value chain, and by most of the retail/wholesale SMEs, but only five manufacturers regard it as highly critical. In terms of value activity interaction support, only one logistics company appears to have implemented an e-commerce solution in this

Figure 2: Automation of Value Activities

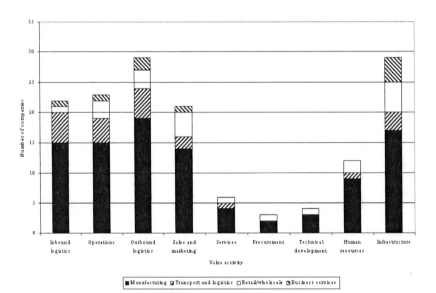

area, however, while five manufacturers and three retail/wholesale companies have done so. The sample's level of internal automation for the services value activity is low.

Procurement was ranked higher than *Services* by manufacturers and not at all high by logistics companies. *Procurement* is the value activity in the sample that is least supported by IT, with only three companies saying they automated it in any way. Two companies, an Italian manufacturer and a German logistics company, use e-marketplaces to support *Procurement to Outbound logistics,* but only for commodity items, such as MRO (Maintenance, Repair, Operations). Three further companies, a UK medical supplies manufacturer, a German fertilizer manufacturer, and another German logistics company, said they use the Internet to search for alternative sources of supply (*Procurement to Sales and marketing*). This is a "Very low" complexity e-commerce solution.

A number of SMEs cited the training and development of their workforce as a critical success factor. But as a value activity, *Human resources* (HR) was ranked the lowest of all. Only one company—a manufacturer—rated HR as highly critical (5). Eight manufacturers, four logistics companies, three services companies, and one retail/wholesaler ranked the activity as critical (4). Only two companies have developed e-commerce solutions in this area, supporting the VAI, *Human resources to Human resources*.

Twenty-two companies rated *Infrastructure* as highly critical or critical. This value activity had the most automated support in the sample: 29 SMEs have implemented some kind of IT system for financial management/quality assurance/planning. Small UK companies are taking the lead in supporting value activity interactions in this area. The solutions here are low to medium complexity.

Complexity of Automation of Value Activities

Medium complexity solutions occur when both value chain partners are carrying out a part of the same value activity: that is, *Outbound logistics to Outbound logistics, Human resources to Human resources, Sales and marketing to Sales and marketing.* Such solutions tend to support one-to-one or one-to-many interactions. The exception is *Procurement to Procurement,* where the "High" complexity e-commerce solution adopted, the e-marketplace, is supporting many-to-many interactions.

The two "High" complexity e-commerce solutions described by respondents (vendor-managed inventory between two Web-enabled enterprise resource management systems and e-marketplaces) were not fully operational at the time of interview. It was expected that, over time, it would be possible to track the development and impact of the different types of e-commerce solutions. It was also assumed that there would be wider adoption of more complex solutions over time.

Impact on the Value Chain

In this section, we examine how the complexity of an e-commerce solution affects an SME's ability to increase its value within its value chain and even transform its role within it. It is evident from experience within the sample that "High" complexity e-commerce solutions have more potential to support value chain transformation than "Low" complexity solutions. The latter are largely helping to streamline companies' supply chains. The explicit motive (strategy) for implementation of these solutions by SMEs is revenue retention.

Position in the value chain does seem to affect the complexity of the e-commerce solution adopted. Some SMEs, most notably those in the middle tiers, such as wholesalers (including e-marketplaces) and logistics companies, are able to provide additional intangible value to their value chain partners through the embryonic creation of new, virtual value chains (Rayport & Sviokla, 1995). Traditional wholesalers and logistics companies are participating in virtual value chains alongside their traditional, physical ones. Over time, at least some of them may use the virtual value chain to create new revenue streams and value chain roles for themselves. The e-marketplaces in the sample have a conscious strategy for virtual value chain intermediation.

Within the KITS sample, there appear to be four ways in which automating VAIs with e-commerce solutions has an impact on each SME's value chain (Table 4). VAI automation may:

1. Streamline the supply chain, taking out risk and cost. The electronic channel to customers/suppliers replaces existing methods of carrying out the value activity interaction (e.g., online ordering replacing phone/fax).

2. Transform the way a value activity is carried out, removing cost and adding new value. The way in which a value activity is automated changes the roles of customers and suppliers (e.g., suppliers carry out *Inbound logistics* on behalf of their customers, matching information about their own capability to deliver information about the customer's production plans and sales through vendor-managed inventory).

3. Capture information (intangible good/service) that adds value to internal processes. For example, a company may gather information on customers through its website and organize, select, and distribute it to improve internal processes, such as sales and marketing.

4. Extend new information (intangible good/service) to external value chain partners' processes. A small portion of this information is being used to generate a revenue stream in its own right (for example, by e-marketplaces, which are synthesizing and distributing information on a subscription basis).

Those companies in the KITS sample that have adopted "Very low" and "Low" complexity solutions are doing so to take cost out of their supply chain and to present a more streamlined interface, primarily to customers. "Medium" to "High" complexity e-commerce solutions are a prerequisite for value chain role transformation. All the VAIs that create intangible good/services, and which therefore enable KITS SMEs to participate in a virtual value chain, are supported with "Medium" or "High" complexity applications.

Table 4: Impact of E-Commerce on the Value Chain

Virtual Value Activity Interaction	E-Commerce Solution	Value Chain Impact	Sample Companies Implementing
Sales and Marketing	Buying/selling online (Medium complexity)	2	UK manufacturer E-marketplaces
Outbound Logistics	Tracking and tracing (Medium/High)	4	3 logistics companies 1 retail/wholesaler 4 manufacturers
	Vendor managed inventory (Medium/High)	2	1 manufacturer (1 manufacturer planning)
	Collaborative scheduling (Medium)	4	1 logistics company
	Sales intelligence (Medium)	2	1 wholesaler
Services	Online technical assistance (Medium)	2	1 wholesaler 3 manufacturers
	Business intelligence synthesised from multiple online sources (Medium)	4	2 e-marketplaces 1 manufacturer
	Performance monitoring (Medium)	4	1 logistics company
Human Resources	Distance learning (Medium)	4	1 wholesaler 1 manufacturer
Infrastructure	Trust services	4	1 e-marketplace
	Credit relationships	4	2 e-marketplaces
	Factoring and administrative service provision	2	1 e-marketplace
	Collaborative quality management	4	1 manufacturer (1 considering)

Future Trends

A number of SMEs in the sample commented on how they saw their value chain role developing over time. Eleven companies in the sample had a vision of their future role in their value chain. Six of these could be described as transformational. However, there is not a complete match between the companies with vision and those supporting virtual VAIs. The Italian wholesaler, UK logistics company, and e-marketplaces have explicit ideas of transforming their value chains, but so, too, does a UK tool manufacturer that has not yet put any "Medium" or "High" complexity e-commerce solutions in place to support virtual VAIs.

Three further companies, a Scandinavian manufacturer, a UK biotech company, and an Italian association of small textile companies, are concerned with 'virtualizing' as many interactions as possible with value chain partners in order to participate in increasingly virtual and global value chains, while remaining competitive in streamlined supply chains.

There are also two SMEs with exciting potential for value chain transformation, the German logistics company and the German farmers' association. The former is creating value chain partnerships, supported by "Medium" complexity e-commerce solutions, that will give it information visibility across different types of organizations (port authority; customers; possibly, in future, other transport infrastructure owners). It will therefore be in a strong position to control the virtual value chain of this information: gathering, organizing, selecting, synthesizing, and distributing relevant information to specific customers.

The German association already possesses and controls a vast amount of specialized knowledge about its value chain, from raw materials to end product. This knowledge (intangible good/service) could be franchised in part, or in its entirety, to sympathetic operators in other country markets. Such operators could use the German association's expertise, information, and processes to bring together small, high-quality meat producers, for example in Italy or the UK, in a way that would give them much greater power in the value chain than they have today. Such operators could even use the German association's soon-to-be "High" complexity e-commerce infrastructure on an outsourcing basis to save the costs associated with investing in their own, and to ensure compliance with the German association's quality standards and brand values.

Conclusion

This project aimed to research and analyze the activities of SMEs engaged in industry value chain relationships with suppliers and customers, in order to identify the triggers for value chain transformation that will encourage them to adopt e-commerce.

Is the Type of Industry Value Chain a Factor in Encouraging SME E-Commerce?

We investigated whether the impetus for adopting e-commerce solutions would differ depending on the type of value chain in which the SME is engaged. At this early stage in the research, there is little detectable effect. SMEs in fragmented value chains are just as likely in the sample to be implementing e-commerce solutions as an SME in a buyer-driven value chain. Within customer-centric value chains, in which the majority of KITS SMEs participate, there is a wide range of e-commerce practice. We would expect, over time, a number of the value chains surveyed to become buyer-driven and we would also expect this to have an impact on SMEs' roles and e-commerce strategies.

We found no absolute correlation between industry sector and type of value chain. For example, in the food sector two UK SMEs see themselves as part of customer-centric food-based value chains. They serve large customers—hotel chains, supermarkets—that need to cater to changing consumer tastes and concerns. An Italian salami producer, in contrast, regards its value chain as fragmented: the production of salami, a traditional national product, is equivalent to a cottage industry, with more than 1,800 manufacturers in the country. An association of SMEs in the food sector perceives a seller-driven value chain, because the association is itself a near complete value chain, stretching from raw material producers (farmers) through associated services, such as slaughtering and veterinary advice, to processing and delivery.

How Does the Stability of the Value Chain Affect SME E-Commerce?

The value chains studied are relatively stable, and the penetration of electronic linkages up and down the chain is low. The SMEs that are automating value activity interactions consider themselves to be market leaders in their sectors. This does not preclude the possibility of competitors moving quickly to copy their success, but overall, the low level of value chain automation is a brake to change. Early adopter SMEs cannot capitalize on their innovation and leadership until the whole value chain is at a critical point for change. The KITS research suggests that the timing is not yet right for this in the value chains studied.

Is the Level of Penetration of Electronic Links with Customers and Suppliers Important?

Many SMEs in the KITS sample anticipated that the number of electronic links they supported would rise sharply over the year following the interviews. Links to customers were a particular priority. This suggests that once SMEs have established the benefits of e-commerce in a few, key relationships, they are motivated to extend its deployment fairly rapidly. They can achieve better return on investment when the solution is extended to a critical mass of value chain partners.

One finding that emerged from this study is that strength in the value chain comes from partnership. Two interlinked SMEs that have synchronized their e-commerce strategies and solutions are more powerful than two individual companies. Business partnerships and alliances are not new, but e-commerce solutions make them easier and less costly to manage, and more likely, other factors being equal, to succeed. The most striking example of partnership in the KITS sample was a German association of more than 1,000 SMEs, which spans an entire value chain. Parts of this value chain are automated: we expect it to be a formidable force in the market when it is entirely automated. At this point, if it were possible to capture the chains of value activity interactions (value chain processes) this value chain executes, this in itself would represent a large intangible good/service, in addition to the association's physical meat-producing value chain. The virtual value chain could potentially be replicated in (sold to) other countries' markets to unite and support other meat producers. The brand values, and even the brand, of the German association could therefore be extended to other markets.

Is Complexity of Automation a Barrier for SME E-Commerce?

It is clear that companies with a vision of how they would like to participate in their value chain in the future are more likely to adopt "Medium" or "High" complexity e-commerce solutions and are beginning a process of value chain education themselves. These companies have considerably more power to effect change in the value chain than might have been expected, even in value chains with powerful customers downstream or dominant suppliers upstream. It has long been recognized that value chains are only as strong as their weakest links, usually thought to be the smallest links, the SMEs. KITS research suggests that SMEs can be equally as innovative at driving value chain change as larger companies, and that they can be faster and more flexible in doing so. The factors holding them back are not e-commerce related (such companies have a great deal of competency in this area), but have to do with risk, timing, and lack of access to the 'visionaries' in suppliers and customers.

Are Value Activity Interactions Important for SME E-Commerce?

In general, KITS SMEs were remarkably free from pressure from customers or suppliers to apply e-commerce to value activity interactions. Even large customers appeared content with the *status quo* in the value chain and, in some cases, can actually make it difficult for SMEs to carry out value activity interactions electronically. Given the current low literacy levels in all of the value chains of the SMEs surveyed, there is little incentive for SMEs to begin to adopt e-commerce solutions. Those that are doing so with the most determination are those that are proactively creating new, intermediary roles in the value chain that would not exist without the Internet. These companies include the e-market-places and the online fulfillment company. Where traditional offline companies are automating value activity interactions, their strategy often appears to be lagging the transformation potential of e-commerce solutions.

Investing in transformation is a high-risk strategy for a small company. The development of new services—either as add-ons to, or in the case of one manufacturer, as a revenue-generating replacement for—an existing physical value chain role, is expensive and the outcome is uncertain.

It is clear from KITS desk research that large suppliers and customers are thinking about how to change their own roles in value chains. Yet they often suffer from the same disconnect that is evident in SMEs: between e-commerce vision and e-commerce solutions in practice. Where the latter have been adopted by large companies, they are more commonly used to streamline the supply chain than for transformational purposes. SMEs are only considered insofar as they are 'black box' suppliers. Some SMEs in the KITS sample complain that their large customers give no thought to new (collaborative) ways of working with them. As a result, large customers fail to capitalize on areas of specialist expertise, or specialist capabilities, that SMEs can offer. In several cases, KITS SMEs suggested they would like a dialogue with customers at a more senior level than the procurement manager, about the development of new collaborative services, but are unsure how to go about this.

Which Value Activity Interactions Should SMEs Automate?

SMEs need to select for automation, value activity interactions that will support their business strategy and e-commerce strategy, and that are appropriate for the level of IT literacy in their value chains. They therefore need to understand the impact particular automated value activities interaction will have on their value chain relationships and the kind of information (intangible good/service) VAIs will yield.

E-commerce solutions should be selected based on the complexity level of partners' IT environments and how critical the VAI is to the business. This will include SMEs' future plans for the VAI—will they want to add more value in this area or link it to a virtual value chain in the future?

Can SME E-Commerce Transform Industry Value Chains?

Where e-commerce solutions support the 'bundling' and/or interlinking of VAIs ("Very high" complexity solutions), we expect a virtual value chain of information-driven intangible goods/services to emerge. In certain circumstances, which need further exploration, SMEs can use such intangible goods/services to generate the benefit of a completely new revenue stream. In the KITS sample, there are already emerging examples of SMEs that could achieve this, although they are using homegrown e-commerce solutions rather than industry-recognized packages.

In summary, although this research has already produced interesting insights into the objectives and practice of SMEs introducing e-commerce in different types of value chains more work is needed to extract benefits and verify best practices. Such validation can only be achieved over time, when the effects of e-commerce solutions can be compared with anticipated impacts and benefits.

Acknowledgments

KITS was supported by the European Commission, Directorate-General Information Society, under the program on Information Society Technologies: New Methods of Work and Electronic Commerce. We also acknowledge the help and cooperation of the SMEs in this study.

References

Baldock, R. (1999). *The Last Days of the Giants? A Route Map for Business Survival.* John Wiley & Sons.

Benbasat, I., Goldstein, D.K., & Mead, M. (1987). The case research strategy in studies of information systems. *MIS Quarterly,* (September), 368-85.

Benjamin, R., & Wigand, R. (1995). Electronic markets and virtual value chains on the information superhighway. *Sloan Management Review,* (Winter), 62-72.

Chen, J., & Williams, B. (1998). The impact of EDI on SMEs: Summary of eight British case studies. *Journal of Small Business Management,* 36(4), 68-72.

Chu, P. (1995). Conceiving strategic systems: What are critical value activities…and how can they help your company? *Journal of Systems Management,* (July/August), 36-41.

Fawcett, S.E., & Magan, G.M. (2001). *Achieving world-class supply chain alignment: Benefits, barriers and bridges.* Center for Advanced Purchasing Studies. Available on the Web: http://www.capsresearch.org.

Hawkins, R. (2001). *The business model as a research problem in electronic commerce.* STAR Issue Report No.4. Available on the Web: http://www.databank.it/star.

Iacovou, C., Benbasat, I., & Dexter, A. (1995). Electronic data interchange and small organizations: Adoption and impact of technology. *MIS Quarterly,* 19(4).

Lockett, N., & Brown, D. (2001). A framework for the engagement of SMEs in e-business. *Proceedings of the Americas Conference on Information Systems.*

Myers, M. (2002). *Qualitative research in information systems.* ISWorld Net. Accessed June 27, 2002 on the Web: http://www.auckland.ac.nx/msis/isworld.

Poon, S., & Swatman, P. (1997). Small business use of the Internet: Findings from Australian case studies. *International Marketing Review,* 14(5), 385-402.

Porter, M.E. (1984). *Competitive Advantage.* New York: The Free Press.

Rayport, J., & Sviokla, J. (1995). Exploiting the virtual value chain. *Harvard Business Review,* (November-December), 75-85.

Ward, J., & Griffiths, P. (1996). *Strategic Planning for Information Systems* (2nd ed.). Chichester, UK: John Wiley & Sons.

Yeh-Yun Lin, C. (1998). Success factors of small- and medium-sized enterprises in Taiwan: An analysis of cases. *Journal of Small Business Management, 36*(4), 43-56.

Yin, R. (1994). *Case Study Research: Design and Methods* (2nd ed.). Thousand Oaks, CA: Sage Publications.

Yli-Renko, H., & Autio, E. (1998). The network embeddedness of new technology-based firms: Developing a systematic evolution model. *Small Business Economics,* 11, 253-267.

Chapter XII

Mass Customization and Product Models

Carsten Svensson, Technical University of Denmark, Denmark

Martin Malis, Technical University of Denmark, Denmark

Abstract

When dealing with complex product models, efficient knowledge distribution is essential to obtain success. This chapter describes how product models can be applied to support the knowledge distribution.

The change toward individualization will radically affect the knowledge application in relation to the product. Through the application of a mass customization strategy, companies have a unique opportunity to create increased customer satisfaction. In a customized production, knowledge and information have to be easily accessible since every product is a unique combination of information. If the dream of a customized alternative instead of a uniform mass-produced product shall become a reality, then the cross-organizational efficiency must be kept at a competitive level. This is the real challenge for mass customization.

A radical restructuring of both the internal and the external knowledge management systems is needed. Management of variety and closer integration with suppliers is necessary when the companies are working in a network.

Introduction

Small and medium-sized manufacturing companies have been offered a unique opportunity by e-commerce. New markets will open, cumbersome administrative processes can be eliminated, and the exchange of knowledge can be executed instantly and effortlessly. At the same time SMEs are realizing that e-commerce is becoming a qualifying attribute. In the future, customers will expect suppliers to be able to integrate business processes and automate transactions. The shift towards increased integration in the supply chain has radically affected the knowledge distribution in relation to "build to order" manufacturing in companies with less than 500 employees—also called small to medium-sized enterprises (SMEs).[1] By use of a mass customization strategy, companies have a unique opportunity to create valuable differentiation. However, mass customization has some industrial preconditions that most SMEs do not meet at present. In mass production, the specifications were made once for each product series; consequently, there were a large amount of products over which to distribute the cost. With increased customization, every product must be individually documented. For this reason, knowledge and information have to be easily accessible.

Because the products of SMEs are often created in networks, the cross-organizational efficiency is critical. A radical restructuring of both the internal and the external knowledge management systems is needed. As a means to respond to this challenge, the application of a product model is introduced in this chapter. By focusing on complex products, the structure of the knowledge needed to generate the product specifications is analyzed.

A product model (short term for product and product-related models) is used to support sales, design of product variants, and production preparation. Product-related models contain knowledge and information regarding the systems related to the product's lifecycle, while the product model itself contains knowledge and information of the product's structure and functional properties (Krause, 1988). The product model is accessed with a configurator, which is the part of the product model that the user can access.

The objective of this text is to illustrate how inter-organizational product models can be applied to support the knowledge distribution within the supply chain, via a configurator. To reduce the total cost of a product, a supplier can apply automation in the specification process for the customized product, thereby enabling e-commerce in a "build to order" manufacturing context. Correctly applied, a product model will support the product through its entire lifecycle from customization to disposal, by maintaining an electronic record of the product structure.

Method

The findings presented here are based on the four-year research program called Centre for Industrialization of Engineering at the Technical University of Denmark. The center is based on a grant from the Danish Ministry of Business and Industry, and is established in cooperation with the Danish Technological Institute, Aalborg Industries A/S, NEG Micon A/S, HV-TURBO A/S, and Nassau Door A/S.

The enterprises have been directly involved as action-research objects. The research is supported by findings made through the Danish Society for Product Modeling (www.productmodels.org). The product-modeling association has approximately 50 participating companies.

The cases presented in the following are examples of interesting applications and good implementations of configurators in a B2B context using a structured procedure for building product models developed by the Centre for Industrialization of Engineering.

Background

The need for increased integration is a reaction to the increased competition manufacturers have experienced over the last 20 years. Manufacturers have focused their efforts around a limited and concise set of technologies and products as suggested by Skinner (1974). To avoid the cost-focused competition of the mass market, some SME manufacturers have chosen to use their responsiveness and agility to differentiate through customization. Customization is rapidly becoming a part of everyday life for many manufacturers. Currently, approximately 50% of Danish manufacturing companies have a production form that can be characterized as mass customization (Christiansen & Bruun, 2002). Until recently, companies could either choose a strategy based on uniformity in large volume at low cost, or they could differentiate themselves by producing small numbers of customized goods at a high cost (Pine, 1993). Through the development of mass customization, the old paradigms from Fordisme have been changed. Mass customization challenges the existing conceptions by combining the efficiency of mass production with the variety of craft production, thereby creating efficient differentiation in a world of uniformity. The progress has been made possible because of the evolution of information technology and production equipment (CAD, CAM, FMS, APS, robotics, etc.). The advances made within technology have enabled manufacturers to treat customized products as uniform products, thereby breaking through the known barriers of manufacturing (Kotha, 1995). When the narrow frames of a specialized production system are no longer restricting product evolution, innovation can run freely through the use of a flexible production system, targeting a dynamic market through continuously adapted products (Boynton et al., 1993). For manufacturers this presents new challenges, as the requirements for information infrastructure increase dramatically when each product is individually specified.

Product Models

To meet the demands for efficient customization, new technology must be applied in product development, production, and logistics. One of the tools that can be used to control the complexity of the construction and production of a customized product is a product model.

In a product model the knowledge is made accessible electronically to other organizational units. Thereby knowledge becomes easily shared and processed both in-house and in relation to the customers and suppliers of the manufacturing company. In a product model the knowledge is formulated as constraints or rules, and thereby product models can validate designs and give cost estimates. An automization in the form of a configurator interface will improve the flexibility and reduce the administrative cost of the trivial B2B interaction. This is particularly useful in production networks where end-manufacturers use customized sub-supplies.

A product model will support the customer selecting the right configuration, as it can find and optimize a solution based on the customer's functional input. To illustrate this, consider the example of a windturbine. The customer has a location that is characterized by some attributes in the form of max/min temperature, average windspeed, and max windspeed. Based on this information the configurator can exclude all solutions that are not valid within the valid solutionspace. The configurator can also optimize against investment and performance.

After the product is sold, the configurators have also proven to be useful as a configurator for supporting maintenance and upgrades of existing products, as they hold the exact specification and can be used for validation of suggested upgrades.

How to Support the Engineering System with Product Models

The following description of product models is based on the work carried out at the Centre for Product Modeling at the Technical University of Denmark (see Hvam, Riis, Malis, & Hansen, 2000). The specification process denotes the part of the engineering system where the specifications for the customized product variants are created, as illustrated in Figure 1.

The activities in the "specification process" include an analysis of the customer's needs, design and specification of a product which fulfills the customer's needs, and specification of, e.g., the product's manufacturing, transportation, erection on site, and service (specification of the product's lifecycle properties). The activities of the specification process are characterized by having a relatively well-defined space of (maybe complex) solutions as a contrast to product development, which is a more creative process.

As stated in Hvam et al. (2000), typical goals for the specification process are the ability to find an optimal solution according to the customer's needs, high quality of the specifications, short lead time, and a high productivity of the work carried out in the specification process. The typical critical goals for the development process are to derive new original concepts of product designs with improved functionality, lifecycle properties, and time to market for the new product designs. The diversification of tasks and goals in the specification and development processes leads to a separation of the two processes, as suggested in Figure 2. The idea is to formalize the knowledge and information related to the products and their lifecycle properties, and to express the knowledge in IT-systems—so-called product models.

Figure 1: The Engineering System

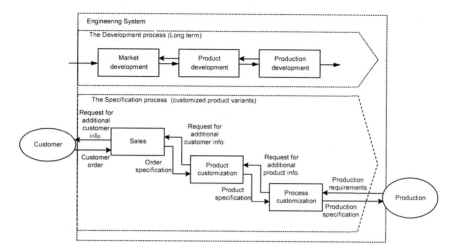

Knowledge Integrated Models

The activities of specifying products can be supported by the implementation of product models containing knowledge and information on products, and models containing knowledge on related systems, e.g., production or assembly.

Knowledge integrated product and product-related models are defined by Hvam (2000b) as:

> *"A knowledge base which contains part of or all of the knowledge and information associated with the product in different phases of the product's lifecycle, e.g., sales, design, production, assembly, service, and reuse."*

Krause (1988) uses the following definition:

> *"Product-related models contain knowledge and information about the systems related to the product's lifecycle, while the product model contains knowledge and information about the product's structure and functional properties."*

Procedure for Building Product Models

Product models implemented in IT-systems, such as sales configuration systems, have been applied in industry during the last 10 to 15 years for relatively simple products such as the configuration of computers and other electronic equipment.

The need for a structured procedure for building product models is stated by Hvam et al. (2000). Experience from a considerable number of Danish companies shows that often product models are constructed without the use of a strict procedure or modeling techniques. Consequently the systems are most often unstructured and undocumented. For this reason they are difficult or impossible to maintain or develop further. Thus there is a need to develop a procedure and associated modeling techniques that can ensure the proper structure and documentation, so that the systems can be maintained continually and developed further.

Another experience is that the product and product-related models are not always designed to fit the business processes they are meant to support. Finally, an important precondition for building product models is that the products are designed and structured in a way that makes it possible to define a general master of the product from which the customer-specific products can be derived.

The procedure (Hvam et al., 2000) includes: an analysis and redesign of the specification processes in focus, an analysis and eventually redesign/restructuring of the products to be modeled, and finally, a structured "language"—or modeling technique that makes it possible to document the product and product-related models in a structured way.

The procedure contains seven phases (described in detail in Hvam et al., 2000). The starting point for the work is an analysis and redesign of the business processes, which will be affected by the product and product-related models (phase 1). In phase 2 the products are analyzed and described in a so-called product master. Phase 3 includes the final design of the product and product-related models by using the object-oriented modeling techniques. Phases 4 to 7 deal with design, programming, implementation, and maintenance of the product models. Phases 3 to 7 follow the general object-oriented project lifecycle.

The procedure is based on a structured "language"—or modeling technique—that makes it possible to document the product and product-related models in a structured way.

Resource Consumption Related to the Implementation of a Configurator

When implementing a configurator the majority of the effort is related to the structuring and modeling of the product program. The effort is naturally dependent on the complexity and nature of the product program. Among the investigated solutions the total number of man-hours used ranged from 200 to 5,000. A variant of the configuration systems is the excel configurator. Excel configurators have been used for less complicated configuration tasks in SMEs with excellent results (Svensson, 2002). Typical excel configurators can be built with little external support. As there is no initial investment, the risk related to such a project is very limited, and the total investment between 200 and 500 man-hours.

Most often, manufacturers choose only to include the most common and standardized part of the product program. A common mistake is to include too many specialized instances, which is time consuming and has little value. Most manufacturers choose to

Figure 2: A Procedure for Building Product Models (Based on Hvam et al., 2000)

Phase	Description
1.	*Process Analysis.* Analysis of the existing specification process (AS-IS), statement of the functional requirements to the process. Design of the future specification process (TO BE). Overall definition of the product—and product-related models to support the process.**Tools:** IDEF0, flow charts, activity chain model, key numbers, problem matrix, list of functional describing characteristics and gap analysis.
2.	*Product Analysis.* Analyzing products and eventually lifecycle systems. Redesigning/restructuring of products. Structuring and formalizing knowledge about the products and related lifecycle systems in a product master. **Tools:** List of features and product master.
3.	*Object-Oriented Analysis (OOA).* Creation of object classes and structures. Description of object classes on CRC-cards. Definition of user interface. Other requirements to the IT solution.**Tools:** Use cases, screen layouts, class diagrams, and CRC-cards.
4.	*Object-Oriented Design.* Defining and further developing the OOA-model for a specific programming tool.
5.	*Programming.* Programming the system. Own development or use of standard software.
6.	*Implementation.* Implementation of the product- and product related models in the organization. Training users of the system, and further training of the people responsible for maintaining the product and product-related models.
7.	*Maintenance.* Maintenance and further development of the product and product-related models.

maintain two order processing streams—a configurator for the orders that fit within the standard product program; the automated order processing is then supported by manual order processing for orders that include solutions that lie beyond the standard options. When determining the details, the manufacturers estimate the total number of products that will include an option, and the cost of programming this option into the configurator versus the cost of manual processing over the product's lifecycle.

SME Manufacturing: Networks of Competence

The days where small manufacturers could turn raw material into complex products are gone. Chapman, Dempsey, Ramsdell, and Reopel (1997) estimate that purchased goods and services can account for 50% to 80% of manufacturers' expenditure nowadays. As a result of the reduced degree of processing, customized products are most often manufactured in a network of specialized suppliers, as it is not possible to contain a sufficient number of competencies within a single SME. Consequently, the network integration must be optimized through automization and other initiatives. Otherwise the benefits will be wasted in transactional friction between organizations in an extensive supply chain. In this specialized environment end-manufacturers will no longer find their core-competence in a manufacturing process. End-manufacturers can discover that their core skills have moved from the materialization of a product to the administrative realization processes that link the need of customers to a design solution.

In some cases independent suppliers handle all contact to the physical product, but most often the final assembly is still kept in-house. Thereby end-manufacturers can canalize and coordinate the competencies of suppliers into a solution. Managing and developing a supplier-network is a new discipline that is critical to the success of the end product. For many SMEs the management of administrative processes is problematic and is often seen as non-value-adding and bureaucratic, because these systems replace informal systems. This resistance must be overcome.

Whatever the strategic importance and the complexity of the task may be, some basic qualifying criteria can be stated. They must be fulfilled in order to qualify as a competent member of an integrated network. The main task of a supply network is still order fulfillment in relation to quality, quantity, and time. To most people this sounds straightforward, but according to Zipkin (2001), fulfillment has proven to be a problem, especially with regards to customized products. It is evident that fare from all SMEs has the sufficient control of their production to meet these qualifying demands. If the basics cannot be accomplished and the data needed are not available, it is not possible to be part of an integrated network.

The obvious barriers to integrated networks are logistics. It is evident that the use of components from a wide range of suppliers is a problem in relation to coordination, lead-times, etc. Another problem that has proven to be an even bigger challenge to the manufacturers is the organizational barriers that exist between customers and suppliers. If we consider the operational data, large customers have been pushing the integration with SME suppliers, as was the case with EDI. This technology squeeze would obligate a supplier to work with different flavors of EDI for each customer, and for the SME supplier this would be challenging; the solution is still to be found (Gulledge, 2001).

With the use of various EDI solutions, the first steps have been taken towards the automation of the simple exchange of production demand data. If we look at the example of a customized product, there is a much more knowledge-intensive transaction between seller and buyer. The customer has a need for which he requires a solution, and in close cooperation the buyer and seller will have to find a solution that will fulfill the need. The iterative process of specifying the configuration is time consuming and inconvenient, as a representative of both the buyer and the seller must be available. The cooperation related to a customized product is much different from selling a standardized product, where the seller presents the product to the customer and subsequently the customer can either accept or reject the product. In this situation the need for a two-way interaction is limited. It is obvious that there is a growing need to automate the interaction between organizations when the number of interactions explodes, and it would be beneficial if the solution could have a generic format so that only one interface should be used. Thereby the setup cost could be distributed over a larger number of customers. By the use of IT technology, an electronic customer interaction is made possible, which in most cases can replace a number of iterations, thereby reducing the transaction cost.

From the supplier's point of view, the ability to collaborate is critical for the overall competitiveness, as is the case with EDI. For customized deliveries customers are increasingly emphasizing the TCO (Total Cost of Ownership); consequently the SMEs must adopt this concept in order to remain attractive suppliers. An increasing number of suppliers are now developing solutions that will enable customers to acquire components with very little transaction costs.

Allocation of Total Cost

Most often the motivation for applying a product model is not only to reduce the internal order processing cost, but also to become a more attractive supplier. Becoming an attractive supplier can be done through a reduction of the total cost related to the relationship. This would include the cost of the product, the cost related to the specification of the product, and other costs. To illuminate these benefits the total cost of ownership model is an industrialized support tool to be used when selecting suppliers. The amount of customers with a broader perspective is increasing. They are starting to look further than the sales price and systematically estimate the tradeoffs made between direct and indirect transaction costs.

Consequently, manufacturers have an interest in focusing on the total cost of ownership (TCO) rather than only on price reductions. However, TCO is not only a matter of considering inventory, price, transportation, and quality as a whole, and this is often a question of synchronizing processes and creating a mutual understanding of business processes. The hidden costs related to purchasing interaction are often a major cost contributor and should be taken in to consideration when selecting suppliers. Ellram (1993) divides this into three areas: pre-transaction, transaction, and post-transaction.

Figure 3: TCO Divided into Three Areas (Ellram, 1993)

Pre-transaction	Transaction	Post-transaction
Identifying need Investigating sources Adding supplier to internal system Education Supplier in firms operations	Price Order placement/preparation Deliver/transportation Tariffs/duties Billing/payment Inspection Return of parts	Defective finished goods rejected before sales Field failures Repair/replacement in field Customer goodwill/reputation of the firm Cost of maintenance and repairs

From this it is obvious that the price is only a part of the picture. In the case of customized products, the cost of order placement, communication, and identification of need is often critical. Therefore suppliers can establish a competitive advantage by offering an automated electronic interface that can reduce the customer's cost related to the transfer of information.

If the purchasing process is to run smoothly, the transfer of knowledge must be well prepared. In reality, drawings are often updated, if updated at all, with handwritten notes, and errors are caught by the experience of the machinists who will double-check if there is an uncertainty. It is not uncommon to see incomplete data being used for production; the tacit knowledge of the employees can compensate internally. These informal safety processes that have prevented errors in SMEs are removed when suppliers perform tasks. When processing takes place outside the manufacturer's work area, the documentation has to be immaculate and unambiguous, since the internal safety valves are removed, or else the total cost will get out of hand. A configurator will support the manufacturer in creating valid documentation and thereby accumulated the experience of the manufacturer in a few drawings, which will be the carrier of knowledge at the operational level of the supply chain.

Procurement

The road to successful networks goes through purchasing. As stated earlier, purchasing is of strategic importance, since purchasing often manages the majority of expenditures. Purchasing is the primary contact interface between a company and its suppliers, and consequently also a cost driver in relation to transaction costs. Despite the strategic role that purchasing has, it is the home of *"engineers who can't add, accountants who can't foot, and operators who can't run their machines"* (Chapman et al., 1997). The competence levels must be raised in order to meet the demands of managing integrated networks, which is much different from just ordering components. Before developing highly sophisticated solutions, the basics must be in place. The primary objective in the supply chain is to ensure that the production is supplied in a timely, cost-efficient manner. Most often the problem is related to the distribution of knowledge. In a recent survey nearly 70% of the companies responded that their supplier *"didn't understand what they where supposed to do"* and that the cost of outsourcing was too high and service was poor (Ozanne, 2000). For most SMEs there is no alternative to a network of suppliers. Consequently they will have to improve the integration issues. To address the current integration challenges, SMEs must be careful in the selection of development of business relationships. Instead of basing the supplier network on the convenient local supplier base, a broader view on expenses must be taken, and for this purpose a total cost model can be used to support the systematic selection of business partners.

Example of Cost-Perspective

An example of the total cost perspective can be found at Nilpeter. Nilpeter is focusing on a closer integration with suppliers. The integration aims at being both flexible and responsive. Nilpeter is a medium-sized manufacturer of label printing presses. Historically, Nilpeter has moved from being a machine shop with a very high degree of processing to being an end-manufacturer with focus on customers, service, education, customization, and technology. Nilpeter has gradually reduced the internal degree of processing and now focuses on core technologies and the satisfaction of the end-customer. Through this process the collaboration with Nilpeter's suppliers has become an issue that is critical for the overall performance of the company. As the processing degree is falling, the dependency of suppliers is increasing (Krause & Ellram, 1997). Therefore the network of suppliers has to be maintained with great care. The response from Nilpeter has been to move towards a higher degree of customization and innovative design. The fact of being able to offer a very extensive product program is only possible through the utilization of a closely knitted supplier network. By the use of new technologies, developed and maintained by suppliers, it is possible to provide customers with cutting-edge equipment. Even core components, such as printing units for the offset and digital presses, are supplied by technology leaders. The decision to buy a large portion of the product from suppliers is made in recognition of the limitation that lies in being a medium-sized manufacturer. If all technologies were developed internally, it would properly only be possible to be at the forefront of one technology; thereby the concept of wide market coverage would be undermined. Instead, Nilpeter turns towards selected suppliers. The integrating with suppliers demands specialized skills, and the transfer of knowledge has become challenging.

When developing products the ability to access knowledge from suppliers must be developed and information must float freely, if the development time shall be acceptable. Finding suppliers that are capable of constructive interaction is critical. The experience from Nilpeter indicates that the formalization of the process would support the process. Only by clearly communicating what the company's intentions are, will it be possible to take full advantage of a relationship. On the operational level the daily interaction with suppliers also calls for skills that are different from the ones required in traditional production. Through the use of suppliers instead of internal production, all the informal networks that would prevent errors are eliminated, as the iterative communication between design and production is replaced by a drawing. In case an uncertainty should arise, the communication will be slow, so if the specifications are not very precise, it can be expensive and time consuming to use suppliers.

Product Models and E-Commerce

As a result of the increased focus on cost drivers, suppliers must expect smaller orders from an increasing number of customers (Soellner & Markham, 2000); consequently the individual order becomes less attractive, it becomes harder to obtain, and this will change the distribution of cost. Most manufacturers indicate that the order-to-tender ratio is falling (Hvolby, Barfod, & Taps, 1999), and that the specification of the individual tender becomes increasingly more time consuming as a result of developments within technology. As a result there are fewer orders over which to distribute the growing specification cost.

An automation of the interaction between business partners can reduce the administrative cost related to the specification of an order significantly. E-business has shown its true potential in the business-to-business market. In the first generation, manufacturers made information widely available on the Internet. The use of updated common online catalogs will reduce overhead and errors dramatically. Simultaneously, manufacturers will be able to update information independently of catalog publications. Manufacturers are increasingly using the interactive opportunity that lies within the information technology. An automation of the interaction between buyer and supplier has been made widely accessible through the XML standards and the use of Web services.

Today suppliers are disqualified if they are not able to integrate automatically with their customers. From the car industry we can already see that EDI is a precondition for being considered as a potential supplier. The ability to transfer knowledge and automated cross-organizational business processes will, in the course of time, be reduced from being an order-winning qualification to being a precondition. The suppliers who do not provide an automated interface will gradually lose ground, because the cost of interaction will overshadow the short-term cost savings they have gained by avoiding investments in the enabling technologies. To improve the integration the supplier of customized products can make a configurator available for its customers, thereby giving easy and instant access to the specification process.

The configurator will thereby reduce the waiting and processing time of the order and at the same time reduce the cost of processing the order. This will make the supplier more attractive, as the cost of integration is reduced and the service is improved, as there is 24 hours access, improved quality of specifications, and a very short throughput time.

Application of Configurators

Two case studies follow in this section. In both cases the structured procedure has been used to build the configurators. In the first case (Demex) a configurator is interacting directly with the costumers. In the second case (Niro) the configurator is used to gather all relevant knowledge about product and processes.

Customer-Oriented Configurator

Demex-electric is a typical SME that has implemented a product model in an advanced e-commerce solution. Demex-electric is a Danish manufacturer of electronic switch-boards. It has more than 100 employees and a turnover of approximately 15 million Euro.

The project of building the configurator through the use of the structured procedure is described in Hvam, Mortensen, and Malis (2002). This case description is based on the same paper.

The sales process prior to implementing a configurator was that the customer indicates to himself, among other things, the power required, the electricity companies that can supply the power, the demands for protection, the switchboard outlets, etc. Then Demex-electric starts specifying the switchboard and prepares a list of parts, makes a sketch, calculates the price, and writes a quotation letter. When the customer has accepted the offer, the list of parts and the sketch are detailed and can now form the basis of purchasing and production.

The lead time for generating quotations is three to five days. Demex-electric uses two to four man-hours for each quotation. The manual processes may lead to frequent errors, and often the time necessary for the optimization of the boards cannot be found.

In order to move towards a higher degree of e-commerce, Demex-electric has made an alliance with Solar A/S, a company that sells electronic equipment. In Denmark Solar A/S has a turnover of 250 million; 50% of the products are sold directly via Solar's homepage.

In the alliance between Demex-electric and Solar A/S, Solar A/S hosts the system for configuring an electronic switchboard as an integrated part of their homepage for selling electronic equipment. When a customer configures and orders an electronic switch-board, Solar A/S ships the parts needed for building a switchboard to Demex-electric. The switchboards are then assembled and shipped. The future process focuses on ensuring efficient quotations by using the Internet. The lead time and the consumption of resources, from the generation of quotations until the specifications are in the production department, are considerably reduced. In connection with the analysis of the existing process at Demex-electric, a number of flow diagrams were made.

With the new product model, the company gets a much more structured process flow, where the knowledge of Demex-electric regarding construction of switchboards is made available to the customers, and complex calculations can be made very quickly. This is illustrated in Figure 4.

The project at Demex-electric has shown how to build a configurator with automatic dimensioning and the specification of complex switchboards. The customers save time, money, and energy when using the configurator. The users can now specify the demands to a switchboard system and then use the configurator as guidance when an optimal configuration is to be selected. Different parameters such as loss of heat and price summarization of the system can be easily displayed. In this way corrections to a configuration will be shown immediately.

The effects of introducing a configurator in Demex electric/Solar A/S can be summarized as follows:

1.   Reduction of lead time from three to four days to 10 minutes when generating quotes.

2.   Possible to optimize a configuration in relation to, e.g., resource consumption. This means up to a 10% reduction of materials.

3.   Significant reduction of specification hours.

Figure 4: The Future Process Flow when Applying a Configurator (Named mexEcon)

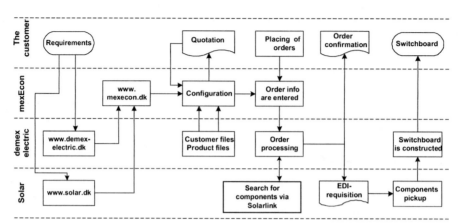

Modeling Knowledge

The structured procedure described early in this chapter has been tested in a case company. A project has been established in cooperation with Niro A/S, a Danish engineering company that has a market leading position within the area of design and supply of spray drying plants. The products are characterized as highly individualized for each project and services that are customized. The project is described more detailed in Hvam and Malis (2001). Briefly, the project concerns the application of product models in extended enterprises. The application of product models has proven to be a very efficient tool for knowledge management. Product-related knowledge has been structured by the use of a technique (see Figure 4), described by Mortensen, Yu, Skovgaard, and Harlou (2000). The objective is to get an overview and a description of the product assortment.

The product variant master is a complete description of the product assortment. Each element is described by attributes that are determined during the configuration. The Object-Oriented Analysis is carried out by the use of a class diagram, as described by Booch, Rumbaugh, and Jacobson (1999). The Unified Modeling Language (UML) is used as notation. CRC-cards (Class, Responsibility, and Collaboration-cards) are being used as a supporting modeling tool. Changes have been made to the traditional CRC-cards described by Bellin and Simone (1997) in order to use them for configuration purposes. They are used as a communication tool between engineers and system maintainers.

A prototype of a configurator has been built through the use of a standard software tool (Oracle). The results from the first testing of the prototype show that the development of the actual configurator has become less complex, since the knowledge is formalized in a way that facilitates the programming process.

Figure 5: Contents of a Product Variant Master (Based on Mortensen et al., 2000)

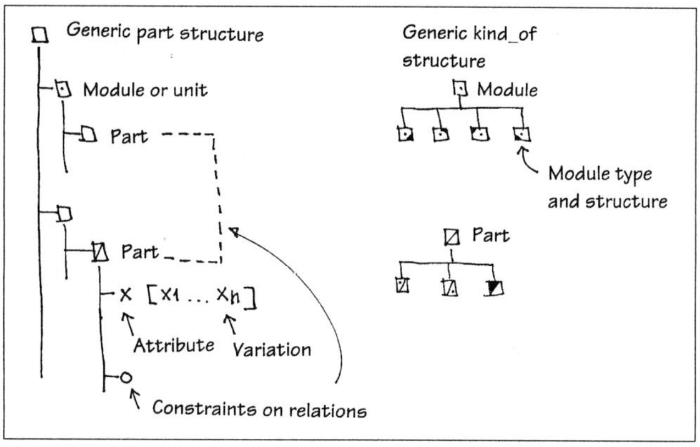

Conclusion and Future Trends

To a large number of manufacturers, success is no longer a question of mastering a production skill to perfection. The efficiency of the internal production will only have a limited effect on the overall performance. Instead, it is the efficiency of integration with suppliers and the ability to acquire knowledge from networks that will create competitive advantages. Manufacturers can use the real-time communication to synchronize production, communicate alterations to design, or provide online information regarding product specifications to create competitive advantages. A configurator can support SME manufacturers in presenting their product program in an easily accessible form, thereby creating a competitive advantage.

For end-manufacturers the core activity moves from manufacturing to management of knowledge. As customization reaches new markets, the amount of work preparation increases. As a result of the increased focus on this subject, the knowledge contained in the work preparation must be moved across organizational borders, which, if done poorly, can undermine the overall efficiency. By formalizing networks and focusing on precision, it is possible to reduce the transaction cost associated with network collaboration significantly. When the formalization has taken place, IT tools can eliminate the need for human interaction, and thereby reduce the cost.

Being part of an extensive network has proven to be the key to competitiveness for Nilpeter and other SMEs; therefore efficiency lies in the ability to interact with the supplier network. This ability is not created by chance, but rather through a structured effort, focusing on the tools that will enable a frictionless transfer of information and product knowledge.

As the Niro case shows, the application of a structured way of building product models can help a company deal with the management and transformation of complex product knowledge. By the use of a product analysis, all relevant information and constraints can be mapped in order to integrate the knowledge into a configurator.

In relation to customized components, product models can push the knowledge of product development to the frontline, thereby giving the best possible solution based on the experience of a company, rather than on the experience of a single sales person. Not only will product models improve the efficiency in the transaction phase, they will also help reduce long-run costs and improve the competitive situation of the supplier.

Endnotes

[1] This is the definition used in the IV European framework program, and this definition is still commonly used in Danish research; please note that the EU definition was later modified.

References

Bellin, D., & Simone, S.S. (1977). *The CRC Card*. Addison-Wesley Longman.

Booch, G., Rumbaugh, J., & Jacobson, I. (1999). *The Unified Modeling Language User Guide*. Addison-Wesley.

Boynton, A.C., Victor, B., & Pine II, B.J. (1993). New competitive strategies: Challenges to organization and information technology. *IBM Systems Journal, 32*(1), 40-64.

Chapman T.L., Dempsey J.J., Ramsdell G., & Reopel, M.R. (1997). Purchasing: No time for lone rangers. *The McKinsey Quarterly,* (2), 30-40.

Christiansen, T., & Bruun, P. (2002). *Facts, based on a questionnaire 2001*. Center for Technology, Economics and Management, The Technical University of Denmark.

The Economist. (2001, July 14).

Ellram, L. (1993). Total cost of ownership: Elements and Implementation. *International Journal of Purchasing and Materials Management*, (Fall), 3-11.

Gulledge, T. (2001). B2B e-marketplaces and small- and medium-sized enterprises. *Proceedings of the SME Conference 2001,* Aalborg, Denmark.

Hayes, R.H., & Wheelwright, S.C. (1994). *Restoring Our Competitive Edge: Competing Through Manufacturing*. New York: John Wiley & Sons.

Hvam, L., & Malis, M. (2001). A knowledge based documentation tool for configuration projects. *World Congress on Mass Customization and Personalization*, Hong Kong (October).

Hvam, L., Mortensen, N.H., & Malis, M. (2002). Construction of product models for the development of product variants specifications. *PDT,* Torino, Italy.

Hvam, L., Riis, J., Malis, M., & Hansen, B. (2000). A procedure for building product models. *Product Models 2000-SIG PM,* Linköping, Sweden (November).

Hvolby, H.-H., Barfod, A., & Taps, S. (1999). Customer order process modeling using activity chains. *Proceedings of PICMET '99 Conference on Technology and Innovation Management: Setting the Pace for the Third Millennium*, Portland, Oregon, USA (July).

Kotha, S. (1995). Implementing the emerging paradigm for competitive advantage. *Strategic Management Journal, 16,* 21-42.

Krause, D., & Ellram, L. (1997). Critical elements of supplier development. *European Journal of Purchasing & Supply Management, 3*(1), 21-31.

Krause, F. (1998). Knowledge integrated product modeling for design and manufacture. *Proceedings of the 2nd Toyota Conference*, Aichi, Japan.

Mortensen, N., Yu, B., Skovgaard, H.J., & Harlou, U. (2000). Conceptual modeling of product families in configuration projects. *Product Models 2000-SIG PM*, Linköping, Sweden (November).

Ozanne, M.R. (2000). *Dun & Bradstreet Barometer of Global Outsourcing*. Dun & Bradstreet.

Pine II, J., Victor, B., & Boynton, A. (1993). Making mass customization work. *Harvard Business Review*, (September/October), 108-119.

Schmitt, E., Manning, H., Paul, Y., Ritter, T., & Tong, J. (1999). Configuration in your future. *The Forrester Report,* (August).

Skinner, W. (1974). The focused factory. *Harvard Business Review*, (May/June), 113-121.

Soellner, N.F., & Markham, W. (2000). From best practices to next practices: Procurement in the decade ahead. *Executive Agenda, 3*(1), 5-17.

Svensson, C. (2002). The configurator that was never meant to be—Experiences from designing, implementing and using a low cost configurator. *Proceedings of the 5th International SMESME Conference,* Danbury.

Zipkin, P. (2001). The limits of mass customization. *MIT Sloan Management Review,* (Spring), 81-88.

Chapter XIII

E-Transformation of Austrian SMEs: A Concept that Fits the Reality

Christoph Auer, evolaris eBusiness Competence Center and
University of Graz, Austria

Reinhard Franz, evolaris eBusiness Competence Center and
University of Graz, Austria

Abstract

This chapter highlights the differences that exist between the e-commerce (EC) perspective of SMEs and the EC perspective from the researchers' point of view. First the main aspects of SME EC found in a literature review are pointed out and then the results of a SME survey are presented. The findings of this survey, conducted with Austrian SMEs in the automotive industry sector, show for example that EC adoption is slower than expected. Consequently, we introduce a concept that was developed to minimize the identified gap between the two EC perspectives, by connecting university research and regional SME networks more efficiently. This action research-based approach enables SMEs to evaluate the impact of EC on their business model.

Introduction

Researchers and academic professionals often attempt to give helpful suggestions and useful guidance regarding the advantages of e-commerce (EC) for small to medium-sized enterprises (SMEs) with their research. This *e-transformation* of SMEs in Austria is also the main aim of the publicly founded evolaris eBusiness Competence Center, a research institution involving various university departments from different disciplines. Through one-and-a-half years of SME research at evolaris, it was found that one of the main factors inhibiting the essential transformation of SMEs towards *e-SMEs* is a dissimilarity in the understanding of e-commerce (EC) by researchers and the SMEs themselves.

This chapter highlights the differences between the EC perspective of SMEs and the EC perspective from the researchers' point of view. Therefore, first these two perspectives—the perspective about SME EC that exists in the literature and the EC perspective that exists in Austrian SMEs—are presented. The main aspects of SME EC found in a literature review are pointed out, as well as the findings of a survey that was conducted with Austrian SMEs in the automotive industry sector, which represent the viewpoint of Austrian SMEs on EC. Consequently, we introduce a concept that we identified as suitable to minimize the identified gap between the two EC perspectives, by connecting university research and regional SME networks more efficiently. The concept is based on a hybrid method approach combining grounded action research (Baskerville, 1999) and other research techniques, such as statistical analysis, semi-structured interviews, and document analysis. Its main characteristic is the direct involvement of the researcher and the SMEs in order to produce a result that is satisfying for both parties.

Background

This part of the chapter presents all necessary definitions, and background information about Austrian SMEs is provided in order to enable the reader to understand the background of our study completely.

The Importance of SMEs in the EU and in Austria

There is no obligatory SME definition for countries in the European Union, but in April 1996 a European Commission guideline suggested the definitions of enterprises by size as shown in Table 1. Within the European Union in 1997, 99.8% of all enterprises (18,765,000) were either very small, small, or medium-sized enterprises employing 66% of all employees in the EU (Sanchez, 2000).

However, the Austrian SME definition differs slightly from the European definition in the way that medium-sized companies employ up to 300 people. As Table 2 shows, in 2001, 99.83% of all Austrian companies were small or medium-sized enterprises, accountable for 69.1% of employment (*Beschäftigte in Österreich*, 2002). Although SMEs obviously

Table 1: Enterprise Size Categories in the European Union

Enterprise Category	Employees	Revenue	Balance Sheet Total	Independency
Very Small Enterprise	1-9	< 7 Mio. €	< 5 Mio. €	< 25 % minority interest
Small Enterprise	10-49			
Medium Enterprise	50-249	< 40 Mio. €	< 27 Mio €	
Large Enterprise	250+	>40 Mio. €	>27 Mio €	N/A

play a crucial role in the European as well as in the Austrian economy, only little research about EC adoption in European and Austrian SMEs is available.

The Characteristics of the Regional SME Network

Following the successful regional business development strategies of northern Italy, the local government of Styria, an Austrian southern state, focused its business initiative on few industry sectors (Cossentino, Pyke, & Sengenberger, 1996). In the automotive industry sector, the government supported the emerging of a cluster of over 400 small to medium-sized enterprises around two large world-leading organizations, AVL List and the Magna Group. The Automotive Cluster Styria (AC Styria) is an initiative of 180 member companies and 250 advising companies in the automotive industry in Austria, trying to enhance innovations and international competitiveness. Members of the cluster are mainly small to medium-sized enterprises that serve as producers, subcontractors, suppliers, and service providers for the major car producers worldwide. The policy initiatives in Styria, which aim to develop a network structure of SME clusters in various industry fields, is comparable to initiatives in New Zealand (Perry, 1999). The literature shows that EC will play a substantial role in SME network structures in the future (Brown & Lockett, 2001; Franke, 1999).

Table 2: The Significance of SMEs in Austria (2001)

Employ.	Size	Category	Number of Enterprises		Employment	
			Number	Percent	Number	Percent
Micro:	1-9	Employees	211,555	83.61%	552,647	19.28%
Small:	10-49	Employees	33,488	13.24%	655,649	22.87%
Medium:	50-299	Employees	6,926	2.74%	744,190	25.96%
Large:	300+	Employees	1,044	0.41%	914,674	31.90%
Total			253,013	100.00%	2,867,160	100.00%

The evolaris eBusiness Competence Center in Graz is a joint venture of major Austrian enterprises from different industries and research institutions. The core values of evolaris are connecting, exploring, and changing. For the business partners of evolaris, this endeavor supports these values by providing the theory behind, and the methodology for transforming their business models. As the local government is a co-founder of evolaris, the research regarding the e-transformation of SMEs is a major issue. However, it also clarifies the potential impact of the Internet in general and within certain industries. Evolaris moderates the entire process of improving an existing business model and provides valuable input through its experience with different industries and strong academic network. In this way an optimum combination of rigor in methodology and relevance of outcomes can be achieved, which is one of the most important success factors of evolaris.

Aiming to strengthen the competitive advantages of the AC Styria, a survey about the adoption of EC applications was conducted by evolaris. Once research results indicated little interest in EC, it was the aim of this project to provide suitable concepts for developing appropriate EC initiatives for the AC Styria.

On the other hand the experience shows that marketplace operators and software vendors are convinced that their products provide the same value to SMEs as large organizations. Hence there is a need for methods that bridge the gap between the perception and the reality in SMEs' EC interest and adoption. It was found that action research (Baskerville & Pries-Heje, 1999) is a suitable concept to connect academic research and business advice for SMEs.

EC SME Research Issues

The research literature shows that common SME characteristics, such as a reluctance to change, a fire-fighting attitude to work, and a constantly changing priority list, have been identified as barriers for the implementation of EC applications (Filson & Lewis, 2000; Corbitt, 2000). The importance of EC especially in supply chain networks, which usually consist of a large number of SMEs, has been discussed in the literature since the emerging of EDI (Caskey, Hunt, & Browne, 2001; Yang, Mason, & Chaudhury, 2001; Chau & Hui, 2001).

Julta, Bodorik, and Dhaliwal (2002) point out that although the use of EC software tools is not measured in most countries, informal evidence suggests a low uptake of EC applications. Their article suggests that governments should support the SME uptake process, and a conceptual model of pertinent metrics of EC readiness for SMEs is provided. However, as no applicable government actions are described by the authors, an implementation of the ideas seems difficult.

Chau and Hui (2001) show that EDI adoption decisions in SMEs are mainly dependent on factors rather than the characteristics of the technology itself. These factors comprise the internal organizational readiness and the external environment, including internal prior EDI experience, perceived level of support from the vendor, influence from business partners, and perceived costs to be incurred.

Also McGregor and Gomes (1999) identified a *"...gap between research examining technology uptake in the manufacturing sector and industry perceptions about their own technology adoption needs...."* To bridge this gap between research and practice, utilizing a suitable research design, where a multidisciplinary team of researcher personally interact with the participating companies, was suggested. Results from the first 20 case studies show that this approach enables the participating SMEs to identify their weaknesses and develop together with the researcher strategies to solve them (McGregor & Gomes, 1999).

Cooperative research approaches, which enable effective research partnerships through applied project work with SMEs, will similarly provide the involved companies with suitable business advice (McGregor & Gomes, 1999). Such qualitative research approaches enable both sides—the company, by receiving a suitable solution to a common problem; and the researcher, by solving a common problem using untested theories—to gain a benefit from the research project. However, the importance of the differentiation between research and consultation has to be considered. The use of grounded action research (Baskerville & Pries-Heje, 1999) is one way to conduct appropriate EC SME research. Action researchers, who take part in the changing process, act out of scientific interest to help the organization itself to learn by formulating various experimental solutions based on an evolving, untested theory, as opposed to consultants who are usually paid to dictate experienced, reliable solutions based on their independent review (Baskerville, 1997).

EC in the AC Styria: An Empirical Investigation

To get better insight into the needs and requirements concerning EC for SMEs, a survey in the AC Styria was conducted. The purpose of the survey was to obtain a first insight concerning the use of Internet technologies in the AC Styria and to get an empirical foundation for further supportive measures towards SME EC. Therefore the members were asked to answer questions about their recent usage of Internet technologies and the integration of Internet technologies into their business model, as well as their assessment of alternative current and future applications.

The survey was conducted online. Contacts with management responsibilities were invited via e-mail to fill out the questionnaire. The survey was online between January 23 and February 2, 2002. Two-hundred-and-forty people were invited to take part in the survey; 42% of them started the session but did not finish. Fifty-seven respondents completed the poll, which is equivalent to a response rate of 23.75%. The reason for the high abruption rate can be found in the length of the survey.

Those who fully completed the questionnaire were mainly production companies (28%) and service providers (13%), but also IT providers, logistics companies, and consulting companies—all as a part of the automotive cluster—took part in the survey.

The majority of the respondents can be assigned to the top management of the companies in the automotive cluster, but also persons responsible for information technology and human resources management took part in the survey.

Recent Usage of Internet Technology in the Automotive Cluster Styria

To achieve an insight into the recent use of Internet technologies, several applications that assist the value chain of the automotive industry were considered. Respondents were asked if the selected EC applications were already in use, in adoption, planned, or not relevant to/for their company. The following applications were tested:

- selling through electronic marketplaces
- buying through electronic marketplaces
- electronic logistics
- selling through the company's website
- electronic collaboration
- optimization of internal processes
- customer relationship management
- finding new suppliers through the Web

Results show that Internet technologies are already in use for searching for new suppliers over the Web; 57.9% of the respondents say that this application is already in operation.

Also the optimization of internal processes with Internet technologies is already well developed in the interviewed companies. More than 55% of all respondents have these

Figure 1: Diffusion of Web Research in the AC Styria

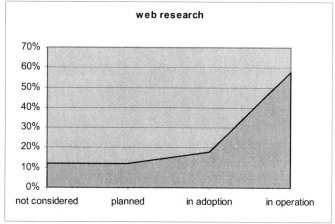

Figure 2: Support of Process Optimization with Internet Technologies

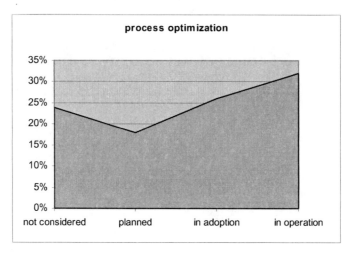

applications already implemented or will implement them soon. The optimization of internal processes is an important requirement for further activities in connecting companies, like the participation in electronic marketplaces or electronic collaboration.

A rather diversified picture shows the status of electronic logistics implementation. While 38.6% of the participants already have these applications in use, 45% do not consider them important for their companies. This leads to the conclusion that companies with logistic processes, which can be supported by Internet technologies, already use EC to facilitate these processes, while other companies do not see any benefit in supporting their logistic processes.

Figure 3: Diffusion of Electronic Logistics in the AC Styria

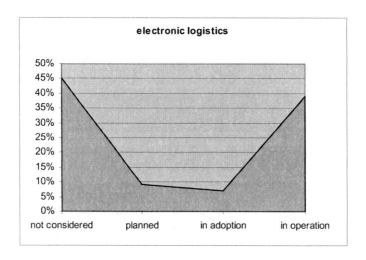

Figure 4: Diffusion of Customer Relationship Management in the AC Styria

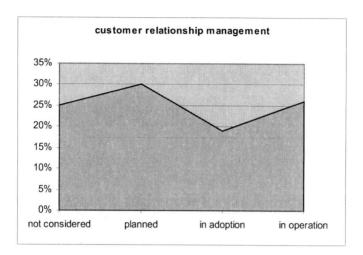

A quite important issue for SMEs in the Austrian automotive industry seems to be customer relationship management with the help of Internet technologies. Many companies are planning to implement services for their customers on the Web. But a quarter of the respondents showed no intention of considering this option in the future.

The rest of the typical EC applications (electronic collaboration, selling through the company's website, buying and selling through electronic marketplaces) show a similar picture. The majority of the companies do not plan to introduce these applications or are in an early state of implementation. This leads to the conclusion that respondents do not see enough benefit in these applications, are afraid of cost-intensive implementations, or have not optimized their internal processes for these applications.

Importance for Business Success

In a second part of the study, respondents had to appraise the importance of the mentioned applications for the general business success. On the one hand respondents had to evaluate the present importance and on the other hand they had to evaluate how the importance of the selected applications will change in the next two years.

Most important for the company success in the opinion of the interviewed companies is the optimization of internal processes through Internet technologies and applications in the field of customer relationship management. Surprisingly, selling and buying in electronic marketplaces is not considered important for business success nowadays. Although these applications will gain importance in the next two years, they still cannot compete with other applications. The only thing that will be less important for a successful business is selling over its own website.

Figure 5: Applications Most Important for Present Business Success

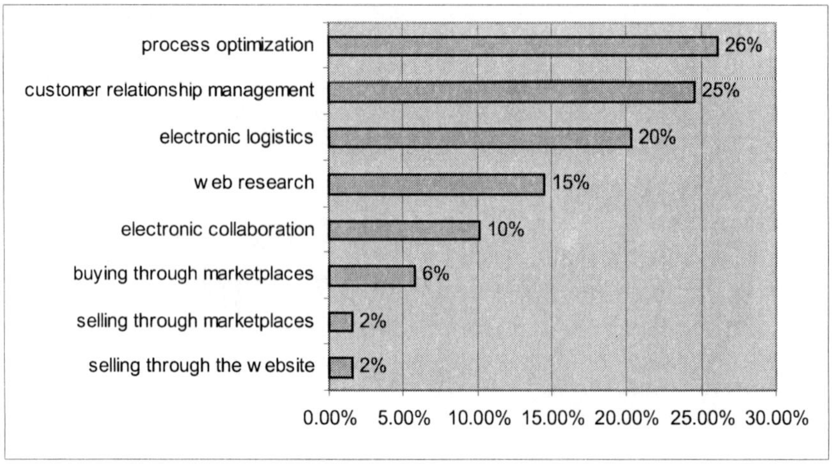

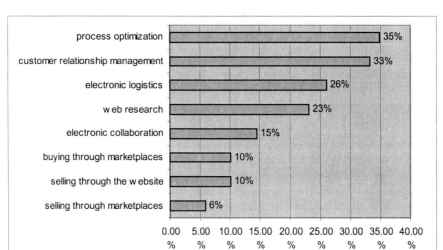

Qualification Requirements

The third part of the survey aimed to find out where representatives of the selected small to medium-sized enterprises see the most urgent need for supportive measures. All measures offered concerned key skills necessary for implementing new Internet-related applications. The most need for additional qualification was identified in the areas of customer relationship management, technical security, strategic matters, change management, as well as supply chain management. Looking at project management for implementing Internet technologies, competence for selling over the website, or legal issues, respondents see no demand for additional training.

Figure 6: Applications Most Important For Business Success in Two Years

Implication of the Findings

In conclusion, the survey results show that the EC adoption in SMEs is slower than expected. Surprisingly, there is no interest in participating in electronic marketplaces either as seller or as buyer. Today only 7% of the interviewed companies think that using electronic marketplaces for buying goods is important for their company's success. On the other hand there is a demand for digitalizing internal processes, since over 30% of the respondents see this central to their future success. This leads to the conclusion that most companies are in an early phase of implementing Internet-related technologies and have not integrated Internet technologies into their business model. If internal processes are not optimized, there is no need for companies to build networks or optimize external processes and networks.

In summary we can say that the applications SMEs are most interested in now, and in the near future, are applications for optimizing internal processes, customer relationship management, and electronic logistics. The Internet as a tool for selling and buying products is not a central issue for SME managers. Small to medium-sized enterprises use Internet applications mainly for optimizing internal processes and serving customers, and not to generate additional revenues.

At first sight it seems quite obvious that SMEs concentrate on the optimization of internal processes, but in the long run, developing their business models towards electronic business seems to be a must as the major companies in the AC Styria Magna and AVL also develop new concepts for electronic business, and as many SMEs in Styria are dependent on these companies, they have to change with them.

Solutions and Recommendations

The results of our survey and the conducted literature review show that the EC adoption in Austrian SMEs is obviously much slower than expected by most researchers and politicians. The presented survey results are only one part of a large research project that is aiming to bridge the digital divide between large companies and SMEs. It was found that successful EC solutions for SMEs can be developed interdisciplinary projects where various interest groups, such as SME mangers, software vendors, politicians, and academic researchers, are participating. Since most Austrian SMEs lack a business model, the formulation of such a business model is a suitable starting point for an SME EC adoption project involving different interest groups. Therefore in this section a concept to initialize such a fruitful cooperation—aiming to minimize the gap between the EC perspectives of different interest groups—is outlined.

A Concept for Supporting SME EC Adoption by Harmonizing Different EC Perspectives

A three-phase concept was developed in order to develop, evaluate, and change the business model of SMEs by bringing different interest groups together. As Figure 9 shows, within the three phases—Understand, Identify the Internet's Impact, and Change—seven specific steps toward the improvement of an existing business model are taken. Based on the principles of action research (Baskerville & Pries-Heje, 1999), this concept is used to help SMEs and researchers better understand the advantages of EC in SMEs and SME networks.

It was found that in order to thoroughly understand the business model of a company, the researchers have to interact intensively with the involved people in the first phase to understand their mental model of their business. Every entrepreneur has an intuitive understanding of how his business works, of the logic, of how it creates value—the business model. It influences all important decisions, but in many cases she or he is not able to communicate it in a clear and simple way. This logic of the system, the business model, is based upon a complex mental model and thus can only be changed if this mental representation of the real world changes first. The mental model can be described as a network of facts and concepts, and its content and structure contain our understanding of social and physical phenomena (Morecroft, 1994). The mental models of researchers and local governments usually differ largely from the entrepreneurs' business logic. Often these diverse mental models are the reason for the different EC perspectives.

Therefore the aim of the first phase—*Understand*—is to understand the logic behind the business of the involved SME or SME network in order to be able to define a business model later in the process. Very different starting points were identified; some companies use a small number of short rules as a strategy; others have complicated (long and hard to communicate) strategies (Eisenhardt & Sull, 2001; Porter, 2001). Depending on the state of the strategy definition of the consulted company, this first stage itself can be very beneficial for an organization. As a result all discussed terms are defined in a glossary so that concepts are equally understood within the organization.

Based on Honegger's six steps for solving a complex problem, four relevant steps, with the objective of understanding the existing mental model of the managers involved, were identified (Honegger, 2001).

In the first step the business model has to be defined in a more detailed way by taking different perspectives into account. As mentioned above, a strategy definition, if it exits, can be used as a basis in this step. However, the researcher should include in this first step the perspectives of as many different stakeholders as possible in order to obtain a complete overview. Also any specific market facts and other important influencing factors should be taken in to account at this early stage.

The identification of the key influencing factors of the business model is the main aim of the second step. This can be done by analyzing every stakeholder's interest in the business model. As a first result the researcher can supply the company with a list of

Figure 9: A Concept for Supporting SME EC Adoption

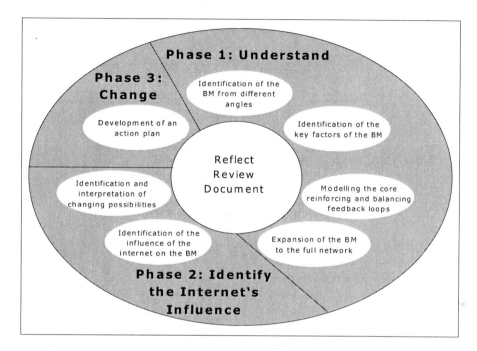

influencing variables within the business model. This list has to be discussed with, and completed by, the involved people from the organization. A glossary with a definition of every variable is another result of these first two steps.

After the definition of variables, the modeling of the core reinforcement or balancing loop is the objective of step three. The search for this central part of the business model has to be done in close relationship with the involved people of the organization. It was found that a workshop lasting either a half day for steps two and three or a whole day for steps two to four is very beneficial with regard to the results and their acceptance within the organization.

During step four the researcher has to expand the model to a full network and identify specific clusters of variables. The results are even better understood and accepted if the involved people are developing the network under the moderation of the researcher. But unfortunately the involved people are often not willing to invest sufficient time for this step. As a result more time has to be invested in explanation and discussion during the following steps.

The second phase—*Identify the Internet's Influence*—has the aim of identifying the impact of the Internet on the business model and all its variables. Once this influence is identified, possibilities of changing the business model towards gaining competitive advantage by using the Internet have to be found. These objectives are reached by providing expert knowledge about the influences of the Internet on specific markets and industry sectors, and by supplying a learning environment for managers to change their mental models. This phase illustrates the true added value of the involvement of a researcher in the process of changing a business model.

The fifth step therefore aims to identify all variables of the business model that are influenced by the Internet. Based on an intensive desk study and the data stored in the case library, the researcher indicates the influence on the business model and discusses his findings in a continuous review process with the client.

Seeking options for changing the business model in order to use the influence of the Internet is the essence of the sixth step. It includes pointing out the risks involved and the opportunities of these options. The combination of the creative potential (knowledge of innovations) of the involved research institution and the knowledge about this specific company helps to generate a variety of change opportunities, which are evaluated by the involved SME and the researcher.

In the third phase—*Change*—an action plan for changing the business model is developed. Either the researcher continues to actively take part in the process and accompanies the change process within the organization, or exits the problem situation here. Either way he has to document and structure the knowledge gained through the application of his findings during the abovementioned phases and steps before. This detailed analysis of every successful or unsuccessful application of the concept helps to extend the knowledge of the experts within the research institution.

It is important to note that during the application of the concept, a continuous review and documentation process is obligatory. Jumping forward or backward from one step to another is explicitly allowed; the concept should be seen as a network rather than a linear sequence of steps. This could mean for example that during the step, 'Identification and interpretation of changing possibilities', another variable of the business model is identified, so that the researcher has to jump back to 'Expansion of the BM to the full network' in order to change the business model network. Now the researcher has to go through the steps within the second phase again to see the implications of the new variable during steps five and six.

The proposed concept was found to generate benefits for all participating interest groups. If the concept is used for SME EC adoption projects involving SMEs, universities, and local government, the following benefits are provided:

1.   The local government is able to provide a useful impulse towards SME EC adoption for their local business environment by initiating such interdisciplinary research projects with local higher education institutions.

2.   The SMEs receive free and valuable advice from the researcher, the involved team members, and other SMEs. If numerous SME projects are conducted, the researcher or the local government is able to establish a network for information exchange and business advice between the participating SMEs.

3.   The researcher benefits through the closer connection between theory and practice, and the opportunity to publish the project results. Besides these benefits for the researcher, such a project also enables the university to provide a rich learning experience for its students.

So far the proposed concept is used to closely link the evolaris eBusiness Competence Center and the AC Styria SME network, providing a win-win situation for academic research, local government, and SMEs.

Future Trends

The need for adequate research in information society technologies and electronic commerce is not only a domestic problem for one particular country, but should also be discussed in an international context. The European Commission has realized that projects that include various interest groups are more successful. In the 6th Framework Program, which is the major EU initiative for funding research projects embracing a 16,270 Mio. Euro budget, primarily integrated projects and networks of excellence are funded. Especially the integrated projects require a large network as well as a clear object focusing on the development concerning EC of SMEs. This presents a large opportunity for further SME and EC research in Europe.

Conclusion

One of the main aims of academic research is to look into the future. On the other hand research should give useful input for companies and show them how to act and react. Especially for SMEs, a look too far into the future does not provide too much value. Hence a more pragmatic way of research has to be implemented to improve business success and transform SMEs. Our research shows that in this case connecting universities, local governments, and SMEs or SME network structures more closely, by initializing action research projects involving all stakeholders, clearly provides benefits for all involved parties. This could also be a way to increase the number of applicable SME research results in the field of EC. So far the results have been promising; e.g., due to our findings, one of the largest Austrian Internet marketplaces changed its strategy to be more successful in the SME field.

References

Baskerville, R.L. (1997). Distinguishing action research from participative case studies. *Journal of Systems and Information Technology, 1*(1), 25-45.

Baskerville, R.L. (1999). Investigating information systems with action research. *Communications of the Association for Information Systems 2* (Article 19). Accessed October 12, 2002 on the Web: http://cais.isworld.org.

Baskerville, R.L., & Pries-Heje, J. (1999). Grounded action research: A method for understanding IT in practice. *Accounting, Management and Information Technologies, 9*(1), 1-23.

Beschäftigte in Österreich. (2002). Wien: Hauptverband der österreichischen Sozialversicherungsträger.

Brown, D.H., & Lockett, N.J. (2001). Engaging SMEs in e-commerce: The role of intermediaries within e-clusters. *Electronic Markets, 11*(1), 52-58.

Caskey, K.R., Hunt, I., & Browne, J. (2001). Enabling SMEs to take full advantage of e-business. *Production Planning and Control, 12*(5), 548-557.

Chau, P.Y.K., & Hui, K.L. (2001). Determinants of small business EDI adoption: An empirical investigation. *Journal of Organizational Computing and Electronic Commerce, 11*(4), 229-252.

Corbitt, B.J. (2000). Developing intraorganizational electronic commerce strategy: An ethnographic study. *Journal of Information Technology, 15*(2), 119-130.

Cossentino, F., Pyke, F., & Sengenberger, W. (Eds.). (1996). *Local and Regional Response to Global Pressure: The Case of Italy and Its Industrial Districts.* Geneva: International Institute for Labor Studies.

Eisenhardt, K.M., & Sull, D.N. (2001). Strategy as simple rules. *Harvard Business Review, 79*(1), 106-116.

Filson, A., & Lewis, A. (2000). Cultural issues in implementing changes to new product development process in a small to medium-sized enterprise (SME). *Journal of Engineering Design, 11*(2), 149-157.

Franke, U.J. (1999). The virtual Web as a new entrepreneurial approach to network organizations. *Entrepreneurship & Regional Development, 11,* 203-229.

Honegger, J. (2001). Wissensmanagement: Vernetzt denken und handeln. *SFZ Technik,* (7/8), 50-53.

Jutla, D., Bodorik, P., & Dhaliwal, J. (2002). Supporting the e-business readiness of small and medium-sized enterprises: Approaches and metrics. *Internet Research, 12*(2), 139-164.

McGregor, J., & Gomes, C. (1999). Technology uptake in small and medium-sized enterprises: Some evidence from New Zealand. *Journal of Small Business Management,* (July), 94-102.

Morecroft, J.D. (1994). Executive knowledge, models, and learning. In J.D. Morecroft & J.D. Sterman (Eds.), *Modeling for Learning Organizations* (pp. 3-28). Portland: Productivity Press.

Perry, M. (1999). *Small Firms and Network Economics.* New York: Routledge.

Porter, M.E. (2001). Strategy and the Internet. *Harvard Business Review, 79*(4), 62-78.

Sanchez, A.O. (2000). *SME Statistics—EU Very Small Enterprises Show Dynamic Growth.* (Rep. No. CA-NP-00-011-EN). Brussels: European Communities.

Yang, H.-D., Mason, R.M., & Chaudhury, A. (2001). The Internet, value chain visibility, and learning. *International Journal of Electronic Commerce, 6*(1), 101-120.

Chapter XIV

Solutions to Support Procurement Activities within Industrial Districts

Aurelio Ravarini, Cattaneo University, Castellanza (VA), Italy

Marco Tagliavini, Cattaneo University, Castellanza (VA), Italy

Carlo Zanaboni, Cattaneo University, Castellanza (VA), Italy

Paolo Faverio, Cattaneo University, Castellanza (VA), Italy

Jennifer Moro, Cattaneo University, Castellanza (VA), Italy

Donatella Sciuto, Politecnico di Millano, Milano, Italy

Abstract

The evolution of information and communication technologies (ICTs) is thought to bring new development opportunities for enterprises by enabling the development of new industrial districts and consolidating existing ones. In fact, small to medium-sized enterprises could largely benefit from this potential innovation, and, specifically, from the improvement of the management of supply chain activities. ICTs, and especially Internet-based technologies, can support the flow of materials with a more efficient way of communicating and sharing information.

In spite of these premises, pioneering organizations providing e-commerce solutions for procurement have experienced many difficulties in sustaining their business. One relevant reason can be identified in the existing misalignment between the characteristics of the available technological solutions and the actual requirements characterizing the industrial district as a whole. The development of these solutions has been mainly based on the specifications of larger companies, which often turn out to be very different from the needs and requirements of SMEs.

This chapter analyzes the characteristics of industrial districts and the features of existing e-procurement solutions, and cross-matches the two dimension in order to verify the adequacy of vendors' offer to demand's needs. The deriving assessment represents the basis to propose a set of prescriptive models of e-procurement solutions that should properly cover industrial districts requirements.

Introduction

One of the most peculiar organizational structures characterizing the way small to medium-sized enterprises[1] (SMEs) manage their relationships with their partners is the *industrial district*. A quite largely agreed definition of industrial district states that it is a network of enterprises, placed in a geographically limited area, that share part of their processes, especially production and logistics (Varaldo & Ferrucci, 1997).

The evolution of information and communication technologies (ICTs), and in particular Internet-based technologies, provides these networks with new opportunities to effectively improve the management of supply chain activities, by supporting the flow of materials with a more efficient way of communicating and sharing information.

Current research and system development regarding business-to-business (B2B) electronic commerce are focusing on solutions that enable enterprises to reengineer their structure and that change them into flexible organizations cooperating with their clients, suppliers, and partners. These solutions aim at creating value along the entire supply chain by improving collaboration, work specialization, information sharing, and quickness of response, i.e., improving those characteristics that make SMEs belonging to industrial districts competitive.

Therefore, it is reasonable to assert that ICT solutions can effectively support the processes of companies belonging to industrial districts. This expectation, combined with the high interest of both researchers and practitioners for e-commerce solutions within SMEs, explains the attempts recently carried out to arrange ICT-based solutions to specifically support procurement activities within industrial districts. However, pioneers experienced many difficulties in providing solutions offering a real competitive advantage, mostly because of a misalignment between the characteristics of the available technological solutions and the actual requirements characterizing the industrial district as a whole (Fink, 1998; OECD, 1998; Micelli & Maria, 2000). In fact, the development of these solutions has been largely based on the specifications of larger companies, which often turn out to be very different from SMEs' (Poon, 1999; Micelli & Maria, 2000).

These remarks show the opportunity to explore the development of ICT solutions specifically designed to satisfy the requirements of those SMEs that belong to industrial districts. This work describes the results of a detailed analysis of the main characteristics of both industrial districts and existing e-commerce solutions to support procurement activities; the deriving outcome is then used to develop and suggest a set of prescriptive models of e-commerce solutions specifically aimed at supporting procurement activities within industrial districts.

Industrial Districts

The industrial districts phenomenon was first introduced in 1922 by Alfred Marshall in his *Principle of Economics* (Marshall, 1922) and has been the object of numerous studies from different disciplines: economy, sociology, history, etc. (Alberti, 2002).

The high number of studies produced a multitude of definitions of "industrial district," and a shared and precise explanation of this concept is still lacking. However, the most accepted definition is the one given by a pioneer and very important scholar of district, Becattini, who defined the industrial district as "a socio-territorial entity which is characterized by the active presence of both a community of people and a population of firms in one naturally and historically bounded area" (Becattini, 1990). This definition highlights the twofold nature of the district, a community of people who share a know-how on a specific sector originated in history and tradition, and a population of firms that use this know-how to generate value and are specialized in the different phases of the same production process.

Italian Industrial Districts

The economic and social importance of the industrial district phenomenon is proven by its diffusion in many countries. Examples of industrial districts can be found worldwide[2] (Alberti, 2002), but the most famous and studied are located in Italy. Italian districts like Murano, Prato, Brianza, and Valenza Po are known worldwide and have been studied as archetypal of the industrial district in order to understand the dynamics and the functioning of this phenomenon.

According to different studies, in Italy there are between 33 and 199 industrial districts,[3] which represent about 25% of the entire Italian population, 30% of the Italian employment, and 42% of the employment in the manufacturing sector (ISTAT, 1997). In addition, belonging to an industrial district has allowed many Italian enterprises to go beyond the typical performance and competitive skills of an SME. Even without considering very special cases—like Benetton and Luxottica—which, starting from their district environment, have become famous multinationals, the belonging to a district enabled many Italian SMEs to be competitive with large enterprises. These remarks are strengthened by the amount of national exportation referred to district enterprises, equal to 43.3% of the total national amount (ISTAT, 1999).

ICT Solutions for Procurement Activities

As for industrial districts, a clear definition of e-commerce solutions for procurement activities is still missing. Due to their recent introduction and rapid development, an acknowledged taxonomy of the different types of electronic solution for procurement activities does not exist yet (Pavlou & Sawy, 2002). This situation makes it necessary to premise any analysis on these technologies with the accurate specification of the taxonomy used by the author. In this work authors use a classification based on the analysis Pavlou and El Sawy made to synthesize several theories about inter-firm relations, but consider just one of the three dimensions employed by Pavlou and El Sawy,[4] *the reach*. It measures the number of potential partners to which a firm has access, i.e., potential trading partners in a B2B exchange. This choice is influenced by the specific needs of this work and because Pavlou and El Sawy themselves finally assume that the *dimension of reach* can almost completely describe inter-firm relations (Pavlou & Sawy, 2002).

The cross-analysis of the dimension of reach of both buyers and suppliers gives as a result a two-dimensional classification scheme (see Figure 1), in which four typologies of inter-firm relations are identified:

- **many to many**, where many customers and many suppliers are able to interact (for example, www.textileitaly.it);

Figure 1: The Two-Dimensional Classification Scheme of Inter-Firm Relations (Pavlou & Sawy, 2002)

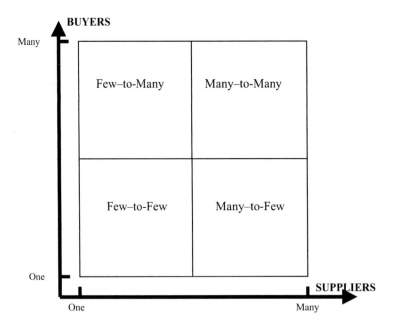

Figure 2: Two-Dimensional Classification Scheme of Electronic Solutions for Procurement (Authors' Elaboration on Pavlou & Sawy, 2002)

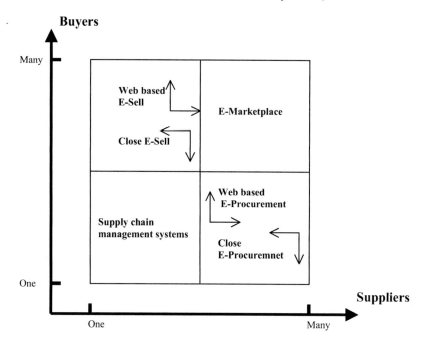

- **few to few**, where a restricted group of buyers and suppliers shares tight and strong strategic and collaborative relations, so that *few to few* in conclusion means: a restricted and selected group of subjects interacting with each other (for example, www.buzzsaw.com) (Pavlou & Sawy, 2002);

- **many to few**, where many suppliers are involved with the procurement process of one enterprise (this case can be referred to as *many to one*) or of few enterprises (for example, www.covisint.com);

- **few to many**, where many customers buy through a sales channel of one enterprise (this case can be referred to as *one to many*) or of few enterprises (for example, www.dell.com).

Each inter-firm relation can be electronically supported by a specific electronic solution for procurement (see Figure 2):

- **E-marketplace (many to many):** Defined as a virtual place where multiple buyers and suppliers are able to transact, buying or selling goods or services, asking for cost estimates, offering, and stipulating commercial relationships (Giamminola, 2001). E-marketplaces make it possible to match demand with offer, so that buyers can reduce procurement costs and suppliers can improve the visibility of their companies and products (Phillips, 2000; Neef, 2001; Raisch, 2001). On the other hand, the number of firms involved in this type of exchange precludes strong interfirm relations (Pavlou & Sawy, 2002).

- **E-procurement (many to few):** Solutions that allow "traditional powerful buyers to capture benefits by leveraging their existing physical into online B2B exchanges" (Pavlou & Sawy, 2002).

- **E-sell (few to many):** A virtual sales channel through which few big suppliers put their products and catalogs at many buyers' disposal, a mechanism that closely follows the primary model for business-to-consumer e-commerce.

- **Supply chain management systems (few to few):** Solutions that support close and strategic relationships between a small number of firms, and benefit from Web-based technologies to exceed the substantial costs that limited the spread of EDI solutions for this type of relationship.

Research Procedure

The main goal of this analysis, as presented so far, is to identify the requirements of different types of industrial districts, suitable to be fulfilled by electronic solutions for procurement. This aim makes it necessary to set some variables which can help to clearly divide the empirically available cases.

In particular, two variables are identified as responding to the task: the *competitive advantages* that a company could achieve thanks to its placement in a specific geographical area (Varaldo & Ferrucci, 1997) and the *critical roles*, i.e., the presence of companies playing key roles within the district supply chain.

Each of these variables points out some peculiarities of the analyzed district and of its composing firms, so that the cross-analysis between *competitive advantages* and *critical roles* allows the identification of a number of district environments and their specific requirements, providing the basis for the development of *ad hoc* models of electronic solutions for procurement.

The Competitive Advantages

The typical competitive advantages that have been referred to industrial districts since Alfred Marshall can be defined as *Marshallian competitive advantage* and divided into *physical economies of localization, social economies of localization,* and *external economies of agglomeration* (Marshall, 1922). These advantages are mainly related to factors that share a considerable decreasing of importance as a consequence of ICT evolution, like the cost reduction due to the small geographical distance between district members and the value of the embedded social know-how sustaining the local labor division.

This appraisal makes it necessary to identify a second kind of advantage, which shares the possibility of being exploited by ICTs and especially by electronic solutions for procurement. According to this requirement, we identified three kinds of *peculiar competitive advantages*:

- the *district brand*, which embeds heterogeneous advantages available to all the district members;

- *district leaders*, which are recognized as district sawyers in the overcoming of the actual difficulties districts are facing; e. Especially, district leaders seem to play a primary role "[...] facilitating the introduction of new technologies and the sharing of codified knowledge, sustaining the demand for workforce in sub-contracting companies, [...] modifying the organizational morphology of the industrial district, acting as boundaries spanners" (Alberti, 2002);

- the *district superior technology*, referred to both products and production cycles, which are the possible results of the typical district labour specialization.

Each of the analyzed competitive advantages (Marshallian, brand, leaders, superior technology) is related to a specific typology of district with its own peculiarities and requirements:

- **Brand districts**, characterized by shared competitive advantages originated from the localization in a region that is famous worldwide for the excellence of both products and production techniques in a specific industry (e.g., in Italy: Murano's glass or Brianza's furniture). These characteristics underline the need to maintain both traditional production techniques and product origin in order to sustain competitive advantages.

- **Ruled districts**, characterized by one or more companies leading the district, thanks to their cultural superiority and their availability of financial and strategic resources. They become the core of the district productions, advantages, and strategic decisions. In this type of district, the leader's interest substitutes the general interest of the district: accordingly, the focus must be on how to valorize and safeguard the leader's competitive advantages.

- **Technologically superior districts**, characterized by a mix of both Brand district and Ruled district characteristics, for the presence of enterprises standing out for their technological products and/or production techniques. Even if these enterprises cannot be considered as district leaders, there is still the requirement to safeguard their competitive advantages (as in Ruled districts), but also to maintain the product origin (as in Brand districts).

- **Marshallian districts**, characterized by enterprises that share only Marshallian competitive advantages, thus not exploiting ICT opportunities. Nevertheless, there is still a purpose that can be carried out through the use of ICTs: the modernization of district infrastructures and of the operative models of district firms.

The Critical Roles

The critical roles are the second variable used to characterize an industrial district, and put the emphasis on the players that could enable and drive technological and organizational innovation. Within a district it is possible to identify six critical roles:

- **Associations, banks, and public administration:** Subjects not-directly involved in the supply chain, but frequently very influential within the district. Their general aim is to increase the value and the competitiveness of the local system as a whole; coherently with this aim, they are considered eligible to play a critical role in all the identified district typologies but the Ruled one, in which the leader's interest substitutes the interest of the district as a whole.

- **Internal suppliers of direct goods:** Subjects belonging to the industrial district capable of pooling many district enterprises with their initiatives in those environments where the supplies have a strategic role, therefore not in the Ruled Districts, where buyers rule.

- **Manufacturing companies:** These subjects could play a critical role in the Ruled and Technologically Superior Districts, in which the chief district production is concentrated in the hands of few enterprises.

- **Intermediaries:** Subjects capable not only of pooling many district enterprises, but also of being promoters and managers of a B2B e-commerce solution in each kind of district.

- **External suppliers of indirect goods:** Usually incapable of playing a critical role, with the exception of those districts where the high cost of labor leads to outsourcing the product manufacture outside the district boundaries.

- **Business clients:** Subjects capable of influencing the district enterprises to join their electronic solutions for procurement, thanks to their importance.

The identification of critical roles and district typologies is not enough to clearly describe the empirically identifiable environments. The aim of the research requires a cross-analysis between the two variables,[5] which gives as a result 16 possible district environments with their own characteristics and requirements (see Table 1).

These results are the basis for the development of *ad hoc* models of electronic solutions for procurements, which are required not only to be suitable to the identified district characteristics and requirements, but also to valorize them so that they become a new truly aspired competitive advantage for district enterprises.

Model Development

The result of the cross-analysis between district typologies and critical rules is the starting point to develop models of electronic solutions for procurement that are suitable for the different district environments. The research procedure could also be an empirical method to identify characteristics and requirements of the analyzed industrial districts, in order to recognize the most suitable model. These research requirements demand a further step before developing the models. In fact, while the existence of the subjects grouped as critical roles is taken for granted, the actual existence of industrial districts strictly belonging to one of the four identified typologies is not. Many districts show

Table 1: Cross-Analysis Between District Typologies and Critical Roles, and 16 Identified District Environments

		District Typologies			
		Brand Districts	Ruled Districts	Technologically superior districts	Marshallian Districts
Critical Roles	None	☒			☒
	Associations, Banks and Public Administrations	☒		☒	☒
	Internal Suppliers				☒
	Manufacturing Companies		☒	☒	
	Intermediaries	☒	☒	☒	☒
	External Suppliers				☒
	Business Clients			☒	☒

characteristics of at least two typologies, such as Murano's glass district, which can be considered as a prototype of Brand District, but where two big firms, La Murrina spa and Venini spa, operate almost as district leaders. There is the need for a variable that is more accurate than the district typology to clearly identify the real requirements of analyzed districts, and the authors' solutions is the development of an index called *Peculiar Competitive Advantage Diffusion* (δ)[6]:

$$\delta = \frac{Number\ of\ enterprises\ which\ benefit\ from\ district\ peculiar\ competitive\ advantage}{Number\ of\ enterprises\ belonging\ to\ the\ industrial\ district}$$

Clearly, δ is still an affected-by-error measure, even if it is more accurate than the simple district typology; but, given the aims of the research, the statistic weight of this error is tolerable.

The eventual values of the *Peculiar Competitive Advantage Diffusion* can be grouped into four ranges; analyzing Table 2, it is possible to understand the link between these ranges and the district typologies.

In this way, given all the necessary tools, it is finally possible to develop a reference framework. Industrial districts can be clustered into 16 environments, each with its own characteristics and requirements. Analyzing these results, six models of electronic solutions for procurement are developed to be suitable for each of these environments (see Table 3): Virtual District, Systems for Large Enterprises, Virtual District Supply Chain Management System, E-Procurement & E-Sell, Participative Solutions.

Table 2: Relationships Between Peculiar Competitive Advantage Diffusion and District Typologies

		Peculiar Competitive Advantage Diffusion			
		Zero $\delta = 0$	Low $\delta \to 0$	Medium $\delta \to 50\%$	High $\delta \to 100\%$
District Typologies	Brand Districts				☒
	Ruled Districts		☒		
	Technologically Superior Districts		☒	Not significant	☒
	Marshallian Districts	☒			

Virtual District

This model is suitable for district environments characterized by a high level of the Peculiar Competitive Advantage Diffusion, and associations, banks, and public administrations playing critical roles. The characteristics and requirements of this environment focus on an exploitation of the district as a whole, as does the need to maintain both traditional techniques of production and product origin in order to sustain competitive advantages. A suitable model, besides supporting the district enterprises, should become the guideline to build the territorial infrastructures that create value for every subject belonging to the district. This effort toward ICT-based competitive advantages is more complex and general than a single electronic solution for procurement: an effort that should involve wiring, training, etc.

Focusing the analysis of the model just on the electronic solution for procurement, there should be a concurrent and more efficient way, besides traditional ways, to manage supplying relationships for all the district enterprises. These remarks lead to the development of a more complex structure than simple vendor solutions.[7] Instead of a structure enabling many-to-many or few-to-many relationships, the *Virtual District* model should enable flexible structures (see Figure 3). In this way, the single enterprise will be able to act as:

- a buyer and/or supplier in an e-marketplace (many to many) to manage left-over stocks and supplies of non-strategic services and goods;

- a buyer and/or supplier in a closed e-procurement (few to many) to manage more strategic relationships;

- a partner in a supply chain management system (few to few) to manage the most strategic relationships as a virtual supply chain, enabling activities like co-planning, co-designing, etc.

Table 3: Reference Framework of Developed Models of electronic Solutions for Procurement

District Categories	Peculiar Competitive Advantage Diffusion	Critical Role	Virtual District	Systems For Large Enterprises	Virtual District SCMS	Vertical District Community	E-Procurement & E-Sell	Participative Solutions
Brand	High	Null	■					
		Ass., Bank, etc.						
		Intermediaries			■			
	Low							
	Zero							
Ruled	High							
	Low	Man. Company						
		Intermediaries		■				
	Zero							
Technologically Superior	High	Ass., Bank, etc.	■					
		Man. Company						
		Intermediaries						
		Business Client						■
	Low	Ass., Bank, etc.						
		Man. Company		■				
		Intermediaries						
		Business Client						■
	Zero							
Marshallian	High							
	Low							
	Zero	Null						
		Ass., Bank, etc.	■			■		■
		Internal Supplier						
		Intermediaries						
		External Suppl.					■	■
		Business Client						■

Figure 3: The Virtual District Model

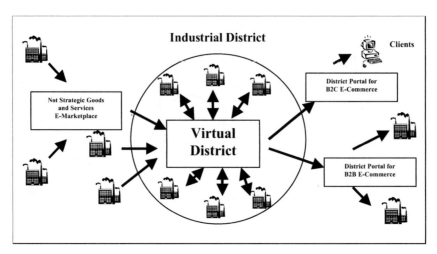

Besides these intra-district relationships, the model could also exploit external relationships, electronics solutions for procurement of stationery and not strategic services, commercialization of district products, and all those non-strategic relationships that could be established with the external environment.

Systems for Large Enterprises

Whenever a district is ruled by a single enterprise, leaders' requirements often substitute the general district requirements. In this case, the most adequate solution appears to be the adoption of existing systems available for large enterprises, making it useless to develop an *ad hoc* model. Besides, it's not coherent with the aims of this research to deepen a system dedicated to large enterprises; the rich literature on this topic is thus referred to Leebaert (1998), Aldrich (1999), Bovet (2000), Wise (2000), Camarinha-Matos, Afsarmanesh, and Raselo (2001), Neef (2001) and Raisch (2001).

Virtual District Supply Chain Management Systems

It is a hybrid model of the *Virtual District* and *Systems for Large Enterprises* that inherits solutions from both. The *Virtual District Supply Chain Management Systems* (SCMSs) should be suited for the need to develop a territorial infrastructure where the needs of large enterprises coexist; this is typical of a district environment characterized by a high diffusion of the peculiar competitive advantage and intermediaries playing critical roles.

Like the *Virtual District* model, the *Virtual District SCMSs* should consist of both an electronic solution for procurement, and a set of services and features producing an exploitation of the district as a whole. However, the presence of some strong and strategic

Figure 4: The Virtual District Supply Chain Management Systems Model

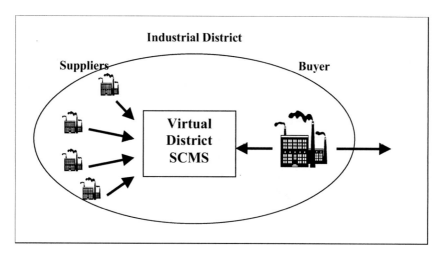

subjects requires a focus on their needs. Thus, according to the *Systems for Large Enterprises* model, the *Virtual District SCMSs* should support relationships between the intermediary and its district partners, besides giving the intermediary the tools to manage the relationships of their supply chain with the external environment of the district (see Figure 4).

Vertical District Community

This model is related to districts where, on one hand, key players (i.e., associations, banks, and public administrations) understand the importance of the community that the district as a whole represents; on the other hand, the enterprises suffer from a low competitive advantage. The most adequate solution in this case is similar to the *Virtual District* solution, but, with respect to that model, the *Vertical District Community* is characterized by a wider opening to external district relationships. There is no need to maintain traditional techniques of production and product origin in order to sustain competitive advantages, because the best partner, supplier, or service might not be found within the district. Nevertheless, in this type of district environment, the feeling of community and the attachment to the territory are still important, not only for the requirements of the key players, but also for that hidden strength that is part of the essence of a district.

Besides all the *Virtual District* model features, this environment requires a model that also acts as an interface with the external environment, enabling enterprises of the district to act as (see Figure 5):

- buyers in e-marketplaces of strategic and not strategic services and goods or in e-sells, or just with their typical supplier;

Figure 5: The Vertical District Community Model

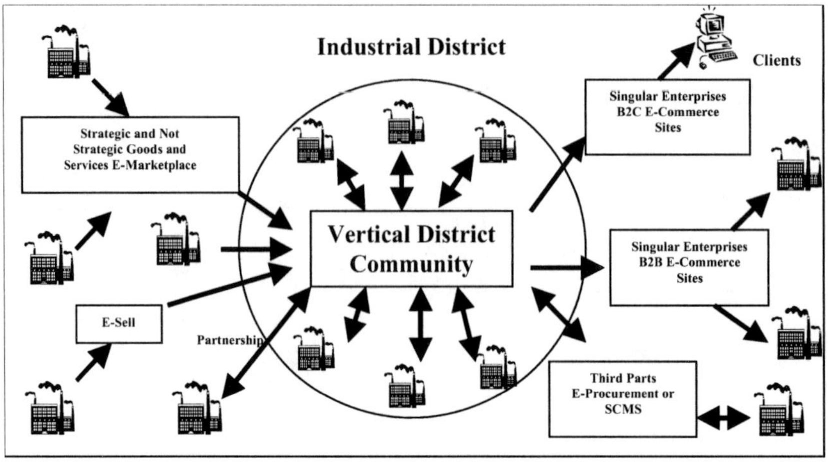

- sellers through owned B2C or B2B sites;
- partners able to manage their relationships with enterprises that are external to the district through a third-party SCMS, or in a traditional way.

E-Procurement and E-Sell

In a district environment where there are no particular competitive advantages, i.e., in a Marshallian district, and few enterprises stand out among the others without being district leaders, district interests and survival tend to lose their importance. In this case, these few enterprises that stand out could undertake the adoption of e-procurement and e-sell systems of the same kind that are already available for large enterprises. There is no need to develop an *ad hoc* model, but the choice to make use of these systems depends on the means of these enterprises. Unfortunately, a district enterprise that is not a leader can seldom afford the investments needed to adopt these systems.

Participative Solutions

This model is related to district environments where enterprises do not share any particular competitive advantage and key roles are absent. In this case, each district enterprise can individually choose to be part of one or more electronic solutions for procurement enabled by subjects not belonging to the district (see Figure **X**) as:

- great e-marketplaces that globally join together demand and supply of enterprises belonging to the same economic sector;

Figure 6: The Participative Solutions Model

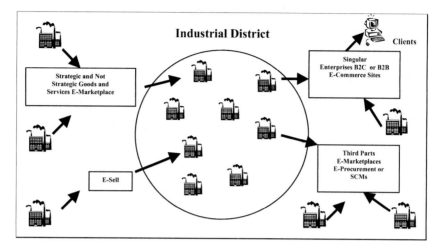

- supply chain management systems and/or e-procurement systems of important business clients;
- e-sell of important suppliers.

Future Trends

The increasing interest toward Knowledge Management Systems (KMSs) could lead the research to investigate how to use them to provide services within industrial districts. In fact, the effect that a KMS could have on an industrial organizational structure whose wealth is based on embedded and shared knowledge, could turn out to be more interesting and advantageous than the use of simpler electronic solutions for procurement, but also more difficult to implement because of the "traditional" culture of SME entrepreneurs.

Conclusions and Future Work

The theoretical models proposed in this chapter are based on real necessities that are expressed by industrial districts and have been pointed out by the developed reference framework. This research procedure leads the obtained results to be a manifesto for both vendors to understand the potentiality of a convergence of district needs and ICT solutions, and district entrepreneurs. In fact, district entrepreneurs can understand how the renewal of district supply chains, based on ICTs specifically developed for their own needs, is a valuable competitive advantage. Ad hoc developed technological solutions, supplemented with district values like know-how and the disposition towards job subdivision and specialization, could strengthen both the competitiveness on markets that are already occupied and the research of new business opportunities.

The six models developed are essentially the archetypes of the strategies that could be undertaken to implement a usable and effective electronic solution for procurement in different industrial districts that are supposed to have some specific characteristics and requirements. Future research will need to empirically test the validity of these results, by trying to match the identified models with the vendors' actual offer, in order to understand if existing systems are suitable to implement some of these models. At the same time, the actual existence of different types of industrial districts and their supposed ICT requirements will be empirically checked through a survey on the field.

Endnotes

[1]   This chapter will refer to the current definition of SMEs provided by the European Community that identifies those companies with less than 250 employees, a turnover lower than 40 million ECU, and owned by less than 25% by non-SMEs, except banks or venture capital companies.

[2]   Some examples are Hollywood, Silicon Valley, and Orange Country in the U.S.; Scotland and Leicester in the UK; Grenoble and Montpellier in France; Gnosjö in Sweden; Baden-Württemberg in Germany; and Castellón in Spain, just to mention some of the best known, but more examples can be found in other countries like Portugal, Brazil, Mexico, and India (Alberti, 2002).

[3]   The mismatch of numbers depends on the already discussed lack of a shared and precise definition of industrial district.

[4]   In their analysis, Pavlou and El Sawy (2002) consider three dimensions to span the interorganizational relations: reach, range, and reciprocity.

[5]   Actually, the district typologies variable could be substituted by the competitive advantages without losing relevant information.

[6]   The value of the numerator must result from an empirical analysis aimed at identifying which is the most considerable particular competitive advantage inside the district.

[7]   Refer to the above-described electronic solutions for procurement.

References

Alberti, F. (2002). *Industrial Districts. Inter-Firm Networks, Entrepreneurial Agency and Institutions.* Guerini Scientifica.

Aldrich, D.F. (1999). *Mastering the Digital.* New York: John Wiley & Sons.

Becattini, G. (1990). The Marshallian Industrial District as a socio-economic notion. *Industrial District and Inter-Firm Cooperation in Italy.* International Institute for Labor Studies.

Bovet, D. (2000). *Value Nets: Breaking the Supply Chain to Unlock the Hidden Profits*: New York: John Wiley & Sons.

Camarinha-Matos, L.M., Afsarmanesh, H., & Raselo, R.J. (2001). *E-Business and Virtual Enterprises. Managing Business to Business Cooperation.* IFIP.

Fink, D. (1998). Guidelines for the successful adoption of information technology in small and medium-sized enterprises. *International Journal of Information Management,* (18), 243-253.

Giamminola, G. (2001). *E-Marketplace.* ISEDI.

ISTAT. (1997). *I Sistemi Locali del Lavoro 1991.*

ISTAT. (1999). *Rapporto Annuale. La Situazione del Paese nel 1998.*

Leebaert, D. (1998). *The Future of the Electronic Marketplace.* MIT Press.

Marshall, A. (1922). *Principle of Economics.* MacMillan.

Micelli, S., & Maria, E.D. (2000). *Distretti industriali e tecnologie di rete: Progettare la convergenza.* Franco Angeli.

Neef, D. (2001). E-procurement. From strategy to implementation. *Financial Times.*

OECD. (1998). *The economic and social impact of electronic commerce: Preliminary findings and research agenda.* Organization for Economic Cooperation and Development. Retrieved on the Web: www.oecd.org.

Pavlou, P.A., & Sawy, O.A.E. (2002). A classification scheme for B2B exchanges and implications for interorganizational e-commerce.

Phillips, C.M. (2000). *The B2B Internet Report.* Morgan Stanley Dean Witter.

Poon, S. (1999). Small business and Internet commerce: What are the lessons learned? *Doing Business on the Internet: Opportunities and pitfalls.* Springer Verlag.

Raisch, W.D. (2001). *The E-Marketplace Strategies for Success in B2B E-Commerce.* McGraw-Hill.

Varaldo, R., & Ferrucci, L. (1997). *Il distretto industriale tra logiche di impresa e logiche di sistema.* Franco Angeli.

Wise, R. (2000). Beyond the exchange: The future of B2B. *Harvard Business Review.*

Chapter XV

SMEs and the Internet: Re-Engineering Core Business Processes and Defining the Business Proposition for Success

Elizabeth Fife, University of Southern California, USA

Francis Pereira, University of Southern California, USA

Abstract

This chapter provides in-depth profiles of two representative small firms and one medium-sized firm from a variety of industry sectors in order to delineate the workflow processes, cost structures, and other aspects about these companies that affect their e-commerce potential. We seek to identify specifically how SMEs can feasibly re-engineer and engage in e-commerce. We consider re-engineering internal business processes as a prerequisite for firms trying to move to e-commerce on the Internet. However, even after re-engineering has occurred, our primary data gathered from key cases—Schober's Machine and Engineering, a small business that designs and builds custom-engineered machines; Castle Press, a small firm specializing in high-quality printing; and Dilbeck Realtors, a medium-sized real estate brokerage—all show that the value proposition for e-commerce still has yet to be realized.

Introduction

Although both large and small firms made substantial IT investments[1] throughout the '90s, small to medium-sized enterprises (SMEs) are far less likely to engage in electronic commerce than large corporations (OECD, 2001; Buckley & Montes, 2002). In addition, small firms collectively have not embarked upon re-engineering to a measurable degree. Even among large firms in the U.S., where re-engineering efforts have been underway for over a decade, implementation has been more difficult than anticipated (El Sawy, 2001). A U.S.-based study found that only a small portion of established companies are actually using the Internet to do business. Overall, financial gains have been observed, yet there is still a long way to go before the Web will be broadly used for rationalizing the internal business processes of SMEs (Park, 2000).[2]

The factors for success that have been identified in re-engineered firms include capital, a knowledgeable IT staff, leadership, and close alignment of the company's culture, product, and organization to the technology. The extent to which these same factors are necessary requirements for re-engineering in SMEs is not yet established, as most SMEs have lacked the essential resources to enable a comprehensive business process re-engineering effort.

This chapter provides in-depth profiles of two representative small firms and one medium-sized firm from different industry sectors in order to delineate the workflow processes, cost structures, industry sector, and other aspects about these companies that affect their e-commerce potential.

We seek to identify specifically how SMEs can feasibly re-engineer their internal business processes to support a move to e-commerce on the Internet. Based upon primary data gathered from our exploration of SMEs, including Schober's Machine and Engineering, a small business that designs and builds custom-engineered machines; Castle Press, a small firm specializing in high-quality printing; and Dilbeck Realtors, a medium-sized real estate brokerage, we find that the value proposition for e-commerce has yet to be realized.

Whether the payback for re-engineering will justify the investment in time and money is not apparent since in many SMEs bureaucracy and inefficiency are not as ingrained as in the large corporation (Hale & Cragg, 1996). The question posed here is *if* an SME does re-engineer its core processes, what benefits can be expected? A related issue for further study is the extent to which these benefits will resemble those of the large corporation.

Challenges for SMEs: Status Report

When considering the challenges for SMEs to re-engineer, it should be recognized that most small businesses are in fact very small. In the U.S., nearly 90% of all sole-proprietorships have annual business revenues less than $100,000 and nearly 70% of these firms have annual business revenues of less than $25,000 (U.S. Census Bureau,

2000). Some 80% of all sole-proprietorships are home-based businesses (Pratt, 1999). Furthermore, some 65% of companies have less than 10 persons, and 80% of all small businesses operate without any employees (Oy, 1998). In the United States, SMEs number some 21 million and comprise more than 60% of all firms.[3,4]

As SMEs are extremely heterogeneous, we have defined them simply according to number of employees. Most research considers companies with less than 100 employees as small (Williams, 1999), and this is the criteria we use in this study. Firms with between 100 and 500 employees are considered medium sized. Various measurements and definitions of small firms can be found, however, ranging from three to less than 500 employees (U.S. Small Business Administration, 2000).

Solutions providers pinned their hopes on small businesses becoming an important market for IT once the large enterprise market was saturated. However, the market has been slow to materialize. An OECD study finds that SMEs have much to gain from employing IT and utilizing e-commerce: from researching global markets, learning about customer tastes and preferences, and reaching targeted audiences, to back-office efficiencies in procurement and production, logistics and coordination, supply processes and inventories, monitoring production costs, and quality control. However, SMEs still lag in their ability to exploit e-commerce (OECD, 2001). In Europe it is estimated that while 70% of SMEs have Internet access, only 40% have websites (Hobly, 2001; Turner, 1997).[5] The results are similar for the U.S., where 62% of SMEs surveyed reported not having websites and only 12% of companies that did have websites reported that they were using them to sell goods and services (*Los Angeles Times*, 1999). The Small Business Administration in the U.S. states that 1.4% of Internet use is related to e-commerce sales (Williams, 1999). Furthermore, an Australian survey attributes the low adoption rates of e-commerce applications by SMEs to many issues: high cost, lack of awareness of the benefits, problems in understanding technical issues, perceptions of risks, concerns about fraud, shortfalls in skills and training, time concerns, and finally, maintenance and upgrade requirements of applications (Switzer, 2001).

Methodology

To establish the limitations and potential for re-engineering of SMEs, we have employed a comparative case study method, examining several SME firms over a three-year period (George, 1979; Eisenhardt, 1995). As has been noted, choosing appropriate cases for small-*n* studies is problematic, as selection bias is an inherent problem (Collier & Mahoney, 1996; Collier, 1995; Geddes, 1990). Controlling for variables is difficult, given the tremendous differences among SMEs. To attempt to mitigate this issue, our small firms share several critical characteristics.

None of the SMEs investigated here have yet re-engineered, but desire to do so and understand the technological and organizational resources needed. The workflow processes of these SMEs are examined to help shed light on how re-engineering could be approached.

Case Study Criteria

The firms we chose have stable structures, a successful track record, and are well-established in their field. All have been in business more than 50 years. Each is run by individuals who have in-depth knowledge and expertise of their own industry and a sophisticated understanding of information technology. We also chose industries that are generally considered good candidates for adoption of Web-based operations because they are information intensive and do not rely on a physical storefront to attract customers. The bulk of customers for nearly all these businesses is local or regional, although this need not be the case except for the real estate brokerage. The solid reputation of the three companies we profile draws in customers from across the U.S. Additionally, all of these companies provide services or products that are unique, can be costly, and are purchased infrequently. Furthermore, they all are vulnerable to a confluence of external pressures that include global competition, and for Castle Press and Schober's, time-to-market pressures and shortened product lifecycles.

In terms of their Internet strategies, all three firms maintain websites that principally provide information. Castle Press's site has increased its interactivity over the past two years, offering downloads and digital printing, as well as estimates. Dilbeck's website has expanded its functionality dramatically in the last two years. Using a case study approach to examining these industries is intended to help:

a.   Gauge the extent to which small firms can re-engineer core processes, and

b.   Identify potential constraints to the process of re-engineering.

The intent is to provide some insights and general findings for SMEs as a whole.

Approach

We examined small firms in the following industries: real estate, high technology (custom machine design and fabrication), consulting, and printing. Interviews were conducted between 2000 and 2003 with CEOs, technical support employees, administrative support, and workers. Yearly site visits were made first to define the workflow process, and then to monitor progress and changes in the firm's Web-based strategies. From this small-scale study, several commonalities are apparent, despite the fact that the workflow processes for each SME are specifically tailored to the business and nature of the product/service.

Initially, each firm completed a survey detailing their motivations for using the Internet and Web-based applications, the extent to which they utilize various services and applications, and the results of their technology investments. The SMEs detailed the Web-based applications that they currently use on the customer and supplier side, and for internal operations. They were also asked about future implementation plans. In addition, they gave feedback about the factors that influenced their decision to set up a website along three categories: corporate functions, customer base, and business efficiencies. Next, companies were asked about services for employees through the corporate intranet, including training, travel reimbursement, news, and job recruitment information. Finally, the firms were asked about the results from current IT efforts in terms of customer satisfaction, information gathering, increased efficiencies in production and administration, cost savings, as well as other benefits. This survey serves as a standard baseline for comparison across case studies.

First, a brief description of each company is provided, along with information about the external environments they operate within. Next, the industry sector is detailed, in addition to analysis of the internal operations, including the cost and labor structure of the company. Based upon interviews and surveying these firms, we consider a theoretical re-engineering of core processes, and enumerate the benefits and challenges that must be overcome for re-engineering to be a viable option. From this point we can begin to describe the critical success factors for re-engineering of core business processes.

Literature Review: Re-Engineering in Theory and Practice

Since the 1980s, the success of Japanese manufacturing and the information technology revolution have dominated the literature on organizational thinking and management. Initially, it was thought that radical redesign of business processes was needed to achieve efficiencies, lower costs, and improve quality (Kuwaiti & Kay, 2000). Specifically, it was concluded that organizations could utilize information technologies (ITs) to change from a hierarchical to a more flexible process-based structure (Morton, 1991). A similar conclusion was advocated by Davenport and Short (1990), who argued that organizations could improve efficiency and effectiveness by adopting process innovations and redesign. Hammer and Champy's (1993) study also pointed to the need for organizations to redesign and re-evaluate their processes, again using IT as a means to improve corporate efficiency and customer support. Although successes were reported, they often were achieved at a price: the downsizing that took place as a part of re-engineering had negative effects like demoralized workforces with little company loyalty. As a result, it became apparent that comprehensive re-engineering needed to include people-oriented factors such as the firm's culture and organization, communications, and employee training. Corporate culture, leadership, inter-firm communication, and other qualitative factors are now considered significant forces in the re-engineering process (Braganza & Myers, 1997).

Re-Engineering Small Firms: Status Report

Much has been written on the topic of re-engineering with respect to the large corporation (Hammer & Champy, 1993). McAdam's (2000, 2002) review of the existing literature concludes that the vast majority of studies on re-engineering concentrate on the large firm, and little research has been carried out on the applicability of the re-engineering concept in theory and practice to the small firm. A few of the more widely known studies that concentrate on this area look at business process re-engineering among 28 Canadian SMEs (Raymond, Bergeron, & Rivard, 1998), an in-depth look at a re-engineered small firm in New Zealand (Hale & Cragg, 1996), and finally, business process re-engineering has been examined in a set of Taiwanese firms (Chang & Powell, 1998). Additional studies have looked at re-engineering and e-commerce in SMEs, but there is still great need for more standardized, structured, focused comparisons.

Given the heterogeneity of small firms, and the differences between small and medium-sized firms, it has thus far been difficult to establish principles with general applicability to the population of these diverse organizations. Most work thus far has examined small numbers of cases to shed light on some dimensions of SMEs' experiences with IT and communications technology.

Despite the difficulties inherent in classification and defining a small firm, most are generally vulnerable to similar factors, including capital shortages, difficulties in finding and retaining skilled labor, and downturns in the economy. Although there are many mitigating factors that can alter the impact of these factors, such as government support for SMEs, studies to this point indicate that these are the major issues faced by small firms. Clearly, more systematically gathered data is needed to establish general principles about how SMEs can optimize their profitability and efficiency of operations. A few small-scale, regional studies have looked at e-commerce activities of SMEs (Smith, 1999; OECD, 2001), but more have looked at IT adoption (Turner, 1997; La Rovere, 1998; Julien & Louis, 1994).

Hammer and Champy (1994) briefly discuss re-engineering and the small firm, recommending that both small and large firms should have a minimal number of processes so that integration between tasks is visible and barriers to the customer are minimal. Although improvements in the areas of product development, customer service, and customer acquisition have been identified, re-engineering among SMEs has yet to materialize to any significant degree for several reasons. The small size and scope of the small firm's operations in addition to resource constraints makes re-engineering a low priority, especially in the face of more immediate challenges (Blili & Raymond, 1993; Chang & Powell, 1998). Also, vulnerability to external conditions—economic, social, and political change—is a constant for small firms in every region of the world (OECD, 2001).

Despite the struggles faced by most small firms, and the resultant lower level of investment in IT per employee compared to large companies (in the U.S.), SMEs in all industries are investing in computers, communications, and IT (Buckley & Montes, 2002). Consistent with these overall statistics for the U.S., the small firms included in this study are using e-mail and make use of the Internet for information gathering. Adoption of IT occurs incrementally, and often there is no clear path to full-fledged e-commerce capabilities. Particularly for small firms that have local, service-based businesses, e-commerce appears to be an added cost that offers limited revenue potential. Contrary to this finding, however, a recent study of small firms in the UK finds that SMEs adopt e-commerce in sequential and progressive stages (Daniel, Wilson, & Myers, 2002). At each stage they gained experience that helped efforts move to more advanced applications.

Our cases do not reveal a clear evolutionary path towards e-commerce. The firms in our study all use IT and communications intensively within their businesses and externally as well. Perhaps reflecting the diversity of SMEs, as well as their inherent flexibility compared to large firms, our small firm cases have adopted a variety of Web-based applications at differing levels of intensity, based upon industry type, capital availability, and customer base.

Furthermore, SMEs are often more focused on niche markets and customers than large corporations.[6] SMEs that focus on customized products, provide services, or carry out research and development, may not ever be able to exploit e-commerce applications that rest upon economies of scale and business efficiencies (Zugelder, 2000). These considerations all influence the potential for SMEs to re-engineer.

Conversely, it is also believed that SMEs have certain advantages over large firms in terms of re-engineering. Leadership is visible, and organizational structures are normally informal. In addition, changes can generally be implemented quicker in a small firm than in a large firm, due to greater flexibility and centralization and less bureaucracy (McAdam, 2000). Winston and Dologite (2002) examine the attitude of small-business owners towards IT, noting that business owners with positive attitudes towards IT are more willing to commit to IT projects. The SME owners in our case studies universally have positive attitudes towards IT, yet are still extremely careful about IT investments and seek a clear understanding of benefits.

Finally, smaller firms usually have a closer proximity to the customer, allowing for more precise analysis of customer needs. All these factors suggest that at least specific SMEs can implement re-engineering under favorable conditions. Raymond, Bergeron, and Rivard's (1998) study found that although the prerequisites for re-engineering success were less favorable for small firms than large firms, SMEs perceived that they had benefited to the same degree as the large corporations. The advantages included increased productivity, cost reductions, and an increase in the overall quality of the organization.

Case Study: Schober's Machine and Engineering

With annual revenues of $2 million, Schober's Machine and Engineering is a small engineering firm located in Alhambra, California, that produces end-to-end, custom-built mechanical and electronic equipment. The company was started in 1917 by Kurt Schober, who specialized in mechanical repair and recovery of airplanes. Today Schober's produces a wide variety of highly specialized customized equipment. Some 24 employees handle projects worth between $60,000 and $500,000.

Sixty percent of Schober's clients are small businesses, while the remaining 40% are large businesses, with the government accounting for some 4% of the latter. About 20% of Schober's clients are from California, while 60% are from other states in the U.S. Fifteen percent of their customers are from outside the U.S. Similar to the other firms detailed here, personal reputation and customer loyalty have been critical factors for success. Face-to-face interaction and word of mouth are the primary means to gain customers. Marty Meschner, owner and chief engineer of Schober's since 1978, has sought to increase the company's business with the maquiadorra in Mexico through personal meetings. He maintains that traveling to Mexico and personally meeting with potential customers is the most effective way to create these business relationships.

Industry Profile

This machine company caters to a niche market, rather than targeting large markets with standardized products that are amenable to IT applications for inventory control, assembly, and delivery. Schober's is unique in its variety of in-house engineering expertise, which allows them to custom-build products from start to finish.

External Environment

Demand for Schober's products rises and falls with economic conditions. Given the resources that the company invests in training, it is costly to reduce staff when revenues fall. Also, in light of the high capital costs for equipment like lathes, drills, presses, and computer hardware and software, any IT or communications technology investment must be integral to the business.

The greatest challenges for Schober's are lack of skilled labor and access to capital, as well as cash-flow problems given the company's high overhead and the lack of upfront payments. Electronic payments could help the latter problem, but technology isn't the definitive solution to any of these issues. In tough economic times, the company has been able to sustain itself due to a combination of its expertise and flexibility in adapting its competencies to new markets.

Schober's Internal Operations: Is Re-Engineering Necessary?

Schober's exemplifies the possible challenges generated by the limited scope of IP-based applications to increase the business efficiencies of SMEs. Operating in a fairly competitive industry, Schober's internal processes are relatively efficient and highly capital intensive, as shown in Figure 1.

Schober's receives preliminary designs or specifications from its clients predominantly through the Internet, in the form of DXF files, although occasionally they do receive such files via post. The company's team of engineers then draw up the blueprints for the machine, based on the received specifications. Once this is finalized, the blueprints are transferred electronically on the company's intranet to the fabrication section, where the individual components are designed and then transferred, once again, electronically to

Figure 1: Work Flow and Process in Schober's Machine and Engineering

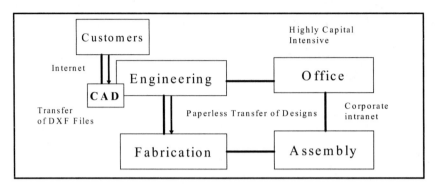

Schober's multi-million-dollar lathe. Because the company produces customized machinery, every product is unique and must be assembled manually. Engineering and fabrication make up 80% of the firm's labor cost, as illustrated in Figure 2.

IT Awareness and Expertise

Marty Meschner, owner of Schober's and a board member of the Small Manufacturer's Association in California, is well aware of the various suites of Web-based applications available.[7] Schober's has found through the years that they are often more technologically advanced than the large corporations they working for. Meschner argues, however, that many Web-based applications are unnecessary for the day-to-day running of the business. The Internet has been extremely useful to his business since the company is in constant collaboration with other manufacturers (Meschner, 2001). For example, the exchange of information has been facilitated by the Internet, and real-time inventory management in the companies they do business with have both created major improvements in efficiency.

Figure 2: Schober's Labor and Cost Structure

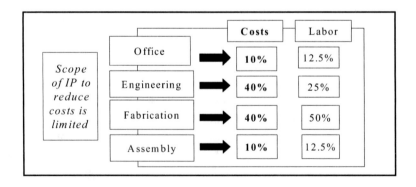

Use of the Internet

The company invests heavily in the training and development of its workforce, which consists of a unique combination of electrical, mechanical, and computer science engineers who work with technicians and apprentices. The diversity of skills represented at Schober's is the company's competitive advantage, and Marty Meschner cultivates the firm's knowledge base by personally recruiting new talent.

Use of the Internet overall, for expanding the company's client base, is somewhat limited from Schober's perspective given the specialized nature of the business and the high cost of each machine that they produce. Other small firms express similar views of their business, seeing the Internet as a complement to their efforts rather than a substitute for traditional business channels (Pereira & Fife, 1999).[8] Schober's has seen no marked increase in sales from the Internet, but finds it useful to have a website for customer support. Figure 3 shows that Schober's uses the Web mainly to provide information and transport files.

Since Schober's generates only 25 to 30 invoices monthly, accounting is minimal. In addition, since the firm's employee base is small, internal coordination and efficiency are not debilitating problems.

Schober's Machine and Engineering: Re-Engineering Model

As noted, some 80% of Schober's cost is associated with engineering and fabrication. However, since engineering and fabrication entail intensive intellectual and mental skills, attempting to reduce costs in these areas is challenging. A "direct from the customer"

Figure 3: Current and Planned Deployment of Web-Based Applications at Schober's Machine and Engineering

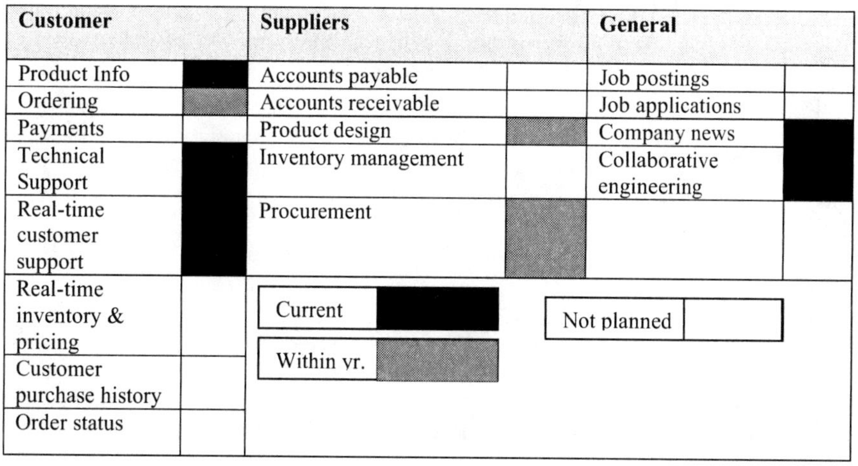

Customer		Suppliers		General	
Product Info	■	Accounts payable		Job postings	
Ordering	▧	Accounts receivable		Job applications	
Payments		Product design	▧	Company news	■
Technical Support	■	Inventory management		Collaborative engineering	■
Real-time customer support	■	Procurement	▧		
Real-time inventory & pricing		Current ■ Not planned ☐			
Customer purchase history		Within yr. ▧			
Order status					

Figure 4: Schober's Re-Engineered Processes

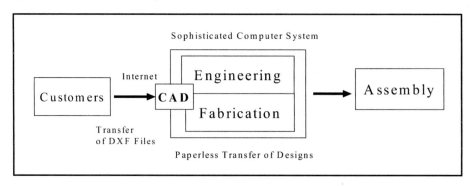

model is illustrated in Figure 4. This would require either customers "acquiring" the requisite skills to design and develop the machinery, or the development of a computer system that would take over that function. It is not clear that the current state of technology would make the latter possible, or if feasible, would make it cost effective.

Case Study: Castle Press

Castle Press is a Los Angeles-based commercial printing company with revenues of some $7 million annually. Founded in 1931, the company employs 70 employees in multiple product lines. Initially a printer of fine limited edition books, today digital printing represents its fastest growing segment. Offset printing is the company's specialization and accounts for 75% of revenues. Greeting cards account for 15% of revenues, and digital printing makes up about 10% of revenues. Castle Press prints limited-edition books, in addition to print advertising and marketing support material, including brochures and catalogs, and annual reports for small companies. Prices for orders range from $3,000 to as much as $500,000.

Printing is very much a regional business. Twenty-five percent of Castle Press's clients are small enterprises, while medium-sized and large enterprises comprise 65% of their client base, with the remaining 10% consisting of individual clients. George Kinney, managing editor of Castle Press, and VP of Marketing, purchased the company with his partner in 1979. He asserts that since printing tends to be a local business, personal relationships are extremely important and "eyeball-to-eyeball" meetings are crucial, which presents major challenges when trying to sell outside the region.

Internal Workflow and Cost Structure

Like Schober's, since Castle Press operates in a highly competitive industry, most internal processes are highly capital intensive and efficient, as shown in Figure 5, with

Figure 5: Workflow and Cost Structure at Castle Press

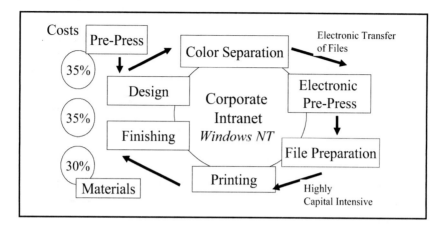

capital investments of at least $1 million.[9] Design, finishing, and materials are where the bulk of costs are incurred. The company uses a corporate intranet to transfer files from one stage of the printing process to the next. Administration and invoicing are not burdensome processes. Like Schober's, Castle Press does not generate large volumes of invoices, only some 100 per month.

Use of the Internet: Current and Planned

Kinney sees some value for e-commerce applications, including product information, technical support, and ordering capabilities, as shown in Figure 6.

Although a keen advocate for modernizing traditional printing processes and adapting to a Web-based environment, Kinney is grappling with what seems to be an insurmountable problem of trying to generate a user-friendly website that will allow his clients, as well as potential clients, to select from more than 1,000 grades of paper, as well as some 3,000 shades of color. Kinney argues that many clients do not know a great deal about printing, but want to create a high-quality item, such as a sales brochure. Customers come to Castle Press because they want a high-quality product, and they can rely on the expertise and reputation of the company. As such, they perform important value-added services like error checks and quality control. In a Web-based environment, much of the responsibility is passed onto the client.

IT and Internet Operations

Like Marty Meschner, Kinney needs to continually upgrade equipment, market aggressively, and retrain workers. These are key expenditures, and having a website has contributed to increased operating costs. Initially, the site was intended to improve

Figure 6: Current and Planned Deployment of Web-Based Applications at Castle Press

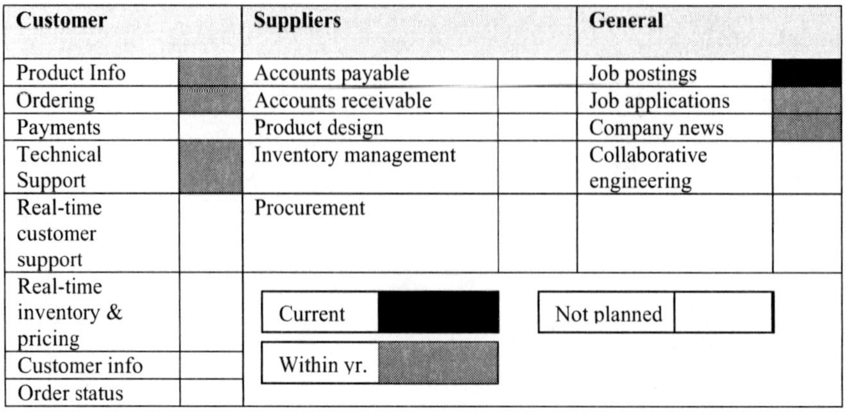

Customer		Suppliers		General	
Product Info	▓	Accounts payable		Job postings	█
Ordering	▓	Accounts receivable		Job applications	█
Payments		Product design		Company news	▓
Technical Support	▓	Inventory management		Collaborative engineering	
Real-time customer support		Procurement			
Real-time inventory & pricing		Current █		Not planned ☐	
Customer info		Within yr. ▓			
Order status					

customer satisfaction, by offering a means to obtain information about the company's services. Increased functionality has occurred in a gradual manner, and presently ordering, estimates, as well as digital printing are possible.

The Future of Printing and Re-Engineering

The potential for the Internet and IP-based applications may be seen in digital printing through the generation of customized products on a mass scale. Although, as Kinney stresses, this represents an increase in costs, the ability to produce customized products, such as sales catalogs tailored to individual tastes, may increase the take-up rate of catalogs that historically has stood at about 2%. Currently, the quality of digital printing is significantly lower than offset printing. Digital printing is suitable for disposable materials like magazines and catalogs, rather than more permanent types of publications like books.

If printing technology improves so that digital printing can equal the quality of offset printing,, then it is conceivable to view a different production process, as shown in Figure 7.[10]

In this scenario, from a single, master digital file of a document, like the *Encyclopedia Britannica*, a file could be sent to a neighborhood print shop after an order was placed. The customer could pick up the order at his or her convenience.

Case Study: Dilbeck Realtors

Dilbeck Realtors is a family owned and operated medium-sized real estate brokerage in Southern California that has provided residential and commercial services since 1950.

Figure 7: Extrapolation of Significant Re-Engineering in Printing Industry

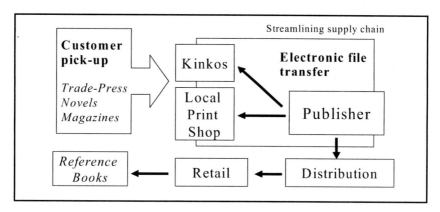

The company has 14 offices in Los Angeles with revenues of over $1 billion.[11] More than 600 independent agents work at Dilbeck. The breakdown of Dilbeck employees is: 28 administrative, 100 general staff, four IT staff, 17 corporate, and four to five relocation staff.

The company has maintained a successful record both before utilizing the Internet, as well as after substantial investments were made to establish a website. Its hope was to both increase efficiencies within its own offices, as well as to meet customers' information-gathering needs in a more convenient manner. Initially, a Web presence was seen as necessary to demonstrate that the company was on top of the latest industry trends.

Industry Characteristics

A traditional "middle-man" business, real estate sales—like stock brokering—is considered an endangered business, due to the Internet. Within the industry, it is believed that there are new opportunities for reducing transaction costs and improving the customers experience if a number of obstacles can be overcome (Oldham, 2000).

Like the other case studies examined here, the real estate business is information intensive, as well as highly competitive. Other relevant features that make real estate well-suited to IT and e-commerce are high transaction costs, and the fact that the experience is cumbersome and legalistic for both clients and agents. Since a house purchase and sale are significant transactions, the involvement of an agent is necessary to make sure that the legal parameters are met. It is necessary to have someone accountable and licensed to oversee the process. Exceptions where an automated process may work might be the sales of large housing tracts where standardization exists. Given the magnitude of a home purchase, it's unlikely that there will ever be a scenario where an agent is not needed in some capacity.

Although a real estate transaction is an extremely information-intensive process that is well-suited to automation, the nature of the product itself mitigates against full e-commerce capabilities. A home is not a static product, and although a virtual tour can give some insight about what to expect, a client still misses crucial aspects of the property such as the surrounding neighborhood, the smell, sounds, and overall ambiance.

Effect of External Factors on Dilbeck Realtors

Dilbeck, like other companies in the real estate industry, is vulnerable to the macro-economy, as interest rate fluctuations, recession, and employment rates affect revenue streams dramatically. The fact that Dilbeck is located in Southern California, however, has helped mitigate these factors, as property values and demand have steadily increased over the last several years.

Nonetheless, as an intermediary, there is increased downward pressure on commissions due to a perception that agents are not working as hard. Thus, the Internet has added pressure to the industry to change the traditional commission-based model.

Re-Engineering and Dilbeck Realtors

Streamlining internal operations has been achieved to some extent at Dilbeck Realtors through IT investment. However, there are limitations to achieving business efficiencies, due to the number of outside players involved in the provision of brokerage services. As shown in Figure 8, the process involves many players who communicate with each other multiple times throughout the transaction.

The buying and selling of residential property is an extremely complicated process involving a myriad of players. Despite widespread interest in making the process more efficient, for the foreseeable future, the Web will be an accompaniment rather than replacement for the physical real estate office.

Figure 8: Workflow Process for Typical Residential Real Estate Transaction

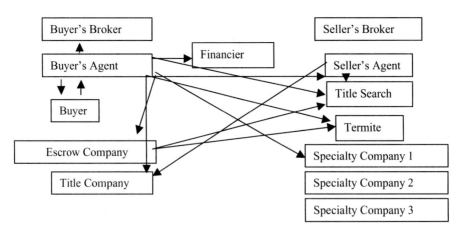

Many players on both the listing and the buying side are involved in a typical residential real estate transaction, including the escrow company, title company, property search company, termite company, and roof inspector, among many others, some whom may not even have e-mail. There is a common misconception that the agent's primary usefulness is during the preliminary part of the transaction, when in fact the greatest amount of time, effort, expertise, and talent is expended after the escrow period. Agents must manage the transaction as it moves among the various participants in as smooth a manner as possible, and often the ease and speed of the transaction depends upon the quality of the agent involved.

Although the Internet is helping consumers tie into the myriad of relationships that make up a real estate transaction, there is still a very long way to go. In the state of California, real estate purchases are becoming increasingly complicated. For example, a purchase agreement which used to be two pages has expanded to 10 pages. To stay within the confines of real estate law requires a voluminous number of forms and disclosures that must be correct. This is a difficult task for the layman and carries a risk of lawsuits.

E-mail communications within the company, and between the company and clients, has sky rocketed. The use of paper has increased, which is a considerable cost. For instance, it costs at least $1,500 each time the company roster is printed and distributed.

Dilbeck's Experience with the Internet

Typically, a real estate company brings in someone from the outside to create a website. Dilbeck instead was able to develop its site internally since the company possessed the unique expertise required. Echoing comments from other small firms we interviewed, Dilbeck maintains that effective websites are developed by people who possess both technical expertise and depth of knowledge about the specific industry. The company noted that most companies' real estate websites "reek of being contracted out" (Seccombe, 2001). In Dilbeck's experience, it is extremely difficult to convey to a technical person the specifics of the industry as well as the internal dynamics of the company.

Unlike the typical real estate company, Dilbeck has been able to create a full-time IT department that has created a high-quality website and a soon-to-be-implemented corporate intranet. Initially the site allowed customers to get information. In addition to personalized home searches and providing an agent, it is now possible to make appointments to see properties. This has proven to be an extremely popular feature, and Dilbeck can trace about four homes that have been sold through the website in the first two months of providing this service.[12]

Dilbeck carefully monitors visits to its site and keeps track of where people go on the site, at what times, and the duration of time spent at the site. The company is also able to mine the subscriber base collected from personalized home searches. As shown in Figure 9, providing information is still the primary use of the website, although Dilbeck hopes to use the Internet more extensively in the future.

Figure 9: Current and Planned Web-Based Applications

Customer		Suppliers		General	
Product Info	■	Accounts payable		Job postings	
Ordering		Accounts receivable		Job applications	
Payments		Product design		Company news	▨
Technical Support		Inventory management		Collaborative engineering	
Real-time customer support		Procurement			
Real-time inventory and pricing		Current ■ Not planned			
Customer info	▨	Within yr. ▨			
Order tracking					

Benefits of Dilbeck's Website for Customers

The Web allows a customer to do a lot of house shopping in a short amount of time. This is one of the principal benefits of the Internet for customers. Nothing will replace a visit in person to a home, but having the visual information at least gives people some insight that will help determine whether a visit in person is worthwhile. Richard Seccombe, Manager of Information Systems, notes that the number of houses that people want to see has been reduced to about three to five from around 10. Overall, because many buyers and sellers are better educated about their transaction, due to the Internet, the time that a house is on the market has generally decreased, the number of houses that a given client needs to see has been reduced, and escrow times have been shortened. A one-stop-shopping experience is still far from a reality, and the Web remains a complement to traditional newspaper advertising and signage, which is still the most important means of informing buyers of open houses.

Impact of the Internet for Dilbeck Realtors

Dilbeck Realtors realizes that it is necessary to have a website to remain prominent in this crowded and competitive industry. The company has made efforts to provide information to customers coming to the site and to give clients a clear picture of what happens in a real estate transaction. Also, Web-based advertising is the cheapest form of advertising that the company now utilizes. Thus far, the website has had measurable success with thousands of visitors recorded in first few weeks the site was up, and a substantial increase in the number of visitors to open houses continues.

In terms of the real estate agent, many have had to obtain training to develop the expertise needed to make use of the Internet and computers. E-mail, Web-based information, digital pictures, and desktop publishing are all ubiquitous and increasingly vital to the success of real estate agents. This has incurred a cost in time and money that represents additional tasks to the agents' duties. In general, agents do not gain clients through the Internet, but through traditional routes—referrals, word of mouth, and reputation. Despite a perception that agents now do less work, in fact the number of tasks needed to promote a transaction has increased, leading many agents to hire assistants. It is true that many buyers and sellers are more educated as a result of the Internet, so escrow times have been cut down, and agents don't need to show as many homes to clients. However, the bulk of the agents' work—customer acquisition and coordinating a transaction to the finish—still remain hidden and time-consuming duties. This is where the Web can potentially have a far-reaching affect on the industry.

Internet-Based Model of the Future

There is a strong movement afoot to automate the entire real estate transaction so that a client could get into a mini-site dedicated to his or her transaction and check on progress. If it were possible to track a transaction, as Dell Computer does, great efficiencies could be achieved for the whole industry. Much of an agent's time is spent calling various players to check on the status of their piece of the deal.

Mark Dilbeck, owner of the company, believes the Internet-based model of the future that could emerge may involve commissions going directly to brokers and agents who are full-time employees (Dilbeck, 2001). The Internet will be a tool to reduce some costs, but more importantly it will tie in the many parties that are involved in lending, escrow and title, inspection, and other services. Brokers will make money through offering a one-stop shop for clients. Customers will use the Internet to guide them, automatically connecting to the forms and information needed for the various pieces of the transaction. The Internet will continue to put pressure on commissions that may lead to bundling of services, like mortgages and escrows along with brokerage services. However, Dilbeck believes that even as use of the Internet grows, the "clicks and mortar" model will be most common for some time to come. Also, there will always be a place for the traditional shop where agents know their clients.

Things can be done today through electronic means that were never before possible, but the ultimate goal, where a whole transaction can be tracked, will require a collective effort and authoritative leadership from a central body to forge agreement and standardization.

Discussion

The human element is a vital component of the success that these SMEs have already achieved in separate, highly competitive businesses that were built over time through establishing a strong reputation. Nonetheless, all have utilized new technologies in slightly different ways to enhance speed, customer service, internal processes, product quality, and innovation.

Schober's and Castle Press operate in highly specialized niche markets, but face challenges common to many small firms: the maintenance of capital flow, and recruiting and maintaining a highly skilled workforce. Thus far, neither Schober's nor Castle Press has used the Internet as a sales distribution channel, but rather both rely on reputation, word of mouth, and face-to-face contact to acquire business. Dilbeck Realtors' success also is grounded in its local reputation, although its website is now propelling measurable sales activity.

Schober's, Castle Press, and Dilbeck Realtors further illustrate the general issues facing SMEs with regard to re-engineering. Overall, the success factors for re-engineering among SMEs have yet to be clearly defined in the literature.[13] Meschner and Dilbeck, and Kinney, echoing the sentiments of other small-business owners, see a limited role for many re-engineering applications in their capital- and knowledge-intensive businesses. Use of the Web is to a large extent a promotional tool, a source of information, and a way to increase visibility for these firms.

Even if suitable SMEs re-engineered their core processes, the value proposition for re-engineering is not yet evident or is still not possible. Certain benefits that re-engineering can bring to a firm, including streamlining of business processes and greater efficiencies, are not critical factors for SMEs. Based upon these cases and secondary data, it appears that internal coordination and communication are generally not problems confronting SMEs.

It is possible that resources could be better placed with information gathered about the external environment, as small firms are vulnerable to change in many forms: economic, political, social, as well as changes in customer preferences and habits (Gunasekaran, Forker, & Kobu, 1998).

Our case studies highlight SMEs that have carefully considered IT investments and yet have uncertainties about whether they should or if they can re-engineer. This still remains a question for further investigation to establish clearly the conditions for re-engineering to be appropriate for SMEs. Slow adoption of Web-based applications reflects the complexities of aligning e-commerce strategies with firms' internal core processes. Greater understanding of how highly specialized small firms can re-engineer will shed light on the potential for SMEs to adopt electronic commerce.

The companies examined in this chapter clearly are keenly aware of e-commerce applications, and slow adoption rates are due to resource constraints and limited applicability. The situations of Schober's Machine and Engineering, and Castle Press, demonstrate that the lack of capital and skilled personnel, the significant and often understated cost of such e-commerce applications and solutions, and the core structure of SMEs remain challenging impediments to the adoption of e-commerce applications. Dilbeck Realtors is faced with the need for industry leadership to help standardize and streamline the transaction process and coordinate players. For Schober's, Castle Press, Dilbeck, and many SMEs, internal coordination is not a problem. However, one of the fundamental challenges facing these SMEs is the continual need to remain competitive. As such, the core business processes of SMEs, including the companies discussed here, were highly efficient even before the Internet and were, in many cases, capital intensive. This presents the second significant challenge to SMEs: While costs are clearly defined, what are the potential benefits from adopting e-commerce applications? As the OECD (2001) concludes, "SMEs are often too busy employing scarce human and financial resources to make their initial business plans succeed and are reluctant to allocate resources to implementing a new electronic commerce strategy without a clearer understanding of the benefits and risks (p. 158).

Conclusion: The Costs of Re-Engineering

Many SMEs are faced with severe cost constraints, such that allocating more than 1% of their total cost structure to Internet-based applications is simply unacceptable (Meschner, 2001). Thus, Castle Press and Schober's have moved slowly with implementation to accommodate their capital requirements. Initially, Castle Press faced difficulties with IT consultants who lacked specific industry knowledge, an issue of general prominence for SMEs (Williams, 1999). On the other hand, Dilbeck Realtors' successful results with their website suggest that great potential exists when the right combination of IT skills and industry knowledge is brought together.

Lessons: Gradual Adoption and Close Communication are Crucial

The cases examined here illustrate the need for:

- **Adaptability:** Dilbeck, Castle Press, and Schober's are learning how to integrate the Internet and IT into their business gradually. The "learn as you go" approach seems well-suited to rapidly changing industry environments in the face of limited resources.
- **Customer-focus:** In all cases Internet-based activities have been undertaken to increase customer satisfaction and retention. Increasing the customer base and increased revenues are secondary benefits.
- **Customization:** Schober's, Dilbeck, and Castle Press all note that commercial off-the-shelf software lacks the nuances and customization needed to truly streamline processes and integrate them with the customer interface. This point has serious implications for providers who serve the small-business market as customization increases cost; the chief stumbling block to a small firm's adoption of e-commerce.

Future Directions

Expansion of this study to include more small firms would allow the potential for systematic data collection and identification of trends. Tracing first the workflow process and then monitoring IT adoption through time can help trace the path of SMEs to adoption of re-engineering and e-commerce. If the process can be broken down, it may be possible to provide targeted support for these efforts. An understanding of key parameters is needed, including the criteria for re-engineering to be a workable option for the SME, amenable industries, optimal organization size, resource base, level of intensity, and evolutionary path.

There remains a need for a wide range of systematically developed case studies of small firms' re-engineering efforts to help identify best practices. Such examples would assist small firms that seek substantiated practices rather than models, and would also allow support agencies and consultants to provide appropriate solutions (Cagliano & Spina, 1998). Also, since the number of cases of re-engineering in small firms is still limited, the development of a systematic method for studying this process would improve validity and reliability. Such a model is beyond the scope of this study, but could be a path forward for research design and implementation.

Endnotes

1   However, on a per-employee basis, SMEs have invested less than large corporations.

2   This study was carried out by the University of Texas and sponsored by Dell Computer Corporation.

3   The European Commission estimates that SMEs make up some 99% of all EU enterprises and provide 66% of all jobs.

4   Additionally, sole-proprietorships comprise 74% of all businesses, although their business revenues amount to only about one-half that of large corporations.

5   Turner's study finds that of the more than 17 million SMEs in Europe, 7% 9% use IT as a matter of course, while 90% are not attuned to the possible advantages of IT utilization.

6   Daniel, Wilson, and Myers (2002) also note that the level of e-commerce adoption attained by a small firm depends on contextual variables at the organizational and industry level.

7   The company has been technologically ahead of many large firms with which it has contracted work. Schober provided Internet access to employees' homes several years before large firms like Ford began to provide connectivity.

8   CTM survey of more than 100 small-business owners in Southern California, through the Marshall School of Business Alumni, University of Southern California.

9   Other SMEs examined in our research also faced highly competitive market environments.

10   Kinkos is a U.S. company that offers photocopying services in addition to other services to businesses and individuals. Operating 1,100 branches in the U.S.,

Europe, and Asia Pacific, they have a ubiquitous presence that seems well-suited to the printing and distribution of electronic publishing materials.

[11]   Dilbeck has grown dramatically in the last year, adding three offices and more than 200 agents.

[12]   Dilbeck had nearly 200 hits in less than three weeks of offering this service at a time when home shopping is traditionally slow.

[13]   The most comprehensive coverage of the literature on re-engineering SMEs is presented in McAdam (2000).

References

Beckenhauer, L. (2001). Personal interview. Branch Manager, Chief Operating Officer, Dilbeck Realtors. La Canada, California (June).

Blili, S., & Raymond, L. (1993). Information technology: Threats and opportunities for small and medium-sized enterprises. *International Journal of Information Management, 13,* 439-448.

Braganza, A., & Myers, A. (1997). *Business Process Redesign: A View from the Inside.* London: International Thomson Business Press.

Buckley, P., & Montes, S. (2002, February). *Main Street in the digital age, how small and medium-sized businesses are using the tools of the new economy.* Washington, DC: U.S. Department of Commerce, Economics and Statistics Administration.

Cagliano, R., & Spina, G., et al. (1998). Designing BPR support services for small firms. *International Journal of Operations and Production Management, 18,* 865-876.

Chang, L., & Powell, P. (1998). Business process re-engineering in SMEs: Current evidence. *Knowledge and Process Management, 5*(4), 264-278.

Collier, D. (1995). Translating quantitative methods for qualitative researchers, the case of selection bias. *American Political Science Review, 89*(2), 461-467.

Collier, D., & Mahoney, J. (1996). Insight and pitfalls: Selection bias in qualitative research. *World Politics, 49,* 56-91.

Daniel, E., Wilson, H., & Myers, A. (2002). Adoption of e-commerce by SMEs in the UK. *International Small Business Journal, 20*(3), 253-270.

Davenport, T.H., & Short, J. (1990). The new industrial engineering: Information technology and business process redesign. *Sloan Management Review,* (Summer), 11-27.

Dilbeck, M. (2001, June). Personal interview. Owner, Dilbeck Realtors. La Canada, California.

Eisenhardt, K.M. (1995). Building theories from case study research. *Longitudinal Field Research Methods,* 65-90.

El Sawy, O. (2001). *Redesigning Enterprise Processes for E-Business.* New York: McGraw Hill.

Fife, E., & Pereira, F. (1999). *The Internet, IP and New Market Opportunities: A Strategic Analysis.* Chicago, IL: International Engineering Consortium.

Fife, E., & Pereira, F. (1999). The Internet: Business efficiencies of merged voice and data communications, networking the future. *Proceedings of FITCE* (August 24-28, pp. 1-8).

Geddes, B. (1990). How the cases you choose affect the answers you get: Selection bias in comparative politics. *Political Analysis, 2,* 131-150.

George, A. (1979). Case studies and theory development: The method of structured, focused comparison. In P. Lauren (Ed.), *Diplomacy: New Approaches in History, Theory & Policy* (pp. 43-68). New York: The Free Press.

Gunasekaran, A., Forker, L., & Kobu, B. (1998). Improving operations performance in a small company: A case study. *International Journal of Operations and Production Management, 20*(3), 316-331.

Hale, A.J., & Cragg, P.B. (1996). Business process re-engineering in the small firm: A case study. *Journal of INFOR, 34*(1), 15-26.

Hammer, M., & Champy, J. (1993). *Re-Engineering the Corporation: A Manifesto for Business Revolution.* London: Nicholas Brealey Publishing.

Hammer, M., & Champy, J. (1994). Avoiding the hottest new management cure. *Inc., 16*(4), 25-28.

Hobly, C. (2001, January). *Just Numbers.* Brussels: Commission of the European Communities Electronic Commerce Team.

James, K. (2001). Be ready to face e-biz reality check. *Business Times Singapore,* (November 8), 24.

Julien, P.-A., & Louis, R. (1994). Factors of new technology adoption in the retail sector. *Entrepreneurship Theory and Practice, 18*(4), 79-88.

Kinney, G. (2000, June). Personal interview. Managing Editor, Owner, Castle Press. Pasadena, California.

Kuwaiti, M.E., & Kay, J. (2000). The role of performance management in business process re-engineering. *International Journal of Operations and Product Management, 20*(12), 1411-1426.

La Rovere, R.L. (1998). Diffusion of information technologies and changes in the telecommunications sector: The case of Brazilian small and medium-sized enterprises. *Information Technology and People, 11*(3), 194-206.

McAdam, R. (2000). The implementation of reengineering in SMEs: A grounded study. *International Small Business Journal, 14*(4), 29-45.

McAdam, R. (2002). Large-scale innovation—reengineering methodology in SMEs: Positivistic and phenomenological approaches. *International Small Business Journal, 20*(1), 33-52.

Meschner, M. (2002, July/1999, October 9). Personal interview. Executive Board Member, Small Business Administration. Alhambra, California.

Morton, M.S. (1991). *The Corporations in the 1990s: Information Technology and Organizational Transformation.* New York: Oxford University Press.

OECD. (2001). *Enhancing SME Competitiveness.* Paris: Organization for Economic Cooperation and Development.

Oldham, J. (2000). Home buying on the Web is still a tough sell. *Los Angeles Times,* (August 6), K1, K8.

Oy, V. (1998). *SME participation in the 4th European Union Framework Programme for Research and Technological Development.* Brussels: European Commission, DG XII.

Park, A. (2000). Most firms are not in B2B, study says, partakers seeing heftier bottom line. *The Houston Chronicle,* (October 1), 6.

Pratt, J. (1999, August). *Home-Based Businesses: The Hidden Economy.* Washington DC: United States Small Business Administration.

Raymond, L., Bergeron, F., & Rivard, S. (1998). Determinants of business process reengineering success in small and large enterprises: An empirical study in the Canadian context. *Journal of Small Business Management, 36*(1), 72-86.

Seccombe, R. (2000, June/2001, June/2002, December). Personal interviews.

Smith, J.A. (1999). The behavior and performance of young micro firms: Evidence from businesses in Scotland. *Small Business Economics, 13*(3), 185-200.

Souza, C. (1999). Entering newly waters charted—as distributors set up global value-added infrastructures, many challenges are surfacing. *Electronic Buyer's News,* (January 25).

Survey—FT Telecomms. (2001). *Financial Times London,* (March 21), 4.

Survey of Small Businesses, Study #427. (1999). *Los Angeles Times,* (May 26-August 19).

Switzer, P. (2001). Online industry off the planet. *Nationwide News Private Limited, Australia,* (September 12), 27.

The Times. (2001). More power to small firms. London. (February 10).

Turner, C. (1997). SMEs and the evolution of the European information society: Policy themes and initiatives. *European Business Journal, 9*(4).

U.S. Census Bureau, Department of Commerce. (2000). *Statistical Abstract of the United States 2000.* Washington, DC.

U.S. Small Business Administration, Office of Advocacy. (2000). *Small Business Expansions in Electronic Commerce.* Washington, DC, June.

Williams, V. (1999). *E-Commerce: Small Business Ventures Online.* Washington, DC: Small Business Administration.

Winston, E.R., & Dologite, D. (2002). How does attitude impact IT implementation? *Journal of End User Computing, 14*(2), 16-29.

Zugelger, M. (2000). Legal issues associated with international Internet marketing. *International Marketing Review, 17*(3), 253-271.

Chapter XVI

Business-to-Business E-Commerce for Collaborative Supply Chain Design and Development

Reggie Davidrajuh, Stavanger University College, Norway

Abstract

SMEs form a virtual enterprise—a short-term loose integration, to meet business opportunities; managers of SMEs are looking for a tool that could help them design the strategic model of the supply chain in which they are collaboratively involved. Though the use of e-commerce tools has a lot of potential to improve an enterprise's collaboration efforts with other enterprises, realizing an e-commerce tool that enables collaborative supply chain design and development is not easy, as collaborating enterprises may each use a different flavor of XML, multiple technology solutions, and have different business rules. This chapter presents a methodology for developing a new e-commerce tool to assist collaborative supply chain management. By this methodology, a new tool that is affordable by the SMEs and offers improved pipeline visibility could be easily implemented.

Introduction

This chapter deals with concepts and a methodology for realizing a new e-commerce tool for collaborative supply chain design and development (CSCDD). The methodology for realizing the new tool is primarily aimed at satisfying the needs of small to medium-sized enterprises (SMEs). First, we present definitions for some of the keywords used in this chapter.

E-commerce enables faster, cheaper, global, and secure means of inter-enterprise collaboration for production and sales of products for achieving enhanced customer value (Davidrajuh, 2002). Turban (2002) provides a typical definition for e-commerce:

Definition 1: E-Commerce. E-commerce enables the business processes (like buying, making, selling, etc.) to take place over the networks, mostly the Internet (Turban, 2002).

Supply chain is a global network of enterprises that collaborate to improve the flows (such as material, information, fund, and work) between them to obtain improved customer satisfaction, low-cost product and/or service, and faster product delivery. The Global Supply Chain Forum defines supply chain as:

Definition 2: Supply Chain. The integration of key business processes from end-user through original suppliers who provide products, services, and information that add value for customers and other stakeholders (Hvolby & Trienekens, 2002).

Definition 3: Small to Medium-Sized Enterprise. By small to medium-sized enterprise (SME), we refer to an enterprise carrying out small to medium-scale manufacturing, employing fewer than 250 employees, and an annual turnover less than EURO 40 million or trade balance less than EURO 27 million (Norwegian Trade Council, 2002).

Collaborative Supply Chain Management

This introductory section on collaborative supply chain design and development covers two interesting concepts: virtual enterprise and collaborative supply chain management. Virtual enterprise is a short-term loose integration of SMEs that bundle their competencies with the help of e-commerce to meet some market opportunity. We believe that SMEs form a virtual enterprise first, before they start collaborating in their supply chain design and development efforts.

After the short introduction to CSCDD, an illustration on the complexity and sophistication in managing collaborative supply chain activities is presented: the iterative nature collaborative supply chain management, and modeling and simulation aspects are given; a basic understanding on these two issues is necessary for realizing a new e-commerce tool.

Virtual Enterprise and Collaboration in Supply Chain Management

During the last decade many SMEs have tried to adapt their supply chains to cope with the increased demands for customized products. This development was caused by changes in the industrial markets (i.e., Hvolby & Trienekens, 2002):

- Customers demanded shorter delivery times and higher delivery frequencies.
- Product lifecycles became shorter and assortments increased.
- Markets were changing rapidly, which increased the risk of investments in new technology, machinery, and other equipment.

In short, the most important pressures on SMEs were reduced delivery times, prices, costs, stocks, and product lifecycles and increased customization, flexibility, and agility; SMEs confronted these pressures by making changes to their supply chains *individually*.

SMEs are now more and more taking part in the global business network, participating in many multi-enterprise supply chains. Nowadays, some of the important issues in supply chain are (Lambert & Cooper, 2000; Hvolby & Trienekens, 2002):

- Supply chain information sharing and monitoring systems.
- Coordination systems of multiple levels for inventory reduction.
- Joint planning systems on different management levels.
- The reduction of supplier bases for better coordination.
- The increase of speed of operations, information, and inventory flows.
- Supply chain costs and benefits sharing systems.

In short, information and cost sharing, coordination, and joint planning have become important issues in supply chain management. Thus, *collaboration* has become the core issue in supply chain design and development for many SMEs.

Jagdev and Thoben (2001) define three types of collaboration in the supply chain between legally independent companies (Hvolby & Trienekens, 2002):

- *Supply chain type of collaboration:* An SME can be viewed as a node in a network of nodes of suppliers, distributors, and customers; all nodes in the chain must operate synchronously to meet customer demands. The supply chain type of collaboration is based on long-term collaboration, but it is less integrated.
- *Extended enterprise type of collaboration:* Information and decision systems and respective production processes of SMEs are integrated. This is the most integrated type of collaboration.
- *Virtual enterprise type of collaboration:* This is the loosely integrated type, where participating SMEs bundle their competencies with the help of e-commerce to meet customer demand. The virtual enterprise can be short-term collaboration between participating companies without system integration.

We believe that SMEs form a virtual enterprise first, before they start collaborating in their supply chain design and development efforts. Virtual enterprise is defined as follows:

Definition 4: Virtual Enterprise. A short-term loose integration of a nucleus enterprise and a number of supply and distribution enterprises to manufacture and sell a class of product; when market requirements are changed, in order to produce a new class of products or an improved version of the product, the nucleus enterprise may seek a new combination of collaborating enterprises that are more suitable to manufacture the new class of products; thus the main aspect of virtual enterprise is dynamic logic of organization and reorganization of collaboration (Davidrajuh & Deng, 2000).

Collaboration between the participating companies of a virtual enterprise to meet a business opportunity is the theme of this chapter. SMEs form a virtual enterprise because they cannot satisfy the business opportunity by acting alone. A virtual enterprise will function only if it generates profits for all the participating companies.

The lifecycle of a virtual enterprise goes through four phases, that may include business opportunity identification phase, collaborator selection phase, formation phase, operation phase, and/or reorganization phase (Enator, 1998; Davidrajuh & Deng, 2000).

Collaborative Supply Chain Design and Development

CSCDD deals with two phases of the lifecycle of a virtual enterprise. In the opportunity identification phase, the nucleus enterprise estimates the profitability of the project (the nucleus enterprise is the one that evaluates the business opportunity and initiates formation of virtual enterprise). After this phase, the right combination of collaborating enterprises (suppliers, distributors, and transporting agents) must be found to manufacture and sell the product; this is the collaborator selection phase. Then the potential collaborating enterprises agree on the global goals (or constraints) for the virtual enterprise, and individually devise local goals to achieve maximum profits while satisfying the global constraints; this is the formation phase. Thus we identify the two most important tasks in the combined collaborator selection and formation phases: (1) establishing a virtual supply chain (inviting and selecting collaborators), and (2) collaboratively developing the supply chain. *We define these two tasks as collaborative supply chain design and development.*

Iterative Nature of Collaborative Supply Chain Design and Development

Figure 1 shows just five enterprises as potential collaborators. It also shows the two planning levels, the strategic planning level and the tactical planning level. Potential collaborators will make tactical decisions (constrained by the strategic decisions) to make profit. To help make tactical decisions, each enterprise's supply chain activities are grouped into the three fundamental groups of activities such as purchasing activities, making activities, and selling activities.

Potential collaborators (in Figure 1) purchase raw materials (by purchasing activities), turn them into products or semi-products (making activities), and then sell (selling activities). Each of these activities changes the state of the material that flows through the supply chain (see Figure 2). When we say "the state" of the material, we limit our scope to: (1) the accumulated cost of material, (2) the time taken for the material to reach its current point from the time it has entered the virtual enterprise, and (3) the total amount (number of units).

Potential collaborators evaluate whether the collaboration is profitable to them by running simulation trials on the fundamental activities. If a potential collaborator could not make a workable tactical decision that will bring in a profit, certainly the enterprise will propose changes to the strategic decisions ('agile', adjusting to the new situation); otherwise, that enterprise will not participate in the virtual enterprise.

A potential collaborator starts with its fundamental activities and verifies whether the change of state (in cost, time, amount) of the product leaving the enterprise conforms to the tactical decisions set by the enterprise for itself. If not, the enterprise must alter the parameters of its activities (e.g., reducing production time by hiring extra human and machinery). When all the potential collaborators individually satisfy their tactical decisions, they can then verify whether the combined activities of the virtual enterprise satisfy the global constraints (on the cost of the final product leaving the virtual enterprise, the quality, delivery time, in right amount, etc.). In case the combined activities do not satisfy the global constraints, even if the local constraints are met individually, a new set of tactical decisions should be made and the collaborating enterprises should start planning their manufacturing activities adhering to the new set of constraints. Thus, the planning effort for formation of a virtual enterprise is an *iterative* process.

How do we allow a potential collaborator to run simulation trials on the supply chain activities? How do we help a potential collaborator verify whether the combined activities of the virtual enterprise satisfy the global constraints? Assuming that the potential collaborator is an SME, we show in the next section how a simple and affordable tool can

Figure 1: Collaborative Supply Chain Design and Development

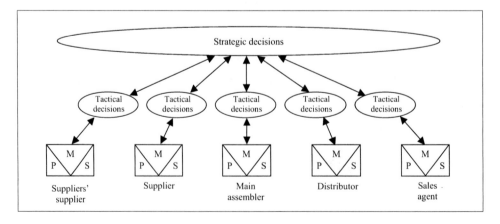

be realized without resorting to complex mathematics. In the following subsection, we present a methodology for modeling and simulation that is simple, yet powerful enough to allow collaborative simulation trials. This methodology is the basis for implementation techniques discussed in the next section.

Modeling Supply Chain Activities

In Figure 2, an activity is represented by a rectangle; circles represent the input and the output (buffers). When an activity is carried out, the input material is removed from the input buffer and the products (or semi-products) are placed into the output buffer. In addition, the state of the material that is subjected to the activity is changed. As shown in Figure 2, the changes to the state of the material owing to the activity are limited to simple arithmetic calculations.

Also in the figure, the supply chain micro activities (or fundamental activities) are represented as Petri nets. Petri net is a simple yet powerful discrete mathematical tool for modeling and simulation of discrete events systems. In Petri nets, the activities are represented by rectangular (called 'transitions'), and circles (called 'places') represent the buffers. A typical definition for Petri net (or 'ordinary' Petri net) is given below:

Definition 5: Petri net. A Petri net is a four-tuple (P, T, A, x_0), where,

P is the set of places (representing conditions or material amounts), $P = [p_1, p_2, ..., p_n]$

T is the set of transitions (corresponds to events), $T = [t_1, t_2, ..., t_m]$

$A \subseteq (P X T) \cup (T X P)$ is a set of arcs from places to transitions and from transitions to places, and

$x = [x(p_1), x(p_2), ... , x(p_{nl})] \in N^n$ is the row vector of markings (tokens) on the set of places, $x0$ is the initial marking (Cassandras & LaFortune, 1999).

As shown in Figure 2, the Petri net model enables the collaborators to estimate the costs, material flow amounts, and times of the micro activities. It is also then possible for a potential collaborator to find its *overall* cost, profit, timing, etc., for participating in the virtual enterprise, by combining the activities. However, it will not be possible to estimate overall estimate for the *whole* virtual enterprise, simply by combining the overall estimates for the individual collaborators. This is because the virtual enterprise may consist of hundreds of potential collaborators, and most importantly, these potential collaborators are dynamically connected in the virtual enterprise during the formation phase; when a potential collaborator is persuaded to join, it enters the supply chain development process by running trial simulations on its activities; then, if not satisfied, it leaves. Therefore, for simulation of a virtual enterprise with hundreds of dynamically connected potential collaborators, a different approach for combining the activities of individual collaborators is needed.

Figure 2: Modeling Supply Chain Activities

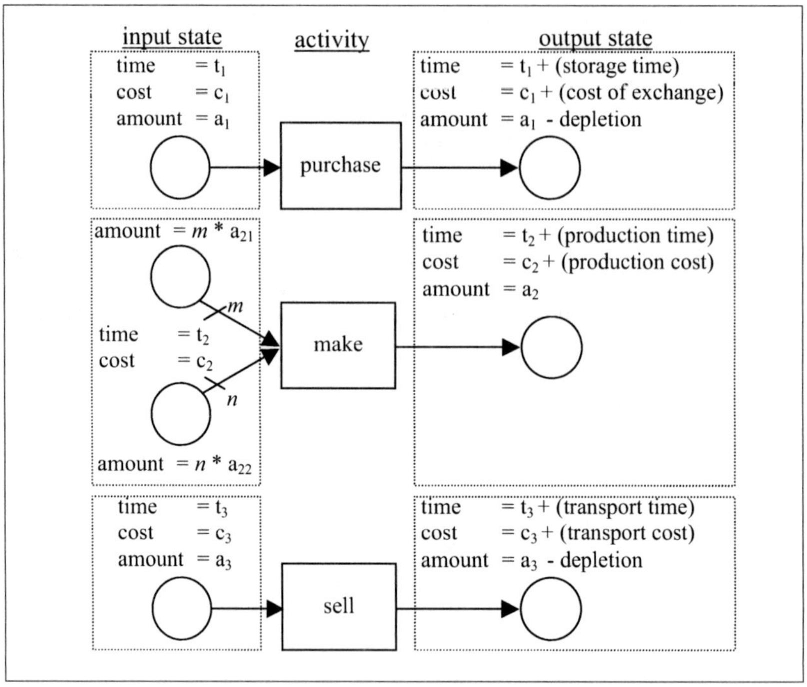

Modeling a Virtual Supply Chain

Figure 3 shows a virtual supply chain consisting of just six potential collaborators (and a customer) of a virtual enterprise. This virtual supply chain can be easily converted into an equivalent Petri net model that can be used for trial simulations. According to Davidrajuh (2000, 2002), in the Petri net model, a single place-transition pair represents each collaborator in the virtual supply chain. In addition to the collaborators (such as material suppliers, part suppliers, e-tailer, and customer), transporting agents are also included in the Petri net model, by representing each transport link by a place-transition pair.

There is a limitation in the approach by Davidrajuh (2000, 2002): basic simulation engine for material flow through supply chain is based on 'pull' material flow principle. In pull material flow, demand triggers the flow. In 'push' material flow principle, material is moved with anticipated demand. As most of the enterprises practice hybrid 'push-pull' material flow, the simulation engine should be upgraded to hybrid type.

Hybrid 'Push-Pull' Engine for Simulation

Figure 4 shows the push engine running in parallel with the pull engine. Though the same transitions have different meaning under different directions (push/pull), they are

Figure 3: A Model of Virtual Enterprise

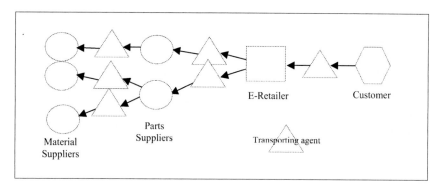

connected to the same place (results are added to the same 'buffer'), as indicated by the thick connecting lines. While the pull engine enables order flow, and the material flow triggered by a customer order, the push engine allows operations such as move for moving material between enterprises in advance as inventory, and store for storing materials in warehouses. A combined pull and push engine is adequate for simulation of a virtual supply chain of potential collaborators of a virtual enterprise.

A Survey on Existing Tools for CSCDD

Literature review provides different names for collaborative supply chain design and development efforts such as "common resource platform" (Fingar & Aronica, 2001); "collaborative, planning, forecasting, and replenishment" (Christopher, 2001; Poirier & Bauer, 2000); supply chain "sharing process" (Govil & Proth, 2002); "dynamic trade" (McCullough, 1999); etc. There is lot of literature proposing a number of concepts, exciting ideas, and examples about collaborative planning efforts; but there is a lack of information on adapting these ideas to specific situations. There is little information on how these ideas can be realized into a set of tools that could help managers of SMEs overcome the complexities of dealing with collaborative supply chain design and development efforts. Even the little information that is available for realizing tools for collaborative planning either use complex techniques such as genetic algorithm (Berry, Murtagh, & Welling, 1998), artificial intelligence (McMullen, 2001), stochastic programming (MirHassani, 2000), and statistical analysis (Reutterer & Kotzab, 1999) that require mathematicians or specialists for using it, or demands very expensive and time-consuming installation of third-party implementation.

Enterprise resource planning (ERP) systems: ERP systems have become popular, especially among large corporations, as a total enterprise-wide application. ERP systems (such as the ones from SAP, PeopleSoft, BAAN, etc.) are said to cover business processes throughout the entire organization and integrate different functional areas of the enterprise (Buck-Emden & Galimow, 1996). ERP systems cannot be considered a tool

Figure 4: Parallel Push and Pull Engines in Action

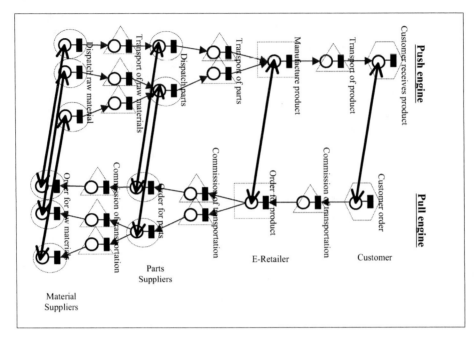

for CSCDD, mainly because they do not support collaborative planning efforts; they are not designed for integrating with another ERP system from a different enterprise for supply chain planning (though some research reports indicate that different ERP systems can be linked together, e.g., Stine, 1999). In addition, ERP systems are very expensive for SMEs to consider; installation and training time for ERP implementation at an enterprise (18 to 48 months) is also prohibitive for an SME (Govil & Proth, 2002). Besides, ERP systems have other limitations too, such as weak on-demand planning, and they do not support quick response to changes in demand (Gormley, Woodring, & Lieu, 1997). Hence, we could conclude that ERP systems are not suitable for CSCDD.

Supply chain planning (SCP) applications: The newer and increasingly popular SCP applications can be considered to be close to tools for CSCDD efforts. SCP applications are from software vendors who specialize in supply chain management (SCM) systems (e.g., i2 Technologies, 2002; Manugistics, 2002). SCP applications are affordable by SMEs, and have a shorter installation and training timeframe than that for ERP systems. As the name implies, SCP applications are specifically designed for supply chain, whereas ERP systems are for 'all' business processes (Govil & Proth, 2002). However, SCP applications have shortcomings too:

1. *Little support for collaboration:* Though SCP applications optimize the internal supply chain of an enterprise, they have little support for inter-enterprise collaborative planning to optimize inter-linked multi-enterprise supply chains.

2. *Limited extensibility:* SCP applications are 'application' packages from independent software vendors (ISVs); as such, the only way to add more functions to the

application, when needed, is to buy standardized modules from the vendor. There is little support available for the enterprise to implement additional functions (other than the ones in the add-on modules) to the applications; outsourcing implementation of customer-specific modules to a software vendor could be very costly.

Statement of the Problem

There is a lack of e-commerce tools to support CSCDD. Managers of SMEs are looking for a tool that could help them design the strategic model of the supply chain in which they are collaboratively involved. The use of e-commerce tools has a lot of potential to improve a company's collaboration efforts with other enterprises; collaboration with other companies that was previously not possible due to coordination problems has now become feasible. But realizing such an e-commerce tool is not easy or cheap.

By definition, SMEs that form a virtual enterprise maintain a short-term relationship to satisfy a business opportunity. Collaborating enterprises may each use a different flavor of XML and have different business rules; Webster (2000) reported that more than 120 standards that extend XML and more than 200 flavors of XML were in use. Thus, a collaborating enterprise is forced to utilize multiple technology solutions. Being SMEs, we cannot expect the collaborating enterprises to invest in newer technologies continually, as they dissolve a virtual enterprise after completion of a project and form new ones later with some other SMEs for some other market opportunities.

An ideal tool for CSCDD should posses the following characteristics:

- *Support collaborative 'inter-enterprise' planning efforts:* The tool should let the managers of collaborating enterprises understand how their strategic decisions, and the ones of their partners, contribute to tactical decisions and thus the success of the whole supply chain.

- *Improve pipeline visibility and demand visibility:* With the tool, the managers should be able to easily evaluate the effect of their simulation trials on the supply chain.

Moreover, to allow SMEs to make use of this tool, the tool should also be:

- *Easily realizable and extensible:* The concept, methodology, and techniques behind the tool development should not be complex. Extensions to the tool should be done easily, and preferably in-house.

- *Not very expensive:* The cost of the tool should not prohibit enterprises from participating in virtual enterprise.

- Quick regarding installation and training.

In the following section, we provide some techniques for realization of a new tool that satisfies the characteristics stated above.

Toward Realizing a New Tool

We presented our methodology for modeling and simulation of virtual supply chain in the previous section; we also presented some of the characteristics of an ideal tool for CSCDD. In this section, we present some techniques for realizing a new e-commerce tool that implements our methodology and satisfies the characteristics of an ideal CSCDD tool as well. The realization is based on the following concepts:

1. Application outsourcing
2. Collaborator commitments
3. Web technology
4. MATLAB programming and Web Server technology

Realization Based on Application Outsourcing

Application outsourcing refers to the emerging trend of deploying applications over the Internet, rather than installing them in the local environment. This shifts the burden of installing, maintaining, and upgrading an application from those SMEs that use the application to the remote computing center (also known as the Application Service Provider, ASP). ASP manages an application package for its clients and allocates related computing resources dynamically (Marchand & Jacobsen, 2001). System administration and application management is performed entirely by the ASP.

Application outsourcing is the best software distribution model for a new e-commerce tool for CSCDD; this is because:

- ASP can charge the SMEs that use the tool on a pay-by-use basis, based on amount of remote system resources consumed (e.g., data storage), application functionality required, transactions executed, or simply based on a periodic or flat fee model (Marchand & Jacobsen, 2001). In other words, SMEs do not bear the total cost of full software license; SMEs can purchase only the services that are needed.

- SMEs can avoid time-consuming set-up and costly business model adaptation (Gilbert & Sweat, 1999; Gill, 1999; Wilson, 1999).

- SMEs need not purchase special hardware and network externality associated with the use of specific software (Marchand & Jacobsen, 2001).

- By application outsourcing, SMEs avoid the high technical risks associated with a large investment in technology that is rapidly changing; application outsourcing provides protection from the high cost of making the wrong decision. If SMEs can reduce their costs by outsourcing their business applications with ASPs, then this offers one option for maintaining profit margins while joining a new virtual enterprise for a new business opening (Gulledge, 2002).

However, the cost of developing and offering an application service can also be very high (i.e., high fixed cost). This is because of the proper implementation of the software, or the licensing of an available solution from a third-party provider (e.g., an independent software vendor, ISV), facilitating file exchange and data formatting through standard intermediaries, the additional per client and per unit of service cost (initial set-up cost per client; continuing support cost per client; allocation of computing resources per unit of service offered; complementary services like data backup, recovery, security). In the next subsections, we provide a solution for further reduction in costs of outsourcing the CSCDD tool:

- Nominating the dominant enterprise or any other collaborator of the virtual enterprise to host the application service (i.e., asking one of the collaborators to be the ASP). This reduces the cost of using independent ASPs or intermediaries, and avoids trust and security problems.

- Using Web technology to achieve zero initial set-up cost per client.

- Using MATLAB to minimize implementation costs of the software.

Hub for Hosting the CSCDD Tool

We suggest that one of the collaborating enterprises acts also as the ASP providing CSCDD tool usage and maintains computer resources relevant to the tool operation. There are many reasons for asking one of the collaborating enterprises to function as the ASP for the CSCDD tool:

- Reducing the costs is the first reason; there is no need to pay an independent ASP. The actual costs of application servicing (such as significant investment in technology and consulting services) can be divided among the collaborating enterprises.

- Collaborating enterprise understands internal operations and business rules better than any independent software vendor or ASP. Since this enterprise is part of a virtual enterprise, it will be willing to share the business rules and technology solutions with the other enterprises of the virtual enterprise.

- The techniques we suggest for implementing the CSCDD tool do not demand high programming expertise. Thus, any collaborating enterprise that has sufficient infrastructure to support implementing a small online application could become the ASP for outsourcing the CSCDD tool.

However, asking one of the collaborating enterprises to outsource the CSCDD tool may cause some problems as well (Gulledge, 2002):

- Lack of trust and an unwillingness to share data with the other enterprises that could be part of any other virtual enterprises.

- Lack of consensus among partners about where functionality should reside.

- High costs of integrating partner back-office systems with the exchange technology.

- Inability to recruit and integrate enterprises.

- Competition among competing software vendors and consultants.
- Political infighting among the collaborating enterprises.

Web-Based Tool

To achieve zero installation at the local environment, and to support collaborative planning efforts of geographically distributed collaborators, we must make use of Web technology. The new tool for CSCDD must be Web-based, offering Web interface to function for running simulation trials on the fundamental activities. The tool should also offer an interface to a database, with a common area with access privileges for all collaborating enterprises, and restricted areas to individual enterprises for their temporary data storage and retrieval.

A simple way of improving pipeline visibility and demand visibility is to offer a public place in a remote database allocated by the ASP where the data of interest to all of the collaborating enterprises can be stored. Individual enterprises have exclusive access to their respective areas in the remote database. This area can be used to store temporary values for simulation of their activities. There are also public data areas where, in addition to other information for common consumption, information about the consumer demands are placed. When an individual enterprise tries to simulate its activities that are of an inter-enterprise nature (say purchasing raw material from raw material supplier), it retrieves data from the public area of other enterprises. However, an enterprise may confine to its private area for operations (e.g., make).

MATLAB Language

Rather than coding the functions for simulation in a general purpose programming language (such as C++ or JAVA), it is highly advisable to program using MATLAB (2002) language. With MATLAB, it is very easy to program complex functions for Petri net manipulation, as MATLAB offers hundreds of built-in mathematical functions. MATLAB programming language is also easy to program. In addition, it is easy to add more functionality to program modules written in MATLAB (easily extensible).

The most important feature of MATLAB for realizing a CSCDD tool is its MATLAB Web Server component. If the CSCDD tool is implemented in MATLAB language and installed with the MATLAB Web Server at the ASP, then the collaborating enterprises only need a Web browser (such as Netscape Navigator or Microsoft Internet Explorer, which are available free of charge these days) to interact with the tool. Since there is inconclusive support for the hypothesis that investment in IT pays off (Brynjolfsson & Hitt, 2000), and due to the newness of e-commerce technologies, managers of SMEs will certainly welcome an e-commerce tool that requires just a Web browser. By using the Web browser, collaborators need not install the tool on their local computers.

With the help of the MATLAB Web Server, in addition to zero installation, training time is also minimized. The users of the tool need not learn the internals of the tool or about MATLAB; they only need to learn how to use the menu-driven Web pages of the tool.

Concluding Remarks

This chapter discusses concepts and a methodology for realizing a new e-commerce tool for collaborative supply chain design and development (CSCDD). The methodology for realizing a new tool is primarily aimed at satisfying the needs of small to medium-sized enterprises.

First, we presented an introduction to CSCDD. The introduction included the characterization of CSCDD, its iterative nature, and our methodology for modeling and simulation of a supply chain in a virtual enterprise environment. Our methodology for modeling the virtual supply chain is based on Petri nets and does not require complex techniques (such as genetic algorithm, artificial intelligence, etc.). Further, the methodology does not require mathematicians or specialists for using it, and does not demand very expensive and time-consuming installation by a third party.

Second, we presented a survey on existing tools for CSCDD, along with reasons for seeking a new tool; we identified the needs for a new tool including: low cost, Web based, faster installation and training, and easily extensible.

Third, we presented some techniques for realizing the new CSCDD tool. The new tool is Web based, application outsourcing based, and hosted by one of the collaborating enterprises. Moreover, realization is fast and easily extensible, owing to our modeling and simulation methodology, and due to implementation with the MATLAB Web Server.

The techniques for realizing a new CSCDD tool described in this chapter have some limitations. These can be considered for further research:

- *Deterministic models:* The models of supply chain (and virtual supply chain) are based on deterministic models; also, the supply chain activities mentioned in this chapter are deterministic. Stochastic components should be added to take care of non-deterministic mechanisms that are elements of any real-life supply chains.

- *Sharing and security:* Sharing, security, and privacy are important issues in any peer-to-peer system; therefore, security measures should be added to the tool to protect individual collaborating enterprises from hacking, hampering, snooping, etc. Questions addressing how to ensure sharing of information, benefits, and losses between collaborating enterprises, are not discussed in this chapter, but must be tackled in any industry-standard tool.

- *Back-office integration with ERP:* To achieve efficiencies and to obtain cost savings, the SMEs would have to integrate internal business applications (back-office integration with ERP), and then integrate with a CSCDD tool. Integrating the CSCDD tool with the other internal and external business applications is beyond the scope of this chapter.

References

Berry, L., Murtagh, B., & Welling, L.D. (1998). Genetic algorithms in the design of complex distribution networks. *International Journal of Physical Distribution & Logistics Management, 28*(5), 11-22.

Brynjolfsson, E., & Hitt, L. (2000). Beyond computation: Information technology, organizational transformation and business performance. *Journal of Economic Perspectives, 14*(4), 23-48.

Buck-Emden, R., & Galimow, J. (1996). *SAP R/3 System: A Client Server Technology.* Addison-Wesley.

Cassandras, C.G., & LaFortune, S. (1999). *Introduction to Discrete Event Systems.* Kluwer Academic Press.

Christopher, M. (2001). Logistics and the virtual supply chain. *Proceedings of the Online Conference on Supply Chain Knowledge* (www. sck2001.com), Cranfield School of Management (November).

Davidrajuh, R. (2000). A Petri net approach for performance measurement of supply chain in agile virtual environment. *MIS Review, 10*(2), 103-132.

Davidrajuh, R. (2001). *Automating supplier selection procedures.* PhD dissertation, Norwegian University of Science and Technology (NTNU), Norway.

Davidrajuh, R. (2002). A methodology for tactical design of virtual supply chain for e-tailing. *Proceedings of the International Conference on E-Commerce Research* (ICECR-5), Montreal, Canada.

Davidrajuh, R., & Deng, Z. (2000). Identifying potential suppliers for formation of virtual manufacturing system. *Proceedings of the International Conference on Information Technology for Business Management* (ITBM'2000), ISBN 3-901882-05-7, Beijing, China.

Davidrajuh, R., & Deng, Z. (2000b). An autonomous data collection system for virtual manufacturing systems. *International Journal of Agile Management Systems, 2*(1), 7-15.

Enator. (1998). *Virtual enterprising.* On the Web: http://195.100.12.162.

Fingar, P., & Aronica, R. (2001). The death of e. FL: Meghan-Kiffer.

Gilbert, A., & Sweat, J. (1999). *Reinventing ERP.* Accessed September 13 on the Web: www.informationweek.com/752/erp.htm.

Gill, P.J. (1999). *ERP: Keep it simple.* Accessed August 9 on the Web: www.informationweek.com/747/47aderp.htm.

Gormley, J., Woodring, S., & Lieu, K. (1997). Supply chain beyond ERP in packaged application strategies. *The Forrester Report.*

Govil, M., & Proth, J. (2002). *Supply Chain: Design and Management.* Academic Press.

Gulledge, T. (2002). B2B e-marketplaces and small and medium-sized enterprises. *Computers in Industry, 49,* 47-58.

Hvolby, H.-H., & Trienekens, J. (2002). Supply chain planning opportunities for small and medium-sized companies. *Computers in Industry, 49,* 3-8.

i2 Technologies. (2002). Available on the Web: http://www.i2.com.

Jagdev, H.S., & Thoben, K.D. (2001). Anatomy of enterprise collaborations. *Production Planning and Control, 12*(5), 437-451.

Lambert, M.D., & Cooper, M.C. (2000). Issues in supply chain management. *Industrial Marketing Management, 29,* 65-83.

Li, Y., Huang, B., Liu, W., Wu, C., & Gou, H. (2000). Multi-agent system for partner selection of virtual enterprise. *International Conference on Information Technology for Business Management* (ITBM'2000), ISBN 3-901882-05-7, Beijing, China.

Manugistics. (2002). Available on the Web: http://www.manugistics.com.

Marchand, N., & Jacobsen, H.-A. (2001). An economic model to study independencies between independent software vendors and application service providers. *Electronic Commerce Research, 1*(1), 315-334.

MATLAB. (2002). Mathworks Inc, USA. Available on the Web: http://www.mathworks.com.

McCullough, S. (1999). *Dynamic supply chains alter traditional models.* Available on the Web: mccullough.ascet.com.

McMullen, P. (2001). An ant colony optimization approach to addressing a JIT sequencing problem with multiple objectives. *Artificial Intelligence in Engineering 15,* 309-317.

MirHassani, S.A. (2000). Computational solution of capacity planning models under uncertainty. *Parallel Computing, 26.*

Norwegian Trade Council. (2002). Available on the Web: http://www.eksport.no.

Poirier, C., & Bauer, M. (2000). *E-Supply Chain.* San Francisco, CA: Berrett-Keohler Publishers.

Reutterer, T., & Kotzab, H. (1999). The use of conjoint-analysis for measuring preferences in supply chain design. *Industrial Marketing Management, 29,* 7-18.

Sarkis, J., & Talluri, S. (2001). Agile supply chain management. In A. Gunasekaran (Ed.), *Agile Manufacturing: The 21st Century Competitive Strategy* (pp. 359-376). Amsterdam: Elsevier.

Stine, W. (1999). *American software adds ERP interfaces to flow manufacturing.* AMR Research. Available on the Web: www.amrresearch.com.

Turban, E., King, D., Lee, J., Warkentin, M., & Chung, H.M. (2002). *Electronic Commerce 2002: A Managerial Perspective.* Prentice Hall.

Webster, J. (2000). *An alphabet soup of B2B standards.* Accessed December 14 on the Web: www.internetweek.com/ebizapps/ebiz121800.htm.

Wilson, T. (1999). *ERP's new Web visage: SAP, PeopleSoft embrace the Net.* Accessed September 2 on the Web: www.internetwk.com/story/INW19990902S0003.

Section VIII

New E-Commerce
Avenues for SMEs

Chapter XVII

What Should SMEs Do to Succeed in Today's Knowledge-Based Economy?

Sushil K. Sharma, Ball State University, USA

Nilmini Wickramasinghe, Cleveland State University, USA

Jatinder N.D. Gupta, The University of Alabama in Huntsville, USA

Abstract

The shift to a knowledge-based economy results largely from developments in information and communications technologies. Knowledge-based economies offer huge opportunities for small to medium-sized enterprises (SMEs) to develop entirely new high-value products and services, add value to existing products and services, reduce costs, develop new export markets, and add value to existing activities. Implicit promises include access to world markets, low-cost entry into new markets, and the ability to gain efficiencies in business processes. However, these promises may be illusory for most SMEs. Technological, organizational, and marketing hurdles are also making it more difficult for SMEs to succeed in knowledge-based economies. This chapter identifies those major factors that are hindering the success of SMEs in knowledge-based economies. The chapter then goes on to suggest a set of guidelines to make SMEs succeed in this new knowledge-based society.

Background

The world has witnessed three distinct ages so far—the Agrarian Age, the Industrial Age, and now the Information Age. Today's Information Age is having a dramatic effect on businesses as well as on the lifestyles of people. Globalization, rapid technological change, and the importance of knowledge in gaining and sustaining competitive advantage characterize this Information Age. Traditionally, economists have seen capital, labor, and natural resources as the essential ingredients for economic enterprise. In recent years, it has been noticed that the new economy of the 21st Century is increasingly based on knowledge, with information, innovation, creativity, and intellectual capitalism as its essential ingredients (Persaud, 2001).

Today's modern economy is based more on intangibles—information, innovation, and creativity—and their abilities to facilitate expanding economic potential (Persaud, 2001) and the exploitation of ideas rather than material things. Many new terms have been coined for this new economy such as "knowledge-based economy," "borderless economy," "weightless economy," and "digital economy," to name a few (Woodall, 2000). This new economy seems to defy the basic economic law of scarcity, which means if a physical object is sold, the seller ceases to own it. In this new economy, however, when an idea is sold, the seller still possesses it and can sell it over and over again (Woodall (2000).

Traditional economic theory assumes that most industries run into "diminishing returns" at some point because unit costs start to rise, so no one firm can corner the market. In the new economy, knowledge-based products and services have "increasing returns" because knowledge-based products are expensive to produce for the first time, but cheap to reproduce. High fixed costs and negligible variable costs give these industries vast potential for economies of scale (Woodall, 2000).

The shift to a knowledge-based economy results largely from developments in information and communications technologies. The facility to communicate information instantaneously across the globe has changed the nature of competition. A company's knowledge assets are inherent in the creativity of its knowledge workers, combined with technological and market know-how (Halliday, 2001). Information can now be delivered with such speed that companies must develop their knowledge assets to solve competitive problems.

The knowledge-based economies offer huge opportunities for small to medium-sized enterprises (SMEs), to develop entirely new high-value products and services, add value to existing products and services, reduce costs, develop new export markets, and add value to existing activities. The Internet has increased the scope of innovation by lowering information and distribution costs. As a result, emerging today are combinations of innovation and equitization, wherein individuals and companies sell equity stakes in good ideas, and use the capital they raise to realize these ideas. The companies are competing predominantly on the basis of knowledge that is in the form of intellectual capital (Persaud, 2001). With past profits and current capital no longer a major constraint, a country's future economic prospects will depend predominantly on knowledge (Acs, Carlsson, & Karlsson, 1999).

Many studies have been conducted on small to medium-sized enterprises, but knowledge gaps continue to exist in relation to the identification of factors affecting SMEs' participation and success in knowledge-based economies. Our study systematically examines the factors affecting successful participation of SMEs in the knowledge-based economy. The study also recommends a set of guidelines for SMEs to exploit opportunities in knowledge-based economy to their advantage.

The Knowledge-Based Economy

In a knowledge-based economy, knowledge drives the profits of the organizations for gaining and sustaining competitive advantage. Intellectual capital—i.e., employees, their knowledge on products and services, and their creativity and innovation—is a crucial source of knowledge assets. The knowledge-based economy is all about adding ideas to products and turning new ideas into new products. Realizing the importance of knowledge assets, many companies have changed their traditional organizations' structures. The traditional command-and-control model of management is rapidly being replaced by decentralized teams of individuals motivated by their ownership in the companies (McGarvey, 2001).

Perhaps the most dramatic evolution in business over the past decade is the dawn of the new economy. The velocity and dynamic nature of the new marketplace has created a competitive incentive among many companies to consolidate and reconcile their knowledge assets as a means of creating value that is sustainable over time. In order to achieve competitive sustainability, many firms are launching extensive knowledge management efforts (Gold, Malhotra, & Segars, 2001). To compete effectively, firms must leverage their existing knowledge and create new knowledge that favorably positions them in their chosen markets (Anonymous, 2001).

The new structure of the economy is emerging from the convergence of computing, communications, and content. Products are becoming digital and markets are becoming electronic. In the old economy, information flow was physical: cash, checks, invoices, bills, reports, face-to-face meetings, analog telephone calls, radio or television transmissions, etc. In the new economy, information in all its forms becomes digital. While evaluating assets of a company, the old economy questions used to be: How much real estate or land assets does a company own? What is the value of facilities, plants? Or how much is the inventory? How many office buildings does the company have at different places? But the knowledge-based economy is based on the application of human know-how to everything we produce, and hence, in this new economy, human expertise and ideas create more and more of the economy's added value. Thus, the knowledge-based economy is all about adding ideas to products and turning new ideas into new products. The knowledge content of products and services is growing significantly, as consumer ideas, information, and technology become part of products. In the new economy, the key assets of the organization are intellectual assets in the form of knowledge.

Elements of the New Economy

Relationships with trading partners, customers and suppliers, distribution networks, intellectual property, patents, image, etc., are all elements of a knowledge economy. These elements represent intellectual capital. Becoming a knowledge-based economy means using knowledge as a core resource for adding value. SMEs have to integrate and leverage intellectual capital (Cowey, 2000) for their participation in the knowledge-based economy. This reality of the new economy presents major challenges to SMEs. Not many SMEs are geared to cope with the demands of high-speed operations and high demands of customers (McGarvey, 2001). In order to understand the factors affecting SMEs' success in this new economy, we must understand seven key elements of the knowledge-based economy and their impact on business practices. Table 1 summarizes these key elements.

Key Issues Affecting Success

It is not enough just to highlight the critical elements of today's knowledge-based economy; we must now understand the various factors affecting the participation and success of SMEs in this economy. We have identified 15 important factors, summarized in Table 2.

Solution and Recommendations for Success

The factors outlined in Table 2 can jointly and separately have a significant impact on the success of SMEs in today's knowledge-based economy Thus, it is imperative that SMEs prepare themselves appropriately to transform to the organizations of customer choice. To accomplish such a transition, we believe the following guidelines will be most beneficial.

Create a Flexible Technology Infrastructure

New technologies, particularly the Internet, have rapidly been changing business models, relationships with customers and partners, processes, and the overall increased pace of business. SMEs face unique obstacles to these changes; they need to deploy a flexible Internet-based technological infrastructure that can respond to dynamic

Table 1: Key Elements in a Knowledge-Based Economy

KEY ELEMENT	DESCRIPTION
The New Economy Is Digital	Information today is in digital form—digital information combined with digital networks for communication has opened a new world of opportunities and allows vast amounts of information to be squeezed or transmitted at high speed.
Virtualization & Molecularization	As information shifts from analog to digital, physical things can become virtual—changing the metabolism of the economy, the types of institutions and relationships possible, and the nature of economic activity itself—in particular the industrial hierarchy and economy is giving way to molecular organizations and economic structures. New enterprises thus will have a molecular structure.
Integration	The new economy is networked, integrating various components such as people, organization, product, and processes, and breaking down walls among companies—suppliers, customers, and competitors (Tapscott, 1996).
Speed	Responsiveness is the key, hence, speed, speed, and more speed is central to knowledge-based economy.
Global Domain	The development of information technology and the vast increases in productivity comprise only one side of the new economy; the other side is the globalization of markets (Fontes, 2001).
Intellectual Capitalism	The capital of the traditional economy is now being transformed into a new form, namely, intellectual capitalism (Granstrand, 2000). In broad terms, intellectual capitalism can be interpreted as resulting from a confluence of a capitalist economy and a knowledge or information economy in which intellectual capital in some sense is dominant (Granstrand, 2000).
Knowledge Assets	A firm's knowledge assets are creativity of knowledge workers combined with technological expertise and market know-how. The generation and exploitation of knowledge is now the predominant factor in the creation of wealth.

business environments, and better manage rapid changes in business processes and relationships. This kind of infrastructure would help to bring customers and suppliers together. New technology architecture should ensure that every business could collaborate successfully with virtually any business partner (Badhwani, 2001).

Customers of tomorrow would expect businesses to serve them via the Internet, anytime, anywhere in the world, on any device, at any time. Therefore, it becomes mandatory to

Table 2: Key Factors for SMEs

FACTORS	DESCRIPTION
Lack of Sustained Technology Developments	While borderless electronic trade and online trading hubs are opening up, along with many more opportunities for small to medium-sized enterprises (Jordan, 2000), sustaining in ever-increasing technological environments is proving to be a difficult task for SMEs. Only 35% of small businesses have an Internet website, and of those only 2% have sites with e-commerce transactions (Kleindl, 2000). Asian SMEs are even further behind the times due to poor penetration of Internet technologies and slow growth of electronic commerce infrastructure (Jordan, 2000). In Hong Kong, more than 65% of SMEs have not engaged in any form of e-business, according to a report by the Institute of Information and Media Industries and IBM. The report found that just 6.5% of Hong Kong SMEs maintained a corporate Web page, while 60% weren't even planning to introduce an e-mail system (Jordan, 2000).
Lack of Proper Information	SMEs require proper guidance in making the right choice of technology suited to their needs. It has been experienced that many SMEs do not have the ability, time, or energy to shift to new technology, either due to lack of expertise at their own level or absence of proper guidance, advice, and support from big companies. Not only do they lack information about the availability and sources of the new technology, but they also lack a resource base for searching for partners (Jordan, 2000).
Inertia to Change	Many small businesses are too content to change, despite the often-surprising rewards of taking that step into the future. For example, SMEs can benefit from powerful enterprise resource planning (ERP) tools and customer relationship management (CRM) software technology solutions without investing in them, because they can rely upon rental-based enterprise solutions such as application service providers (ASPs) to provide these solutions.
Slow to Adapt E-Commerce	The Internet and the Web environments are bringing fundamental changes in traditional business models. SMEs often lack the resources of larger firms and may not have the brand name recognition of Internet first movers.

create a Web-based infrastructure that can integrate back-office management systems, customers, and business partners to respond to any situation. Such an infrastructure can also help to create self-service capabilities. Properly designed Web portals can provide trusted business partners with a secure, flexible environment for activities ranging from self-service to collaborative commerce (Badhwani, 2001).

Table 2: (continued) Key Factors for SMEs

FACTORS	DESCRIPTION
Encroachment by Big Corporations into Niche Areas	The Internet and the online environments are having a major impact on how businesses operate. The Web environments allow customers to easily search and find competitive information and new sources of supply (Kleindl, 2000). SMEs have traditionally been able to gain the advantage over larger competitors by developing personalized relationships with customers, customizing their offerings, and efficiently targeting niche markets (Kleindl, 2000).
Commoditization of Suppliers	SMEs face additional pressure due to the commoditization of suppliers. This occurs when the customer can find a large number of suppliers with relatively similar offerings and then have them bid for the sale.
Competition from First Movers	SMEs face competition with online competitors who have first mover advantages. Firms that are Web pioneers already have cost advantages as they move along experience curves that relate to personnel training and management in Web practices.
Weak Supply Chains	Online communication and developing links with suppliers are impacting almost all businesses including SMEs.
Lack of Expertise	The Internet allows SMEs to communicate and transact business at any time. SMEs can use the Internet and information technologies to create unique products and services for their customers that differ from the competition.
Barriers for International Trade	Export and internationalization are important to the survival of many SMEs because of their tremendous potential for enhancing sales growth, increasing efficiency, and improving quality (Masurel, 2001). SMEs find it difficult to jump to internationalization trade due to many barriers such as difficulties in forming international partnerships, a lack of managerial experience and competence, and difficulties in gathering information.
Lack of Awareness of Management Processes	As our economy becomes more connected to the global marketplace, SMEs need awareness of management processes and tools to create competitive advantage (Monk, 2000).

Adapt New Standards of Valuation

Identifying and leveraging organization assets is the most important element in building a successful business in the new economy. The encompassing challenge that SMEs face in this new environment is how to identify and leverage all sources of value, not just the assets that appear on the traditional balance sheet. These important assets include

Table 2: (continued) Key Factors for SMEs

FACTORS	DESCRIPTION
Long Lead Times	The rapid economic and technological developments in the globally oriented business world make the strategic use of information technology (IT) essential, yet SMEs are generally found somewhat behind regarding the application of IT (Knol & Stroeken, 2001).
Poor Management and Accounting Practices	The role of finance has been viewed as a critical element for the development and participation of small to medium-sized enterprises (Cook, 2001). Levy has highlighted the limited access to financial resources available to smaller enterprises compared to larger organizations and the consequences for their growth and development (Levy, 1993).
Intense Market Competition in International Trade	Many SMEs are relatively inexperienced operators in international trade. SMEs face the challenge of intense market competition for trade promotion. Adapting to a new global trading environment presents a challenge to SMEs.
Inefficient Value Chains	The rapid development of the World Wide Web as a communication and marketing medium offers SMEs tremendous opportunities of access to world markets, low-cost entry into new markets, and the ability to gain efficiencies in business processes (Kleindl, 2000). However, SMEs require restructuring of value chains because business models of a knowledge-based economy are very different than the earlier traditional businesses.

customers, brands, suppliers, employees, patents, and ideas. The new economy demands a new standard of valuation for the new knowledge-based assets. Old ways of managing and measuring assets no longer suffice since traditional approaches to management and measurement are no longer adequate in fast-changing business environments. The SMEs have to start valuing their assets differently. It could be the way the equity markets value companies for market capitalization and book value based on intangibles such as innovations, creativity, customer base, employees, and ideas. SMEs have to value relationships, intellectual property, and leadership, along with their physical assets and financial capital for creating value (Boulton, Libert, & Samek, 2000).

Build and Adapt an Asset-Based Business Model

Every business uses a particular combination of assets to build a business model unique to its needs and goals. The new economy demands SMEs to adopt new business models. In these emerging models, intangible assets such as relationships, knowledge, people, brands, and systems are taking center stage. SMEs can leverage these intangible assets for creating most value for their stakeholders. In the new economy, SMEs need to create a business model that links combinations of assets to value creation. For example, though not reflected in the balance sheet, employees and supplier assets are important in the world of intangible value. Each component in the employee and supplier asset category, including all members of the supply chain, is considered a partner in producing products and services.

Outsourcing, mergers, and alliances are the steps in acquiring asset base of customers, expertise, and brands to gain new efficiencies in the value chain. Companies offer stock options to employees to acquire and retain employee assets and their knowledge. SMEs' new business models must consider assets of both the tangible and intangible kind for value creation. SMEs should not consider employees as expenses and customers as targets, but both should be treated as partners.

SMEs must identify assets, of all value-tangible and intangible sources, and must assess how these contribute to create value. SMEs also need to find ways through which these assets can be enhanced to create further value. They can expand into new product or service markets, or change or develop new products to achieve value-creating synergies (Boulton et al., 2000).

Provide Support for Digital Infrastructure

Both virtual and semi-virtual companies seem to realize today that what differentiates successful from failing e-ventures is often the existence or lack of appropriate infrastructure. SMEs offering e-commerce must understand that they would need appropriate infrastructure for customer service support, auxiliary services, or timely delivery to succeed. The value and cost of inventory management, deliveries, or customer care would be very important for business (Kupiec, 2000).

Many nations are developing their information technology infrastructures for the growth of e-commerce or e-trade, but few countries are still ready to support e-trade for their SMEs (Said, 2000). Many countries have started a process of liberalization of the telecommunications sector, and new legislative framework for information practices. Such a legislative framework includes, but is not limited to an Electronic Commerce Bill that provides the legal basis for the safe but free conduct of electronic commerce, and a Data Protection Bill that safeguards citizens from the potential abuse of their personal data through information systems (Said, 2000).

The various agencies, including the government, have to create a supportive infrastructure for SMEs to enable their participation in the digital economy. The interventions could be, for example, to allow SMEs to exploit business information resources, turning them into accessible, visible products, thus creating favorable conditions for firms to access business information, know-how, training, and technology (Said, 2000).

Design Flexible Organizations

The knowledge-based economy has forced almost every type of company to find new ways of measuring success and create organizational models that consistently deliver shareholder value (Clieaf, 2001). The designs of SMEs should allow organizations to respond quickly, and decision-making authorities are truly adding value to the organization. Moreover, the talent pool needs to be assessed, selected, and developed based on new measures of work complexity and the capabilities required to succeed (Clieaf, 2001).

In rapidly changing markets reflected in customer changes, SMEs require a rapid and flexible business process and organizational change. At times SMEs suffer with scarcity of funds, lack of expertise, and lack of effort to re-engineer their process. SMEs may find, at times, the financial cost too high to re-engineer and prepare themselves for changing technology and markets (McAdam, 2000).

Exploit Economies of Global Scale

SMEs have the opportunity to expand their operations to global markets for larger revenues and a larger asset base, but have a challenge to create economies of scale. The economies of scale can be by spreading fixed costs, reducing capital and operating costs, pooling purchasing power, and creating critical mass.

SMEs require collaborations, partnership, or alliances to increase their market reach to global markets, as well as to exploit economies of global scale. However, each of these opportunities is associated with significant obstacles and challenges that often prevent SMEs from exploiting them optimally. To overcome these challenges, SMEs need to have collaborations and partnerships (Gupta & Govindrajan, 2001).

Use a Customer-Focused Approach

The confluence of changing customer demands, emerging marketing theories, and available technology underlie a dramatic shift in the way organizations relate to customers (Kandell, 2000).

A knowledge-based economy presents numerous challenges to SMEs, as customers of the 21st Century are more knowledgeable, powerful, and highly informed. Customer relationship management is replacing the traditional "Four Ps" of marketing: product, price, place, and promotion. Since product lifecycles are reduced, it is very important for SMEs to invest in long-term relationships with customers for their growth and stability in an increasingly dynamic market (Kandell, 2000).

SMEs have to shift from being product centric to customer centric, making customers a part of the organization. The new marketing approach of SMEs must focus on customization and long-term relationships. Since most SMEs are organized around product lines, one of the greatest organizational challenges is the art of being customer centric.

Implement Interactive Web Portal

SMEs must understand and utilize the power of the interactive channel offered by Web technology, which can include customers and third-party providers as partners within the enterprise. The Web portal of SMEs should ensure that all front-office activities and customer interactions are integrated with supply chains. Integration has to be across all types of interaction— marketing, sales, service, and support systems. In order to be effective, customer relationship management (CRM) systems must link with the back-office systems that assist the enterprise with all facets of operational planning. The critical success factors for most firms will be the competencies of how to integrate their business effectively into information networks and of how to respond rapidly to changing customer perceptions of value (Soren et al., 1999).

Focus on Customer Relationship Management

CRM is all about building a long-term learning relationship with customers. Globalization and the Internet have changed customers' expectations and behavior. Today, customers are just a click away from the competition. Many SMEs lack information about their customers. In the digital economy, SMEs must have full information of their customers so the products and services can be customized to the expectation of customers. SMEs need to build CRM solutions to take care of the dynamic needs of customers that will increase SMEs' competitive edge and enable them to compete with bigger firms. Customer relationship management is rapidly becoming a key factor for the success of SMEs (Karkoviata, 2001). Internet-based customer relationship management promises to streamline processes, lower costs, and enhance customer loyalty. However, SMEs need CRM solutions that could be implemented fast at an affordable pricing and should have a rapid return-on-investment (Badhwani, 2001).

Need to Become a Learning Organization

Lastly, it is vital for SMEs to incorporate knowledge management techniques into their strategies and become learning organizations. To succeed, knowledge management must be articulated clearly at the strategic level and fostered by senior management, as has been the practice in many of the large consulting companies that have successfully adopted knowledge management strategies (Wickramasinghe, 2002). By becoming a learning organization, we believe that SMEs will be able to continuously address the other nine preceding guidelines critical to their enjoying success and achieving a sustainable competitive advantage. Figure 1 highlights the key areas that SMEs need to adopt in order to become a truly learning organization.

Future Trends

The Internet and IT revolution have provided many opportunities for small to medium-sized enterprises since the beginning of the most dramatic economic turnaround in modern times (Mars, 2000). A large percentage of small businesses are looking to the Web for business, but don't know how to start. This has opened the door to a number of e-

Figure 1: Key Attributes of a Learning Organization

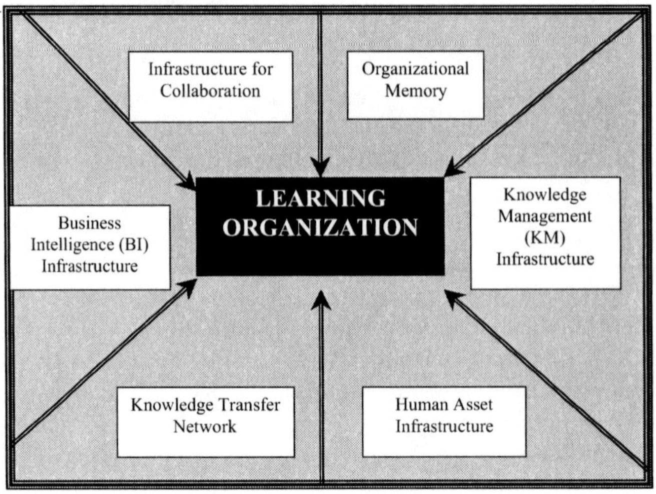

commerce facilitators. Two key areas we believe need to be addressed are changing customers and changing business models.

Changing Customers

Shifts in technology are causing a number of changes regarding customers. Customers are no longer just viewers or listeners, but are active users of interactive services and information. Many companies are offering opportunities for customers to produce their own products and services by providing interactive models (Stewart, 2000). The easy access that buyers have to competitive information is placing pressure on prices and is encouraging customers to search for substitutes.

Changing Business Models

New business models are emerging in every industry of the new economy. In these emerging models, intangible assets such as relationships, knowledge, people, brands, and systems are taking center stage (Boulton et al.; 2000, McGarvey, 2001). The relationship and interaction of various stakeholders such as customers, suppliers, strategic partners, agents, or distributors is entirely changed. Moving into e-commerce may require a major change in the commerce models that businesses use. Because companies are creating value in new ways, they need new business models that accurately reflect 21st Century business realities. The key to survival in the new e-business environment depends upon SMEs' ability to adapt to a new, more collaborative, corporate-competition model.

Conclusion

We believe that SMEs should find many more new opportunities in today's knowledge-based economy, but at the same time may be threatened in competitive environments that can force SMEs to modify or completely abandon many current business practices. SMEs must consider new business models that take advantage of existing and emerging Internet-based technologies in order to stay competitive. SMEs have to introduce new technologies to enter into global markets and find ways to attract customers if they want to compete in global scenarios. As larger organizations are entering into Internet-enabled businesses, SMEs have to upgrade their tools and techniques to equip themselves with the abilities to compete with large organizations. In addition, more has to be done to encourage stability and growth in the SME business sector, and to establish globally competitive firms. Many small manufacturers do not have the resources required to transform their businesses in response to the digital economy's rapid evolution. It may be necessary for SMEs to redesign many of their traditional business processes to compete in the new economy. SMEs face the challenges of fast-changing technology and business scenarios in the knowledge-based economy. Combining the right business strategy along with the most effective technology tools would improve the chances of SMEs' participation in knowledge-based economy.

We have outlined 10 key areas that SMEs must focus on in order to enjoy success and maximize the new opportunities in today's knowledge economy. We strongly urge researchers interested in the knowledge-based economy and the competitiveness of SMEs to explore the issues outlined in this chapter even further. Our understanding of the factors affecting successful participation of SMEs in the knowledge-based economy has convinced us that a crucial if not the critical step for SMEs is to embrace knowledge management strategies and become learning organizations. We are confident that our guidelines will enable SMEs to develop sustainable competitive advantages and enjoy success in today's knowledge economy.

References

Acs, Z.J., Carlsson, B., & Karlsson, C. (1999). *The Linkages Among Entrepreneurship, SMEs and the Macroeconomy.* Cambridge: Cambridge University Press.

Anonymous. (2000). Web returns for SMEs. *Management Accounting, 78*(5), 14.

Anonymous. (2001). What knowledge economy? *Information World Review,* (170), 1.

Boulton, R.E.S., Libert, B.D., & Samek, S.M. (2000). A business model for the new economy. *The Journal of Business Strategy, 21*(4), 29-35.

Budhwani, K. (2001). Becoming part of the e-generation. *CMA Management, 75*(4), 24-27.

Clieaf, M.V. (2001). Leading and creating value in the knowledge economy. *Ivey Business Journal, 65*(5), 54-59.

Cook, P. (2001) Finance and small and medium-sized enterprise in developing countries. *Journal of Developmental Entrepreneurship, 6*(1), 17-40.

Cooper, J. (2001). Enhancing the competitive success of Canadian SMEs. *CMA Management, 75*(5), 16-21.

Cowey, M. (2000). Knowledge economy—fact or fad? *New Zealand Management, 47*(4), 54-55.

Cowey, M. (2001). Managing in the new economy. *New Zealand Management, 48*(3), 66-67.

Duhan, S., Levy, M., & Powell, P. (2001). Information systems strategies in knowledge-based SMEs: The role of core competencies. *European Journal of Information Systems, 10*(1), 25-40.

Fjeldstad, O.D., & Haanaes, K. (2001). Strategy tradeoffs in the knowledge and network economy. *Business Strategy Review, 12*(1), 1-10.

Fontes, M., & Coombs, R. (2001). Contribution of new technology-based firms to the strengthening of technological capabilities in intermediate economies. *Research Policy, 30*(1), 79-97.

Gold, A.H., Malhotra, A., & Segars, A.H. (2001). Knowledge management: An organizational capabilities perspective. *Journal of Management Information Systems, 18*(1), 185-214.

Granstrand, O. (2000). The shift towards intellectual capitalism—the role of infocom technologies. *Research Policy, 29*(9), 1061-1080.

Gulisano, V. (2001) Succeeding in the digital logistics age, *World Trade, 14*(5), 42-43.

Gupta, A.K., & Govindarajan, V. (2001) Converting global presence into global competitive advantage. *The Academy of Management Executive, 15*(2), 45-58.

Halliday, L. (2001). An unprecedented opportunity. *Information World Review,* (167), 18-19.

Heneman, R.L., Tansky, J.W., & Michael Camp, S. (2000). Human resource management practices in small and medium-sized enterprises: Unanswered questions and future research perspectives. *Entrepreneurship Theory and Practice, 25*(1), 11-26.

Jordan, T. (2000). Transform your business. *Asian Business, 36*(5), 30-32.

Kandell, J. (2000). CRM, ERM, one-to-one-decoding relationship management theory and technology. *Trusts & Estates, 139*(4), 49-53.

Karkoviata, L. (2001). Making the customer king. *Asian Business, 37*(2), 47-48.

Klaas, B.S., McClendon, J., & Gainey, T.W. (2000). Managing HR in the small and medium enterprise: The impact of professional employer organizations. *Entrepreneurship Theory and Practice, 25*(1), 107-124.

Kleindl, B. (2000). Competitive dynamics and new business models for SMEs in the virtual marketplace. *Journal of Developmental Entrepreneurship, 5*(1), 73-85.

Knol, W.H.C., & Stroeken, J.H.M. (2001). The diffusion and adoption of information technology in small and medium-sized enterprises through IT scenarios. *Technology Analysis & Strategic Management, 13*(2), 227-246.

Kupiec, E. (2000). Shifting strategies: Challenging the traditional business knowledge. *CMA Management, 74*(4), 15-17.

Levy, B. (1993). Obstacles to developing indigenous small and medium enterprises: An empirical assessment. *The World Bank Economic Review, 7*(1), 65-83.

Lu, J.W., & Beamish, W. (2001). The internationalization and performance of SMEs. *Strategic Management Journal, 22*(6/7), 565-586.

Mars, R.D.D. (2000). SMEs flourish. *Asian Business, 36*(5), 53-54.

Masurel, E. (2001). Export behavior of service sector SMEs. *International Small Business Journal, 19*(2), 80-84.

McAdam, R. (2000). The implementation of reengineering in SMEs: A grounded study. *International Small Business Journal, 18*(4), 29-45.

McGarvey, R. (2001). New corporate ethics for the new economy. *World Trade, 14*(3), 43.

McMahon, R.G. (2001). Business growth and performance and the financial reporting practices of Australian manufacturing SMEs. *Journal of Small Business Management, 39*(2), 152-164.

Persaud, A. (2001). The knowledge gap. *Foreign Affairs, 80*(2), 107-117.

Peursem, K.A.V., & Wells, K. (2000). Contracting practices in professional accounting SMEs: An analysis of New Zealand firms. *International Small Business Journal, 19*(1), 68-82.

Said, A.J. (2000). Helping small firms trade effectively with the Internet. *International Trade Forum*, (3), 16-19.

Stewart, T.A. (2000). Three rules for managing in the real-time economy. *Fortune, 141*(9), 332-334.

Tapscott, D. (1996). *Digital Economy—Promise and Peril in the Age of Networked Intelligence.* McGraw-Hill

Tapscott, D., Lowy, A., & Ticoll, D. (1998). *Blueprint to the Digital Economy—Creating Wealth in the Area of E-Business.* McGraw-Hill.

Warren, L., & Hutchinson, W.E. (2000). Success factors for high-technology SMEs: A case study from Australia. *Journal of Small Business Management, 38*(3), 86-91.

Wickramasinghe, N. (2002). Do we practice what we preach: Are knowledge management systems in practice truly reflective of knowledge management systems in theory? *Business Process Management Journal.*

Woodall, P. (2000). Survey: The new economy: Knowledge is power. *The Economist, 356*(8189), 27-32.

Chapter XVIII

Community and Regional Portals in Australia: A Role to Play for Small Businesses?

Arthur Tatnall, Victoria University, Australia

Stephen Burgess, Victoria University, Australia

Mohini Singh, RMIT University, Australia

Abstract

The importance of Web portals to small business has increased considerably in recent years. There are many different types of portals, but this chapter examines the use of community and regional portals by small businesses in Australia. In the chapter, two Australian regional portals are contrasted with the more generic e-malls, and the advantages of each are discussed. We show how portals can be used to advantage by small businesses in several different settings. Benefits to small business include: greater customer loyalty, improved business relationships, enhanced e-business trust, lower cost of infrastructure, ease of access to advice, and expanded business opportunities.

Introduction

There are many differences in the ways in that small businesses adopt and use information technology (IT) in comparison with medium to large-sized businesses. Small businesses are constrained by a lack of resources (time, money, and expertise) and the strategic, longer term focus necessary to plan effective use of IT. These differences extend to the adoption and use of the Internet and electronic commerce (e-commerce). This chapter examines the evolving concept of *portals* and speculates on the potential use of community and regional portals by small businesses as part of their online strategy. A potential list of benefits that portals can provide to small businesses is provided, and two existing regional portals are contrasted against the more generic e-mall to determine the benefits that portals are currently providing for small businesses.

Background

A portal is a special website designed to act as a *gateway* to give access to other related sites (Phillips, 1998). It is intended as a base-site that users will keep returning to after accessing these other sites, and is often seen as a starting point for specific groups of users when they access the Web. The *Oxford Dictionary* defines a portal as:

> "A door, gate, doorway, or gateway of stately or elaborate construction; the entrance, especially of a large or magnificent building. Hence often poetic for door or gate. A space within the door of a room, partitioned off, and containing an inner door; also such a partition itself." (Oxford, 1973)

What is new about Web portals is the way that these special sites are now being used to facilitate access to other sites that may be closely related, in the case of special purpose portals, or quite diverse in the case of general portals. Portals now offer a range of services including trading facilities, as banks look to partner them (Internet.com, 1999).

In this chapter, "Internet business use" is defined as being all of those modern uses of Internet technologies by a business, including communications technologies (such as e-mail) and using the Internet for business research and electronic commerce (use of the Internet to conduct business with external partners, such as suppliers, customers, and government). The definition of e-commerce can be expanded to include other technologies (such as Electronic Data Interchange), but our definition is suitable for this chapter.

Web managers are discovering that increased sales and advertising income result from attracting more people and *retaining* them longer. Websites with successful portals that attract large numbers of browsers who linger can charge more for Web advertising (Schneider & Perry, 2001). Portal sites have been projected to be the conduit for more than 40% of all commerce revenue and to gain 67% of advertising dollars (Kleindl, 2001). As such, portals can play an important part in the e-commerce strategy of a business.

One of the attractions of portals is the amount of traffic that travels through them. The portal is viewed as a means of advertising to a large audience via banner advertisements.

New Internet jargon has emerged as businesses operating portals attempt to increase the number of their 'eyeballs' (visitors to the site) and their 'stickiness' (the amount of time they stay at the site) (Zikmund & d'Amico, 2001).

Eduard (2001) refers to portal websites as being the **fourth** stage of development of business websites. The earlier stages are:

Stage One: Dumb Website. For mainly one-way transfer of information from a business to its customers. The purpose of the portal at this stage is to acquire new users (increase 'eyeballs'). As suggested by Eisenmann (2002), to encourage new users, portal awareness is created by online and offline advertising and by word of mouth.

Stage Two: Simple Interactive Website. Browsers of the website can conduct basic searches and place simple queries. Replies from the company usually come in the form of e-mail or traditional communications. Orders may be placed by e-mail, for instance, but the transaction is handled using traditional methods. Stage Two aims to turn new users into repeat visitors by collecting user information, displaying ads, and selling goods.

Stage Three: Transactional Interactive Website. Trading transactions, such as online payments, are conducted by automated means. In many cases this will require some integration between a company's online 'front end' (which may be its 'storefront') and its 'back end' (existing computerized systems). In many cases this requires that the systems and/or the business processes need to be redesigned, requiring a deal of IT expertise (Eduard, 2001).

The fourth stage of website development according to Eisenmann (2002) is where the business attempts to become a focus of attention for customers (and perhaps suppliers). It becomes the first 'port of call' for that group for many of their needs, perhaps linking through to other businesses. This opens up options for other forms of revenue, such as advertising of sales commissions, but for many small businesses, a 'stage three' website will be the highest level they could hope to achieve.

Types of Portals

Portals come in several flavors, including:

1. **General portals,** sometimes known as mega portals, try to be the 'one-stop port-of-call' for all (or at least many) user needs. Many of these have developed from being simple search tools (e.g., Yahoo), Internet service providers (e.g., AOL), and e-mail services (e.g., Hotmail). Many general portals include services such as: free e-mail, links to search engines and categories of information, membership services, news and sports, business headlines and articles, personalized space with a user's selections, links to chat rooms, links to virtual shopping malls, and Web directories. Other Web services that have transformed themselves into portals are large software distributors (such as Netscape) and sites that initially offered free services, such as e-mail. These sites tend to become portals, as it is realized that a large amount of Internet traffic is moving through the site (Amor, 2000).

2.   **Community portals** are often set up by community groups such as Launceston in Tasmania (http://www.elaunceston.com/) and Manchester in the UK (http://www.mymanchester.net), or are sometimes based around special group interests such as the needs of older people (http://www.greypath.com) (Tatnall & Lepa, 2001).

3.   **Vertical industry portals** are usually based around specific industry areas and are sometimes known as vortals. Vortals tend to be more specialized, offering their services in one particular interest or industry area. Some of these are open to all Internet users, such as the Singapore government's Ecitizen website (www.ecitizen.org.sg), which provides access to government services (Al-Kibsi, de Boer, Mourshed, & Rea, 2001). Many vertical portals, however, have services for business partners or 'members' only. Ernst & Young (2001) has developed a portal that is, in many ways, a form of extranet (http://www.esecurityonline.com/) for their partners to access the company's knowledge and tools related specifically to online security. The CPA2Biz site (www.cpa2biz.com) is supported by the American Institute of Certified Practicing Accountants (AICPA). It offers services related to training courses, publications, conferences, accounting software, and so forth to members of the society (Rogozinski, 2002). Interestingly, there is a vortal called Portals Community (www.portalscommunity.com) that provides the "definitive enterprise portals resource" (their description). Membership, which is free, provides access to further information on portals.

4.   **Horizontal industry portals** are based around a group of businesses in an industry or a local area. One example discussed later is Bizewest (Tatnall & Burgess, 2002). United Overseas Bank's B2B portal in Singapore is a horizontal portal, allowing small businesses to set up an online storefront, with payments for purchased goods to be settled through the bank (Guan et al., 2001). Lynch (1998) suggests that portals can be described as horizontal when they are utilized by a broad base of users across a horizontal market, and vertical when their content is tightly focused toward a particular audience such as a specific industry or group of industries.

5.   **Enterprise information portals** serve as the gateway to a corporate intranet. There is a recent trend for larger businesses to set up their own 'internal' portals for employee use as part of their intranet services. An enterprise information portal offers a single point of entry that brings together the employees, business partners, and consumers at one virtual place (Turban et al., 2002). These are not investigated in this chapter, given its small business focus.

6.   **E-marketplace portals** are extended enterprise portals that offer access to a company's extranet services. An example is Covisint (www.covisint.com), launched by automotive companies General Motors Corporation, Ford Motor Company, and Daimler Chrysler. This portal aims to eliminate redundancies and burdens for suppliers through integration and collaboration with promises of lower costs, easier business practices, and marked increases in efficiencies for the entire industry (Turban et al., 2002). The name Covisint clearly indicates the purpose of the portal, in which 'Co' represents connectivity, collaboration, and communication; 'Vis' represents the visibility that the Internet provides and the vision of real-time information on the supply chain; and 'Int' represents the integrated solutions the venture provides, as well as its international scope.

The importance of reliable, efficient, and easy-to-use portals will be seen increasingly as the amount of information available on the Internet continues to expand at a rapid rate (Amor, 2000).

The Internet and Small Business in Australia

Small businesses face a number of barriers to the successful implementation of information technology. These barriers typically include (Burgess, 2002):

• the cost of IT;

• the lack of time to devote to the implementation and maintenance of IT;

• a lack of IT knowledge combined with difficulty in finding useful, impartial advice;

• a lack of use of external consultants and vendors;

• short-range management perspectives;

• a lack of understanding of the benefits that IT can provide, and how to measure those benefits; and

• a lack of formal planning or control procedures.

This list also reflects many of the differences between the ways in which small businesses adopt and use IT in comparison with medium to large-sized businesses. Interestingly, the barriers facing small-business adoption and use of the Internet virtually match those listed above for IT (Burgess, 2002). However, a comprehensive survey of 1,800 small and medium-sized businesses in Australia (Telstra Corporation, 2002) revealed that 79% of small and 94% of medium-sized businesses are connected to the Internet, so small businesses are showing that they are willing to 'dip their toes into the water.' The main usages of the Internet are to communicate via e-mail and obtain reference information, look for products and services, and access directories (such as the Yellow Pages). The first three uses were identified by more than 50% of businesses as 'essential' applications. Lesser identified areas of usage are those more associated with the term 'e-commerce'—placing orders, paying for goods, providing extra customer service, networking with other members of the industry, and offering online sales (Telstra Corporation, 2002). This is typical for small businesses, which will initially tend towards those applications that are easiest to set up and provide easily identifiable efficiency improvements (Burgess, 2002).

It is notable that 60% of respondents in the Australian survey indicated that the use of the Internet made employees more effective, up from 51% in 2001 and 49% the previous year (Telstra Corporation, 2002, 2001), so there is a recognition that the Internet is starting to deliver identifiable benefits in those favored applications.

Portals and Small Business

Internet business use is well known for new, evolving, and interchangeable terminologies. Two years ago, what we now know as portals were generally known as e-malls, either generic or specialized, especially in the retail industry. More recently portals also include a very narrow vertical structure such as www.rmit.edu.au/ebusiness/, which is aimed at a small community with specific information.

To date, most small businesses involved with portals usually do so as a *user* of the portal, rather than setting up the portal themselves (Eduard, 2001). The bottom line is that most small businesses still view the Internet as being mainly a mechanism for information provision, and may fail to take advantage of some of the added value and other opportunities that Internet applications, such as portals, can provide (Eduard, 2001). One of the best mechanisms by which small businesses can become involved with portals is through regional and community portals, and one way of 'testing the water' can be by becoming involved in a portal.

Benefits to Small Business

So, what benefits can portals provide for small businesses? Portals perform many different functions, but their main core elements, described by Eisenmann (2002), are search, content, community building, commerce, and personal-productivity applications. The key questions for small businesses are whether portals are going to provide these services on a more cost-effective or efficient basis than they could themselves, or provide services beyond what they could normally expect to achieve. Some of the advantages that portals offer to small businesses are:

A Secure Environment

Portals provide a secure online environment to small businesses to set up a cyber business. The capital outlay for e-commerce can be significant for a small business. The capital and integration headache for small businesses is eliminated, however, by being part of a portal, enabling them to concentrate on customer-focused services to improve 'stickiness' and expand business. Portals generally have a payment infrastructure that enables small businesses to integrate their accounts receivable and payable to the portal back-end systems.

Search and Directory Services

Search engines and directories, and 'shopping bots' that list the portals, will automatically enable Web users to find the gateway to small online shops on the Web via these portals, saving substantially on costs. Advertising on portals is generally in the form of banner ads linked to certain directory entries or search keywords and sponsorships of contextually relevant content.

New Partnerships

E-commerce opens up the opportunity for small businesses to sell to new buyers, tap into the 'cyber' supply chain and win new business, offer complementary products with other businesses, and procure goods electronically. Suppliers to large organizations can participate in online bidding processes and obtain free training to use technology as well as new buyers.

Community Building and Regional Relationships

Community building features such as chat rooms, message boards, instant messaging services, online greeting cards, applications for digital photos, FAQs, and other Web services are included in the portal infrastructure that small businesses can capitalize on.

In addition to all of these benefits, regional portals provide the advantage that participating small businesses can feel that they are contributing to the local community. There are also cost and efficiency benefits through dealing with businesses in the local area, especially where physical products are being transacted. This is in addition to the goodwill that can eventuate through dealing in the local area.

Strategy, Management, and Business Trust

Small businesses are usually constrained by resources and expert advice on online business, which lead to a lack of strategy for the management and implementation of e-business. Portals enable small businesses to uptake a common structure for e-business that helps them to attain the management support or share ideas with others businesses and attain success.

Factors affecting trust identified by Farhoomand and Lovelock (2002) include reputation, willingness to customize, expertise, frequency of business contact, anticipated future transactions, intention for future interactions, frequent business contact, size, publicity, confidential information sharing, length of relationship, and perceived power. Establishing trust in an electronic environment is a bigger challenge for small businesses due to complexity, the need for tight integration, and interdependence between business partners and the Internet itself, which is an anonymous, impersonal medium, lacking visual, non-verbal cues usually taken for granted in off-line communication. On a portal a small business has the opportunity to overcome most of the trust-building factors as the infrastructure and communication is the same for all the parties on the portal as compared to a single online business.

Improved Customer Management

As suggested by Farhoomand and Lovelock (2002), customer acquisition is a critical aspect of an online firm's overall marketing strategy. Portals can make deals with Internet retailers for the 'eyeballs' that will also benefit small businesses that are part of the portal.

Regional and Community Portals

One of the problems with trying to identify community and regional portals is that definitions can vary quite widely. The top 10 results of a search on the directory Yahoo (www.yahoo.com) in October 2002 for the term 'community portal' revealed what the authors would classify as:

- Four regional portals
- Three vertical (industry) portals
- One horizontal portal
- One Internet solution provider
- One portal that was a listing of various regional portals

A similar search for the term 'regional portal' revealed:

- Seven regional portals
- Two Internet solution providers
- Another portal that was a listing of various regional portals

The problem is that many of the sites that we would classify as regional portals were called community portals. Another popular term for community portal was 'interest portal.'

In this chapter we are primarily interested in regional portals, as they can provide small businesses with the opportunity to become involved in e-commerce without having to worry a great deal about setting up the infrastructure.

Portals for Small Business in Australia

A number of regional and community portals exist in Australia, primarily to service the needs of small businesses. The rest of the chapter discusses some examples of Australian portals and their relative importance to small businesses. Two regional portals are contrasted against the more generic e-mall. In each instance, the portals are examined to see whether they provide the benefits indicated previously.

In the instance of the first regional portal and the e-malls, the authors gathered details of the portals via observation of the actual portals themselves. For the second regional portal, details were gained from a series of interviews with various stakeholders in the portal. Further details are provided in the following text.

Regional Portals

Example One: Ebiznet

Ebiznet (www.ebiznet.com.au) was set up in 1997 by a number of regional development boards in South Australia for the purpose of increasing awareness and use of communication technologies in the regions to boost economic development and employment growth (Ebiznet, 1999a). A number of separate websites were set up within the project, including the Adelaide Hills Regional Portal (www.adelaide-hills.com.au), and there are now five separate websites in the project. Information about the operation of the websites was extracted from the websites by the authors in October 2002. The Adelaide Hills Regional Portal offers a number of services (Ebiznet, 2000):

- **Come Visit.** Links to accommodation, dining, events, and shopping information, as well as details about local attractions and location maps.

- **Go Shopping.** Links to regional businesses that have successfully taken their business online and are utilizing e-commerce.

- **Do Business.** Links to information websites on government and other business services.

- **Live Here.** This section is more for individuals and families.

We suggest that small businesses would primarily be interested in the 'Go Shopping' and 'Do Business' links. To set the project up, IT personnel in the regions formed part of a project team that:

> *"...involved a series of inter-related stages, providing awareness of the Internet and its business applications, with an emphasis on electronic commerce. These stages included the development of cost-effective e-commerce solutions, the establishment of a range of demonstration websites with e-commerce capacities, including shopping carts, and training in IT business applications and use of the Internet. The project was specifically targeted to small regional businesses that were unlikely to find solutions or acquire the necessary skills without the opportunity to participate in a project of this nature." (Ebiznet, 1999a)*

Functions provided by local Web service providers were project management, strategic planning, Web design, hosting, e-commerce, Web marketing, Web maintenance, and training (Ebiznet, 1999b).

Initially, information seminars were run for small businesses, but were not well attended. It was felt that this was because of a lack of advertising dollars and effort. Those that did attend found the seminars to be very useful and were particularly interested in the e-commerce applications. Training courses were subsidized and were oversubscribed, with extra courses being run. It was felt that *local* examples were most important to the success of the courses (Ebiznet, 1999a).

Nine businesses currently operate using secure online payments on the Adelaide Hills website. These range from accommodation, to provision of food and wine, a general store, and an online recruitment agency. Other community portal sites within Ebiznet offer a similar structure to Adelaide Hills. A total of 26 businesses are part of the secure online shopping area of the Ebiznet sites.

Usefulness to Small Businesses

The benefits to small businesses that became involved in Ebiznet (as reported on the website) were the opportunities to receive subsidized training, and the technology and secure payment processes already set up and available to be used. They also have the chance of traffic heading to their own websites through the portal, and there is also the opportunity to support the local region.

Example Two: The Bizewest Portal

In June 2000, the Western Region Economic Development Organization (WREDO), a not-for-profit organization sponsored by the six municipalities that make up the western region of Melbourne (Australia), received a government grant for a project to set up a business-to-business portal. The project was to create a 'horizontal portal'—*Bizewest*—that would enable small businesses in Melbourne's west to engage in an increased number of e-commerce transactions with each other. The western region of Melbourne contains around 20,000 businesses and is regarded as the manufacturing, transport, and distribution hub of South-Eastern Australia.

Electronic commerce that is external to an organization occurs mainly between three groups: business, government, and consumers. In setting up the Bizewest portal, it was noted that the majority of electronic commerce activity currently occurs on a business-to-business level (Department of Industry, 1998). It is estimated that transactions of this type comprise 80% of all electronic commerce (Conhaim, 1999) and that this is likely to remain the case in the near future (Straub, 1998) for reasons described by Viehland (1998) as follows:

- Businesses are generally more computerized and networked than homes.
- Many businesses only sell their goods and services to other businesses.
- The supply chain for many businesses goes from business-to-business (for instance, manufacturer to wholesaler to distributor to retailer to customer).

The main objective of the Bizewest portal project, in its initial stages, was to encourage small to medium-sized enterprises in Melbourne's west to be more aggressive in their up-

Figure 1: Bizewest Portal Site

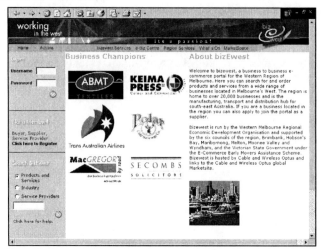

take of e-commerce business opportunities, and to encourage them to work with other local enterprises in the region also using the portal. The project was to create a 'true' business-to-business portal on which online trading was to occur. It was also intended to encourage and facilitate transactions between local government and small business. The initial plan was to gain the participation of about 300 SMEs from the local region in the use of the portal to facilitate their business-to-business and business-to-local-government interactions. Another important project goal was youth involvement, and students from the local high schools and colleges, who were studying IT-related subjects, were to be given the opportunity to 'consult' with SMEs on a one-to-one basis in the development of their Web pages for the portal. When the portal was launched, a payment gateway was not initially included. This meant that orders could be placed on the portal, but that full transaction processing functionality was not initially available. It was always intended that a payment gateway be added to the portal as soon as this was practically possible.

After some initial delays, the Bizewest portal went online in June 2001, and the data that forms the basis of this chapter was collected later that year. The research project to investigate adoption of the portal consisted of three stages (Tatnall & Burgess, 2002). This chapter relates only to the first of these stages:

Stage 1 (second half of 2001) began with interviews of the 'business champions' identified by WREDO. This was followed by further interviews resulting from the first set of interviews.

Stage 2 (second half of 2002) will involve returning to the businesses interviewed earlier and checking whether things are progressing as they thought they would.

Stage 3 (first half of 2003) will check these same businesses to see if any change in the way they do business has resulted from their use of the portal.

Qualitative data collection techniques are important investigation tools and, in particular, focus groups and interviews allow the researcher to explore the formation and development of alliances built along the way. In this research project, interviews were used, as they provided the opportunity for feedback in clarifying questions, allowing the interviewer to probe for a clearer or deeper response, allowing a lengthier period of questioning and generally affording a much higher response rate (Zikmund, 2000; Leedy, 1997). Interviews are now a well-established means of qualitative data collection in the information systems field (Myers, 1999).

The research began by identifying some of the important actors, starting with the portal project manager at WREDO. An interview with the project manager revealed why the project was instigated, and identified some of the other actors. One line of inquiry resulting from this interview was to approach the portal software designers and programmers, and another suggested interviews with the proprietors of the local businesses themselves. The project manager suggested some 'business champions' to interview first, to find out why they had adopted the portal and what had influenced them in doing so. Some of these business people then pointed to the influence exerted by the computer hardware or software as a significant factor. From this point on the key was to seek out interactions, and all negotiations between the actors were carefully investigated.

The portal's proponents, including those from WREDO, negotiated with the SME proprietors to convince them that business-to-business interactions are best performed using the e-commerce solutions offered by the portal. For the project to be successful, the portal needed to be seen by the proprietors of the SMEs as a necessary point of entry to using e-commerce and business-to-business transactions. The proprietors of the SMEs needed to be convinced that this technology was more worthwhile and offered them better business prospects than the approaches they had previously used, and to convince them to stop sending orders by post or fax, but instead to use the portal.

In summary, the first set of interviews showed that most businesses adopting the portal did so because it seemed to them to be 'a good idea' rather than because they had any clear idea of its benefits. Few had looked objectively at the characteristics of portal technology or B2B e-commerce. Common reason for adoption included:

> "If other businesses adopt it and we don't, we will be left behind."

> "All the talk is about e-commerce and how it is the way of the future."

> "It doesn't look too hard to make it work and we have little to lose."

> "My kids tell me that everyone will be on the Internet soon and we had better be too."

When looked at in this way, the process of adopting, or choosing not to adopt the portal begins to be seen in its true complexity, not just as a yes/no decision, but as a complex set of negotiations between actors. Our research made use of actor-network theory (Callon, 1986; Latour, 1986, 1996; Law 1999) in analyzing these interactions and negotiations.

Usefulness to Small Business

There is a distinct contrast between the 'usefulness' to small business as reported on the website of Ebiznet and that resulting from actual interviews with small businesses participating in Bizewest. The interviews indicated that there were some less obvious reasons for linking with the community portal, such as "It seemed like a good idea" and "We didn't want to be left behind."

E-Malls

An e-mall consists of a number of e-shops, and serves as a gateway through which a visitor can access other e-shops. An e-mall may be generalized or specialized depending on the products offered by the e-shops it hosts. Revenues for e-mall operators include membership fees from participating e-shops and customers, advertising, and possibly a fee on each transaction if the e-mall operator also processes payments. E-shops, on the other hand, benefit from brand reinforcement and increased traffic, as visiting one shop on the e-mall often leads to visits to 'neighboring' shops. When a brand name is used to host the e-mall, the level of trust and readiness to purchase is generally raised among consumers. Visitors to e-malls benefit from the convenience of easy access to other e-shops and ease of use through a common interface (Farhoomand & Lovelock, 2001). One example is Internet Marketing (http://www.e-mall.com.au/index.htm), which is a community directory that lists local businesses and community services in the area west of Sydney. The e-mall website (visited in November 2002 by the authors) promotes itself as offering solutions from website development to listings in local business directories, allowing the move to a Web presence to be "cheap and easy." The Australian Internet Shopping Mall (http://dkd.net/mall/holesale.html, visited November 2002) offers a range of services, including a national presence and regional divisions. Both of these enterprises have therefore recognized the value of regional or local influences on their participants.

Usefulness to Small Business

E-malls enable small businesses to promote their business, tap into the infrastructure for online business already set up for transactions, expand market reach by acquiring new users, and be listed on search engines. They also allow these businesses to participate in community building, supplement their hardware sales with revenues from online services, partner with other providers and increase the value of their products and services, retain traffic to their websites, invest in marketing activities at reduced costs, and remain innovative. Where they have differed from regional portals is that, although there are benefits in relation to cost efficiencies and possible market expansion, they have not tapped into community relations. The examples provided above indicate that this may be changing.

Discussion

Do the portals examined provide the benefits to small businesses as outlined in the

Figure 2: Australian Internet Shopping

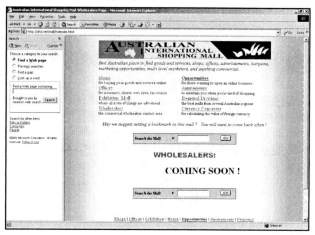

'Benefits to Small Businesses' section earlier? Table 1 summarizes the findings of the authors in this respect.

Table 1: Benefits of Example Portals

Potential Benefits	Ebiznet	Bizewest	E-Malls
A Secure Environment	Secure catalogue, order and payment facility provided	Secure environment currently under development	Not all e-malls offer ordering and purchasing. Some just offer links to business websites (cheapest solution). Others offer the full service.
Search and Directory Services	Directory, but no search provided	Search and Directory options are provided	Search and Directory options are provided
New Partnerships	No service for 'bidding' for business; but training was provided	No service for 'bidding' for business; links to providers of training are provided	Will sometimes link to printed directories
Community Building and Regional Relationships	Community news; community notice boards; community contact details	'Regional' services include maps; government services; youth services	Starting to introduce 'regional' categories for their services
Strategy, Management and Business Trust	Infrastructure is identical for all participants	Infrastructure will be identical for all participants	Again, it depends upon the e-mall. Those that only offer links to business websites do not offer identical infrastructure for all participants
Improved Customer Management	No 'special deals' in relation to attracting customers are apparent	No 'special deals' in relation to attracting customers are apparent	Some can provide cross-promotional opportunities

Figure 3: E-Mall Internet Marketing

The two regional portals investigated here are still in the early stages of development. They offer regional services, a consistent infrastructure, and search and directory services to allow businesses and consumers to find the products and services they are after. E-malls offer some of these services (depending upon the mall), with the added advantage of having access to a wider market—*if* that is what the small business desires. In the end, the small business must balance the benefits of regionality against what an e-mall may offer. It still seems, however, that there is potential for the regional portals we have examined to develop further, especially in the areas of fostering new partnerships and improving customer relationships.

Conclusion

With developments in the Internet, and its increased application to business since 1994, portals have developed, largely from being directories and search engines to new e-business model selling and advertising goods and services. Within the e-business model, portals are generic, specific to an industry, vertical or community based. There has been considerable growth in community portals in recent years and more small businesses have capitalized on this and achieved revenue growth. Small-business benefits anticipated from community portals include: increased customer loyalty, improved business relationships, enhanced trust in e-business, lower infrastructure costs, easy access to expert advice, increased market share, and expanded business. Regional portals add the benefit of community participation, a very strong part of many small businesses, to the list of portal strengths (although e-malls are beginning to address this). The investigation of portals in this chapter indicates that there is some scope to increase the level of benefits that they can provide to small businesses.

References

Al-Kibsi, G., de Boer, K., Mourshed, M., & Rea, N.P. (2001). Putting citizens on-line, not in line. *McKinsey Quarterly, Special Edition,* (2), 64-73.

Amor, D. (2000). *The E-Business (R)evolution: Living and Working in an Interconnected World.* NJ: Prentice-Hall.

Burgess, S. (Ed.) (2002). *Information Technology and Small Business: Issues and Challenges.* Hershey, PA: Idea Group Publishing.

Callon, M. (1986). The sociology of an actor-network: The case of the electric vehicle. In Callon, M., Law, J., & Rip, A. (Eds.), *Mapping the Dynamics of Science and Technology* (pp. 19-34). London: Macmillan Press.

Conhaim, W.W. (1999). The business-to-business marketplace. *Link-Up, 16*(1), 5-12.

Department of Industry, Science and Tourism. (1998). *Getting Business Online.* Commonwealth of Australia, Canberra.

Ebiznet. (1999a). *What is Ebiznet?* Accessed October 12, 2002 on the Web: http://www.ebiznet.com.au/what/index.htm.

Ebiznet. (1999b). *Who is using Ebiznet?* Accessed October 12, 2002 on the Web: http://www.ebiznet.com.au/who/index.htm.

Ebiznet. (2000). *Adelaide Hills Regional Portal.* Accessed October 12, 2002 on the Web: http://www.adelaide-hills.com.au.

Eisenmann, T. (2002). *Internet Business Models: Texts and Cases.* New York: McGraw-Hill Irwin.

Farhoomand, A., & Lovelock, P. (2001). *Global E-Commerce: Text and Cases.* Singapore: Prentice-Hall.

Internet.com. (1999). *Portals to capitalize on e-commerce.* Available on the Web: http://cyberatlas.Internet.com/market/retailing/keenan.html.

Kleindl, B.A. (2001). *Strategic Electronic Marketing: Managing E-Business.* Cincinnati, OH: South-Western College Publishing.

Latour, B. (1986). The powers of association. In Law, J. (Ed.), *Power, Action and Belief. A New Sociology of Knowledge? Sociological Review Monograph 32* (pp. 264-280). London: Routledge & Kegan Paul.

Latour, B. (1996). *Aramis or the Love of Technology.* Cambridge, MA: Harvard University Press.

Law, J. (1999). After ANT: Complexity, naming and topology. In J. Law & J. Hassard (Eds.), *Actor Network Theory and After* (pp. 1-14). Oxford: Blackwell Publishers.

Lynch, J. (1998). Web portals. *PC Magazine.*

Oxford. (1973). *The Shorter Oxford English Dictionary* (3rd edition, reprinted with corrections and revisions). Oxford: Clarendon Press.

Phillips, M. (1998). *Successful E-Commerce: 10 Case Studies to Show Small Business How to Profit from Online Commerce*. Melbourne: Bookman.

Schneider, G.P., & Perry, J.T. (2001). *Electronic Commerce* (2nd ed.). Boston, MA: Course Technology.

Straub, D. (1998). *Competing with Electronic Commerce (seminar notes)*. Melbourne: Melbourne Business School, University of Melbourne.

Tatnall, A., & Burgess, S. (2002). Using actor-network theory to research the implementation of a B2B portal for regional SMEs in Melbourne, Australia. *Proceedings of the 15th Bled Electronic Commerce Conference—eReality: Constructing the eEconomy,* Bled, Slovenia, University of Maribor.

Tatnall, A., & Lepa, J. (2001). Researching the adoption of e-commerce and the Internet by older people. *Proceedings of the We-B Conference,* Perth, Australia.

Turban, E., Lee, J., King, D., & Chung, H.M. (2002). *Electronic Commerce: A Managerial Perspective*. NJ: Prentice-Hall International.

Viehland, D. (1998). E-commerce course notes. Melbourne: Institute of Chartered Accountants in Australia.

Zikmund, W.G. (2000). *Business Research Methods* (6th ed.). Dryden.

Zikmund, W., & d'Amico, M. (2001). *Marketing: Creating and Keeping Customers in an E-Commerce World.* Cincinnati, OH: South-Western College Publishing.

Section IX

E-Commerce Outsourcing and the Impact of APSs on E-Commerce Success in SMEs

Chapter XIX

Analyzing the Risk Factors of Moving to a Remote Application Outsourcing Model

Vishanth Weerakkody, Brunel University, UK

D.E.S. Tebboune, Brunel University, UK

Wendy L. Currie, Brunel University, UK

Naureen Khan, Brunel University, UK

Bhavini Desai, Brunel University, UK

Abstract

In the last few years there has been much interest in the delivery of software-as-a-service. The concept of remote application outsourcing, or application service provision (ASP), has emerged as a solution aiming to offer organizations, mainly small to medium-sized enterprises (SMEs), access to key applications that were previously unaffordable. This chapter examines this model of software delivery, focusing on the potential risks that could be associated with it. The authors identify shared risks with traditional IS/IT outsourcing and proprietary risks of this model. The chapter concludes by giving a classification of these risks.

Introduction

In this current age of globalization, overall business integration, and rapidly evolving trading environments, new technologies are constantly being introduced, as old ones become obsolete. Businesses are prone to continuous changes and rapid evolution (Clark, Zmud, & McCray, 1995). Technology today has become a strategic enabler and is no longer relegated to the task of automating processes and functions (Currie, 2002). To cope with pressures exerted within this competitive and constantly evolving business environment, small to medium-sized enterprises (SMEs) may have to invest heavily in new technology to maintain a competitive edge. For many years firms have been engaged in the practice of transferring the cost of these investments to an external source through outsourcing, and it has appeared as one viable option to overcome the problem of keeping pace with technology advances (Linthicum, 2000). Outsourcing involves the transfer of a firm's need for IT infrastructure, people, and technology to external sources (Currie & Seltsikas, 2001).

In the last few years there has been much interest in the delivery of software-as-a-service. The concept of remote application outsourcing, or application service provision (ASP) as it is popularly known, has captured the imagination of many analysts. According to the ASP Industry Consortium, an ASP *"manages and delivers application capabilities to multiple entities from a data center across a wide area network"* (CherryTree&Co., 1999). Being a form of application outsourcing, the model consists in its simplest form, deploying, managing, and remotely hosting software applications through centrally located servers.

The ASP model claimed to leverage the power and flexibility of the Internet to deliver high performance applications to firms at a fraction of the cost of having to run and maintain the systems in-house or by traditional bureau type outsourcing. The ASP model would be different from traditional outsourcing, as the software applications are priced on rental basis (based on usage per seat). By taking away the day-to-day hardware and systems management duties, the ASP model promises to give firms the opportunity to focus on their core functions (Columbus, 2000). It is a new model in software distribution that delivers software as a service.

The emergence of the ASP model has been stimulated by many facts; mainly, a segment, SMEs, was almost excluded from the enterprise applications market, due to its incapability to afford them. The model offers these SMEs the possibility of leveraging costs as a result of the economies of scales characterizing it. Based on the principle of one-to-many, the ASP model is believed to create enormous cost savings of the order of 20% to 50% (Miley, 2000).

Despite the hype surrounding the introduction of the ASP concept and the claim that the solution was aimed at the SME market, it has failed to fulfill predictions for success in terms of market growth (Dean, 2000). Further, the ASP model's adoption has been slower than expected (Clancy, 2001), proving many analysts' predictions wrong, including those of IDC and the Gartner Group (2001).

Although many independent software vendors (ISVs) and other companies such as Telcos have embraced the ASP concept, few have managed to deploy this business model profitably. Throughout the year 2000, numerous such firms entered the market as self-styled ASPs promising to offer industry-focused (vertical) or business focused (horizontal) software applications to customers (Currie, Desai, Khan, Wang, & Weerakkody, 2003). However, to date, vested interests within IT departments, problems of customer positioning within the market, and fears about data security and infringement have prevented many companies from fully investigating and integrating the ASP business model (Currie et al., 2003). Furthermore, the ASP model remains essentially embryonic and immature, causing the business environment in which ASPs operate to be extremely dynamic and unpredictable (Desai, Weerakkody, Currie, Tebboune, & Khan, 2002). Moreover, a competitive analysis (Porter, 1985) of the ASP market shows low barriers to entry as a major weakness of the model.

This chapter will evaluate the ASP business model and identify the potential risks that SMEs would face if they remotely outsource applications using this model. The authors argue that the ASP model needs further revision to attract customers. These challenges relate to technical, organizational, and cultural imperatives, as well as cost and pricing issues. The results of an industry survey,[1] undertaken by the authors, will be analyzed to present a synopsis of the current ASP market in Europe. The chapter will present an overview of the current state of the ASP market and the future impact of remote application outsourcing on European SMEs. The authors will relate ASP to traditional IS/IT outsourcing, identifying the shared (with IS/IT outsourcing) and proprietary risks of this model.

The chapter concludes by suggesting that the current risks relating to the ASP model for SMEs are a major inhibitor and will need to be overcome if the model is to gain acceptance. The chapter will also identify areas for potential research opportunities.

Background: The Emergence and Impact of ASPs on SMEs

With the new millennium, the information technology and information systems (IT/IS) markets witnessed a new breed of enterprise, flourishing from the provision of promoting 'software as a service.' This phenomenon, popularly referred to as application service provision (ASP), is aimed at delivering applications and computer services from remote data centers to multiple users via the Internet. The ASP concept is considered as a sub-sector of the IT application outsourcing marketplace, also referred to as the third wave of outsourcing (Currie & Seltsikas, 2000) or net sourcing (Kern, Kreijger, & Willcocks, 2002).

As a third-party service that maintains and distributes software applications on a selective outsourcing basis, ASPs could be seen as the ideal solution to sell technology and ERP outsourcing benefits to SMEs. Some of the biggest ASP players are actually ERP solution vendors, such as SAP, BAAN (now Invensys), and Oracle, who saw ASP as a means of penetrating the SME sector.

The emergence of the ASP model has been stimulated by many factors, notably a desire for technology sector firms to penetrate the SME sector with new software applications delivered via a remote (Internet) model. The model offers these SMEs the possibility of leveraging costs as a result of economies of scale. Based on the principle of one-to-many, it has been suggested that the ASP model may create enormous cost savings of the order of 20% to 50% (Miley, 2000). Yet no studies have emerged that confirm such statements.

The generic process view for an ASP includes the establishment of a basic business and technical infrastructure to support the distribution of one or more marketable software applications over the Internet or virtual private networks on an agreed charging model. This should also be backed up with additional help-desk-type support and training to customers.

There are different types of ASP models that have emerged in the market in recent years, as revealed in our research. These are shown in Table 1.

The ASP concept draws on traditional IT outsourcing, but is highly influenced by the advancement in telecommunication media and the Internet (Tebboune, Weerakkody, & Currie, 2002). For the purpose of setting the scene for the rest of this chapter, it would be worthwhile to briefly revisit some of the IS/IT outsourcing literature.

IS/IT outsourcing is defined by Willcocks and Lacity (1998, p. 3) as the *"handing over to third-party management of IS/IT assets, resources, and/or activities for a required result."* The main drivers that led managers to think about outsourcing IS/IT are several. The most obvious one is, undoubtedly, the search for cost efficiency (Takac, 1994; DiRomualdo & Gurbaxani, 1998). In fact, as organizations are becoming increasingly dependent upon IT, chief information officers (CIOs) are expected to demonstrate value for money. The search for improving business performance is another driver to outsourcing IS/IT (Weerakkody & Currie, 2002) where the high pace of development of IS/IT and the resulting lack of skills has led outsourcing to become a valuable choice. However, even if outsourcing IT seems to be very beneficial, it has many drawbacks. Some of these drawbacks as cited by many authors (Currie & Willcocks, 1997; Earl, 1996; Takac, 1994; Prahalad & Hamel, 1990) include the possibility of losing control of key IT activities, issues concerning service quality and performance, and hidden costs that are usually difficult to predict.

All these advantages and disadvantages have previously created a debate on whether outsourcing IS/IT is an appropriate business strategy. As with any strategy, looking at the risks involved could help to better understand the validity of IS/IT outsourcing.

In the following section, the authors will discuss the major IS/IT outsourcing risks, as found in the literature. Moreover, relating ASP to traditional IS/IT outsourcing will help

Table 1: Variations of the ASP Business Model

No.	Name (Type)	Main Features
1.	Pure Play	A start-up firm which enters into partnerships with ISVs to deliver software on a remote model over the Internet.
2.	ASP enablers	Telecos with the necessary IT infrastructure (backbone) to deliver software using a remote model
3.	Vertical	An ISV or start-up ASP focusing upon a specific industry-sector
4.	Enterprise	A large ISV or start-up ASP which aims to deliver enterprise-wide or ERP software to the end-user via a remote model or via a virtual private network (VPN)
5.	Horizontal	An ISV or start-up firm which delivers 'business' software such as HRM or payroll as well as collaboration tools like groupware

in deriving the risks involved in this strategy. A further analysis will use the results of a survey conducted by the authors, in order to identify the risks proprietary to ASP, independently of traditional IT/IS outsourcing.

Risks of Remote Application Outsourcing

The first phase of the ASP market suggested that the ASP model would have a revolutionary impact on firms, requiring extensive revisions to how IS outsourcing is carried out (Tebboune et al., 2002). The main thrust of its revolutionary impact was the potential of the Internet and all its possibilities for re-engineering business through networking technologies, enabling the remote delivery of software applications to new customer sectors, notably SMEs (CherryTree&Co., 2000). Others, however, were more cautious, and argued that the ASP model was simply another form of service bureau outsourcing on a pay-as-you-go model (see Currie, 2002). If so, the same risks would apply whether outsourcing used traditional methods or remote methods of service delivery.

The issue of risk mitigation from IT outsourcing has gained much attention. The study conducted by Earl (1996) discusses many aspects for which IT outsourcing deals have become risky. It is, therefore, useful to start from the 11 risks of outsourcing IT as described by Earl (1996) (see Table 2), as a basis for studying the risks of moving into remote application outsourcing, provided that ASP has partially evolved from IT outsourcing.

From the 11 risks cited in Table 2, it could be argued that most of these could be applied to the case of ASP. In the following, we analyze these 11 cited risks and relate them to the case of ASP.

1. *Possibility of weak management:* As with traditional IT outsourcing, the role of senior management is critical in achieving best value from the outsourcing decision. The success of the decision to outsource software applications to a third-party service provider may depend on the vendor/customer relationship. If the relationship breaks down, then the IT outsourcing contract may become difficult to manage.

2. *Inexperienced staff:* Such a risk will always exist, especially in the current period, where skilled IT staff scarcity is reaching record levels. However, contrary to traditional IT outsourcing deals, ASP does not involve staff shifting from the customer's side to the vendor's.

3. *Business uncertainty:* This risk also seems to be relevant in the case of ASP, where the urge to get access to key applications may lead customers to underestimate certain parameters, and therefore a risk of inhibiting future business developments.

4. *Outdated technology skills:* Contrary to traditional IT outsourcing, ASP does not usually involve outsourcing legacy systems (applications in this case) that may stay frozen in old technology. ASP is based on offering applications owned by the service provider, including the upgrades that may be available.

5. *Endemic uncertainty:* As it is an outsourcing deal, ASP customers may face endemic uncertainty concerning the services received. Again, flexibility should always be sought as recommended by Earl (1996).

6. *Hidden costs:* Concerning software applications, costs estimation is always a difficult task to do, where the components involved such as deployment costs, training costs, and several other components can easily be underestimated. Thus, hidden costs are also a major risk for the success of an ASP deal.

7. *Lack of organizational learning:* As the customer in any ASP deal would not be involved with managing its applications, learning becomes limited if not absent, and therefore a risk of losing the understanding of systems capabilities becomes a serious issue.

8. *Loss of innovative capacity:* Again, similarly to traditional IT outsourcing, the loss of innovative capacity is a potential risk in ASP deals, as managing applications will not be a task that the customer achieves.

9. *Dangers of an eternal triangle:* Communication between service providers and customers might be an issue when it comes to vendors unaware of the business side of their customers. However, as more and more vertical ASPs—specialized in a certain sector or industry—are joining the market, such a risk is enormously reduced.

10. *Technological indivisibility:* Such a risk is highly relevant in the case of ASP, especially when applications of daily use, such as office and communication applications, are outsourced.

11. *Fuzzy focus:* Compared to traditional IT outsourcing, ASP also needs to bring innovative ideas important for business development. As many customers rushed into having quick access to key applications, this risk could be faced by firms, especially when knowledge about future business development requirements is uncertain.

The above risks were only based on the work of Earl (1996) and focus on the evolutionary aspect of ASP as related to traditional IS/IT outsourcing. However, as ASP has a revolutionary character, a further investigation of the proprietary risks, which can emerge with this model only, is needed. For this purpose, the authors conducted a survey on SMEs' perspective of the ASP model.

Research Methodology

This research progressed through many phases. Initially, a pilot study was conducted in the Silicon Valley (USA) and Europe, to identify the key issues relating to the ASP model. In particular, we were concerned how vendors intended to offer the remote delivery of software applications to SME customers (Currie, 2000). Semi-structured interviews were conducted with 28 firms in the U.S. and Europe about their perceptions of the ASP market (Currie & Seltsikas, 2001). This research suggested a mismatch between supply-side offerings and demand-side requirements, with many customers

Table 2: Eleven Risks of Outsourcing IT (adapted from Earl, 1996)

Risk	Explanation
1. Possibility of weak management	Management issues are of major importance, where there is a risk that complex IT management responsibilities that an outsourcing customer want to reduce, turn to be the same, if not worse, when outsourced to a third party. Earl (1996, p. 27) highlights that if a given firm selects outsourcing as a strategy, *"the executives also have to know how to manage contracts and relationships with third parties."*
2. Inexperienced staff	Capable IT staff is rare, and there is risk that the service provider might not have the required staff. This is especially true when the customer's staff move to work with the vendor.
3. Business uncertainty	Uncertainty about the future business developments that any organization may need to do, could lead to use outsourcing as a solution for emerging problems. This is particularly true when it comes to outsourcing IT, as it usually comes into scrutiny when costs need to be reduced. Thus, IT Outsourcing may have a long-term risk of inhibiting business development.
4. Outdated technology skills	Earl (1996) argues that as legacy systems are outsourced, there are serious risks that the market will be frozen in old technology, and therefore customers may not have access to any current technology.
5. Endemic uncertainty	In outsourcing contracts, customers should seek for flexibility, as IT and business requirements are always due to change. Therefore, Earl (1996, p. 29) recommends that *"IT contracts of any sort should first agree on a process of conflict resolution and problem solution for the inevitable uncertainties."*
6. Hidden costs	Firms usually underestimate the costs involved in outsourcing deals, including setup and management costs, where a basic comparison of vendors' costs with current costs is done.
7. Lack of organizational learning	Usually, firms develop their learning on IT capability, by managing it themselves. By outsourcing IT, firms limit this learning.
8. Loss of innovative capacity	There is a risk that outsourcing IT might inhibit customers from maintaining IT innovative capacity. Earl (1996, p. 30) adds that while it is not sure that innovation cannot be bought, it is suggested that *"partners have their limitations and that expectations must be properly managed."*
9. Dangers of an eternal triangle	In outsourcing deals, it is often the case where firms' managers want vendors who understand their business and their culture, resulting in vendors aiming to reskill their specialists and make them more aware of the business issues and building organizational relationships. Such a change may lead some organizations to stand still in their IT evolution, and this is what Earl (1996) qualifies as *"the eternal triangle"*.
10. Technological indivisibility	Mentioning the classic example of desktop outsourcing, Earl (1996) cites technological indivisibility as a potential risk of outsourcing IT. He (ibid) argues that current information systems *"are increasingly integrated or interconnected, and problems can occur at the interface of responsibility between different vendors or between the vendor's domains and the customer's domain"* (p. 31).
11. Fuzzy focus	Earl (1996, p. 32) states that a serious problem with outsourcing is that it *"concentrates on the **how** of IT, not on the **what**."* As such, outsourcing frequently fails to bring innovative ideas that may be important for businesses.

suggesting that, unless the ASP model offered them business benefits of cost reduction and increased efficiency, they could see no real benefit in accessing their software applications over the Internet. Few potential customers were interested in software integration, especially if the firm was small (two to 50 employees).

Questionnaire Survey

Following the initial research study, a questionnaire survey was designed to capture the performance measures used to evaluate benefits and risks from the ASP model. It was recognized that many respondents in the SME sector may not use the ASP model, though they may be considering it as part of their IT outsourcing strategy. The questionnaire survey was therefore intended to elicit data and information on user perceptions of the ASP model, whether they had actually deployed ASP as a solution or not. Respondents were asked to evaluate, on a scale of 1 to 4, how important they perceived specific performance indicators. Initially, questionnaire surveys were sent to 50 respondents, though this was deemed inappropriate given that IT directors, CIOs, and others with IT responsibilities are reluctant to fill in and return questionnaires. A more appropriate method of data collection was to attend conferences and trade fairs where IT professionals were interviewed, face-to-face, on their perceptions of the list of performance indicators. This method of data collection increased the validity and reliability of the data as respondents could clarify the meaning of specific questionnaires (Yin, 1994). One-hundred-and-fifty responses were obtained from the various visits to UK venues over a six-month period. All respondents gave their job title, company address, and other details about product/service offerings and size of company. Firms were targeted in the SME sector, up to 500 employees, from a range of sectors, including retailing, education, financial services, technology and communications, and travel. More responses were received from the financial services, and technology and communications sectors.

The authors focused the survey results on identifying the key issues of remote application outsourcing under the categories of delivery and enablement, management and operations, business transformation, and client/vendor relationships. The survey aimed to identify the level of importance of each of these key areas to its audience (SMEs), and the responses were based on Likert scales varying from (1) *Not important*, to (4) *Highly important*.

Modified from the ASP Industry Consortium's list of performance indicators, the survey identified five categories of performance measurement: delivery and enablement, management and operations, integration, business transformation, and client/vendor relationships. Four categories are discussed in this chapter. The category of integration was not a sufficient issue for SMEs, and is not one that is particularly relevant to Earl's (1996) study.

Under the key area of *delivery and enablement*, the survey focused on finding how significant SMEs perceived 'data security' and 'disaster recovery' to be. These issues were considered due to the insecure nature of the Internet, particularly for a task such as software application delivery. Since the data is held usually in a remote data center in an ASP outsourcing model, security issues such as access authentication, application security, data encryption, intrusion detection, real-time assessment, anti-virus, and physical security are vital to the outsourcer. As shown in Figure 1, SMEs that responded to our survey indicated that the issue of data security would be highly important for them if they outsource applications to an ASP.

The second key area in the questionnaire, *management and operations*, covers issues such as the significance of reducing costs by using the services of an ASP and the focus on core competencies to gain competitive advantage. Issues such as total cost of ownership (TCO) of technology were considered as relevant by the vendors selling ASP solutions. They reasoned that SMEs would adopt the ASP solution to reduce their IT costs, though many did not equate the size of the firm with the size of the IT budget. For example, one telecommunication firm, selling an ASP solution, found that few SMEs spent more than £1 million per annum (inclusive) on its IT functions.

Under the third key area, *business transformation*, the survey aims to identify the significance of IT and the services provided by the ASP in the context of business improvement. The passing of responsibility for core applications to an ASP vendor can be for any SME something to approach with caution. The fear of loss of control within the organization is a valid concern for many companies. For an organization with a significant internal IT department, use of an ASP is likely to be seen as a significant threat to the 'power' of the IT/IS department, and thus to future employment prospects (Ovum, 2000).

Finally, the fourth key area in the survey questionnaire covers the important topic of *client/vendor relationship*. Under this area, the importance of vendors' status to the customers, their financial stability, mergers and acquisitions between vendors, market turbulence and uncertainty, and vendors' responsiveness to ICT changes are considered.

The survey results concerning the four categories discussed above are summarized in Figure 1. These results represent the average response of the targeted SMEs. These interpret the views of SMEs' executives concerning the significance of each criterion under each corresponding category. Whereas the above results do not determine precisely the potential risks emerging form ASP adoption, these give an idea about the most critical aspects according to SME executives' views. This could, accordingly, be translated into the criterion that have to be satisfied by the ASP model, and thus could be seen as representing the potential risks proprietary to this model. However, due to the immaturity of this model, proving this idea is still difficult. Consequently, having a definite idea about the potential risks cannot be set until more SMEs have enough experience with the model adoption.

As we have compiled results from two different sources (IS/IT outsourcing literature and ASP survey), a correlation of these results seems logical. In the following, we consider the survey's results shown in Figure 1, explaining them on the basis of Earl's (1996) work (see Table 1).

1. *24/7 applications availability:* This criterion is about the continuous availability of applications delivered by the vendor. According to the survey results, this criterion was of a medium to high importance for SMEs. In relation to Earl's (1996) work, this aspect corresponds to the set of risks stated under *"possibility of weak management"* and *"outdated technology skills."* In fact, as the vendor will be in charge of providing the applications, the reduced responsibility of the customer can be a source of risk, where weak management capabilities of the former can affect the whole IT activity. Furthermore, outdated technology skills of the vendor could be a risk of failing to deliver applications on a 24/7 basis.

2. *Data security and integrity:* This aspect focuses on the security and integrity issues of customers' data. Relating these aspects to the work of Earl (1996), these are linked to the risks of *"hidden costs"* and *"technological indivisibility."* These issues tend to be neglected as a cost of outsourcing, as potential customers mainly focus on analyzing the direct financial costs when faced with the outsourcing decision. This is further enhanced in the case of ASP, as data is stored on a remote location, away from the customer's premises. Technological indivisibility, as described by Earl (1996), is also very relevant in this context, as data is highly

Figure 1: Survey Results of Key ASP Issues as Seen by SMEs

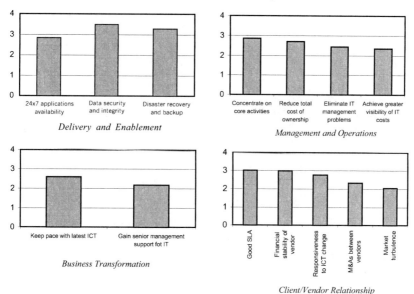

integrated among the different business processes, making it indivisible from the organization.

3. *Disaster recovery and backup:* This aspect, as seen in Figure 1, is considered to be very important to SMEs. According to Earl's (1996) work, this aspect could face the risk of hidden costs, as financial costs are not the only ones to be considered, as explained above concerning data security and integrity. Moreover, outdated technological skills of the vendor may impact the effectiveness of data recovery and backup. Finally, for the same reasons as in *"data security and integrity,"* technological indivisibility could be a potential risk for prospective ASP customers.

4. *Concentrate on core activities:* Concentrating on core competencies is frequently mentioned as a reason for outsourcing IT; this is further confirmed by our survey, where it is stated as very important. However, going back to Earl's (1996) work, this aspect could be related to many risk sources. The possibility of weak management on the vendor's part can result in poor management of customer processes, thus exposing the SME to a high level of risk. Business uncertainty could, also, contain major risk, where such uncertainty could lead SMEs to jump on the ASP model in order to get quick access to key applications, without thorough consideration about future business developments. Finally, *"fuzzy focus"* could also be a potential risk, resulting in customers failing to receive innovative ideas from their vendors.

5. *Reduce total cost of ownership:* This criterion is also a very frequently cited incentive for outsourcing. While this aspect is shown to be very important, in the results of our survey, it could involve the risk of underestimating the hidden costs, as stated in Earl's (1996) work in Table 2.

6. *Eliminate IT management problems:* This aspect refers to the risks that could emerge from the possibility of weak management on the vendor's side, as explained above.

7. *Achieve greater visibility of IT costs:* Again, the risk of not considering the hidden costs associated with the activity is relevant in this case.

8. *Keep pace with latest ICT:* If compared to the risk of outdated technology skills stated in Table 2, where Earl (1996) mentions the risk of the market being frozen in old technology, the case of ASP is less likely to face this problem as the market is new and competition is so high that the latest applications are offered. However, in the longer term, such a risk could take place.

9. *Gain senior management support for IT:* This criterion was not of a very high importance according to the survey results. However, the risk of weak management of the vendor might have an impact on this support.

10. *Good SLA:* Service level agreements are of very high importance when dealing with ASPs, and the survey results in Figure 1 confirmed this. Compared to Earl's (1996) 11 risks, the risk of endemic uncertainty can be considered for this case. In fact, as the ASP environment is still highly dynamic, conflict resolution process should take part in any SLA.

11. *Financial stability of vendor:* Traditional outsourcing vendors were typically large organizations that did not particularly suffer financial stability problems. However, in the case of ASPs, as these are mainly new start-ups, financial stability could become a major risk. According to our survey result, this aspect is ranked very important.

12. *Responsiveness to ICT change:* Similarly to the criterion *"keep pace with latest ICT"* cited above, this criterion could face the risk of outdated technology skills. Furthermore, if a weak vendor's management is included, it could have a major impact on the responsiveness to ICT change.

13. *M&As between vendors:* As the ASP model relies highly on alliances, mergers, and acquisitions in order to aggregate the required skills (Tebboune et al., 2002), choosing the right partners is extremely important for the success of this model. Failing to do so could have an impact on the quality of the services offered. Contrary to ASPs, traditional outsourcing organizations did not face this problem, as they could offer an end-to-end service themselves.

14. *Market turbulence:* This criterion is, again, particular to the case of ASP, where the environment is so dynamic that it causes a potential risk for customers. As stated by Tebboune et al. (2002), the ASP market has been accessed by too many vendors with similar offerings, which caused confusion for potential customers.

Future Trends

In the previous section, we analyzed the 14 key aspects of the ASP model, as seen by European SMEs. After we related these aspects to the risks of IS/IT outsourcing, as identified by Earl (1996), we derived the potential risks that could be faced by SMEs when

Figure 2: Classification of the Potential ASP Risks According to their Impact

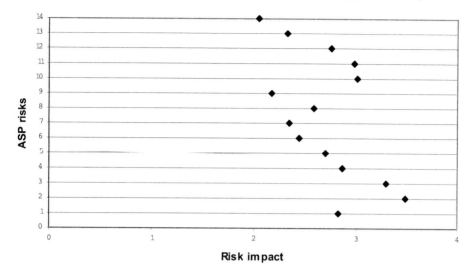

adopting the ASP model. Furthermore, we identified other risks that are proprietary to the ASP model that may not necessarily apply to traditional IS/IT outsourcing. However, we found that the intensity of these may differ from one risk to another according to the importance given to each criterion by the SME executives (see Figure 1). Therefore, a classification of the 14 risks, as identified above, can be made according to their impact on SME customers. This classification is illustrated in Figure 2 [the risk numbers (Y axis) in Figure 2 correspond to their order in the classification described above].

The classification in Figure 2 is based on the SME executives' views of the importance of each criterion as found in the survey (see Figure 1). However, these risks, as derived, need to be further validated and presented to potential SME customers as risks, and not aspects of the ASP model. This opens a large window on further research to be undertaken in this area, whereby these risks can be further validated, along with new risks being discovered that this study may have failed to identify. Furthermore, new developments are happening in the market, where the recent emergence of Web services would enhance the integration of software applications across business processes (Currie et al., 2003). Such developments will certainly have other impacts on customers and probably involve other risks previously unidentified.

Conclusion

This chapter has this far illustrated that the ASP model and remote application outsourcing in general has failed to impact the SME sector in Europe as expected. Research by the authors exposed SMEs' views regarding 14 key aspects, which were categorized under the headings: delivery and enablement, management and operations, business transformation, and client/vendor relationship. Relating these key ASP criteria to the 11 risks of traditional IS/IT outsourcing identified by Earl (1996), we have attempted to identify and define potential risks that SMEs could face when adopting the ASP model.

Although market predictions for the ASP model are many and varied (i.e., Ovum, 2000; CherryTree&Co., 2000), this chapter has shown that the European ASP market is still in an *embryonic* stage. Therefore, identifying the potential risks associated with this model can prove to be difficult. However, when relating ASP to traditional IS/IT outsourcing, a set of risks was derived. Moreover, using the survey results, we identified the shared (with traditional outsourcing) and proprietary risks that SMEs may face if ASP is adopted. A classification of these risks was drawn according to the impact these could have on customers.

As a conclusion, this study has shown that many risks can be associated with the ASP model, but further research needs to be undertaken, in order to validate these results. Such research would certainly help potential SME customers to have a clearer view of the ASP model and stronger basis for decision making about vendor selection (Currie, et al., 2003).

Endnotes

[1]   This research is supported by grants from the Engineering and Physical Sciences Research Council (EPSRC) and Economic and Social Research Council (ESRC): Principal Investigator: Professor W.L. Currie.

References

Butler, J. (2000). Web enabling the enterprise: The management service provider options. *Information Systems Management*, (Fall), 8-13.

CherryTree&Co. (1999). *Application service providers. Spotlight report.* Accessed January 2001 on the Web: http://www.cherrytreeco.com/res_rep.htm.

CherryTree&Co. (2000). *2ⁿᵈ generation ASPs. Spotlight report.* Accessed January 2001 on the Web: http://www.cherrytreeco.com.

Clancy, M. (2001). *The insidious resistance to ASPs.* Available online on the Web: http://www.aspnews.com.

Clark, T.D., Zmud, R.W., & McCray, G.E. (1995). The outsourcing of information services: Transforming the nature of business in the information industry. *Journal of Information Technology, 10,* 221-237.

Columbus, L. (2000). *Realizing E-Business with Application Service Provision.* Sams.

Currie, W. (2002). Application outsourcing: A new business model for enabling competitive electronic commerce. *International Journal of Services and Technology Management, 3*(2), 139-153.

Currie, W. (2003). A knowledge-based risk assessment system for evaluating Web-enabled application outsourcing projects. *International Journal of Project Management*, (Forthcoming: December).

Currie, W., & Seltsikas, P. (2001). Exploring the supply-side of IT outsourcing: The emerging role of application service providers. *European Journal of Information Systems, 10*(3), 123-134.

Currie, W.L., & Seltsikas, P. (2000). Evaluating the application service provider (ASP) business model. *Executive Publication Series.* Brunel University, CSIS2000/004.

Currie, W., & Willcocks, L. (1997). *New Strategies in IT Outsourcing: Major Trends and Global Best Practice.* London: Business Intelligence.

Currie, W.L., Desai, B., Khan, N., Wang, X., & Weerakkody, V. (2003). Vendor strategies for business process and application outsourcing: Recent findings from field research. *Proceedings of the 36th Hawaii International Conference on Systems Sciences (HICSS-36)* (January).

Dean, G.H., & Jackson, G.A. (2000). *Application Service Providers—Exploring the Theory of Evolution.* Baird E- Services Publications.

Denzin, N.K. (1978). *The Research Act: A Theoretical Introduction to Sociological Methods.* New York: McGraw-Hill.

Desai, B, Weerakkody, V., Currie, W., Tebboune, S., & Khan, N. (2003). Market entry strategies of application service providers: Identifying strategic differentiation. *Proceedings of the 36th Hawaii International Conference on System Sciences (HICSS-36)* (January).

DiRomualdo, A., & Gurbaxani, V. (1998). Strategic intent for IT outsourcing, *Sloan Management Review*, (Summer), 67-80.

Earl, M.J. (1996). The risks of outsourcing IT. *Sloan Management Review,* (Spring), 26-32.

Galliers, R.D. (1991). Choosing appropriate information systems research approaches: A revised taxonomy. In H.E. Nissen, H.K. Klein, & R. Hirscheim (Eds.), *Information Systems Research: Contemporary Approaches and Emergent Traditions* (pp. 327-345). North Holland.

Gartner Group. (2001). Sanity check on the ASP opportunity. *Gartner Group's Research Brief.* Available on the Web: http://www.gartner.com.

Keen, P.G.W. (1991). Relevance & rigor in information systems research: Improving quality, confidence, cohesion and impact. In H.E. Nissen, H.K. Klein, & R. Hirscheim (Eds.), *Information Systems Research: Contemporary Approaches and Emergent Traditions* (pp. 27-49). North Holland.

Kern, T., Kreijger, J., & Willcocks, L. (2002). Exploring ASP as sourcing strategy: Theoretical perspectives, propositions for practice. *Journal of Strategic Information Systems, 11,* 153-177.

Lehman Brothers. (2000*). Severs in the sky: The application service provider.* Available on the Web: http://www.lehman.com.

Linthicum, D.S. (2000). To ASP or not to ASP. Accessed May 2001 on the Web: http://www.SoftwareMag.com.

Miley, M. (2000). Reinventing business: Application service providers. *Oracle Magazine*, (November/December), 48-52.

Ovum. (2000). Application service providers: Opportunities and risks. *Ovum Report.*

Porter, M.E. (1985). *Competitive Advantage: Creating and Sustaining Superior Performance.* London: Macmillan.

Prahalad, C.K., & Hamel, G. (1990). The core competence of the corporation. *Harvard Business Review,* (May/June), 79-91.

Takac, P.F. (1994). Outsourcing: A key to controlling escalating IT costs? *International Journal of Technology Management, 9*(2), 139-155.

Tebboune, D.E.S., Weerakkody, V.J.P., & Currie, W.L. (2002). Application service provision: Revolution or evolution? Forthcoming paper in the *Business Information Technology (BIT) Conference*, Manchester Metropolitan University, Manchester, UK.

Tesch, R. (1990). *Qualitative Research: Analysis Types and Software Tools.* New York: Falmer.

Weerakkody, V., & Currie, W. (2002). Facilitating business process improvement through application outsourcing. *Business Process Management Journal: Special Issue on Application Service Provision*, (Autumn).

Willcocks, L.P., & Lacity, M.C. (eds.). (1998). The sourcing and outsourcing of IS: Shock of the new? *Strategic Sourcing of Information Technology: Perspectives and Practices.* Chichester, UK: John Wiley & Sons.

Yin, R.K. (1994). *Case Study Research—Design and Methods* (2nd ed.). London: Sage Publications.

Chapter XX

The Role of Application Service Providers in the Development of Small and Medium-Sized Enterprises

Yuroung Yao, Louisiana State University, USA

Kevin C. DeSouza, University of Illinois at Chicago, USA

Edward Watson, Louisiana State University, USA

Abstract

This chapter explores the role of application service providers (ASPs) in the development of small to medium-sized enterprises (SMEs) in e-commerce era and guides clients to successfully collaborate with ASPs for competitive advantages. It extensively discusses the advantages and risks SMEs will take when renting applications from ASPs. Furthermore, a five-stage model is presented to investigate the process by which SMEs can establish cooperation with ASPs. At each stage, the factors SMEs need to account for when choosing ASPs, as well as management strategies during relationship building, are examined in detail. Practical recommendations are provided for SMEs to follow in order to set up a successful relationship with ASPs. By understanding this

relationship establishment process through the stage model, practitioners facing the
real challenge may learn a well-grounded methodology for ASP selection based on
particular characteristics of their organizations.

Introduction

In this era of e-commerce, characterized by change and uncertainty, companies continue
to struggle to achieve and maintain their competitive edge. Technological advances
become important weapons for companies that expect to compete in this environment.
Those initiatives that were once a competitive advantage quickly became competitive
imperatives as time passed, such as front-office and back-office automation in a 24/7
environment, enterprise application integration within the organization, and enterprise
integration (and particularly the facilitation of communications) between internal and
external applications (Heart & Pliskin, 2002). Companies, both large and small, find it very
difficult to afford the hardware and software required to run their operations.

Though there is no well-agreed definition of the class of companies referred to as small
to medium-sized enterprises (SMEs), they are doomed to confront the most daunting e-
commerce challenges such as limited people resources, shrinking budgets, and the
constant barrage of competitive threats (SAP, 2002). The U.S. National Institute of
Standards and Technology found in a survey that SMEs invest large amounts of capital
in IT consulting services and tend to purchase piecemeal applications that are not
appropriately scaled for their businesses. Furthermore, it is reported that, "they are not
training their staffs appropriately to use the IT solutions in which they've just invested.
Many IT hardware and software solutions sit idle, are used inappropriately, or are not
used to their maximum advantage" (Heart & Pliskin, 2002). Thus, the IS infrastructure of
many SMEs resides on fragmented platforms and separate databases, which are too
expensive to maintain and too complex to manage. SMEs are faced with the dilemma of
having a serious lack of IT competency and requiring unaffordable IT investments. IT,
the essential component for any SME to achieve its e-commerce solution, turns out to
be the bottleneck to many SMEs' business initiatives.

The Application Services Provision model emerged in the late 1990s and offers several
intriguing benefits, particularly for SMEs that hope to cope with rapid change, high
uncertainty, and keen competition (Lacity & Willcocks, 2001). The ASP Industry
Consortium (2001) defines an application service provider (ASP) as a company that
"manages and delivers application capabilities to multiple entities from a data center
across a wide area network." Forrester predicted that 90% of small business would rely
on external providers to host their sites when launching e-business ventures (Gerwig,
1998). In this chapter we explore the role of ASPs as strategic contributors to the growth
and development of SMEs.

Practitioners and researchers have a tendency to incorrectly equate ASPs with traditional
outsourcing models (Yao & Murphy, 2002). Unlike traditional outsourcing contracts,
which are generally long and complicated, the ASP model strives for simplicity with
shorter term agreements (Gillan et al., 2000). Moreover, traditional outsourcing models

usually suggest specific long-term projects or strategic alliance between two large organizations, whereas ASPs tend to strive for economies-of-scale and repetition (i.e., delivering similar solutions to multiple clients), especially for small to medium-sized companies. In the traditional IS outsourcing model, customers purchase and own both hardware and software assets, while ASPs host the application on their central servers. Also, unlike traditional outsourcing vendors that tend to be large-sized organizations, ASPs are more likely to be newly established smaller companies. In short, the ASP model clearly differs significantly from the traditional IS outsourcing model from several perspectives: extent of application customization, customer markets that are targeted, characteristics of the vendor, solution and service offerings, asset ownership, and contract type (Yao & Murphy, 2002). However, since the traditional IS outsourcing model has been tossed around for about two decades now, much research has focused on understanding its intricacies (Lee, Huynh, Kwok, & Pi, 2002). On the other hand, the research on ASPs, particularly in the SME domain, is relatively scarce.

In this chapter, we explore the role of ASPs in the development of SMEs. We discuss the advantages and risks SMEs take when renting applications from ASPs. Furthermore, we investigate the process by which SMEs can establish cooperation with ASPs through the implementation of a five-stage model. In so doing, we will examine factors SMEs need to account for when choosing ASPs, as well as management strategies during relationship building. Practical examples borrowed from ongoing research projects involving several ASPs are used to illustrate these issues. The benefits and risks associated with the ASP models have been discussed extensively. These ASP examples provide a good understanding for real-world application.

The major contribution of this chapter is to examine, in a holistic sense, the contribution of ASPs to the development of SMEs and to provide a stage model for SMEs to follow when selecting and working with ASPs. This chapter has implications for both curious minds as well as practitioners facing real challenges. Practitioners may gain from the discussion as they learn a well-grounded methodology for ASP selection based on particular characteristics of their organizations. For those with just curious minds, we set the stage for an in-depth investigation into the various factors related to ASP adoption by SMEs and the contract negotiation phase between ASPs and SMEs.

The remainder of the chapter is organized as follows. The following section examines benefits ASPs posit for SMEs. Then we explore risks associated with contracting services from ASPs, and then we present a stage model for ASP adoption. Concluding the chapter, we look at managerial and research implications.

Advantage of ASPs in E-Commerce for SMEs

ASPs offer several intriguing benefits for SMEs. We explore some of the prominent pros of "renting" applications for SMEs here.

Compensate for Lack of IT Expertise

Most SMEs lack knowledge and expertise on how to strategically leverage information technology capabilities (Yao & Murphy, 2002). SMEs face hurdles related to IT deployment due to lack of expertise in requirements gathering, system analysis and design, and application selection.

Moreover, recruiting adequate IT expertise is not a trivial issue. U.S. government statistics estimate that about 4 million technology jobs will be unfilled by 2003 (Applegate, Auston, & McFarlan, 2002). Hence, to attract needed talent, SMEs have to compete by offering high incentives in the form of compensation packages. Offering high salaries coupled with benefits and allowances can take a toll on an SME's limited financial budget. Furthermore, it takes about three to four years to internally train professionals and reap subsequent benefits. SMEs do not have the luxury of time, to wait years before gaining returns on their investments.

ASPs are strategically positioned to alleviate these burdens. With sound IT expertise, ASPs can guide clients in choosing technology functions, and provide reliable application and maintenance support. To most SMEs, an ASP can take on the role of an external "IS department black box." By taking a one-to-many model (Gillan et al., 2000), ASPs may provide standard IT functions suitable for most SMEs such as office productivity software and enterprise financials, operations, and human resources application suites. Moreover, ASPs that provide a domain focus, in an industry such as automobile manufacturing or retailing, are more likely to understand specific needs of the customers and offer highly tailored solutions. ASPs that strive for specializing in specific industries are referred to as vertical service providers (VSPs). VSPs are flourishing in industries such as telecommunications, healthcare, and insurance industries (CherryTree&Co., 2001). Through specialization, they are able to significantly improve service performance and lower their cost (Clemons, Hitt, & Snir, 2000).

Cost Reduction

An ASP operating as a central service delivery center can provide multiple financial benefits to its customers. Firstly, a common pricing approach may entail an initial charge plus service fees based on time or user sign-ons (Koch, 2000). One practitioner characterized acquiring ASP services as similar to buying voicemail services from a telephone company (Koch, 2000). Morgan Stanley Dan Witter estimated that cost can be reduced by as much as 80% to 90% by outsourcing management of IT infrastructure (Applegate et al. 2002). International Data Corporation (IDC) also found that ROI from outsourcing services can reach 300%, with a payback time on the investment of only 120 days (Applegate et al., 2002). Compared with tremendous investment for in-house information system implementation projects, this typical "pay-as-you-use" model relieves SMEs from heavy financial pressure to purchase software and hardware, and from large systems installation. This pricing approach by usage or user number enables the customers to predict the costs more precisely before the actual usage. It reduces the risks and simplifies the decision process by quantifying the costs. Moreover, by renting from ASPs, SMEs are able to afford the expensive high-end software packages such as enterprise resource planning, customer relationship management systems, which would not be possible otherwise.

Secondly, ASPs deliver applications over the Internet that can be easily accessed with low setup cost. Moreover, all training and help functions for the software are also deployed online (Selwitz, 2001). For example, employees can use a property management system offered by external vendors within 24 hours' training, resulting in tremendous cost savings (Selwitz, 2001). Especially, ASPs are responsible for operations, maintenance, and associated troubleshooting to provide reliable 24/7 applications (Gillan et al., 2000).

Thirdly, Applegate et al. (2002) compared purchase-and-subscribe cash flows for renting services from ASPs versus a traditional investment in IT. Traditional IT expenditures involve buying software, hiring consultants, installing, testing, and maintaining. They reported that a traditional IT investment requires huge up-front outlays but produces uncertain benefits due to an unpredictable project failure rate. The traditional IS project also has a relatively long lifespan. Meanwhile, collaboration with ASPs eliminates the need to make huge purchase outlays upfront, resulting in quicker cash flows. For example, SMEs can rent Oracle's Small Business Suite for a mere fee of $99/month (*Asian Business,* 2001).

Flexibility

In the current information economy—IT market relative to the traditional industrial economy—the product lifecycle is much shorter and there are subsequently many more product upgrades to manage. Without a strong financial foundation and sufficient internal IT professionals, it is relatively difficult for SMEs to stay abreast of new technology and to maintain their strategic competence (Cleaver, 2000). By managing the software application and hardware in a central data center, an ASP can upgrade software regularly so to provide current applications and functionality to all customers in a timely and convenient manner. Thus, ASP clients can enjoy the latest released software versions without making any significant investments.

Flexibility is also shown when extending functionality. As SMEs are not always certain about their requirements in the very beginning, they are likely to make adjustments to their requirements after having some experience (Koch, 2000). In traditional purchasing or outsourcing, negotiations may be lengthy. Even so, these pre-evaluations may not guarantee later usage quality and performance. By shifting all these risks and uncertainty to ASPs, SMEs find a viable way to extend or terminate some applications based on their needs. In most cases, clients can sign a short-term contract for a trial version of the application in order to examine the suitability of application(s) before making a final decision (Yao & Murphy, 2002). If the customers are satisfied with the services, they may decide to rent additional applications from the ASP.

SMEs that only rent standard applications from ASPs find it much less painful to switch to another vendor than to make a termination decision in the middle of a time-consuming and money-intensive installation project. When knowledge about information technology accumulates, SMEs can have more control in service delivery and enjoy more flexibility.

Also, in the ASP context, they can benefit from high scalability by providing similar applications to those newly added SMEs. Centrally hosted applications enable ASPs to have the economies of scale.

Strategic Goals Realization

ASPs play an important role in assisting SMEs to realize their strategic objectives. It will help SMEs significantly reduce the time of getting new products to market. Usually, first movers in this area who look to adopt some new technology or business model can expect revenue realization to present a struggle (Kerin, Varadarajan, & Peterson, 1992).

In today's environment, adoption of a Web-hosted ASP package may help SMEs carve out their e-commerce strategy without any significant additional efforts (Applegate et al., 2002). Though no offerings of two companies are exactly alike, most include tools for electronic business, such as secure payment processing, supply chain management and digital certificate processing, customer relationship management, ongoing support, and so on. It is also important for an ASP to integrate with a company's existing legacy systems and corporate data (CIO, 2002). This is often achieved by developing new interfaces and integration subsystems. The primary reason for a multi-unit hotel owner to outsource their applications to Statability, an ASP that delivers reporting functionality, is to present an integrated view of their internal systems. Statability will develop different style reports by accessing data from different sources.

NAPAonline.com gets an all-in-one solution from IBM; this has proven to ease the organization's e-commerce anxieties. With a well-supported website, NAPAonline.com has expanded its market share overall and extended the NAPA brand online. Currently it dominates the online market in this industry. The manager is quoted as saying, "By outsourcing our e-commerce functions, we've been able to focus more on our core business and the thing that is most important—taking care of our customers" (CIO, 2002).

Risks of SMEs to Take ASP Alternatives

When ASPs create benefits, or value-add, to their client companies, SMEs must also be aware of the potential risks that often accompany success. In this section we examine the principal risks that SMEs should assess when evaluating the ASP model.

Technological Problems

PMP Research (2001) listed that the most important issues associated with technology are connectivity and security. Breakdown or latencies caused by system shutdown or telecommunication issues may make online delivery rather tenuous (Heart & Pliskin, 2001). For companies or hotels that absolutely require reliable connections and quick response times from their customer reservation systems, this breakdown would present serious issues that could ultimately lead to dissatisfied customers, loss of market share, loss of reputation, or lower customer retention rates (Selwitz, 2001).

Moreover, the security of data storage and data transfer is another major risk for SMEs. The potential risk of critical data abuse often weighs higher among ASP selection determinants (Clemons et al., 2000). Particularly, leakage of critical information, such as customer information, financial, and sales data will result in great damage to the SME. The maturity of network technology and applications will further impact ASP adoption (Heart & Pliskin, 2001). It is often the case that technological functions that are too advanced may not be suitable for online outsourcing (Lacity & Willcocks, 2001), as they may introduce more uncertainty.

Most ASPs established in the earlier years are new start-up companies and are often short on credibility in their respective industries. Clients are often not clear about the ASPs' capabilities to understand business requirements and application specifications or functional specifications (Kern, Willcocks, & Lacity, 2002). Therefore, customers don't have enough confidence to put the important data in these unknown parties. However, successful cooperation requires mutual trust and intensive constructive communications to overcome any uncertainty related to the technology or the operations of the business. In the business world, trust is often the foundation on which collaborative relationships are built. Thus, if managers are not comfortable with their ASP(s), they will be reluctant to fully cooperate with them, and this will influence service quality and service satisfaction (Keegan, 1999). For example, in the hospitality industry, most small or medium hoteliers are not comfortable leaving customer history information in the hands of a third party (Paraskevas & Buhalis, 2001). Currently, since the ASP market is relatively young, customers are in the early stages of tackling trust issues with the ASP business model and individual ASPs. Without the general issues of trust worked out, the decision toward ASP adoption will be deterred.

Contract Management

As SMEs lack IT expertise, they are not able to evaluate product quality adequately and match exactly ASPs' capabilities with their own expectations when negotiating with ASPs. ASPs generally will take the dominant position during the early stages of contract negotiation (Kern et al., 2002). Even with traditional outsourcing activities, contract issues are a fundamental driver of risk (Clemons et al., 2000). Information asymmetry puts SMEs in a disadvantageous position to judge the feasibility of contract items (Oliver, 1990). This ultimately leads to unrealistic customer expectation towards the ASP, or in some cases it may lead to incomplete or inflexible contracts (Kern et al, 2002). Most traditional outsourcing contracts include detailed items (Lacity & Willcocks, 1998) related to the responsibilities and performance evaluation criteria. Any misinterpretations or outright negligence of contract items lead to higher risks; subsequent issues with cooperation or performance measurement will result.

Without IT expertise, SMEs probably have loose control on ASPs' behaviors in the negotiation and late performance (Grover, Teng, & Cheon, 1998). Contract with unclear items cannot effectively protect SMEs from ASPs' opportunistic behaviors, i.e., ASPs can't upgrade the services probably or provide satisfied services. A good service level contract is a prerequisite condition for successful cooperation.

Dependence

According to various levels of customization, SMEs will differ in the extent of dependence on ASPs. Usually, a highly customized application will better suit the needs of clients than standard packaged products (Lacity & Willcocks, 2001). This is also the reason for the emergence of vertical service providers. Many VSPs deliver value-added applications in a certain domain, providing a better fit with the clients' requirements. But by renting the unique and value-added applications from VSPs, SMEs will depend more on VSPs' services, and switching costs may go up as well.

Dependence is an important determination in outsourcing (Grover et al., 1998). The high level of customization that results in unique applications increases the difficulty for customers to switch from their current ASP to a new ASP that will deter their decision for ASP cooperation (Kern et al., 2002). This relationship with totally unbalanced power will make clients feel insecure about their business. Especially since SMEs generally lack significant ASP experience, they may not be able to anticipate, control, or prevent the overly opportunistic behaviors of the ASP and potential cost rising. When an ASP goes out of business or reduces the service quality without any notice, it creates a major problem for its clients, especially if there is a high level of dependency. In summary, dependence has to be considered closely: the right level of dependence will lead to a long-term cooperation, but too much dependence will be a detriment to the ASP adoption decision.

Seemingly, there is a tradeoff between high-quality performance and costs associated with adopting the ASP business model. Based on organization situations and requirements, the customers should be able to weigh benefits versus risks and make a rational, logical decision. Usually, if the company is anxiously looking for the benefits (e.g., cost reduction, professional compensation, or integration realization) offered by an ASP, especially under pressure situations, they might underestimate their risks and expect— or hope—that the ASP can solve the problems quickly.

The benefits and risks are summarized in Table 1.

SMEs should consider all these benefits and risks comprehensively prior to making important ASP adoption decisions. The characteristic of a company's outsourced applications suggest that ASP clients will weigh these factors differently. For instance, outsourcing core business activity, immature technology, or "too" advanced technology will result in higher levels of uncertainty (Heller, 2001). Thus ASP clients must assess risks and benefits seriously, along with internal strategic planning and financial budget concerns, prior to making the final decision for ASP adoption.

Table 1: Benefits and Risks of Adopting an ASP in SMEs

Benefits	Risks
Compensate for lack of IT expertise • Provide necessary IT professionals • Offset needed domain-focused IT expertise • Focus on core business • Accumulate knowledge about IT functions from ASP	**Technical Problems** • Disconnect network and application service delivery • Lengthen response time • Abuse customers' critical data • Lack trust on ASP's capabilities: business understanding and application delivery • Lack ability to judge ASP's ability
Cost Reduction • Save initial software and hardware investment • Save training expenses • Start to harvest profits immediately	**Contract Management** • Increase conflicts due to unclear contract items • Lack detailed evaluation items • Lack IT ability to negotiate a good contract
Flexibility • Gain access to latest technology • Easily extend the functionalities • Easily switch to ASP for standard software • Reduce the time to market	**Dependence** • Increase dependencies associated with highly customized products • Increase switching cost to another ASP • Lack control on possible cost rising • Lack control on opportunistic behaviors
Strategic Goals Realization • Integrate internal legacy system with new systems • Provide facilities for website building	

Stage Models for ASP Adoption

In previous IS outsourcing studies, few empirical IS studies have examined the development of IS relationships. Lasher, Ives, and Jarvenpaa (1991) and Klepper (1998) proposed a stages model for the development of the relationships between outsourcing vendors and customers (Yao & Murphy, 2002). Kern (1997) also provided a relationship development model along those same lines.

Lasher et al. (1991) presented outsourcing as a strategic partnership evolving from large-scale, long-duration projects that require substantial customization and intensive mutual learning. Five stages for outsourcing vendor-client partnership development are developed, including establishing the purpose, finding a partner, defining the partnership, maintaining the partnership, and institutionalizing the partnership. Klepper (1998) used a model borrowed from Dwyer, Schurr, and Oh (1987) to identify four stages for the traditional outsourcing of the vendor-client relationship development process—awareness, exploration, expansion, and commitment—by using two cases studies. Kern (1997) provided an IT outsourcing relationship model to examine various types of vendor-client relationships that change over time, such as social and personal bonds; investments in resources, knowledge, and time, communication and information exchange; financial exchange and the exchange of products and services.

These IS studies reflect the complexity of institutionalized relationships between traditional outsourcing vendors and clients. However, Yao and Murphy (2002) found that vaguely defined boundary stage models are not appropriate for describing the ASP relationship development process. In particular, as the ASP business model represents high flexibility, a long-term strategic partnership may be inappropriate for ASPs and their clients (Gillan et al., 2000). Furthermore, as mentioned before, ASPs differ greatly from traditional outsourcing, and we believe that potential ASP clients will make ASP adoption decisions based on factors that are quite distinct from traditional IS outsourcing decision factors.

Two general classes of theories are of interest here: economic factor models and marketing behavior models. Economic factor models, such as Agency Cost Theory (e.g., Jensen & Meckling, 1976) and Williamson's (1975) Transaction Cost Economics, focus on the advantages and limitations of different types of relationships (such as contracts) for achieving effective and efficient service delivery. Marketing relationship research (e.g., Anderson & Narus, 1990; Ganesan, 1994; Landeros, Reck, & Plank, 1995; Lee & Kim, 1999) has examined the influence of communication, conflict resolution, and reputation related to perceptions and behavior in an economic setting. Based on these two types of theories and practical ASP experiences, we explore the viable path for these customers to follow in order to find a suitable ASP, and to establish a satisfactory and effective relationship. A conceptual model is presented to explain this process. Practical cases are provided for illustration purposes.

Below is the conceptual stage model for clients to select and develop relationships with ASPs (Figure 1).

In this model, we classify the whole process into five iterative stages: selection, initial trial contract, contract negotiation, performance evaluations, and reaction to changes. In the model, SMEs will set up initial contact with a certain ASP and adjust their

Figure 1: Stage Model for ASP Selection and Relationship Development

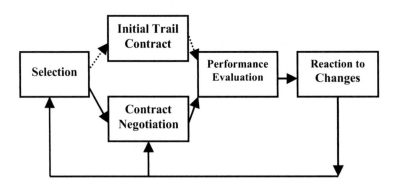

relationship in the subsequent collaboration. In this study, this model is only developed for applications selection based on one-to-one negotiation. In some cases, clients may rent a group of applications from several ASPs simultaneously. As these ASPs will generally not have mature collaborative protocol in place, the ASP client still needs to negotiate with them individually. Negotiations, or collaboration, at the group level could present additional challenges. Also, several customers might group together and negotiate with the same ASP, but it generally requires more effort in order to coordinate properly. Thus, the individual ASP selection and working experience are the basic components in forming this coalition. Thus, the model presented here is valuable in guiding customers under *most* conditions.

Selection

The process of ASP selection is very important and a critical step in any ASP relationship. At this point in the ASP adoption process, customers have already assessed the benefits and drawbacks of this business model, and decided to move forward on the ASP model for one or more of their applications.

Based on a cross-industry survey regarding strategic sourcing, the Gartner Group (2002) argued that it is perhaps most effective and efficient to select vendors from only two potential partners. Otherwise, it will take a long time to evaluate and compare the candidates before making the final decision. The tedious and time-consuming process of comparing and discussing candidates may cause both ASP clients and ASPs to lose initial interest before finally selecting the most appropriate ASP. So, selecting an ASP vendor from an initial pool with two candidates would be a reasonable approach to ensure timely decisions. Furthermore, when SMEs lack IT expertise, it is very difficult for them to accurately and comprehensively compare ASP vendors properly. The ASP industry, being relatively recently established, lacks generally accepted standards necessary to classify and evaluate ASP vendor capabilities (Linder, Jacobson, Breitfelder, & Arnold, 2001). All these factors combined increase the complexity of the assessment. If necessary, a third-party consultant, for instance, may be involved in the evaluation process. This may adequately compensate any deficiency in IS competency experienced by a customer.

Generally speaking, ASP capabilities, reputation, and match between expectation and capabilities form the basis for ASP vendor selection decisions. DiRomualdo and Gurbaxani (1998) regard ASP capability as a critical factor in building the relationship between ASP vendors and clients. Sufficiently powerful and secure servers, effective relationships with hardware and software vendors, a sound financial foundation, and an experienced staff form the basis for an ASP to deliver on its promises (Yao & Murphy, 2002). Prospective clients will rely heavily on non-specific indicators of the vendors' capabilities such as endorsements by major vendors or metrics of size and coverage. Particularly, many ASP vendors partner with third-party software, telecommunication, or hardware companies to enhance their competencies (Lee et al., 2002). This coalition can facilitate the ASPs and their partners to share the customer base and gain significant trusts from the customers. The number of partners an ASP has, and the popularity of these partners, are critical indicators used by inexperienced customers to evaluate the ASP vendor's capabilities. Also, Grover et al. (1998) argue that a set of requirements—software functions, problem response time, data security, transaction cost, and agency cost—form a client's outsourcing expectations. A key motivation for seeking ASP outsourcing is to complement internal IT shortcomings (Cleaver, 2000). Also, an ASP vendor's reputation in an industry may at least partially be determined by the personal reputation of the founders; this will add weight to a customer's ASP decision.

Furthermore, Lacity and Willcocks (2001) investigated 102 sourcing decisions in European countries and in the U.S. They found that sourcing decisions made by both senior executive and IT managers have higher success rates (76%) compared to sourcing decisions make only by IT-oriented personnel, because these persons examine the same issues from distinct perspectives. So when clients select an ASP vendor, they should try to get more input from various sources, at least including both business and technical personnel, so as to have a broader perspective.

Statability, the ASP vendor previously mentioned that provides enhanced business reporting capabilities for companies in the hospitality industry, is regarded highly in this industry. The founders' 10 more years' working experience in hotels helps them gain insight about clients' requirements. As most clients are multi-unit franchisees, owning the hotels belonging to the different hotel chains, Statability can help them alleviate internal burden for data collection, repackage, distribute, and work out effective reports. Lewis Dawley, the director of World Reservation Sales at International Marriott, commented that "Statability has helped us improve an existing program and add value to our internal customers. The new service by Statability has allowed me to focus my time on other parts of our business that are strategic to the organization" (Statability, 2002). These successful stories further enhance their reputation, attracting more clients to Statability. It is also regarded as evidence for good expectation-capability matches.

Based on the above discussion, we recommend that:

Recommendation 1a: Customers can effectively and efficiently select a vendor from an initial pool with two principle ASPs candidates.

Recommendation 1b: Customers can select ASPs based on their high capabilities, including hardware, software, number of IT professionals, and partnership with other infrastructure companies.

Recommendation 1c: More managers from both business and technical sides involved in this selection processes will increase the possibility to make correct decisions.

Initial Trial Contract

Initial trial contract, in the first instance of cooperation, is expected to be relatively short and characterized by clients providing more information to the specific vendor than vice versa.

Even though this initial trial is not a necessary step for every customer to choose an ASP, we strongly believe that a first short-term contract is significantly important for SMEs to set up a working relationship with ASPs (Yao & Murphy, 2002). The "trialability" of a standardized service via short-term contract reduces the duration and intensity of negotiations. In some cases, when trial contract is not possible in reality, detailed demos can also help to clarify the misunderstandings and give clients a more concrete impression of the ASPs' capabilities.

As only limited information is available about the needs of the client, so standard terms are expected to have a significant influence on the perceptions of matching expectations. Also, only the standard applications should be included in the contract. Customized applications will increase negotiation efforts. Immature technologies are not recommended in this stage, even for the later regular contract, as customers will be exposed to too many risks (Kern et al., 2002). Besides, the contract length should be restricted within six months. Too long a contract will increase risks while too short a contract is not enough for both sides to know each other. During the execution of a short-term contract, both the ASP and the clients learn more about each other, with the potential for a mismatch to emerge between their mutual perceptions (Landeros et al., 1995). Then they can make a good preparation for future cooperation. Lakota Technologies Inc. (LTI), an IT service company in an Indian reservation, has worked for the National Library of Medicine (NLM) to produce 1,957 medical journals electronically. Before it secured the five-year contract, NLM also had a relatively short-term service experience with LTI to build confidence on its capabilities (CIO, 2001).

Changes to the standard contract terms may be conceived of as indicating both a better or worse "match." The willingness to modify a contract for special terms may signal to a client that the ASP is supportive and flexible. Yet, when the vendor can accommodate a client's needs within the terms of an existing contract, clients with lower IT expertise may be more comfortable that there is a fit. Likewise, a vendor will perceive a customer who accepts a standard agreement as being a closer fit to their capabilities than a client who asks for contract changes (Yao & Murphy, 2002).

Thus, based on the above discussion, we recommend:

Recommendation 2a: If the customers have no idea about their internal requirements and ASPs' capabilities, they can request the short-term trial contact to gain more knowledge about this business model.

Recommendation 2b: The trial contract should only cover those standard applications and matured technologies. And the contract length should be around three to six months.

Recommendation 2c: Customers should carefully examine the items of standard contract in the initial stage in order to achieve the best fit between their expectation and the ASPs' capabilities. The unchanged contract indicates a good fit.

Contract Negotiation

Contract Negotiation refers to mutual discussions for a regular contract. When ASPs and clients know each other well, they can go directly into a regular contract. But usually, it happens after two parties have some working experience. During the *initial trial contract*, clients can better evaluate an ASP's capabilities, both in business understanding and technology application delivery. Also, the ASP will know more about the client's requirements in order to provide better services. Through the intensive communications and conflict solutions, both parties need to work out a better way to prevent problems and achieve better performance. As two parties have adjusted expectations and requirement understandings, it's necessary to renegotiate contract items to reflect these changes, including service scope, service quality, evaluation criteria, and so on.

Contract negotiations should take place as quickly and carefully as possible. In the contract, performance measures must be stated clearly, and associated true costs must be realistically assessed. Meanwhile, contract terms also need to be flexible enough for inevitable changes occurring during the course of collaboration (Gartner Group, 2002). The Gartner Group (2002) even argues that third-party involvement in this process will help to bring a healthy and streamlined process for both parties, leaving them clear about the reasonable expectations and moving forward together.

These renewing contracts are still not long, about two or three years, as in a dramatically changing market, ASPs should maintain flexibility and build committed relationships with clients as well (Lacity & Willcocks, 2001). Clients might change their applications and switch to other vendors accordingly. Also, a shorter contract can motivate ASPs to provide better services, as they notice that clients could opt to change a supplier. The IS manager at the Civil Aviation Authority commented that when it was near to contract expiration, service quality became better (Lacity & Willcocks, 2001).

Statability works hard to satisfy customers' requests. Usually, it will redesign its standard contract for renewing clients. In most cases, renewing clients would ask for more customized products or wider scope services after an initial trial contract. More work will demand more investment on the ASP's side. In order to balance their efforts and profits, Statability will require a longer contract to secure their cooperative relationship (Statability, 2002).

Thus, we recommend that:

Recommendation 3a: Customers should sign a relatively shorter contract, such as two or three years, to keep the flexibility in the functionality extensions and terminations.

Recommendation 3b: Customers and ASPs should quickly and carefully negotiate the contract items in order to reduce the potential conflicts and achieve the mutual benefits. If necessary, a third party, such as a consulting company, can be involved in this negotiation to give customers subjective guidance.

Recommendation 3c: In the renewed contract, customers can ask for the customized products based on the experience of the initial product usage and accumulated knowledge about internal IT requirements. However, the extent of customization should be controlled at an acceptable level, e.g., it's possible that other alternatives still can be found.

Performance Evaluation

The collaboration allows both vendors and clients to learn more about each other through service delivery, training, help-desk operations, and especially resolving conflicts. Three years is regarded as the time period for SMEs to know their own IT requirements well and assess the "match" between the ASP's capabilities and the client's needs (Lacity & Willcocks, 2001). The client is gaining the ability to monitor the ASP's performance by referring to the contract items. This evaluation also goes along with intensive communications and conflict resolutions, which clarifies misunderstandings and adjusts expectations in the cooperation.

Efficient monitoring of the performance is a guarantee for a successful relationship (Kern et al., 2002). Assign a specific person to the key elements of the deal and keep them working toward the target. During the collaboration, the circumstances might shift in capacities, and opportunities to innovate will occur constantly. So benchmarking should be set carefully to make these evaluations feasible in various situations. Without probable monitoring and regulation, SMEs' relationship with ASPs will go out of alignment as quickly as a New York taxi.

Generally, the performance will involve three basic components: cost evaluation, service quality evaluation, and application quality evaluation (Gartner Group, 2002). Cost evaluation means the assessment of exact cost saving, which can give clients a clear idea about economic benefits by using an ASP. Service quality evaluation refers to the check on troubleshooting and daily maintenance. An efficient technology supporting center or help desk will increase satisfaction and clients' trust. Application quality evaluation means assessment of IT functions' productivity. Do applications really meet the needs of the clients and facilitate their business?

In the cooperation, as two parties have more of a sense about the ASP's application delivery, the assessment criteria become more reasonable and objective for both sides. It will be easier for clients to value an ASP's performance, compared with the initial contract period.

iVASP, an New Zealand's leading ASP, emphasizes the importance of the service-level agreement. Its customers can evaluate latency, service quality, and security protections based on a well-designed and customized contract. With the strong guarantee and support of a service-level agreement, many customers even put some strategic business in the ASP's hands (Heller, 2000).

Thus, we recommend that:

Recommendation 4a: Clients need to monitor ASPs' services during the cooperation, even assign a specific person responsible for this performance monitoring.

Recommendation 4b: Clients can evaluate ASP performance from three perspectives: cost, service quality, and application quality.

Recommendation 4c: Based on the working experience with ASPs, customers should evaluate the match between ASPs' capabilities and their expectations for the decision on continuous cooperation.

Reaction to Changes

In this market, any reluctance and several rounds of negotiation will lead to dramatic change in business environment. So SMEs should be well prepared for any potential alteration in cooperation and make adjustment accordingly. Both parties should take this change into account when initially reassessing the deal. It's the only way to keep a working relationship fresh and alive (Gartner Group, 2002).

In addition to external environment, internal relative dependence between the two parties will also change. Dependence in the context of ASP relationships is related to the need of one party to perform for the other to achieve their goals (Ganesan, 1994). Research suggests that mutual dependence has a positive influence on relationship development (Lee & Kim, 1998). However, unbalanced dependence will lead to unstable relationship. Besides, customization will undoubtedly lead to better performance, especially to large and complicated ERP systems (Yao, 2002). Increased dependence will grant one party more power than the other. SMEs will face the risk of increasing switch cost and the potential ASP's optimistic behavior.

So facing these changes, SMEs should carefully think about further actions based on performance evaluations in the past cooperation: stay with this ASP but modify contract items, or start to find another ASP? There is another scenario: the clients are totally satisfied with current services and keep the contract unchanged. But it rarely happens.

If ASPs do not satisfy SMEs within existing contract items, and clients do not believe the current ASP can meet their needs later, they will terminate the cooperation and go back to the very first stage to select a new ASP. Then SMEs have to go through the whole circle again from *selection*, unless they give up on the outsourcing plan and build their own in-house systems instead.

If SMEs are satisfied with current applications, and explore more stable and secure relationships with this ASP, they might ask for customization or function extension. Either action will need more bargaining and negotiation in renewing a contract. Two parties will go back to *contract negotiation* to assess the possibility of signing a longer term contact (like three years). A tradeoff between stability and flexibility would be considered when SMEs decide the length of renewed contracts (Clemons et al., 2000).

For clients of Statability, usually after the first contract, they will hope to add more functions to the initial designed reports, such as reporting sales and revenue not only based on areas but also on salesmen, providing market comparison with other hotel brands, etc. They come to know what kind of functions they really need. A new contract will be signed according to these changes. As Statability has strong domain knowledge, no clients have terminated the service delivery because of unsatisfied service (Statability, 2002).

Thus, we recommend that:

Recommendation 5a: Clients and ASPs need to be alert to external environment changes and internal relative dependence changes, and make changes accordingly to keep the mutual benefits.

Recommendation 5b: Based on the performance evaluations, unsatisfied clients should stop the cooperation with current companies and search for another capable ASP or terminate their outsourcing plan as soon as possible, to prevent further loss and risk.

Recommendation 5c: Satisfied clients can renegotiate with ASPs for more customized and wider scope applications, but they should be cautious about the increasing dependence on the ASPs. The tradeoff between benefits and dependence should be considered before renewing the contract.

Conclusions and Contributions

The objective of this study is examining the role of ASPs in the development of SMEs in this e-business era, and guiding clients to successfully collaborate with ASPs for competitive advantages.

The chapter has two principal contributions. The first is investigating the exact advantages and risks to SMEs when they initiate the cooperation with ASPs. The advantages include devices cost saving, avoiding internal IT professional shortage, flexibility in software update and maintenance, and good support for strategic development. The risk will take account of dependence, data security, customization cost, and so on. Another contribution is presenting a stage model to shed insight on this complicated selection and cooperation process, which involves five stages: selection, initial contract, contract negotiation, performance evaluation, and reaction to changes. This model presents a good guide for SMEs to follow when they adopt an ASP business model.

In this fluid industry, our study about the role of ASPs in SMEs is still in its early stage. There are many other aspects that need further examination. Firstly, in order to test this conceptual model, empirical studies—especially longitudinal studies—should be conducted to assess the customer-ASP relationship development process. Secondly, more empirical studies are needed to examine continuing changing characteristics of ASPs, such as large independent service vendors that set up their online hosting centers, and their potential contribution to the development of SMEs. These changes will lead to the variations in the decision-making and relationship development process. Thirdly, until now, more research investigates the problem from the customers' perspective. We call for studies to examine the problems on the ASP side, such as service contract design and positioning strategy.

References

Anderson, J.C., & Narus, J.A. (1990). A model of distributor firm and manufacturer firm working partnerships. *Journal of Marketing*, 54, 42-58.

Applegate, L.M., Auston, R.D., & McFarlan, F.W. (2002). *Creating Business Advantage in the Information Age*. Boston, MA: McGraw-Hill Irwin.

Asian Business. (2001). Targeting SMEs. *37*(8), 19.

ASP Industry Consortium (Industry Trent or Event). (2001). Intelligent enterprise. (January 1), 4, 8.

CherryTree&Co. (2001). *Vertical industry specialization*. Spotlight report available on the Web: http://www.cherrytreeco.com. Retrieved on May 21, 2001.

CIO. (2001). *Homegrown talent*. Case study reports available on the Web: http://www.cio.com/archive/100101/homegrown.html. Retrieved on May 21, 2001.

CIO. (2002). *Outsourcing: E-business*. Executive summary available on the Web: http://www.cio.com/summaries/outsourcing/ebiz/. Retrieved on November 13, 2002.

Cleaver, J. (2000). Small business turning to ASPs to make life easier: The basics preferred over 'killer apps'. *Crain's New York Business, 16,* 27.

Clemons, Hitt, & Snir (2000). *A risk analysis framework for IT outsourcing.* Unpublished manuscript.

DiRomualdo, A., & Gurbaxani, V. (1998). Strategic intent for IT outsourcing. *Sloan Management Review, 39*(4), 67-80.

Dwyer, F., Schurr, P., & Oh, S. (1987). Developing buyer-seller relationships. *Journal of Marketing, 51,* 11-27.

Ganesan, S. (1994). Determinants of long-term orientation in buyer-seller relationship. *Journal of Marketing, 58,* 1-25.

Gartner Group. (2002). *Strategic Sourcing.* CT: Gartner Group.

Gerwig, K. (1998). Concentric offers hosting options. *Internetweek,* (November 16), 36.

Gillan, C., Graham, S., Levitt, M., McArthur, J., Murray, S., Turner, V., Villars, R., & Whalen, M. (2000). *The ASP's impact on the IT industry.* Available on the Web: http://www.idc.com. Retrieved on April 20, 2001.

Grover, B., Teng, J.T.C., & Cheon, M.J. (1998). Towards a theoretically based contingency model of information systems outsourcing, in IS outsourcing. In L.P. Willcocks & M.C. Lacity (Eds.), *Strategic Sourcing of Information Systems: Perspectives and Practices* (pp. 79-102). New York: John Wiley & Sons.

Heart, T., & Pliskin, N. (2001). IS e-commerce of IT application services (ASP) alive and well? *The Journal of Information Technology Theory and Application, 3,* 33-41.

Heart, T., & Pliskin, N. (2002). Business-to-business e-commerce of information systems: Two cases of ASP-to-SME e-rental. *Information and Operation Research, 40*(1), 23-34.

Heller, M. (2000). *Sound off—taking sides on critical IT issues.* Available on the Web: http://comment.cio.com/soundoff/042600.html.

Jensen, M.C., & Mecking, W.H. (1976). Theory of the firm: Managerial behavior, agency costs and ownership structure. *Journal of Financial Economics, 3,* 305-360.

Keegan, P. (1999). Is this the death of packaged software? *Upside, 11*(10), 138-147.

Kerin, R.A., Varadarajan, P.R., & Peterson, R.A. (1992). First-mover advantage: A synthesis, conceptual framework, and research propositions. *Journal of Marketing, 56*(October), 33-52.

Kern, T. (1997). The gestalt of an information technology outsourcing relationship: An exploratory analysis. *Proceedings of the 18th International Conference in Information Systems* (pp. 37-58).

Kern, T., Willcocks, L.P., & Lacity, M. (2002). Application service provision: Risk assessment and mitigation. *MIS Quarterly Executive, 1*(2), 113-126.

Klepper, R. (1998). The management of partnering development in IS outsourcing. In L.P. Willcocks & M.C. Lacity (Eds.), *Strategic Sourcing of Information Systems: Perspectives and Practices* (pp. 305-326). New York: John Wiley & Sons.

Koch, C. (2000). Monster in a box. *CIO Magazine,* (May 1).

Lacity, M., & Willcocks, L.P. (1998). *Strategic Sourcing of Information Systems: Perspectives and Practices.* Chichester, UK: John Wiley & Sons.

Lacity, M., & Willcocks, L.P. (2001). *Global Information Technology Outsourcing in Search of Business Advantage.* Chichester, UK: John Wiley & Sons.

Landeros, R., Reck, R., & Plank, R. (1995). Maintaining buyer-seller partnerships. *International Journal of Purchasing and Materials Management,* 3-11.

Lasher, D., Ives, B., & Jarvenpaa, S. (1997). USSA-IBM partnerships in information technology: Managing the Image Project. *MIS Quarterly, 15*(4), 551-565.

Lee, J., & Kim, Y. (1999). Effect of partnership quality on IS outsourcing success: Conceptual framework and empirical validation. *Journal of Management Information Systems, 15*(4), 29-61.

Lee, J.N., Huynh, M.Q., Kwok, R.C.W., & Pi, S.M. (2002). Current and future directions of IS outsourcing. In R. Hirschheim, A. Heinzl, J. & Dibbern (Eds.), *Information Systems Outsourcing: Enduring Themes, Emergent Patterns, and Future Directions.* Heidelberg: Springer-Verlag.

Linder, J., Jacobson, A., Breitfelder, M.D., & Arnold, M. (2001). *Business transformation outsourcing: Partnering for radical changes.* Research Note, Institute for Strategic Change, Accenture.

Oliver, C. (1990). Determinants of interorganizational relationships: Integration and future directions. *Academy of Management Review, 15*(2), 241-265.

Paraskevas, A., & Buhalis, D. (2002). Outsourcing IT for small hotels: The opportunities and challenges of using application service providers. *Cornell Hotel and Restaurant Administration Quarterly, 43*(2), 27-39.

PMP Research. (2001). *Software as a service.* Available on the Web: http://www.itscrviccsandsolutions.co.uk'200 /july/article1.asp. Retrieved on May 15, 2001.

SAP. (2002). Available on the Web: www.sap.com. Retrieved on November 12, 2002.

Selwitz, R. (2001). PMS suppliers cite ease of use, cost as bonuses of ASP model. *Hotel and Motel Management, 216*(5), 50.

Statability. (2002). Available on the Web: www.statability.com. Retrieved on November 12, 2002.

Williamson, O.E. (1975). *Markets and Hierarchies: Analysis and Antitrust Implications, A Study in the Economics of Internal Organization.* New York: The Free Press.

Yao, Y., & Murphy, L. (2002). Client relationship development with application service providers: A research model. *Proceedings of the 35th Hawaii International Conference in Information System,* Big Island, Hawaii (January 9-12).

About the Authors

Nabeel A.Y. Al-Qirim is a lecturer of Information Systems and module coordinator of Electronic Business in the School of Computer and Information Sciences, Faculty of Business, Auckland University of Technology, Auckland, New Zealand. He has a bachelor's degree in Electrical Engineering, Cert. (Tertiary teaching), GradDipInfoSys. (Hons. with distinction), MBA, and PhD (candidate). His research interests and publications are in IT and e-commerce in small business, SCM, mobile commerce, health informatics & telemedicine, NGOs and developing countries. He worked in the IT industry for 12 years as a consultant and in managing total IT solutions with international companies including IBM, Compaq, Data General, Group Bull, and Siemens Nixdorf.

* * *

Angsana Achakulwisut is a doctoral candidate at the Carlson School of Management, University of Minnesota, USA. Her research interests include adoption and diffusion of information technology, IT in SMEs, and IT acceptance.

As key account manager at the evolaris eBusiness Competence Center, **Christoph Auer** is responsible for all research projects with companies from the utility sector. evolaris is a partly publicly funded research institution, with close connections to various international universities, including the University of Graz, where Mr. Auer lectures senior courses in the field of Management Information Systems. He has an MSc in Mechanical Engineering from the Technical University of Graz and the University of Bristol, UK, and is a certified e-business project manager. He has successfully managed projects in Austria, the UK, and Brazil, and was recently assistant of the board of the third largest health insurance group in Austria, responsible for the coordination of all e-business activities within the group.

Stephen Burgess is a senior lecturer in the School of Information Systems at Victoria University, Melbourne, Australia. He has a bachelor's degree in Accounting and a

Graduate Diploma in Commercial Data Processing, both from Victoria University, Australia; a Master's of Business (Information Technology) from RMIT, Australia; and a PhD from Monash University, Australia, in the area of small business to consumer interactions on the Internet. His research and teaching interests include the use of IT in small business, the strategic use of IT, B2C e-commerce, and IT management education.

Tanya Castleman is professor of Information Systems at Deakin University, Australia, and director of research in the School of Information Systems. The main focus of her research is the organizational and social aspects of information and communication technologies, especially the Internet and e-commerce. Her research is practically oriented, and she has conducted a broad range of research and consultancy projects. Professor Castleman has published internationally on issues including the adoption and implementation of e-commerce by small to medium-sized enterprises, employment implications of e-commerce applications, the Internet and regional sustainability, ICT in health and human service delivery, and government electronic service delivery.

Caroline Chappell has more than 20 years of experience in the IT industry, gained as a practitioner and consultant. She co-founded The Trefoyle Partnership (UK) in 1993 to exploit her research interests in e-commerce, Internet security, and multimedia. Over the past five years she has worked on two research projects investigating the adoption of e-commerce by European SMEs for the European Commission, including a three-year study of the use of e-commerce in SME value chains in the UK, Germany, and Italy. Before joining The Trefoyle Partnership, Ms. Chappell worked for Ovum, where she was responsible for managing and executing large market research projects in business technology and telecommunications areas. Earlier in her career, she carried out software development for British Aerospace, and worked as a journalist editing and writing leading UK ICT publications. She continues to contribute articles on business and technology topics for UK and international magazines and journals.

John K. Christiansen is professor in Management of IT, Project, and New Product Development at Copenhagen Business School, Denmark, which is among the largest in Europe. He has produced nearly 70 papers, book chapters, and edited books on topics such as IT strategy, implementation, project organization, project management, and product development. He is currently head of the PhD school at CBS in Managing Technologies and engaged in several research projects, including several with cooperation between companies and universities.

Wendy Currie is professor of Strategic Information Systems and director of the Centre for Strategic Information Systems (CSIS), Department of Information Systems and Computing, Brunel University, UK. She currently holds three research grants from the EPSRC and ESRC for the study of application service provisioning (ASP) and Web services. Dr. Currie has published several books and journal articles on management and strategy. She holds a PhD from Henley Management College and is an associate editor for the *MISQ Journal*.

Reggie Davidrajuh received his MS degree in Control Systems Engineering in 1994, and PhD in Industrial Engineering in February 2001, both from the Norwegian University of Science and Technology (NTNU). He is currently an associate professor of Computer Science in the Department of Electrical and Computer Engineering at Stavanger University College, Norway. His current research interests include e-commerce, agile virtual enterprises, discrete event systems, and modeling of distributed information systems. His URL is: http://ied.ux.his.no/?U=reggie.

Kevin C. Desouza is a doctoral candidate in the Information and Decision Sciences Department at the University of Illinois at Chicago, USA. He has authored *Managing Knowledge with Artificial Intelligence* (Quorum Books), and several articles either published or forthcoming in journals such as *Communications of the ACM, International Journal of Healthcare Technology Management, Competitive Intelligence Review, Business Horizons, Emergence: A Journal of Complexity Issues in Organizations and Management, European Management Journal,* and *Business Process Management Journal.* His research interests include knowledge management, data mining, and management of medical technology. He received his BSc (distinction) from the University of Illinois at Chicago, and his MBA from the Stuart Graduate School of Business, Illinois Institute of Technology.

Bhavini Desai is currently employed under the ESRC (Economic and Social Sciences Research Council) grant facility studying the *"role of application service providers (ASPs) in vertically and horizontally integrated sectors."* Her main area of interest is the study of the ASP business model. As part of previous work, she has investigated the role of ASP as a potential outsourcing channel. Her specific interests lie in the study of factors that have hindered and impeded the take-up of ASPs as an outsourcing channel.

Zakia Elsammani is a lecturer and a PhD research student in the Department of Business Information Technology, Manchester Metropolitan University, UK. She completed her BSc in Physics at the University of Khartoum, Sudan, and MSc in Information Systems at Liverpool University. Her current research focuses on acceptance of e-commerce with particular interest in the adoption of EC by SMEs. She can be reached via e-mail at: Z.Elsammani@mmu.ac.uk.

Paolo Faverio received his degree in Business Administration from Cattaneo University, Italy, in 1999. Since 2000, he received a research grant at Cattaneo University from the Information System Department and he has been member of the CETIC research center. He has been researching in the field of Information Systems, with a specific focus on issues related to the adoption and use of ICTs. At the moment his research interests cover the topics of the management of business information systems and the adoption of ERP systems, especially focusing on the peculiarities of small to medium-sized enterprises.

Sylvie Feindt is currently managing director of SFC (Germany), which she founded in 1997. She is involved in several European projects (KITS, ASP-Net) and has undertaken a number of studies for the European Commission and the European Parliament. Her experience focuses on e-commerce, SMEs, start-up companies, e-government, and the socio-economic impact of the Information Society. She has researched and co-authored more than a dozen reports and articles in these fields. She belongs to a network of trainers and consultants, with whom she has set up the KIZ Akademie (www.kiz.de).

Elizabeth Fife is a principal researcher at the Center for Telecom Management at the University of Southern California, USA, where she is the editor of the *Telecom Outlook Report*. She received her PhD in International Relations from USC, where she is a lecturer in the field of Business and Technical Communications. Her areas of research include European telecommunications, e-commerce, SMEs, and R&D innovation. She has seven years research experience in the telecommunications field.

Reinhard Franz is key account manager and research analyst at the evolaris eBusiness Competence Center since December 2000. He is responsible for different projects focusing on online content, market research, and online advertising. His research is mainly focused on customer needs online, online marketing, online market research, as well as virtual communities. Professor Franz has studied economics at the University of Graz, Austria, where he still lectures practical courses in the field of market research and virtual communities.

William Golden is a member of the Centre for Innovation and Structural Change and a lecturer in Information Systems at NUI, Galway, Ireland. He has held this position since 1991. He completed his doctorate on B2B e-commerce at the University of Warwick, UK. He has presented papers at both national and international conferences. He has co-authored a book, contributed chapters to other texts, and published papers in the areas of e-commerce and information systems in *Omega, The International Journal of Management Science, International Journal of Electronic Commerce, Journal of Agile Management Systems,* and *Journal of Decision Systems.*

James Griffin received his PhD in 2002, studying the field of Internet adoption and implementation in SMEs. His thesis, "An Examination and Analysis of the Internet Adoption Experience in SMEs in the Republic of Ireland," was awarded by the University of Limerick, Ireland. He has published and presented papers over the last three years on the factors influencing the Internet adoption decision process in SMEs at the University of Twente, Holland, the Manchester Business School, UK, and Edith Cowan University, Perth, Australia. He is a lecturer in e-business and strategic information systems planning at the Tipperary Institute, Ireland. He can be reached via e-mail at: jgriffin@tippinst.ie.

Jatinder N.D. Gupta is currently eminent scholar of Management, professor of Management Information Systems, and chairperson of the Department of Accounting and Information Systems in the College of Administrative Science at the University of Alabama in Huntsville, USA. Most recently, he was professor of Management, Information and Communication Sciences, and Industry and Technology at Ball State University,

Muncie, Indiana. He holds a PhD in Industrial Engineering (with specialization in Production Management and Information Systems) from Texas Tech University. Co-author of a textbook on operations research, Dr. Gupta serves on the editorial boards of several national and international journals. Recipient of the Outstanding Faculty and Outstanding Researcher awards from Ball State University, he has published numerous papers in journals such as *Journal of Management Information Systems, International Journal of Information Management, INFORMS Journal of Computing, Annals of Operations Research*, and *Mathematics of Operations Research*. More recently, he served as a co-editor of a special issue on "Neural Networks in Business of Computers and Operations Research" and a book entitled, *Neural Networks in Business: Techniques and Applications*. His current research interests include information and decision technologies, scheduling, planning and control, organizational learning and effectiveness, systems education, and knowledge management. Dr. Gupta is a member of several academic and professional societies including the Production and Operations Management Society (POMS), the Decision Sciences Institute (DSI), and the Information Resources Management Association (IRMA).

Ray Hackney is director of Business Information Technology Research within the Manchester Metropolitan University, UK. He has contributed extensively to research in the field of information systems, with publications in numerous national and international conferences and journals. He has taught in a number of MBA programs, including at MMU, Manchester Business School, and the Open University. He leads the organizing committee for the annual BIT and BITWorld Conference series, and is a member of the Strategic Management Society and Association of Information Systems. Dr. Hackney has served on the board of the UK Academy for Information Systems since 1997 and was also the vice president of research for the Information Resource Management Association (IRMA). He currently serves as associate editor of *JGIM, JEUC, JLIM*, and *ACITM*. His research interests are the strategic management of e-business within a variety of organizational contexts. Dr. Hackney was president of IRMA during 2001/2002 and is now an executive member of the Information Institute (www.information-institute.org).

Xueli (Charlie) Huang is a senior lecturer in Marketing at Edith Cowan University, Australia. He earned his PhD from Monash University. His research interests range from innovation and management among SMEs to e-work in China. Dr. Huang has published widely in scholarly marketing journals in the area of e-business. He can be reached via e-mail at: x.huang@ecu.edu.au.

Sid L. Huff is professor and Ericsson chair of Information Systems at Victoria University of Wellington, New Zealand, and is the head of the School of Information Management. He has been teaching and researching in the information systems field for more than 25 years. His current research focuses on e-commerce and its in SMEs, as well as IS strategy and senior management roles in IT. He has taught at universities in the USA, Canada, and New Zealand, and has published extensively in the leading information systems journals. He has written more than 50 teaching cases, and is the lead author of *Cases in Electronic Commerce*, the second edition of which was recently published by Irwin/McGraw-Hill.

Martin Hughes is a member of the Centre for Innovation and Structural Change, and a lecturer in Information Systems at NUI, Galway, a position he has held since 2000. He is currently pursuing a PhD in Inter-Organizational Systems at the University of Bath, UK. His research interests include e-commerce and the small firm, inter-organizational systems and risk, and e-government. He has been published in leading international IS conferences in these areas.

Judith Jeffcoate is head of the Department of Information Systems at the University of Buckingham, UK. She is program director for the University's program of post-graduate studies in e-commerce. She is a graduate of the Open University and holds a PhD in Numerical Analysis from the University of Salford. Professor Jeffcoate has 22 years of experience in the IT industry, in a career that has ranged from academic research, to hands-on experience of commercial systems analysis and design, to high-level consultancy studies. She has researched and co-authored more than a dozen reports on markets for emerging technologies. She was an advisor to the UK Labour Party's policy forum on the Information Superhighway.

Naureen Khan is working as a research associate in an EPSRC (Engineering and Physical Sciences Research Council) project, investigating the deployment, hosting, and integration of business-critical information systems by the application service provider (ASP) industry. Currently she is doing her PhD in the area of offshore IS/IT outsourcing. Her research interests include issues related to global outsourcing strategies, their inhibitors and drivers, and their capabilities and risks.

Chalermsak Lertwongsatien is an IT specialist at the Information & Communication Technology Center, Ministry of Finance, Thailand. He has also served as a visiting lecturer at several universities in Thailand. He holds a PhD in Management Information Systems from Rensselaer Polytechnic Institute, New York. His research interests include strategic implications of IS resources, and capabilities and diffusion of e-commerce. Dr. Chalermsak's research has been published in the proceedings of the *International Conference of Information Resource Management Association (IRMA), Americas Conference on Information Systems (AMCIS),* and *Annual International Conference in Information Systems (ICIS).*

Martin Malis is working as an industrial researcher at the Technical University of Denmark under the Centre for Product Modelling. His main research interest is the B2B collaboration in extended enterprises. The primary focus is the transformation of product-related data through the use of configurators as a tool to facilitate agile and instant communication, which is considered to be of profound strategic importance in a dynamic global market.

Jennifer Moro received her degree in Business Administration from Cattaneo University, Italy, in 2000. She presently works under a research grant from the CETIC Research Center at Cattaneo University. Her research interests concern CIO competencies, the management of business information systems, and Internet-based technologies, especially focusing on the peculiarities of SMEs.

Francis Pereira is a principal researcher at the Center for Telecom Management. He is also an assistant professor of Clinical Information and Operations Management at the University of Southern California, USA. He received his PhD in Political Economy and Public Policy from the University of Southern California and teaches courses in e-commerce, economics, and statistics. His areas of research include trade and financial flows in the Association of South-East Asian nations. Current research focuses on e-commerce applications, particularly in the SME market. He has seven years of research experience in the telecommunications field.

Simpson Poon is chair professor of Information Systems at Charles Sturt University, Australia. He earned his PhD in Information Systems from Monash University, Australia, and was the founding director of the Centre of E-Commerce and Internet Studies at Murdoch University, Australia. Dr. Poon has been an e-business consultant, and has worked with both government and business organizations in Australia and Asia. He has published widely in the area of e-business in both academic and professional journals.

Fuatai Purcell, a Samoan consultant, has worked in both public and private organizations in Samoa, and is currently studying at Victoria University to become an academic researcher. She works part time as a finance and information system (IS) analyst in New Zealand while studying. Since 1997, she has attained a Certificate of Management Studies and a postgraduate diploma in IS Management from Victoria University of Wellington. She has completed her thesis for a Master's of Commerce and Administration degree in IS Management. She will be studying toward a PhD degree, after which she will return to Samoa as a full-time academic researcher. Ms. Fuatai's research interests are SME development, the diffusion of the Internet, e-commerce, and information and communication technologies (ICTs) in developing countries.

Michael Quayle is the director of the Business School and Robert Bosch professor (chair) in Purchasing & Supply Chain Management at the University of Glamorgan, UK. The university's business school is the largest in Wales and 14th largest (out of 120) in the UK. Before entering academia, he gained significant procurement and project management experience in the European electronics and defense industries. An advisor to the UK HM Office of Government Commerce (OGC), Professor Quayle is a registered purchasing and supply management specialist with, and senior consultant to, the United Nations (UNCTAD). He has published extensively in the fields of management development, purchasing, materials management, logistics, and e-business. He is also the UK Chartered Institute of Purchasing & Supply (CIPS) ambassador to Wales.

Pauline Ratnasingam, an assistant professor in the Department of Computer Information Systems of the Harmon School of Business Administration at Central Missouri State University. Previously, she was an assistant professor of MIS in the School of Business

Administration at the University of Vermont, received her Bachelor's in Computing (Information Systems) and Honors in Information Systems from Monash University, Melbourne, Australia. She received her PhD, with a thesis titled "Inter-Organizational Trust in Business-to-Business Electronic Commerce," from Erasmus University, Rotterdam School of Management, The Netherlands. She has lectured on topics such as project management, management of information systems, and e-commerce in Australia, New Zealand, Europe, and America. She is an associate member of the Association of Information Systems, and is a member of the Information Resources Management Association and the Academy of Management. Her research interests include business risk management, Internet-based business-to-business e-commerce, organizational behavior, inter-organizational relationships, and trust. She is a recipient of a National Science Foundation Grant and has published several articles related to this area in national and international conferences and refereed journals.

Aurelio Ravarini received his degree in Management Engineering in 1994 at Politecnico di Milano, Italy. In 1998 he obtained a master's, with a thesis titled, "Training Trainers," at ISMO, Milano. Assistant professor in Information Systems at the Faculty of Business Administration at Cattaneo University, Castellanza, Italy, Mr. Ravarini's activity involves empirical research, action research, and consultancy. His research focuses on organizational issues of the adoption and use of ICT (and in particular Internet-based information systems), especially within SMEs. He has published approximately 30 papers in international journals and conferences, and is a member of the editorial board of the *Journal of Electronic Commerce in Organizations,* and of the program committee of IRMA international conference.

Lucy Ruane recently completed a research master's in Information Systems at National University of Ireland Galway, Ireland.

Donatella Sciuto received her PhD in Electrical and Computer Engineering in 1988 from University of Colorado, Boulder. She is currently a Full Professor at the Dipartimento di Elettronica e Informazione of the Politecnico di Milano, Italy. She is member IEEE, IFIP 10.5, EDAA. She is member of different program committees of EDA conferences, and associate Editor of the *IEEE Transactions on Computers* and the *Journal Design Automation of Embedded Systems*, Kluwer Academic Publishers. Her research interests cover mainly the methodologies for co-design of embedded systems and the analysis of the impact of Information and Telecommunication technologies on business.

Philip Scown earned his Psychology degree from Warwick University in 1979. In 1985, after some years in public- and private-sector industries, he earned his master's degree (Cognition, Computing, and Psychology), again from Warwick. For the last 15 years he has lectured in British universities. His PhD in human factors for complex real-time systems was earned at Loughborough University. In recent years he has been involved in the usability analysis of hundreds of websites.

Sushil K. Sharma is currently assistant professor of Information Systems and Operations Management at Ball State University, Muncie, Indiana, USA. He received his PhD in Information Systems from Pune University, India, and taught at the Indian Institute of Management, Lucknow, for 11 years before joining Ball State University. Prior to joining Ball State, Dr. Sharma also held the position of visiting research associate professor in the Department of Management Science, University of Waterloo, Canada. Dr. Sharma's primary teaching interests are e-commerce, computer communication networks, database management systems, management information systems, and information systems analysis and design. He has extensive experience in providing consulting services to several government and private organizations, including World Bank-funded projects in the areas of information systems, e-commerce, and knowledge management. Dr. Sharma is the author of two books, and has numerous articles in national and international journals. His current research interests include database management systems, networking environments, e-commerce, knowledge management, and corporate information systems.

Mohini Singh is a senior lecturer in E-Business in the School of Business Information Technology at RMIT University, Australia. She holds a PhD in New Technology Management from Monash University, where she received the Helen M. Schutt Award for Outstanding PhD Student in 1995. Dr. Singh has successfully completed a number of funded research projects, published and presented widely in the areas of e-business, and new technology and innovation management. Her research interests include e-business relationship management, evolving e-business models, e-markets, B2B issues, and e-commerce regulatory issues.

Carsten Svensson is an industrial researcher at the Technical University of Denmark under the Centre for Product Modelling. He is currently working in a project that is studying the implementation of a mass customization strategy in medium-sized Danish enterprises seen from an administrative perspective. The main goal is to establish a decision-making platform supporting the sales situation. The decision-making platform is based on real-time data from the manufacturing system that will eliminate much of the uncertainty related to build-to-order production. Prior to mass customization, Mr. Svensson worked with supply chain management and business process reengineering, which is strongly influencing his current research.

Marco Tagliavini earned his degree in Computer Science from the University of Milan in 1992. In the same year he obtained a master's in Information Technology at the CEFRIEL Research Center in Milan. He is assistant professor of Information Systems, and has been teaching Computer Science and Information Systems for two universities: the Cattaneo University in Castellanza (since 1993) and the Catholic University in Milan (since 1998). His research work concerns the management of business information systems and Internet-based technologies, especially focusing on the peculiarities of SMEs. He is member of the program committee of IRMA (Information Resource Management Association) international conference. He has published about 30 papers in international journals and conference proceedings, including one entitled, "An Evaluation Model for Electronic Commerce Activities Within SMEs," in *Information Technology Management* (Baltzer Science Publishers—2(2), 211-230).

Arthur Tatnall is a senior lecturer in the School of Information Systems at Victoria University in Melbourne, Australia. He holds bachelor's degrees in Science and Education, a graduate diploma in Computer Science, and a research Master of Arts in which he explored the origins of business computing education in Australian universities. His PhD involved a study in curriculum innovation in which he investigated the manner in which Visual Basic entered the curriculum of an Australian university. His research interests include technological innovation, information technology in educational management, information systems curriculum, project management, and e-commerce.

D.E. Sofiane Tebboune is a doctoral student in the Department of Information Systems and Computing, Brunel University, UK. He is a member of the Centre for Strategic Information Systems (CSIS) at Brunel University. Mr. Tebboune holds an MA in Information Systems Management, and researches the area of IS outsourcing and collaborative strategies in the context of application service provision. He has previously been involved in research on e-procurement and supply chain management. He has also published in conferences and journals.

Janet Toland is a lecturer in Information Systems at Victoria University of Wellington, Australia. She has 20 years of experience in the field of Information Systems, both in industry and as an academic. She has worked in the UK, Botswana, Fiji, and New Zealand. Her areas of research are systems analysis and design, virtual organizations, the virtual university, computer-mediated communication, the digital divide, and computer-supported cooperative work. She is currently investigating the development of e-commerce in the South Pacific, and the development of learning regions in New Zealand.

Edward Watson is the E. J. Ourso professor of Business Analysis, and director of the SAP UCC and Enterprise Systems Programs at Louisiana State University, USA. Dr. Watson's interests include ERP and e-business systems implementation and organizational impact, logistics information management, process engineering, and performance analysis. His doctoral and master's degrees are in Industrial Engineering from Penn State, and his BS in Industrial Engineering and Operations Research is from Syracuse University. He has published in such journals as *Decision Sciences, Decision Support Systems, IEEE Transactions on Computers, International Journal of Production Research, Interfaces, European Journal of Operational Research,* and *Communications of the Association for Information Systems.* He is active in the information systems and decision sciences communities, and is a regular contributor and speaker at related conferences and workshops.

Vishanth Weerakkody is a lecturer in the Department of Information Systems and Computing at Brunel University, UK. He holds an MSc in Business Systems Analysis and Design from City University in London, and a PhD in Process Management and

Information Systems from the University of Hertfordshire. Dr. Weerakkody has published several journal and conference articles, and has held various IT positions in multinational organizations.

Nilmini Wickramasinghe first graduated from the University of Melbourne, Australia, with a Bachelor of Science in Mathematics and Computing, then completed her MBA at Melbourne Business School. In August 1995, she accepted a full scholarship to undertake PhD studies with Michael Ginzberg at Case Western Reserve University, Ohio, USA. During this time she was involved with many research projects focusing on healthcare issues. In April 1999, she was awarded her PhD in Management Information Systems. Upon completion of her PhD, Dr. Wickramasinghe returned to Australia, where she was a senior lecturer of Business Information Systems at the University of Melbourne, in the Faculty of Economics and Commerce. Currently, she is an assistant professor in the Computer and Information Science Department at the James J. Nance College of Business Administration at Cleveland State University, Ohio. She teaches Information Systems at the undergraduate and graduate levels, in particular, knowledge management, as well as e-commerce and m-commerce, IT for competitive advantage, and organizational impacts of technology. She is currently carrying out research and is published in the area of management of technology, in the field of health care, as well as focusing on IS issues, especially as they relate to knowledge work and e-business. She can be reached via e-mail at: n.wickramasinghe@csuohio.edu.

Nitaya Wongpinunwatana is an assistant professor at the Faculty of Commerce and Accountancy, Thammasat University, Thailand. She holds a PhD in Information Systems from the University of Queensland, Australia. Her research interests include expert systems for security auditing, e-learning, and e-commerce. She has presented papers at several international conferences, and published papers in several domestic and international journals.

Yuroung Yao is a doctoral candidate and research associate in the Department of Information Systems & Decision Science at Louisiana State University, USA. She has had several articles published in books and highly ranked conference proceedings. She received her BSc in International Business and Computer Science and Engineering, and MSc in Computer Science and Engineering from Shanghai Jiao Tong University in China. Her research interests include application service provision, electronic government, and strategic issues of information technology.

Carlo Angelo Zanaboni received his degree in Business Administration from Cattaneo University, Italy, in February 2002. He is currently working under a research grant from CETIC Research Center at Cattaneo University. His research interests are mainly focused on ICT solutions to support SME aggregations, like industrial districts and industrial associations.

Index

Journal of Electronic Commerce in Organizations (JECO)

The International Journal of Electronic Commerce in Modern Organizations

ISSN: 1539-2937
eISSN: 1539-2929
Subscription: Annual fee per volume (4 issues):
Individual US $85
Institutional US $185

Editor: Mehdi Khosrow-Pour, D.B.A.
Information Resources
Management Association, USA

Mission

The *Journal of Electronic Commerce in Organizations* is designed to provide comprehensive coverage and understanding of the social, cultural, organizational, and cognitive impacts of e-commerce technologies and advances on organizations around the world. These impacts can be viewed from the impacts of electronic commerce on consumer behavior, as well as the impact of e-commerce on organizational behavior, development, and management in organizations. The secondary objective of this publication is to expand the overall body of knowledge regarding the human aspects of electronic commerce technologies and utilization in modern organizations, assisting researchers and practitioners to devise more effective systems for managing the human side of e-commerce.

Coverage

This publication includes topics related to electronic commerce as it relates to: Strategic Management, Management and Leadership, Organizational Behavior, Organizational Developement, Organizational Learning, Technologies and the Workplace, Employee Ethical Issues, Stress and Strain Impacts, Human Resources Management, Cultural Issues, Customer Behavior, Customer Relationships, National Work Force, Political Issues, and all other related issues that impact the overall utilization and management of electronic commerce technologies in modern organizations.

For subscription information, contact:

Idea Group Publishing
701 E Chocolate Ave., Ste 200
Hershey PA 17033-1240, USA
cust@idea-group.com
URL: www-idea-group.com

For paper submission information:

Dr. Mehdi Khosrow-Pour
Information Resources Management
Association
jeco@idea-group.com